Plan Like a Grandmaster

PLAN LIKE A GRANDMASTER
Alexei Suetin

Translated by Ken Neat

B. T. Batsford Ltd / David & Charles Inc

First published 1988
© Alexei Suetin 1988

ISBN 0 7134 5830 5 (limp)

Typeset by W. Turner & Son Ltd, Halifax
Printed and bound in Great Britain by
Biddles Ltd, Guildford and King's Lynn
for the publishers, B.T. Batsford Ltd
4 Fitzhardinge Street, London W1H 0AH

Published in the U.S.A. by:
David & Charles Inc.
North Pomfret, VT 05053

A BATSFORD CHESS BOOK
Adviser: R. D. Keene GM, O.B.E.
Technical Editor: Ian Kingston

CONTENTS

FOREWORD

The present book is devoted to one of the most important topics in chess theory — the strategic problem of the opening and its close connection with the middlegame. The author, GM Alexei Suetin, has long been working fruitfully in this field, and he first expressed his ideas in *Modern Chess Opening Theory* (Pergamon Press, 1965).

This book has little connection with the previous one, although the author's basic conception has remained practically unchanged. Suetin attaches the greatest importance to the dynamic handling of a position, and to the harmonious connection between opening mobilization and the subsequent development of ideas in the middlegame.

In the book an attempt is made to create a system of opening theory instruction on the basis of a differentiated classification and a large number of practical examples. It is well known that chess thinking constitutes an organic synthesis of visual and verbal ideas, i.e. tactical and strategic.

Since in young chess players it is visual thinking which predominates, we consider this approach by the author to be interesting and correct.

In Part I of the book, intended for less experienced players, the theoretical discussion is somewhat limited for this type of chess literature. but there are very many practical examples, which should enable the reader to improve his mastery of opening play, and also to expand his general horizons, especially in the field of attacks and combinations.

In Part II of the book, basic questions of opening strategy are examined, and certain generalizations in this field are made.

The book is intended for a wide range of players (Elo grades approx. 1700-2200; BCF 135-200) and coaches.

GM Lev Polugayevsky

PART I
BASIC PRINCIPLES AND TASKS
OF THE OPENING

MOBILIZATION OF THE FORCES IN THE OPENING

The scale of relative piece values and its significance in the opening

A study of chess usually begins with an acquaintance with the scale of relative values of the pieces, in which the unit of measurement is taken to be the pawn. A minor piece — bishop or knight — is roughly equal to three units, a rook to four and a half, and the queen — the strongest piece — to nine units.

A special position is occupied by the king. Its value in the opening and middlegame is difficult to express in numerical terms, but in the endgame, when the king is rarely threatened with an attack and itself becomes an active piece, its numerical equivalent is fairly high — roughly five units.

In practice, a player very quickly comes to the conclusion that this generally-accepted scale of values is a very arbitrary and loose concept. And yet the scale is necessary! It is the starting point for the first, crude assessment of any position. As he gains experience, a player sees ever more deeply (in the second approximation) that any position is an indivisible group of actions of the forces, where each piece rarely acts in accordance with its scale value. In the position there are usually both strong pieces, operating at the forefront of the battle, and also weak, isolated pieces, standing as though to one side.

In the main, the same relative forces operate in the opening as in the middlegame, but in the former case there are specific features. In particular, it is very important to understand the opening role of the weakest unit — the pawn. With a large number of forces on the board, the weakness of the pawn also constitutes its strength. The point is that a pawn risks much less than any other piece. Thus, for example, when a pawn attacks a square, an opponent's piece can stand there only under exceptional, combinational circumstances. This is why pawns are so important in controlling the centre, by driving away enemy pieces.

Pawns can only move forward, and sometimes their advance can result in irreparable weaknesses. But at the same time, by advancing, pawns gain space for activity by the pieces. Here it is desirable that a pawn phalanx should be mobile, and also that the mobility of the pawns should coordinate with the play of the pieces.

The role of pawns in the opening is very varied. A pawn is by no means a 'functional' quantity, subject to general aims. In many cases, right from the opening it is a strong and independent fighting unit. It is sufficient to say that, other things being equal, the win of a pawn normally creates the necessary preconditions for winning the game, while at the same time, for example, the obtaining of a strong passed pawn guarantees a definite advantage.

In general, in the opening, pawns take a very active part in the play. But as for the heavy pieces — queen and rook — at the start of the game they usually play a very modest role. Space on the chess board is cramped, and is literally overrun with attacks by the pieces. This applies especially to the opening stage, when in the majority of cases the heavy pieces feel uncomfortable, or even clumsy.

The start of the game gives scope mainly to the minor pieces — the bishops and knights.

Thus, after a move (or moves) by a central pawn (or pawns), beginners are recommended first to develop the minor pieces, and to deploy the bishops as actively as possible. For example, after 1 e4 e5 2 ♘f3 ♘c6 the light square bishop is best developed at c4 or b5. On the contrary, it would be very bad to play 3 ♗d3?, blocking the development of the Q-side, while 3 ♗e2 is rather passive.

We will dwell on one further factor. Inexperienced players are recommended not to make premature attacks with the bishop. They are initially more committing than 'solid' developing moves by the knights.

Consider the following example.

No. 1 Morphy-Allies
Paris, 1853
Philidor's Defence

1 e4 e5 2 ♘f3 d6 3 d4 ♗g4?

The initial cause of Black's troubles. Now White forces the exchange of the g4 bishop for the knight at f3, and in an open pos-

ition (which is what the resulting position is) bishops are normally stronger than knights.

4 de ♗xf3 5 ♕xf3 de 5 ♗c4 ♘f6 7 ♕b3 ♕e7 8 ♘c3!?

Of course, White could have won a pawn by 8 ♕×b7, but after 8...♕b4+ 9 ♕×b4 ♗×b4+ 10 c3 Black would have exchanged queens, depriving White of an attack and reducing matters to the simple realization of an advantage. As if foreseeing the spectacular finale, Morphy ignores the prosaic gain of material, which, however, would have robbed the play of its interest. (I think also that a far from minor role in Morphy's decision was played by the low standard of his opponents). In general, such pawns should not be declined!

8...c6 9 ♗g5 b5? 10 ♘xb5 cb 11 ♗×b5+ ♘bd7 12 0-0-0 ♖d8

Now White commences a spectacular combination, one which has become thematic.

13 ♖×d7! ♖×d7 14 ♖d1 ♕e6 15 ♗xd7+ ♘×d7 16 ♕b8+!! ♘×b8 17 ♖d8 mate!

The following example is also still very instructive.

No. 2 Knorre-Chigorin
St. Petersburg, 1874
Italian Game

1 e4 e5 2 ♘f3 ♘c6 3 ♗c4 ♗c5 4

0-0(?) ♘f6 5 d3 d6 6 ♗g5 h6 7 ♗h4? (7 ♗×f6 was essential).

The combination of White's early castling with his bishop development on move 6 is unsuccessful, the more so in that he persists in maintaining the pin along the h4-d8 diagonal. Now Black launches a very strong counterattack on the opponent's castled position.

7...g5!

By attacking the bishop, Black advances his K-side pawns with gain of tempo for an attack on the king. It is very important that he has not yet castled, so that he can boldly move the pawns in front of his own king.

8 ♗g3 h5! 9 ♘×g5

On 9 h4 there could have followed 9...♗g4 10 hg h4 11 ♗h2 ♘h7, again with a strong attack for Black, but even so this was the lesser evil for White.

9...h4! 10 ♘×f7 10 hg 11 ♘×d8 ♗g4! 12 ♕d2

Black also has a spectacular win after 12 ♕×g4 ♘×g4 13 ♘×c6 ♗×f2 14 ♖×f2 gh+! when, despite his enormous material advantage, White cannot defend against the mate.

12...♘d4 13 ♘c3 ♘f3+ 14 gf ♗×f3 0-1

Development of the pieces and the role of the centre

The squares on the chess board are not all equivalent.

Their 'market value' depends largely on the specific situation on the board, but normally a particularly important role is played by the centre, by which we understand the group of four squares d4, e4, d5, and e5.

Any piece deployed in the centre can not only in principle exert its maximum influence on the position, but can also be switched quickly to any part of the board. This is readily apparent if one compares the actions of centralized pieces with pieces on the edge of the board (although the real strength of the pieces' actions depends mainly on the specific situation). If one controls the centre, it is normally easy to 'govern' the flanks, whereas the opponent's forces will be disunited and restricted in mobility.

The central squares are of particular significance in the opening, and therefore, until an area of specific conflict is determined, it is advisable to direct the development of one's forces towards the centre. The neglect of the centre in the opening can lead to great difficulties, and sometimes even to a swift catastrophe.

This is confirmed by an example, taken from a game between two beginners. In an Italian Game after 1 e4 e5 2 ♘f3 ♘c6 3 ♗c4 ♗c5 4 c3 ♘f6 5 0-0?!, instead of taking an important central pawn by 5...♘xe4, Black engaged in inappropriate prophylaxis, and played 5...a6?

This allowed White after 6 d4 ed 7 cd ♗a7 8 d5 ♘e7 9 e5! to begin a powerful pawn offensive in the centre, and under its cover to quickly build up a decisive piece attack on the black king: 9...♘g4 10 h3 ♘h6 11 d6 ♘g6 12 ♗g5 f6 13 ef gf 14 ♖e1+ ♔f8 15 ♗xh6 mate!

Thus the basic struggle in the opening revolves around the centre. In graphic terms, the centre is a most important transit point, through which all strategic plans 'pass' (and are sometimes decided!) Therefore the development of the pieces and the struggle for the centre in the opening are inseparably linked.

The unpleasant consequences of loss of tempi

The aimless moving of one and the same piece early in the game is normally likely to have unpleasant consequences. This is eloquently confirmed in the following examples, in which

White irrationally wasted precious tempi in the opening on moves by his pieces.

In the first game — 10 ♕d2? and 11 ♗e3?, and in the second game — 8 ♘e5? and then the inappropriate queen manœuvre ♕×c4-c7? Each time, exploiting his lead in development, Black replied with a timely opening of the centre, with a subsequent attack on the opponent's king, which was caught there.

No. 3 Rotlewi-Rubinstein
Lodz, 1908
Queen's Gambit

1 d4 d5 2 ♘f3 e6 3 e3 c5 4 c4 ♘c6 5 ♘c3 ♘f6 6 dc ♗×c5 7 a3 a6 8 b4 ♗d6 9 ♗b2 0-0 10 ♕d2? ♕e7 11 ♗d3? (11 cd ed 12 ♗e2 is better) 11...dc 12 ♗×c4 b5 13 ♗d3 ♖fd8 14 ♕e2 ♗b7 15 0-0 ♘e5 16 ♘×e5 ♗×e5 17 f4(?) (17 h3) 17...♗c7 18 e4? ♖ac8 19 e5 ♗b6+ 20 ♔h1 ♘g4 21 ♗e4 ♕h4 22 g3 (22 h3 ♖×c3!) 22...♖×c3 23 gh ♖d2!! 24 ♕×d2 ♗×e4+ 25 ♕g2 ♖h3! 0-1

No. 4 Belin-Lipnitsky
Riga, 1950
Queen's Gambit

1 d4 ♘f6 2 c4 e6 3 ♘f3 d5 4 ♗g5 h6 5 ♗×f6 ♕×f6 6 ♘c3 ♗b4 7 ♕a4+ ♘c6 8 ♘e5? ♗d7 9 ♘×c6 (9 ♘×d7 ♕×d4!) 9...♗×c3+ 10 bc ♗×c6 11 ♕b3 dc 12 ♕×c4 0-0 13 f3 e5! 14 d5 ♗d7 15 ♕×c7? e4! *(1)*

16 ♖c1 ♖ac8! 17 ♕×d7 e3! 18 ♕a4 ♖×c3 19 ♖d1 ♖fc8 20 g3 ♖c1 21 ♗h3 ♖×d1+ 22 ♕×d1 ♕c3+ 23 ♔f1 ♕d2! 24 ♔g2 ♖c1!! 0-1

Incidentally, both here and later, for illustrative purposes, use will be made of short games, in which the crisis occurs at an early stage. They reveal very clearly the typical opening mistakes.

Short games are mainly good catylysts for remembering various characteristic opening mistakes, but their division by opening, which has become traditional in many books, essentially explains little. After all, the attack, say, on f7 lies in wait for Black in literally every opening, and this is the main basis of many short games with similar swift attacks, irrespective of the specific opening situation from which such an attack arises.

We give some examples to confirm this.

No. 5 Suetin-Arnaudov
Albena, 1970
Pirc Defence

1 e4 g6 2 d4 ♗g7 3 c3 d5 4 ed ♕xd5 5 ♘f3 c5 6 ♗e3 cd 7 cd ♘c6?

7...♘f6 is correct. The position of the knight at c6 allows White to mount an offensive in the centre with gain of tempi.

8 ♘c3 ♕d8 9 ♗b5 ♗d7? (better 9...e6) 10 0-0 a6 11 ♗e2 ♗g4 12 d5 ♗xf3 13 ♗xf3 ♘e5 14 d6!

The most efficient continuation, opening up the position for a decisive piece attack.

14...♘xf3+ 15 ♕xf3 ♕xd6 16 ♕xb7 ♖b8 17 ♕a7 ♖c8 18 ♖fd1 ♕c7 19 ♕xa6 ♘f6 20 ♖ac1 ♕c6 21 ♕a7 ♖a8 22 ♘b5! 1-0

No. 6 Kupreichik-Pedersen
Teesside, 1974
Pirc Defence

1 e4 g6 2 d4 ♗g7 3 ♘c3 d6 4 ♗e3 c6 5 ♕d2 ♘d7 6 0-0-0 b5 7 e5!? d5? (7...♘b6 is correct) 8 h4 ♘b6 9 h5 gh 10 ♘h3 f6? 11 ♘f4 ♗g4 12 f3 fe 13 de ♗f5 14 ♘xh5 ♗f8

White would also have won after 14...♔f8 15 g4 ♗g6 16 ♗xb6 ♕xb6 17 ♕f4+ or 14...♗xe5 15 ♗d4 ♕d6 16 ♘g7+.

15 ♘xb5 cb 16 ♗xb5+ ♔f7 17 g4 ♗g6 18 ♗d4 e6 19 ♕f4+ ♗f5 20 gf 1-0

No. 7 Kapengut-Pavlenko
Riga, 1975
Nimzowitsch Defence

1 e4 ♘c6 2 d4 d5 3 ♘c3! de 4 d5 ♘b8 (4...♘e5 is better) 5 ♗f4 ♘f6 6 ♗c4 g6 7 f3! ef 8 ♘xf3 ♗g7 9 0-0 0-0 10 ♕e2 c6 11 ♖ad1! cd 12 ♘xd5 ♘xd5 13 ♖xd5 ♕b6+ 14 ♗e3 ♕xb2 15 ♖b5 ♕c3 16 ♖c5 ♕a3 17 ♘g5 ♗g4 18 ♖xf7! ♖xf7

Not 18...♗xe2 19 ♖xf8++ ♔xf8 20 ♖c8 mate, while 18...♘d7 19 ♖xe7+ ♔h8 20 ♖xg7 ♘f6 21 ♖cc7! is also bad, as is 20...♔xg7 21 ♗d4+ ♔h6 22 ♘f7+ ♖xf7 23 ♕d2+ etc., each time with a win for White.

19 ♕f2 ♗f5 (19...♗f6 20 ♘xf7!) 20 ♖c8+! ♗f8 21 ♗xf7+ ♔g7 22 ♗d4+ 1-0

Premature inclusion of the heavy pieces in the play

It is inadvisable to bring the heavy pieces — queen and rooks — into the game early, since they can easily come under fire from the less important forces — the minor pieces and pawns, which leads merely to loss of time. It is for this reason that an attack such as 1 e4 e5 2 ♕h5 is unconvincing, since it can be successfully parried by Black. Those who like gambit play can be advised to continue 2...♘f6 (of course, 2...♘c6 3 ♗c4 g6 4 ♕f3 ♘f6 5 g4? ♘d4! etc. is also good) 3 ♕×e5+ ♗e7 4 ♗c4 ♘c6 5 ♕f4 0-0 6 ♘f3 d5!

After completing his mobilization, Black should immediately take active measures. It is readily apparent that, at a slight cost, Black has obtained a very strong attack, which White can hardly parry successfully.

Also instructive is the following example, where in an eccentric variation Black committed a serious mistake as early as the 3rd move. Instead of developing his minor pieces as quickly as possible – 3...♗d6 etc., he inappropriately brought his queen into play, and it soon became merely a vulnerable target for White to attack.

No. 8 Boleslavsky-Lilienthal
Moscow, 1941
King's Pawn Opening

1 e4 e5 2 ♘f3 d5?! 3 ♘×e5 (3 ed is objectively stronger, e.g. 3...e4 4 ♕e2 f5 5 d3 ♘f6 6 de fe 7 ♘c3 ♗b4 8 ♕b5+! c6 9 ♕×b4 ef 10 ♗g5!, and White won quickly in Tal-Lutikov, Tallinn 1964) **3...♕e7? 4 d4 f6 5 ♘d3! de 6 ♘f4 ♕f7 7 ♘d2 ♗f5 8 g4! ♗g6 9 ♗c4 ♕d7 10 ♕e2 ♕×d4 11 ♘e6! ♕b6**

12 ♘×e4 ♘bd7 13 ♗f4 ♘e5 14 0-0-0 ♗f7 15 ♘4g5! fg 16 ♗×e5 ♗×e6 17 ♗×c7! 1-0

The danger of leaving the king in the centre

In the opening and middle-game the most vulnerable piece is the king. In the opening, in the overwhelming majority of cases one should remove the king from the centre and castle as soon as possible, since if the centre is quickly opened it will become a target for attack. (Also of considerable importance is the fact that castling brings into active play the rook, which in one leap moves from the edge of the board almost to the centre).

Leaving the king in the centre when behind in development can very often lead to a rapid defeat. This is a very important topic in the practical sense, and we offer several typical examples.

No. 9 Em. Lasker-Pirc
Moscow, 1935
Sicilian Defence

1 e4 c5 2 ♘f3 ♘c6 3 d4 cd 4 ♘×d4 ♘f6 5 ♘c3 d6 6 ♗e2 e6 7 0-0 a6 8 ♗e3 ♕c7 9 f4 ♘a5 10 f5!? ♘c4? (leads to catastrophe; 10...e5 is better) **11 ♗×c4 ♕×c4 12 fe fe** *(2)*

13 ♖xf6! gf 14 ♕h5+ ♚d8 15 ♕f7 ♗d7 (15...♗e7 16 ♘f5! ♖e8 17 ♘xd6 ♗xd6 18 ♗b6+ ♗c7 19 ♖d1+! is crushing) 16 ♕xf6+ ♚c7 17 ♕xh8 ♗h6 18 ♘xe6+ ♕xe6 19 ♕xa8 ♗e3+ 20 ♚h1 1-0

No. 10 Smyslov-Euwe
The Hague/Moscow, 1948
Spanish Game

1 e4 e5 2 ♘f3 ♘c6 3 ♗b5 a6 4 ♗a4 ♘f6 5 0-0 ♘xe4 6 d4 b5 7 ♗b3 d5 8 de ♗e6 9 ♕e2 ♘c5?! 10 ♖d1 ♘xb3 11 ab ♕c8 (3)

12 c4! dc 13 bc ♗xc4 14 ♕e4

♘e7 15 ♘a3! c6 16 ♘xc4 bc 17 ♕xc4 ♕b7 18 e6! f6 19 ♖d7 ♕b5 20 ♕xb5 cb 21 ♘d4 ♖c8 22 ♗e3 ♘c6 23 ♖xa6 ♘e5 24 ♖b7 ♗c5 25 ♘f5 0-0 26 h3! 1-0

No. 11 Unzicker-Stahlberg
Amsterdam OL, 1954
French Defence

1 e4 e6 2 d4 d5 3 ♘c3 ♘f6 4 ♗g5 ♗e7 5 e5 ♘fd7 6 h4 f6 7 ♕h5+! ♚f8

White also retains the initiative after 7...g6 8 ef! ♘xf6 (8...gh? 8 fe!) 9 ♕e2 c5 10 dc ♘c6 11 0-0-0 etc.

8 ef ♘xf6 9 ♕f3 c5 10 dc b6?! 11 h5! bc 12 h6! g6 13 0-0-0 ♘bd7 14 ♖e1 ♕b6 15 ♗b5! ♚f7 16 ♘h3 a6 17 ♗xd7 ♗xd7 18 ♗xf6 ♗xf6 19 ♘g5+! 1-0

No. 12 Tal-Minev
Munich OL, 1958
Queen's Gambit

1 c4 c5 2 ♘c3 ♘c6 3 ♘f3 ♘f6 4 e3 e6 5 d4 d5 6 cd ♘xd5 7 ♗c4 ♘b6? (7...cd 8 ed ♗e7) 8 ♗b5 a6 9 ♗xc6+ bc 10 0-0 ♗b7? 11 ♘e4 ♘d7 12 ♕c2 ♕b6 13 ♘e5! cd 14 ♘xd7 ♚xd7 15 ed ♚e8 16 ♗e3 ♕c7 17 d5! ed 18 ♖ef1 ♚d8

Black's position is hopeless. White also wins after 18...de 19 ♕xe4+ ♗e7 20 ♗c5!, or 19...♕e7 20 ♕d3! ♖d8 21 ♕b3 etc.

19 ♕b3 c5 20 ♘xc5! 1-0

No. 13 Suetin-Holmov
Minsk, 1962
Sicilian Defence

1 e4 c5 2 ♘f3 ♘c6 3 d4 cd
4 ♘xd4 ♘f6 5 ♘c3 d6 6 ♗g5 ♗d7
7 ♕d2 ♖c8 8 ♗e2 ♘xd4 9 ♕xd4
♕a5 10 f4 ♕c5 11 ♕d3 e6 12 0-0-0
♗c6 13 ♗xf6 gf 14 ♔b1 h5 15 h4
a6 16 ♗f3 b5 17 ♘e2 f5?! 18 ef
♗xf3 19 gf ♕xf5 20 ♕d2 ♗h6? 21
♕xd6! ♕xc2+ 22 ♔a1 ♗g7 23
♘c3!! 1-0

No. 14 Tal-Bilek
Amsterdam, 1964
Sicilian Defence

1 e4 c5 2 ♘f3 d6 4 d4 cd 4 ♘xd4
♘f6 5 ♘c3 a6 6 ♗g5 ♘bd7 7 ♗c4
h6 8 ♗xf6 ♘xf6 9 ♕e2! e6 10
0-0-0 ♕c7 11 f4 e5 12 ♘d5! ♘xd5
13 ed ♗e7 14 fe de *(4)*

15 ♘e6! ♕d6
White also wins after 15. . .fe
16 ♕h5+ ♔f8 17 de ♗f6 18 e7+!
♕xe7 19 ♖d8+ ♕xd8 20 ♕f7

mate.

16 ♘xg7+ ♔f8 17 ♘e6+! ♔e8
18 ♖hf1 ♗g5+ 19 ♔b1 b5 20 ♕h5
♗f4 21 ♗b3 a5 22 ♘c7+! ♕xc7 23
d6! 1-0

No. 15 Tal-Bronstein
USSR Ch, 1971
Caro-Kann Defence

1 e4 c6 2 c4 d5 3 ed cd 4 d4 ♘f6
5 ♘c3 ♘c6 6 ♗g5 ♗g4? 7 ♗e2!
♗xe2 8 ♘gxe2 dc 9 d5 ♘e5 10 0-0
h6 11 ♗f4 ♘g6 12 ♕a4+ ♕d7 13
♕xc4 ♖c8 14 ♕b3 e5 15 de ♕xe6
16 ♕xb7 ♗c5 17 ♘d4! ♗xd4 18
♖ae1 0-0 19 ♖xe6 fe 20 ♗d6
♖fd8 21 ♗c7 ♖f8 22 ♘b5! ♗e5 23
♗xe5 ♘xe5 24 ♕xa7 ♘d5 25
♕d4 1-0

No. 16 Suetin-Spiridonov
Brno, 1975
Caro-Kann Defence

1 e4 c6 2 ♘c3 d5 3 ♘f3 ♗g4 4 h3
♗xf3 5 ♕xf3 ♘f6 6 d3 e6 7 a3 ♗e7
(the alternative plan is 7. . .♘bd7
and then 8. . .g6) 8 g4 de 9 de
♘fd7 10 ♗d2 ♗g5 11 0-0-0 ♗xd2+
12 ♖xd2 ♕h4?

12. . .h6 was stronger, with the
possible continuation 13 ♕e3 e5
14 f4 ef 15 ♕xf4 ♕e7, when Black
has gained an important tempo.

13 ♕e3 e5 14 f4 ef 15 ♕xf4 ♕e7
16 h4 h6 17 ♘e2! ♘e5
Thus Black has gained the e5
post for his knight, which was

the aim of his dark-square strategy, but he is behind in development, and has by no means equalized.

18 ♘d4 g6 19 h5 ♕g5 20 ♕g3 ♕e7 21 hg fg

Here some conclusions can be drawn: Black's e6 square is hopelessly weakened. In addition his king is caught in the centre, and White wins quickly.

22 ♕b3!

Now Black has no defence.

22...♕f7 23 ♘e6 ♔e7 24 ♕b4+ ♔f6 25 ♖f2+ ♔xe6 26 ♗c4+ 1-0

No. 17 Veresov-Zhelyandinov
Minsk, 1969
Veresov Opening

1 d4 ♘f6 2 ♘c3 d5 3 ♗g5 ♘bd7 4 ♘f3 e6 5 e4 h6 6 ♗h4 g5 7 ♗g3 ♘xe4 8 ♘xe4 de 9 ♘d2 ♗g7 10 h4! ♗xd4 11 c3 gh? (11...♗e5 is correct) **12 ♖xh4! ♗f6 13 ♕h5! ♗g5 14 ♘xe4 ♖g8 15 ♖d1 a6 16 ♖g4 e5 17 ♗c4 ♕e7 18 ♗h4 ♘f6 19 ♖xg5! hg 20 ♗xf7+ ♔f8 21 ♘xf6 1-0**

In the majority of the examples, success was achieved by a sacrifice of material, leading to an abrupt opening of the position and to the elimination of important defensive barriers.

The pursuit of material to the detriment of development

At an early stage of the game you should not try at any cost to win material, to the detriment of your development (cf. games Nos. 5 and 11). We give several more games to illustrate this.

No. 18 Alekhine-Nimzowitsch
Bled, 1931
French Defence

1 e4 e6 2 d4 d5 3 ♘c3 ♗b4 4 ♘ge2 de 5 a3 ♗xc3+ 6 ♘xc3 f5? (6... ♘c6) **7 f3!? ef 8 ♕xf3 ♕xd4(?) 9 ♕g3! ♘f6 10 ♕xg7 ♕e5+? 11 ♗e2 ♖g8 12 ♕h6 ♖g6 13 ♕h4 ♗d7** (13...♖xg2 14 ♗f4 ♕d4 15 ♖d1 leads to a win for White) **14 ♗g5 ♗c6 15 0-0-0 ♗xg2 16 ♖he1 ♗e4 17 ♗h5 ♘xh5 18 ♖d8+ ♔f7 19 ♕xh5 ♔g7 20 ♘xe4 fe 21 ♗h6+ 1-0**

No. 19 Tolush-Boleslavsky
USSR Ch, 1945
Queen's Pawn Opening

1 d4 ♘f6 2 ♗g5 c5 3 dc ♘e4 4 ♗f4 ♘c6 5 ♕d5? f5! *(5)* **6 ♕xf5 d5 7 ♕h5+ g6 8 ♕h4 ♘d4 9 ♗e5 ♘xc2+ 10 ♔d1 ♘xa1 11 ♗xh8 ♕a5 12 ♘c3 ♘xc3+ 13 ♗xc3 ♕xa2 14 e3 ♕b1+ 15 ♔e2 d4! 16 ♕xd4 ♗d7 17 ♕b4 0-0-0 18 f4**

♘c2 19 ♕a5 ♕c1 20 ♗d4 ♘xd4+ 21 ed ♕xb2+ 22 ♔f3 ♕xd4 23 ♘e2 ♗c6+ 24 ♔g4 h5+ 25 ♔h4 ♕f6+ 26 ♔g3 e5 0-1

No. 20 Enevoldsen-Andersen
Denmark, 1940
Queen's Gambit

1 c4 ♘f6 2 ♘f3 e6 3 ♘c3 d5 4 e3 ♗e7 5 b3 0-0 6 ♗b2 b6 7 d4 ♗b7 8 ♗d3 dc 9 bc c5 10 0-0 cd 11 ed ♘c6 12 ♕e2 ♘xd4? 13 ♘xd4 ♕xd4 14 ♘d5! ♕c5 15 ♗xf6 gf 16 ♘xe7+ ♕xe7 17 ♕g4+ ♔h8 18 ♕h4! 1-0

No. 21 Rovner-Kotov
Leningrad, 1949
Slav Defence

1 d4 d5 2 c4 e6 3 ♘c3 c6 4 e4 de 5 ♘xe4 ♗b4+ 6 ♗d2 ♕xd4 7 ♗xb4 ♕xe4+ 8 ♗e2 ♘a6 9 ♗c3 ♘e7 10 ♗xg7 ♕xg2?

Black should have played 10. . . ♖g8 11 ♗c3 ♘d5!

11 ♗f6! ♘c5 (11. . .♕xh1 12

♕d6 0-0 13 ♕g3+ ♘g6 14 ♗f3! leads to a win for White) 12 ♕d6 0-0 13 ♗f3 ♕g6 14 ♗xe7 ♘d3+ 15 ♔e2 ♘xb2 16 ♖c1 ♖e8 17 ♘h3, and White won.

No. 22 Geller-Nahlik
Szczawno Zdroj, 1957
Petroff's Defence

1 e4 e5 2 ♘f3 ♘f6 3 d4 ed 4 e5 ♘e4 5 ♕xd4 d5 6 ed ♘xd6 7 ♘c3 ♘c6 8 ♕f4 ♗f5 9 ♗b5 ♗xc2? 10 ♘e5! g5 11 ♕e3 ♗e7 12 ♘xc6 bc 13 ♗xc6+ ♔f8 14 ♗xa8 ♕xa8 15 0-0 ♘f5 16 ♕e5 ♖g8 17 ♕d5 ♗e4 18 ♕xe4 1-0

No. 23 Tal-Uhlmann
Moscow, 1971
French Defence

1 e4 e6 2 d4 d5 3 ♘d2 c5 4 ♘gf3 ♘c6 5 ♗b5 de 6 ♘xe4 ♗d7 7 ♗g5 ♕a5+ 8 ♘c3 cd 9 ♘xd4 ♗b4 10 0-0 ♗xc3 11 bc ♕xc3 *(6)*

12 ♘f5!! ef 13 ♖e1+ ♗e6 14 ♕d6 a6 15 ♗d2! ♕xc2 16 ♗b4!

ab 17 ♕f8+ ♔d7 18 ♖ad1+ ♔c7 19 ♕xa8 1-0

No. 24 Kondratiev-Gašić
Olomouc, 1975
Albin Counter-Gambit

1 d4 d5 2 c4 e5 3 de d4 4 ♘f3 ♘c6 5 g3 ♗e6 6 ♗g2!? ♗xc4 7 0-0 ♗e6? (7...d3!) 8 ♕a4 ♕d7 9 ♖d1! ♖d8 10 ♘c3! ♗c5 11 ♗g5 ♘ge7 12 e3 ♗g4 13 ♗xe7 ♘xe7 14 ♕c4! ♗b6 15 ed ♗xf3 16 ♗xf3 ♗xd4 17 ♘b5 ♘f5 18 ♘xc7+ ♔f8 19 ♗g4 ♕e7 20 ♗xf5 ♕xe5 21 ♘b5 ♗xf2+ 22 ♔xf2 ♕xf5+ 23 ♔g1 1-0

No. 25 Uhlmann-Liebert
East Germany, 1976
English Opening

1 c4 ♘f6 2 ♘c3 d5 3 cd ♘xd5 4 g3 c5 5 ♗g2 ♘c7 6 ♘f3 ♘c6 7 ♕a4 ♕d7 8 0-0 g6 9 ♕c4?! b6 10 b4?! ♗g7 11 bc b5! 12 ♕b3 b4! 13 ♘g5 0-0 14 ♗xc6? ♕xc6 15 ♕xb4 ♖b8 16 ♕f4 ♗b7 17 ♘f3 ♘e6! 18 ♕e3 ♗d4! 19 ♕h6 ♗a8! 20 ♖b1 ♖xb1 21 ♘xb1 ♕e4! 22 ♘c3 ♗xc3 23 dc ♕xe2 24 ♘d2 ♖d8! 25 ♕e3 ♖xd2!! 26 ♗xd2 ♘g5!! 27 ♕xe2 ♘h3 mate!

It will be noticed that in these games too the "punishment" involved strong tactical measures, and in certain cases a decisive attack on the opponent's king.

Diversions in the opening

One of the logical principles of opening play is that, if the opponent has not made a serious mistake, forcible measures to obtain an advantage are doomed to failure. Therefore early, ill-prepared diversions in the opening, in which a small number of pieces participate, are inadvisable. If such 'pseudoactive' operations cannot be supported by the main forces, they are quickly refuted.

In this respect the following game is an instructive example.

No. 26 Botvinnik-Denker
USSR-USA, 1945
Slav Defence

1 d4 d5 2 ♘f3 ♘f6 3 c4 c6 4 cd cd 5 ♘c3 ♘c6 6 ♗f4

Here, instead of the natural continuation of his development, Black embarked on an unfortunate diversion (there is no other word for it) on the Q-side.

6...♕a5 7 e3 ♘e4(?) 8 ♕b3 e6 9 ♗d3 ♗b4 10 ♖c1

White very calmly meets the opponent's impulsive attack, completing his development and thus neutralizing the opponent's ephemeral threats.

10...♘xc3 11 bc ♗a3 12 ♖b1 b6 13 e4! (7)

A timely switch to genuinely

decisive action, opening up the centre, which is aided by White's considerable lead in development.

13...de (13...⌗a6 is bad because of 14 ⌗×a6 ⌗×a6 15 ed ed 16 ⌗×d5) 14 ⌗b5! ⌗d7 15 ⌗d2 a6 16 ⌗×c6 ⌗×c6 17 ⌗c4 ⌗f5 18 ⌗d6! e3 19 ⌗×e3 ⌗×b1+ 20 ⌗×b1 ⌗×d6

By giving up material Black tries to weaken White's onslaught, but without success.

21 ⌗×b6 ⌗d7 22 ⌗b3 ⌗ab8 23 ⌗c2 ⌗b5 24 0-0 ⌗h5 25 h3, and White has a won position.

Harmony in the development of the flanks

The development of the flanks should also be harmonious. Mobilization can hardly be considered complete if the pieces on one flank are well developed, but those on the other are totally undeveloped. In such cases the mobilization

'balance arm' is as though disturbed, and the weight of the undeveloped flank will sometimes overturn the entire set-up.

In this respect the following game is instructive for players of any standard.

No. 27 Keres-Botvinnik
Absolute USSR Ch
Moscow, 1941
Nimzo-Indian Defence

1 d4 ⌗f6 2 c4 e6 3 ⌗c3 ⌗b4 4 ⌗c2 d5 5 cd ed 6 ⌗g5 h6! 7 ⌗h4

It soon transpires that 7 ⌗×f6 would have been better, but it is very tempting to maintain the pin on the knight.

7...c5 8 0-0-0 *(8)*

White would appear to have successfully solved his main opening problems. He has already castled, and is actively pressing against Black's central d5 pawn. But in aiming for this position, White failed to take account of a highly significant factor — the totally undeveloped state of his K-side. It is this circumstance, together with the possibility of favourably opening the position on the Q-side, which allows Black to begin a very strong attack on the white king.

8...♗xc3! 9 ♕xc3 g5! 10 ♗g3 cd!

Disregarding positional weakenings, Black conducts the attack with colossal energy. His main problem is to assail the opponent's king while White's K-side is still bottled up. In addition, by ...g5! Black has temporarily shut out of the game another of the opponent's pieces — his dark-square bishop.

11 ♕xd4 ♘c6 12 ♕a4 ♗f5 13 e3 ♖c8 14 ♗d3 ♕d7!, and soon Black completely overran his opponent's position.

The following example on the same theme is no less attractive and convincing.

No. 28 Larsen-Spassky
USSR-Rest of World
Belgrade, 1970
Nimzowitsch Larsen Attack

1 b3 e5 2 ♗b2 ♘c6 3 c4 ♘f6 4 ♘f3 e4 5 ♘d4 ♗c5 6 ♘xc6 dc 7 e3 ♗f5 8 ♕c2 ♕e7 9 ♗e2?! (9 d4!) **9...0-0-0! 10 f4?** (10 a3 is better) **10...♘g4! 11 g3 h5!** *(9)*

A correct and highly energetic

plan. Black opens up the position on the K-side, which assists the development of his initiative. Only in this way can he exploit the 'freezing' of White's Q-side.

12 h3 h4! 13 hg

Interesting variations arise after 13 ♗xg4 ♗xg4 14 hg hg 15 ♖g1 ♖h1! 16 ♖xh1 g2 17 ♖g1 ♕h4+ 18 ♔e2 ♕xg4+ 19 ♔e1 ♕g3+ 20 ♔e2 ♕f3+ 21 ♔e1 ♗e7 or 20 ♔d1 ♕f2 21 ♕xe4 ♕xg1+ 22 ♔c2 ♕f2!, when Black wins.

13...hg 14 ♖g1 ♖h1!! 15 ♖xh1 g2 16 ♖f1 (or 16 ♖g1 ♕h4+ 17 ♔d1 ♕h1 18 ♕c3 ♕xg1+ 19 ♔c2 ♕f2 20 gf ♕xe2 21 ♘a3 ♗b4 with a decisive attack for Black) **16...♕h4+ 17 ♔d1 gf♕+ 0-1**

Excessive prophylaxis

Excessive prophylaxis in the opening is often a significant mistake, and common but unnecessary pawn moves such as ...h7-h6 (or h2-h3) are especially to be condemned.

And yet how tempting it is at times to make such a move, in order, for example, to avoid a pin. Especially since in a number of cases such prophylaxis is indeed useful. Thus in the main line of the Spanish Game after 1 e4 e5 2 ♘f3 ♘c6 3 ♗b5 a6 4 ♗a4 ♘f6 5 0-0 ♗e7 6 ♖e1 b5 7 ♗b3 d6 8 c3 0-0, although this position has occurred a countless number of times, players with White have been unable to, and are unlikely to, devise anything better than the flexible 9 h3!

But in the given case this is not a significant loss of time (in addition the position is not an open one), and it restricts Black's counterplay (it radically prevents . . .♗g4 etc). In short, it is a justified decision. But such moves, made out of a fear of what might happen, without specific reason, are a simple waste of time.

One of the simplest examples of what can result from unnecessary moves of the rooks' pawns is the famous Legall mate: 1 e4 e5 2 ♘f3 d6 3 ♗c4 h6? 4 ♘c3 ♗g4? 5 ♘xe5 ♗xd1 6 ♗xf7+ ♔e7 7 ♘d5 mate.

Suppose that instead of 3. . . h6? Black had played any useful developing move, e.g. 3. . .♘c6 or 3. . .♗e7. Then not only would the sacrifice on e5 (5 ♘xe5) have been impossible, but White would not have even gained any immediate advantage.

In playing . . .h7-h6 (or correspondingly h2-h3) inexperienced players are usually motivated by a desire to avoid either a knight attack on f7, or the 'unpleasantness' resulting from a pin on the h4-d8 diagonal, which usually arises after ♗c1-g5. It is not hard to show that in the majority of cases these threats can easily be parried.

For example, in the variation 1 e4 e5 2 ♘f3 ♘c6 3 ♗c4 ♗c5 4 d3 Black has no reason to fear 5 ♘g5 or 5 ♗g5. Without wasting time on 4. . .h6, he should continue his development with 4. . .d6 or 4. . .♘f6. If on 4. . .d6 White plays 5 ♘g5, after 5. . .♘h6 Black easily parries the threat against f7 and simultaneously completes the development of his K-side.

4. . .♘f6 is equally safe, there being no reason to fear the pin after ♗c1-g5. Moreover, in many cases one can ignore this threat, and resort to. . .h7-h6 for a counterattack on the bishop in the event of the pin.

Advantageous opening of the centre

From the examples examined earlier it will be apparent that the exploitation of a lead in development invariably involves the advantageous opening of the centre.

It is in an open position that a lead in development proves most significant. GM Rudolf Spielmann maintained, for example, that in the majority of cases in an open game a lead of three tempi should almost automatically ensure a won position, which logically it should be possible to find.

Here are some examples from his games.

No. 29 Spielmann-Flamberg
Mannheim, 1914
Vienna Game

1 e4 e5 2 ♘c3 ♘f6 3 f4 d5 4 fe ♘xe4 5 ♘f3 ♗g4 6 ♕e2! ♘c5? (6...♘xc3 7 dc ♘c6 is better, but Black considered 7 d4 to be unfavourable for White; nevertheless...) 7 d4! ♗xf3 8 ♕xf3 ♕h4+ *(10)*

In his calculations Black considered only 9 ♕f2 here, after

which 9...♕xf2+ 10 ♔xf2 ♘e6 11 ♘xd5 c6 and 12...♘xd4 leads to a favourable ending for him. But Spielmann's thinking is on a broader plane. In the best traditions of Paul Morphy, the founder of opening principles in open games, he sacrifices two pawns, and for purely strategic aims — to open the centre to his advantage. Black is unable to avert this dangerous turn of events.

9 g3! ♕xd4 10 ♗e3 ♕xe5 11 0-0-0 c6 12 ♘xd5 cd 13 ♖xd5 ♕e6 14 ♗c4 ♕e4 15 ♗xc5! 1-0

No. 30 Bernstein-Spielmann
Ostend, 1906
Tarrasch Defence

1 d4 d5 2 c4 e6 3 ♘c3 c5 4 cd ed 5 dc(?) d4 6 ♘a4 ♗xc5 7 ♘xc5 ♕a5+ 8 ♕d2? (the start of an incorrect plan; 8 ♗d2 was better) 8...♕xc5 9 b4 ♕b6 10 ♗b2 ♘c6 11 a3 ♗e6 12 ♘f3 ♖d8 13 ♕g5? *(11)*

A typical mistake, which experienced players commit very

rarely, usually as a result of an oversight, and weak players make fairly often, due to a lack of understanding of basic principles.

Of course, the queen move looks tempting: White tries to disorganize the development of Black's K-side. But, as the winner correctly remarked in his notes to the game, can Black's natural development really be disrupted in such an 'unlikely way'?

White wanted to gain a tempo by threatening to capture on g7. With his next move Black directs his opponent's actions precisely to this place; he gives up the pawn, but in turn gains a highly important tempo for the development of his pieces. And with the position being an open one, Black's lead in development becomes decisive.

13...♘f6! 14 ♕xg7? (14 ♕c5 was better) **14...♔e7!** (with the unequivocal threat of 15... ♘xb4!) **15 ♕h6 ♖hg8 16 ♖d1 a5! 17 ♕d2 ♘e4 18 ♕c2 f5 19 ba ♕xa5+ 20 ♘d2 ♘e5 21 ♗c1 ♖d6 22 f3 ♘c3 23 g3 ♖b6 24 ♔f2 ♖c8 25 ♔g1 ♘xe2+ 0-1**

No. 31 Shories-Spielmann
Scheveningen, 1905
Spanish Game

1 e4 e5 2 ♘f3 ♘c6 3 ♗b5 a6 4 ♗a4 ♘f6 5 0-0 ♘xe4 6 d4 b5 7 ♗b3 d5 8 de ♗e6 9 c3 ♗c5 10 a4 b4 11 ♕e2 0-0 12 ♗c2 f5!

It can be said that, although the game was played more than 80 years ago, this is a perfectly modern pawn sacrifice. White accepts the challenge, reckoning that after 13 ♗e3 ♗xe3 14 ♕xe3 f4 15 ♕d3 ♗f5 or 15 ♕e2 ♗g4 Black has an undisputed advantage.

13 ef ♕xf6 14 ♗xe4 de 15 ♕xe4 ♗b3! 16 c4? (16 ♗e3 is rather better) **16...♕d6! 17 ♘bd2** (17 ♕d5+ was essential, agreeing to an inferior ending) **17...♖ae8 18 ♕b1 ♘d4! 19 ♘e4 ♘xf3+ 20 gf ♕g6+ 21 ♔h1 ♖xf3 22 ♖e1 ♖xf2 23 ♗g5 ♕h5 24 ♘f6+ gf 25 ♖xe8+ ♔f7 0-1**

We will also examine two striking examples from the games of Alekhine.

No. 32 Alekhine-Seitz
Hastings, 1925-26
Budapest Counter-Gambit

1 d4 ♘f6 2 c4 e5 3 de ♘g4 4 e4 ♘xe5 5 f4 ♘ec6 6 ♗e3 ♗b4+ (6...♘a6 followed by...♗c5 is better) **7 ♘c3 ♕e7 8 ♗d3 f5 9 ♕h5+! g6 10 ♕f3 ♗xc3+ 11 bc fe?** (this opening of the game is inappropriate; it merely allows White to begin a decisive attack) **12 ♗xe4 0-0 13 ♘d5+ ♔h8 14 ♘h3 d6 15 0-0 ♗xh3 16 ♕xh3**

♕d7 17 f5! gf 18 ♖ab1 f4 19 ♗xf4 ♕xh3 20 ♗e5+! 1-0

No. 33 Alekhine-Marshall
New York, 1927
Queen's Pawn Opening

1 d4 ♘f6 2 c4 e6 3 ♘f3 ♘e4? 4 ♘fd2! ♗b4 5 ♕c2 d5 6 ♘c3 f5 7 ♘dxe4 fe 8 ♗f4 0-0 9 e3 c6 10 ♗e2 ♘d7 11 a3 ♗e7 12 0-0 ♗g5 13 f3! ♗xf4 14 ef ♖xf4 15 fe ♖xf1+ 16 ♖xf1 e5 17 ♕d2! c5 18 de! d4 19 ♕f4! dc 20 ♕f7+ ♔h8 21 bc *(12)*

This underlines the hopelessness of the position for Black, who is in an unusual type of zugzwang. After 21 e6? ♘f6 22 e7 ♕g8 23 ♖xf6 ♗g4! 24 ♕xg8+ ♔xg8 25 ♖d6 ♖e8, on the contrary, it is White who would have been in a difficult position.

21...♕g8 22 ♕e7 h6 23 ♗h5! a5 24 e6 g6 25 ed ♗xd7 26 ♖f7! 1-0

Retribution for routine play

A chess player's practical thinking must be specific, and this applies also to the development of the pieces in the opening. It is not enough to be able to deploy the pieces competently — from the very first moves of the game he must get to the essence of the struggle.

Apart from direct mistakes, there is nothing more ruinous than routine play, the aim of which is mechanical development. This is clearly demonstrated by the following examples.

No. 34 Portisch-Benko
Las Palmas, 1972
English Opening

1 ♘f3 c5 2 c4 g6 3 d4 cd 4 ♘xd4 ♘f6 5 ♘c3 d5 6 ♗g5 dc 7 e3 ♗g7 8 ♗xc4 0-0 9 0-0 ♗d7 10 ♕d2 ♘c6 11 ♖fd1 ♘xd4?

An instructive mistake. Black appears successfully to relieve the tension in the centre and to achieve full equality, but White has not only a lead in development, but also very active pieces. He has available a clever tactical possibility.

12 ♕xd4 ♗c6 13 ♗xf7+!

This is where the weak spot is revealed! — if 13...♔xf7 14

♕c4+! etc.

13...♔h8 14 ♕h4 ♕c8 15 ♗c4 (but not 15 ♗×g6? ♕g4 16 ♕×g4 ♘×g4 etc. with counterchances for Black) 15...♘g4 16 f3 ♘e5 17 ♗e2 ♕e6 18 e4 ♖fe8 19 ♔h1 ♘f7 20 ♗e3 ♖ed8 21 ♕f2 a6 22 ♗b6 ♖f8 23 ♗d4 ♘e5 24 ♕g3 ♖f7 25 f4 1-0

No. 35 Portisch-Lombard
Biel IZ, 1976
Queen's Gambit

1 c4 ♘f6 2 ♘c3 e6 3 ♘f3 d5 4 d4 c6 5 ♕b3 ♘bd7 6 ♗g5 ♗e7 7 e3 0-0 8 ♗d3 dc?! 9 ♕×c4 a6 10 ♗c2 b5 11 ♕d3 ♗b7 12 e4! g6 13 ♗h6? *(13)*

This natural move proves to be a mistake, with serious consequences. Correct was 13 e5! ♘d5 14 ♗×e7 ♕×e7 15 ♘×d5 ed 16 0-0 with an obvious advantage to White.

13...♖e8 14 e5 ♘g4! 15 ♗f4 c5 16 ♘e4 cd 17 h3 f5!

The point of Black's idea is that his forces in the centre are sharply activated and develop very strong counterplay, while at the same time the white pieces are driven back from their active positions with gain of tempo. As a result the white king, caught in the centre, becomes a vulnerable target.

18 ♘ed2 (18 ♘eg5 ♗×g5 19 ♗×g5 ♘g×e5 is bad for White, as is 18 ♘g3 ♗×f3! etc) 18...♘c5 19 ♕f1 d3! 20 ♗d1 g5 21 hg gf 22 ♕g1 ♖f8 23 ♕h2 ♖f7 24 gf ef 25 ♕×f4 ♗d5 26 ♖h5 ♘e6 27 ♕g3+ ♖g7 28 ♕h2 ♗b4 29 a3 ♕a5 30 ♖h6 ♖e8 31 ♕h5 ♖ee7 32 ♖c1 ♗×d2+ 33 ♘×d2 ♘f8! 34 ♗f3 ♖×e5+ 35 ♔d1 ♗b3+ 0-1

We give some further examples on the same theme.

No. 36 Bronstein-Averbakh
USSR Ch, Moscow, 1963
Nimzo-Indian Defence

1 d4 ♘f6 2 c4 e6 3 ♘c3 ♗b4 4 e3 0-0 5 ♗d3 d5 6 ♘f3 c5 7 0-0 ♘c6 8 cd ed 9 ♘e2? c4! 10 ♗c2 ♖e8 11 ♗d2 ♗d6 12 b3 cb 13 ♗×b3 ♗g4 14 ♘c3 ♘e4!

White's position is already very difficult, a consequence of his feeble, routine play. The threat of 15...♗×f3 16 gf ♕g5+ 17 ♔h1 ♕h4 is pretty significant.

15 ♖e1? (he could have held on by 15 ♘e2) 15...♗×f3 16 gf ♘×f2! 17 ♔×f2 ♕h4+ 18 ♔e2 ♕×h2+ 19 ♔d3 ♘b4 mate!

No. 37 Kupreichik-Estrin
Leningrad, 1965
Centre Game

1 e4 e5 2 d4 ed 3 ♕×d4 ♘c6 4
♕e3 ♘f6 5 ♘c3 ♗b4 6 ♗d2 0-0 7
0-0-0 ♖e8 8 ♗c4 d6 ♘h3! ♘e5(?)
10 ♗b3 ♗e6 11 f4 ♘c4 12 ♗×c4
♗×c4 13 e5! ♘d7?

13...de is better. Now White
obtains a very strong attack on
f7.

14 ♘e4 ♗×d2+ 15 ♖×d2 ♗b5
16 ♕b3 ♗c6 17 ♘eg5 d5 18 ♘×f7!
♔×f7 19 ♘g5+ ♔f8 20 ♖×d5 h6

Black's position is hopeless,
e.g. 20...♖e7 21 ♘×h7+ ♔e8 22
♖×d7 and 23 ♕g8+, or 20...
♗×d5 21 ♕×d5 ♘×e5 22 ♘×h7+
♔e7 23 ♕×e5+ ♔d7 24 ♖d1+
etc.

21 ♘h7+ ♔e7 22 f5! ♗×d5 23
♕×d5 ♕c8 24 f6+ ♔d8 25 f7 1-0

No. 38 Fokin-Suetin
Daugavpils Otborochnii, 1978
Slav Defence

1 d4 d5 2 c4 c6 3 ♘f3 ♘f6 4 ♘c3
e6 5 e3 ♘bd7 6 ♗d3 dc 7 ♗×c4 b5
8 ♗d3 a6 9 e4 c5 10 d5!? c4 11 de
fe 12 ♗c2 ♕c7 13 ♗g5? ♗c5 14
♕e2 ♗b7 15 0-0 0-0 16 ♖ad1?
(14)

White has made solid developing moves, and appears to be
completing his mobilization, but
this essentially brings about his
catastrophe. Now follows a

forcing, combinational attack by
Black.

14

16...♘g4! 17 h3 (also bad is 17
g3 ♘de5 18 ♗f4 ♘×f2! 19 ♖×f2
♘×f3+ 20 ♕×f3 e5 etc) 17...
♘de5! 18 ♘×e5

White also loses after 18 hg
♘×f3+ 19 gf ♕g3+! 20 ♔h1
♕h3+ 21 ♔g1 ♖×f3, or 18 ♘d4
♗×d4 19 ♖×d4 ♘f3+ etc.

18...♘×f2! 19 ♖d7 ♕×e5 20
♗e3 ♘×h3+ 0-1

Flexibility of development in the opening

Another 'delicate' rule is that
mobilization should as far as
possible be flexible.

During the initial moves it is
advantageous to retain as wide a
choice as possible of further
opportunities, while devoting
the main attention to general
opening tasks, i.e. the mobilization of the pieces and the
struggle for control of the central
squares, without tying oneself,

until a certain time, to committing operations.

Usually one should avoid an early fixing of the central formation or early exchanges, if this is to the detriment of the basic tasks of mobilization. To explain this we will consider the initial moves of the Sicilian Defence: **1 e4 c5 2 ♘f3 ♘c6 3 d4 cd 4 ♘xd4 ♘f6** *(15)*

With his last move Black has attacked the e4 pawn and created pressure on the central squares. White's strongest reply is undoubtedly 5 ♘c3, since it assists the development of the pieces in their most active positions and increases White's influence on the centre.

Other ways of defending the pawn are significantly worse. Thus 5 f3 leads to a premature weakening of White's K-side, and 5 ♘xc6 bc 6 ♗d3 to a strengthening of Black's pawn centre.

In the French Defence the immediate gain of space by White with 3 e5 is also very debatable. The position in the centre becomes blocked, and Black, who has not yet begun mobilizing his pieces, acquires very convenient ways of undermining White's pawn centre. In a short time Black often seizes the initiative.

After the moves pursuing the general tasks of the opening, the main struggle gradually develops.

If, in particular, we continue the variation of the Sicilian Defence considered above for just one more move, it becomes clear that after 5 ♘c3 d6 6 ♗c4 (as an example we will take the Sozin Attack) the struggle begins to take on a more specific character.

Although 6 ♗c4 strives mainly for the rapid mobilization of the pieces, it also determines the subsequent plan of active pressure along the a2-g8 diagonal, and there are already concrete threats: 7 ♘xc6 bc 8 e5! de 9 ♗xf7+, with which Black has to reckon.

The advantage of the first move and the initiative

In the initial chess position there exists a natural equality of force of the two sides, and this determines their roughly equal chances in the opening struggle.

A tangible positional advantage can be achieved in the opening only after definite mistakes by one of the sides, in particular after disturbance of the equilibrium in the opening, disregard for opening principles, nonconcrete approach to the position, and so on.

However, the character of the opening struggle is also significantly influenced by the right of the first move, which belongs to White and makes him the active side. It gives White a certain initiative at the start of the game, expressed in his active aspirations and slightly greater choice of different plans.

To a certain degree Black must submit to White's initiative, and his plans depend on those of the active side. Thus in many cases the player with Black, before creating his active counterplan, must weigh things up with great care.

In the following game Black committed an instructive mistake, in playing an early . . .b5. In the given variation this is in general his basic plan of counterplay, but . . .b5 should have been prepared after completing his development, and tactically should have been weighed up very thoroughly. After playing

. . .b5 on the off chance, Black's idea met with a decisive refutation.

No. 39 Taimanov-Aronin
Leningrad, 1951
Sicilian Defence

1 e4 c5 2 ♘f3 d6 3 d4 cd 4 ♘xd4 ♘f6 5 ♘c3 ♘c6 6 ♗g5 e6 7 ♕d2 a6 8 0-0-0 h6 9 ♗f4 ♗d7 10 ♗g3 b5? *(16)*

11 ♗xd6! ♗xd6 12 ♘xc6 ♗xc6 13 ♕xd6 ♕xd6 14 ♖xd6 ♗xe4 15 ♘xe4 ♘xe4 16 ♖xa6!! and White won easily.

Or take the problem of the struggle for a critical point in the centre, when a typical pawn tension exists (white pawns on d4 and e4, black pawns at d6 and e5). Releasing the tension by d4×e5 d4×e5 is normally favourable to Black, since he thereby gains equality in the centre. White in turn will try to provoke the exchange . . .e5×d4, after which he gains a definite advantage in space.

In many cases the opening struggle revolves around this, and often logic dictates that Black has to make certain concessions, by being the first to release the tension in the centre. Instructive in this respect is the classic Steinitz Variation of the Spanish Game: 1 e4 e5 2 ♘f3 ♘c6 3 ♗b5 d6 4 d4 ♗d7 5 ♘c3 ♘f6 6 0-0 ♗e7 7 ♖e1.

It now transpires that Black cannot hold his e5 point, since after 7...0-0 there follows 8 ♗×c6 ♗×c6 9 de de 10 ♕×d8 ♖a×d8 11 ♘×e5 ♗×e4 12 ♘×e4 ♘×e4 13 ♘d3 f5 14 f3 ♗c5+ 15 ♘×c5 ♘×c5 16 ♗g5! ♖d5 17 ♗e7, when Black loses by force, since against the threat of 18 c4 he has no defence. This was how the game Tarrasch-Marco (Nuremberg, 1892) concluded. In the event of 10...♖f×d8 11 ♘×e5 ♗×e4 12 ♘×e4 ♘×e4 13 ♘d3 f5 14 f3 ♗c5+ White wins by 15 ♔f1.

Thus, truly with mathematical authenticity White compels his opponent to concede the centre by 7...ed 8 ♘×d4 0-0. But although this is forced, it does not signify that Black has conceded any great advantage. In the resulting typical structure in the centre (pawn on e4 against pawn on d6) it is true that White has a certain spatial advantage,

but Black has no vulnerable points in his pawn formation, and the mobilization of his forces is largely complete. All this provides the basis for gradual equaliziation of the game by Black, which is often what in fact occurs.

However, White's chances are nevertheless preferable, since he enjoys a slight but persistent initiative thanks to his greater freedom.

Does this mean that in the opening Black is doomed to passive defence and deprived of activity? By no means! On the contrary, in modern opening set-ups his activity is growing ever greater. Black merely has greater difficulties and bears more responsibility for his actions. While a slight mistake by White usually entails only the loss of his initiative, a similar mistake on the part of Black can often have much more serious consequences.

It is natural that in the opening stage White should aim to consolidate and increase his initiative, whereas Black in turn will try to neutralize such aspirations of White and if possible to seize the initiative.

In master play the firm possession of the initiative is regarded as a definite achievement, and, as is customarily stated in chess literature, it ensures a slight but persistent advantage.

Thus in the modern opening the factor of the initiative plays a most important role. It indicates the degree of preparedness for carrying out an active plan. Therefore it is only if the initiative is held that there are real preconditions for putting one's plans into action.

It will be apparent that the struggle for the initiative in the opening revolves around the central squares. Both active and defensive means are constantly being improved, and it is this that advances the development of opening theory.

Move order in the opening

Move order in the opening is often of great practical importance. Sometimes a change in the order of even two adjacent moves can lead to completely different systems of play, Take, for example, the main line of the Spanish Game: 1 e4 e5 2 ♘f3 ♘c6 3 ♗b5 a6 4 ♗a4 ♘f6 5 0-0 ♗e7 6 ♖e1 b5 7 ♗b3. At first sight the difference between 7...0-0 and 7...d6 seems significant. In both cases after 8 c3 d6 (or 8...0-0) 9 h3 ♘a5 10 ♗c2 c5 11 d4 etc. the basic Closed Vari-

ation arises. And in many instances of course that is what in fact happens. But at the same time, after 7...0-0 8 c3 Black has the possibility of playing the sharper 8...d5!? leading to the Marshall Attack. On the other hand, after 7...0-0 White has the quite effective continuation 8 a4, with which Black now has to reckon.

Often the correct move order in the opening has a different, more significant practical importance. The mechanical reproduction of moves in the opening and a mix-up in their order can quickly lead to catastrophe.

As an illustration let us examine the Dragon Variation of the Sicilian Defence: 1 e4 c5 2 ♘f3 d6 3 d4 cd 4 ♘×d4 ♘f6 5 ♘c3 g6 6 f4!? Here 6...♗g7 simply 'asks' to be played, but before making this reply Black must weigh things up very carefully, since after 7 e5! White gains a very dangerous initiative. Correct is 6...♘c6!, and if 7 ♗e3 only now 7...♗g7, when 8 ♗e2 leads to one of the Classical Variations, normally reached via a different move order: 6 ♗e2 (instead of 6 f4!?) 6...♗g7 7 ♗e3 ♘c6 8 f4 etc.

Or take another elementary example, again from the Marshall Attack: 1 e4 e5 2 ♘f3 ♘c6 3 ♗b5 a6 4 ♗a4 ♘f6 5 0-0 ♗e7

6 ♖e1 b5 7 ♗b3 0-0 8 c3 d5 9 ed ♘xd5 10 ♘xe5 ♘xe5 11 ♖xe5 ♘f6 12 d4 ♗d6 13 ♖e1 ♘g4 14 h3 ♕h4 15 ♕f3. Here Black plays 15...♘xf2, when it is un-favourable for White to capture: 16 ♕xf2? (16 ♖e2! or 16 ♗d2! is correct) 16...♗h2+ 17 ♔f1 ♗g3, with a very strong attack for Black. But even in serious tourna-ment games Black sometimes 'automatically' plays 15... ♗h2+?? 16 ♔f1 and here takes with the knight on f2. This trans-position of moves has irrepar-able consequences, since after 17 ♕xf7+!! Black is mated (17...♖xf7 18 ♖e8 mate!)

The following is also a charac-teristic example.

No. 40 Fischer-Tal
Bled, 1961
Sicilian Defence

1 e4 c5 2 ♘f3 ♘c6 3 d4 cd 4 ♘xd4 e6 5 ♘c3 ♕c7 6 g3 ♘f6? *(17)*

A careless violation of the correct move order. Correct was first 6...a6 and only then 7... ♘f6. Now White gains a powerful initiative.

7 ♘db5! ♕b8 8 ♗f4! ♘e5 (8...e5 8 ♗g5 a6 10 ♗xf6! ab 11 ♗g5 etc. favours White) 9 ♗e2! ♗c5 (after 9...d6 10 ♕d4 ♘c6 11 ♘xd6+ ♔d7 12 ♗b5 ♗xd6 13 0-0-0! Black stands badly) 10 ♗xe5 ♕xe5 11 f4 ♕b8 12 e5 a6 (12...♘g8 13 ♘e4! ♗e7 14 ♕d2 would have given White an over-whelming advantage) 13 ef ab 14 fg ♖g8 15 ♘e4 ♗e7 16 ♕d4 ♖a4 17 ♘f6+ ♗xf6 18 ♕xf6 ♕c7 19 0-0-0 ♖xa2 20 ♔b1 ♖a6 21 ♗xb5! ♖b6 22 ♗d3 e5 23 fe! ♖xf6 24 ef ♕c5 25 ♗xh7 ♕g5 26 ♗xg8 ♕xf6 27 ♖hf1 ♕xg7 28 ♗xf7+ ♔d8 29 ♗e6!, and White won easily.

Such instances should be very carefully watched for, especially in sharp variations, full of com-binational possibilities. Opening theory is 'spelled out' move by move, normally with mathemat-ical accuracy, where behind the bare symbols there is in each case a 'physical' sense.

Thus a transposition of moves can not only take play along com-pletely different lines, but can also, and this is much more im-portant, lead to disaster.

two

ACTIVE OPERATIONS IN THE OPENING

Combinations, early attacks and counterattacks

As is shown by the majority of examples given above, the basic struggle in the opening very often arises before the completion of development. In many variations it is only a few initial moves which can truly be called mobilizing, when there is not yet the required contact between the two sides' forces.

But barely do the two sides' forces come into contact, when mobilization has to be combined in some way or other with active operations, and sometimes even with a direct attack (in the Open Games usually on the opponent's king). It is this that comprises the serious practical difficulty of playing the opening. It can be said that successful play in the opening demands not only an understanding of basic rules, but also great ingenuity and skill.

Essentially, any developing move must be carefully considered in connection with the specific conditions of the struggle. A move which does not accord with an active plan is a waste of time. This is confirmed by an example from the CaroKann Defence: after 1 e4 c6 2 ♘c3 d5 3 d4 de 4 ♘xe4 the manœuvre 4...♗f5 5 ♘g3 ♗g6 is highly expedient, since Black develops his bishop on the active b1-h7 diagonal. But the same manœuvre in an analogous variation: 1 e4 c6 2 ♘c3 d5 3 ♘f3 de 4 ♘xe4 ♗f5? 5 ♘g3 ♗g6? (5...♗g4 is correct) is unsatisfactory, since after 6 h4 h6 7 ♘e5 ♗h7 8 ♕h5! g6 9 ♗c4! Black comes under a crushing attack, e.g. 9...e6 10 ♕e2 ♘f6 11 ♘xf7! ♔xf7 12 ♕xe6+, and mate next move is inevitable.

The difference between these variations is that in the second of them, thanks to the move 3 ♘f3, the specific conditions arose for an attack on f7, by exploiting the gain of tempo in attacking the bishop at g6: h2-h4, ♘f3-e5!, ♕d1-h5 etc.

The triumph of tactics

Often, at a very early stage of the game, combinational motifs arise, when the outcome can be quickly decided by tactical blows, basically of the same nature as in the middlegame. But opening features can sometimes be very tangible, since at the start of the game, when almost all the forces are still on the board (although the greater part of them may be inactive), combinational difficulties may be caused by the congestion of the pieces. We give some examples on the theme of the 'smothering' of the queen or king.

No. 41 Gibaud-Lazard
Paris, 1924
Queen's Pawn Opening

1 d4 ♘f6 2 ♘d2 e5!? 3 de ♘g4. Here, suspecting nothing, White impulsively made the natural move 4 h3?, but after 4...♘e3! he was forced to resign.

An analogous situation arose in Vasyukov-Giterman (Odessa, 1960; Spanish Game): 1 e4 e5 2 ♘f3 ♘c6 3 ♗b5 ♗c5 4 c3 f5 5 d4! fe 6 ♘g5!? ♗e7? (6...♗b6! is correct) 7 de ♘xe5? 8 ♘e6!! 1-0.

And here is a rather different way of trapping the queen.

No. 42 Euwe-Rubinstein
Bad Kissingen, 1928
Queen's Gambit

1 d4 d5 2 c4 e6 3 ♘f3 ♘f6 4 ♗g5 ♘bd7 5 e3 ♗e7 6 ♘c3 0-0 7 ♖c1 c6 8 ♗d3 a6 9 cd ed 10 0-0 ♖e8 11 ♕b3 h6 12 ♗f4 ♘h5? 13 ♘xd5!, and 13...cd fails to 14 ♗c7! White went on to realize his advantage.

The same idea was employed in Alekhine-Rubinstein (San Remo, 1930; Queen's Gambit): 1 d4 d5 2 ♘f3 ♘f6 3 c4 e6 4 ♗g5 ♘bd7 5 e3 ♗e7 6 ♘c3 0-0 7 ♖c1 ♖e8 8 ♕c2 a6 9 cd ed 10 ♗d3 c6 11 0-0 ♘e4? 12 ♗f4 f5 13 ♘xd5! etc.

In the above examples it was the queen that was trapped. We now give some similar situations with the king, as a consequence of which the queen had to be given up.

No. 43 Fine-Yudovich
Moscow, 1936
Queen's Gambit

1 d4 d5 2 c4 e6 3 ♘c3 ♘f6 4 ♘f3 c5 5 ♗g5 cd 6 ♘xd4 e5 7 ♘bd5? a6 8 ♘xd5? ab 9 ♘xf6+ ♕xf6! 10 ♗xf6 ♗b4+ 11 ♕d2 ♗xd2+ 12 ♔xd2 gf, and being a piece down, White soon resigned.

One of the characteristic tactical ideas, especially in the ancient Open Games, is the diagonal attack on the enemy king which is restricted by its own pieces and pawns. The following examples confirm this.

No. 44 Blackburne-Teichmann
Two Knights Defence

1 e4 e5 2 ♘f3 ♘c6 3 ♗c4 ♘f6 4 ♘g5 d5 5 ed ♘×d5? 6 d4 ed 7 0-0 ♗e6 8 ♖e1 ♕d7 9 ♘×f7 ♔×f7 10 ♕f3+ ♔g8 11 ♖×e6! ♖d8 12 ♖e4 ♘a5? 13 ♖e8!! 1-0

No. 45 Maroczy-Vidmar
Ljubljana, 1923
Two Knights Defence

1 e4 e5 2 ♘f3 ♘c6 3 ♗c4 ♘f6 4 d4 ed 5 0-0 ♗c5 6 e5 d5 7 ef dc 8 ♖e1+ ♗e6 9 ♘g5 ♕d5 10 ♘c3 ♕f5 11 ♘ce4 ♗f8 12 ♘×f7! ♔×f7 13 ♘g5+ ♔g8 14 g4 ♕×f6? (better 14...♕g6) 15 ♖×e6 ♕d8 16 ♕f3 ♕d7 17 ♖e7!! 1-0

Another well known combinational tactic in the opening is the luring of the enemy queen into a trap. This can happen in a variety of ways, one of which is to lure the queen deep into one's own territory and then surround it.

No. 46 Kubanek-Flohr
Prague, 1930
Spanish Game

1 e4 e5 2 ♘f3 ♘c6 3 ♗b5 a6 4 ♗a4 d6 5 d4 b5 6 ♗b3 ♘×d4

7 ♘×d4 ed 8 ♗d5 ♖b8 9 ♕×d4 ♘e7 10 ♗g5 f6!? 11 ♗×f6?

Black lures the white queen, which is lost as a result of White's incorrect combination.

11...gf 12 ♕×f6 ♘×d5 13 ♕×h8 ♘f6!

This reply was obviously overlooked by White. Now the trap snaps shut.

14 0-0 ♕e7 15 f4 ♔f7 16 e5 ♗g7 0-1

No. 47 Botvinnik-Spielmann
Moscow, 1935
Caro-Kann Defence

1 e4 c6 2 d4 d5 3 ed cd 4 c4 ♘f6 5 ♘c3 ♘c6 6 ♗g5 ♕b6 7 cd ♕×b2?

A hazardous journey, after which Black's queen can no longer escape from the quagmire. He should have played 7...♘×d4, although here too White has a strong initiative after 8 ♘f3!

8 ♖c1 ♘b4 9 ♘a4 ♕×a2 10 ♗c4 ♗g4 11 ♘f3 ♗×f3 12 gf 1-0

If the queen is developed early, it will often come under fire in the middle of the board.

No. 48 Tolush-Aronson
USSR Ch, 1957
Chigorin Defence

1 d4 d5 2 c4 ♘c6 3 cd ♕×d5 4 ♘f3 ♗g4? 5 ♘c3 ♕a5 6 d5 0-0-0 7 ♗d2 ♗×f3 8 ef ♘b4? 9 a3

♘xd5? 10 ♘a4!, and the black queen is trapped.

No. 49 Robatsch–S. Garcia
Sochi, 1974
English Opening

1 c4 c5 2 ♘f3 g6 3 d4 ♗g7 4 e4 ♕a5+?! 5 ♘c3 ♘c6? 6 d5! ♘d4 7 ♗d2 ♕b6 8 ♘xd4 ♗xd4

Black is already in considerable difficulties. 10...cd is very strongly met by 11 ♘b5!

9 ♖b1 d6 10 ♘b5 ♗g7 11 ♕a4 ♗d7 12 ♗a5! ♕a6 13 ♘c7+ ♔f8 14 ♕a3! 1-0

No. 50 Krogius–Arotovsky
Saratov, 1945
Philidor's Defence

1 e4 e5 2 ♘f3 d6 3 d4 ♘d7 4 ♗c4 c6 6 ♘g5 ♘h6 6 a4 ♗e7? 7 ♗xf7+! ♘xf7 8 ♘e6 ♕b6 9 a5 ♕b4+ 10 c3 ♕c4 11 ♘c7+ ♔d8 12 b3 1-0

In the opening clever combinational situations sometimes arise, when the outcome is quickly decided by the threat of a pawn promoting. Here is an example from a well known variation of the Slav Defence: 1 d4 d5 2 c4 c6 3 ♘f3 ♘f6 4 e3 ♗f5 5 ♕b3 ♕b6 6 cd ♕xb3 7 ab ♗xb1? 8 dc! ♗e4. Black's calculations seem justified, but after 9 ♖xa7!! he has to resign: 9...♖xa7 10 c7!

'Lightning from a clear sky'

struck in the opening of Razuvayev–Kupreichik (Dubna, 1970; English Opening): 1 c4 e5 2 ♘c3 ♘c6 3 ♘f3 f5 4 d4 e4 5 ♗g5 ♘f6 6 d5? ef 7 dc fg 8 cd+ ♘xd7!! 0-1 *(18)*

If 9 ♗xd8 Black obtains a new queen by 9...gh♕, winning a rook in the process, while after 9 ♗xg2 ♕xg5 he is a piece up.

And now another example.

No. 51 Panov–Yudovich
USSR Ch, Tbilisi, 1937
French Defence

1 e4 e6 2 d4 d5 3 ♘c3 ♘f6 4 ♗g5 ♗e7 5 e5 ♘fd7 6 h4 f6 7 ♗d3?! (7 ♕h5+! is correct) 7...c5 8 ♕h5+ ♔f8 9 ♘xd5 fg! 10 ♖h3 g4! 11 ♘f4 ♘xe5 12 de gh! 13 ♗xh7? ♖xh7 14 ♕xh7 h2!! 15 ♔e2 h1♕ 16 ♘g6+ ♔f7 17 ♘h8+ ♕xh8 18 ♕xh8 ♘c6 19 ♕h5+ ♔g8 20 ♘h3 ♕xg2! 21 ♕e8+ ♗f8 and Black won.

Thus tactical blows lie in wait at the very start of the game, and in many cases are thematic in nature. Here are some examples of double attacks.

No. 52 Tartakower-Capablanca
New York, 1924
King's Gambit

1 e4 e5 2 f4 ef 3 ♗e2?! d5 4 ed ♘f6 5 c4 c6 6 d4 ♗b4+! 7 ♔f1 cd 8 ♗×f4 dc!

This looks like a crude oversight, but is in fact a subtle positional decision, based on precise calculation.

9 ♗×b8? *(19)*

White rises to the bait. 9 ♗×c4 was the lesser evil.

9...♘d5!

A double attack. The e3 and b4 squares are put under fire, allowing Black to regain his piece with interest.

10 ♔f2 (10 ♗g4 ♕f6!) **10... ♖×b8 11 ♗×c4 0-0 12 ♘f3 ♘f6 13 ♘c3 b5! 14 ♗d3 ♘g4+ 15 ♔g1 ♗b7 16 ♗f5 ♗×f3 17 gf ♘e3! 18 ♗×h7+ ♔h8! 19 ♕d3 ♗×c3 20 bc**

♘d5 21 ♗e4 ♘f4 22 ♕d2 ♕h4 23 ♔f1 f5 24 ♗c6 ♖f6 25 d5 ♖d8! 26 ♖d1 ♖×c6 27 dc ♖×d2 28 ♖×d2 ♘e6 29 ♖d6 ♕c4+ 30 ♔g2 ♕e2+ **0-1**

In the following example the double blow has the nature of a latent attack.

No. 53 Petrosian-Ree
Amsterdam, 1971
English Opening

1 c4 e5 2 ♘c3 ♘f6 3 ♘f3 ♘c6 4 g3 ♗b4 5 ♘d5 ♘×d5 6 cd ed4? 7 dc ef 8 ♕b3! 1-0

The next example demonstrates the idea of a discovered attack, which early in the game occurs quite often.

No. 54 Monticelli-Prokeš
1926
Queen's Indian Defence

1 d4 ♘f6 2 c4 e6 3 ♘f3 ♗b4+ 4 ♗d2 ♗×d2+ 5 ♕×d2 b6 6 g3 ♗b7 7 ♗g2 0-0 8 ♘c3 ♘e4?! 9 ♕c2 ♘×c3 10 ♘g5!! and White wins.

The similar tactical operation is not possible in this analogous variation: 1 d4 ♘f6 2 c4 e6 3 ♘f3 b6 4 g3 ♗b7 5 ♗g2 ♗e7 6 0-0 0-0 7 ♘c3 ♘e4 8 ♕c2 ♘×c3. Now on 9 ♘g5 Black can interpose the check 9...♘×e2+!, when it is White who loses. Thinking by analogy in such situations is dangerous, if not fatal.

The cause of defeat in the opening stage is quite often the overloading of a key defender. Here are several typical examples.

No. 55 Flohr-Gilg
Zurich, 1934
Nimzo-Indian Defence

1 d4 ♘f6 2 c4 e6 3 ♘c3 ♗b4 4 ♕c2 d5 5 cd ♕xd5 6 e3 0-0 7 ♘ge2 c5 8 ♗d2 ♕d8 9 a3 cd 10 ♘xd4 ♗a5 11 ♗e2 ♗b6 12 ♘f3 ♘c6 13 0-0 ♕e7 14 ♖fd1 e5 15 ♘g5 h6? 16 ♘d5! 1-0

No. 56 Euwe-Kramer
Holland, 1946
French Defence

1 e4 e6 2 d4 d5 3 e5 c5 4 c3 ♘c6 5 ♘f3 ♕b6 6 ♗e2 ♘ge7? (6...cd 7 cd ♘ge7) 7 dc! ♕c7 8 ♘d4 ♘xe5? 9 ♘b5! ♕xc5 10 ♕d4! 1-0

No. 57 Krogius-Martyushov
Tula, 1948
Queen's Indian Defence

1 d4 ♘f6 2 c4 e6 3 ♘f3 b6 4 g3 ♗b7 5 ♗g2 ♗e7 6 0-0 0-0 7 ♕c2 ♗e4 8 ♕a4 c5 9 d5! ed 10 ♘c3 ♘c6 11 cd ♗xd5 12 ♘xd5 ♘xd5 13 ♘h4! ♘c7? (better 13...♗xh4 14 ♗xd5 ♗g5) 14 ♖d1 ♕e8 15 ♘f5 ♘e6 16 ♖xd7 ♕xd7 17 ♗xc6 ♕c7 18 ♗xa8 ♖xa8 19 ♕c6!! 1-0

No. 58 Hasin-Lilienthal
Moscow, 1955
Scotch Game

1 e4 e5 2 ♘f3 ♘c6 3 d4 ed 4 ♘xd4 ♗c5 5 ♗e3 ♕f6 6 c3 ♘ge7 7 ♗c4 ♘e5 8 ♗e2 d5 9 0-0 h5? 10 ♘b5! ♕b6 11 ♗xc5 ♕xc5 12 ♕d4! 1-0

Significant among such tactical devices is the pin, most often along the h4-d8 diagonal for White and a5-e1 for Black.

No. 59 Kan-Botvinnik
Odessa, 1929
Evans Gambit

1 e4 e5 2 ♘f3 ♘c6 3 ♗c4 ♗c5 4 b4 ♗b6 5 a4 a6 6 ♘c3 ♘f6 7 ♘d5! ♘xe4 (better 7...♘xd5 8 ed e4) 8 0-0 0-0 9 d3 ♘f6 (not 9...♘d6 10 ♗g5 ♕e8 11 ♘f6+ gf 12 ♗xf6 etc) 10 ♗g5 d6 11 ♘d2 ♗g4 12 ♗xf6 ♕c8 13 ♘xb6 cb 14 f3, and White won.

No. 60 Boleslavsky-Peterson
Minsk, 1957
Nimzo-Indian Defence

1 d4 ♘f6 2 c4 e6 3 ♘c3 ♗b4 4 e3 b6 5 ♘ge2 ♗a6 6 ♘g3 0-0 7 e4 d6 8 ♗d3 e5? 9 0-0 ♗xc3 10 bc ♘c6 11 ♘f5 ♗c8 12 ♗g5! ed 13 ♘xd4 ♘e5 14 f4! ♘g6 15 e5! de 16 fe ♘xe5 17 ♗e4 ♗g4 18 ♕e1 ♕d6 19 ♗xf6 gf 20 ♕h4 f5 21 ♗xa8 ♘g6 22 ♕f2 ♖xa8 23 h3 ♗h5 24 ♕xf5 1-0

No. 61 Tarrasch-Bogoljubow
Germany, 1920
Queen's Indian Defence

1 d4 ♘f6 2 c4 e6 ♘f3 b6 4 ♗g5 ♗b7 5 e3 h6 6 ♗h4 ♗b4+ 7 ♘bd2? g5! 8 ♗g3 *(20)*

8. . .g4 9 a3 gf 10 ab fg 11 ♗xg2 ♗xg2 0-1

Since then this type of trap has often been repeated. Here is an example from one of Karpov's early games.

No. 62 Sangla-Karpov
USSR Teams Ch, Riga 1968
Queen's Pawn Opening

1 d4 ♘f6 2 ♘f3 e6 3 ♗g5 c5 4 c3 cd 5 cd ♕b6 6 ♕b3 ♘e4 7 ♗f4 ♘c6 8 e3 ♗b4+ 9 ♘bd2? g5! 10 ♗xg5 ♗xd2+ 11 ♘xd2 ♕a5 0-1

The pin is an effective tactical device in the opening, but the reverse consequences of a premature pin should also not be forgotten.

Up till now we have mainly been examining elementary tactical ideas, but in the opening stage fairly complex tactical operations are often encountered. Many of these have typical features. Thus the following combinational structure is widely known: rook at d1, bishop at g5, with mate on the 8th rank at d8 (known as Morphy's mate − cf. Game No. 1)

To illustrate this we give several examples, each of which is a little masterpiece.

No. 63 Reti-Tartakower
Vienna, 1910
Caro-Kann Defence

1 e4 c6 2 d4 d5 3 ♘c3 de 4 ♘xe4 ♘f6 5 ♕d3?! e5? (5. . .♘bd7) **6 de ♕a5+ 7 ♗d2 ♕xe5 8 0-0-0 ♘xe4 9 ♕d8+! ♔xd8 10 ♗g5++ 1-0** (10. . .♔e8 11 ♖d8 mate; 10. . . ♔c7 11 ♗d8 mate!)

No. 64 Nimzowitsch-Alapin
Carlsbad, 1911
French Defence

1 e4 e6 2 d4 d5 3 ♘c3 ♘f6 4 ed ♘xd5 5 ♘f3 c5 6 ♘xd5 ♕xd5 7 ♗e3! cd 8 ♘xd4 a6 9 ♗e2 ♕xg2? 10 ♗f3 ♕g6 11 ♕d2 e5 12 0-0-0 ed 13 ♗xd4 ♘c6 14 ♗f6! ♕xf6 15 ♖he1+ ♗e7 (15. . .♗e6 16 ♕d7 mate!) **16 ♗xc6+ ♔f8** (16. . .bc 17 ♕d8 mate!) **17 ♕d8+! ♗xd8 18 ♖e8 mate!**

No. 65 Vukovic–N. N.
Yugoslavia, 1926
Spanish Game

1 e4 e5 2 ♘f3 ♘c6 3 ♗b5 ♘f6
4 d4 ed 5 e5 ♘e4 6 ♗f4 f5 7 ♗xc6
dc 8 ♕xd4 ♕d5 9 ♘c3 ♕a5? 10
♖d1 ♗e7 11 ♗d2 ♕b6? 12 ♘e2
♗c5? 13 ♕d8+! ♔xd8 14 ♗g5++
♔e8 15 ♖d8+ ♔f7 16 e6+! ♔xe6
17 ♘f4+ ♔f7 18 ♘e5 mate!

No. 66 Bronstein–N. N.
Simultaneous display, 1950
Centre Game

1 e4 e5 2 d4 ed 3 ♕xd4 ♘c6
4 ♕a4 ♘f6 5 ♘c3 d5 6 ♗g5 de
7 ♘xe4 ♗e7 8 0-0-0 ♕xe4?
9 ♖d8+! ♔xd8 10 ♕xe4 1-0

No. 67
Bonch-Osmolovsky v. Baranov
Moscow, 1953
Petroff's Defence

1 e4 e5 2 ♘f3 ♘f6 3 d4 ed 4 e5
♘e4 5 ♕xd4 d5 6 ed ♘xd6 7 ♗d3
♕e7+ 8 ♗e3 ♘f5? 9 ♗xf5 ♗xf5
10 ♘c3 ♕b4 11 ♕e5+ ♗e6 12
0-0-0 ♘c6 13 ♕xc7 ♖c8 14 ♕f4
♕a5 15 ♕g5 ♕a6 16 ♖he1 ♘b4 17
♘d4 ♖xc3 *(21)* 18 ♕d8+!! ♔xd8
19 ♘xe6++ ♔e7

Black loses after 19...♔c8 20
♖d8 mate!, or 10...♔e8 20
♘xg7+ ♗xg7 21 ♗g5+! etc.
20 ♗g5+ f6 21 ♘d8+! 1-0

21

We now give another typical
combinational idea, which involves shutting out the
opponent's queen and then
attacking his king. This too is
accompanied by considerable
material sacrifices and demands
exceptional imagination.

No. 68
Anderssen–Kieseritzky
London, 1851
King's Gambit

1 e4 e5 2 f4 ef 3 ♗c4 ♕h4+
4 ♔f1 b5 5 ♗xb5 ♘f6 6 ♘f3 ♕h6
7 d3 ♘h5 8 ♘h4 ♕g5 9 ♘f5 c6 10
g4! ♘f6 11 ♖g1 cb 12 h4 ♕g6 13
h5 ♕g5 14 ♕f3 ♘g8 15 ♗xf4 ♕f6
16 ♘c3 ♗c5? 17 ♘d5 ♕xb2 18
♗d6! ♕xa1+ 19 ♔e2 ♗xg1 (19...
♕b2!) 20 e5!! ♘a6 21 ♘xg7+ ♔d8
22 ♕f6+! ♘xf6 23 ♗e7 mate!

The following example too
has not lost its charm.

No. 69   Alekhine-Levenfish
St. Petersburg, 1912
Benoni Defence

1 d4 c5 2 d5 ♘f6 3 ♘c3 d6 4 e4 g6 5 f4 ♘bd7 6 ♘f3 a6? 7 e5 de 8 fe ♘g4 9 e6 ♘de5 10 ♗f4 ♘xf3+ 11 gf! ♘f6 12 ♗c4 fe 13 de ♕b6 14 ♕e2! ♕xb2 *(22)*

15 ♘b5!! ♕xa1+ 16 ♔f2 ♕xh1 17 ♘c7+ ♔d8 18 ♕d2+ ♗d7 19 ed 1-0

In the examples below this motif appears in rather different form.

No. 70   Rodzinsky-Alekhine
St. Petersburg, 1913
Philidor's Defence

1 e4 e5 2 ♘f3 d6 3 ♗c4 ♘c6 4 c3 ♗g4 5 ♕b3?! ♕d7 6 ♘g5? (6 ♕xb7 ♖b8 7 ♕a6 ♖b6 8 ♕a4 f5 gives Black an excellent game) 6...♘h6 7 ♗xf7+? ♘xf7 8 ♘xf7 ♕xf7 9 ♕xb7 ♔d7! 10 ♕xa8 ♘c4! 11 f3 ♗xf3! 12 gf ♘d4! 13 d3 ♕xd3 14 cd ♗e7! 15 ♕xh8 ♗h4 mate!

No. 71   Euwe-Reti
Amsterdam, 1920
Two Knights Defence

1 e4 e5 2 ♘f3 ♘c6 3 ♗c4 ♘f6 4 d4 ed 5 0-0 ♘xe4 6 ♖e1 d5 7 ♗xd5 ♕xd5 8 ♘c3 ♕a5 9 ♘xd4 ♘xd4 10 ♕xd4 f5 11 ♗g5? (better 11 ♗d2) 11...♕c5! 12 ♕d8+ ♔f7 13 ♘xe4 fe 14 ♖ad1 ♗d6 15 ♕xh8 ♕xg5 16 f4 ♕h4 17 ♖xe4 ♗h3! 18 ♕xa8 ♗c5+ 19 ♔h1 ♗xg2+ 20 ♔xg2 ♕g4+ 0-1

The number of such combinational motifs, and especially of practical examples, is very great.

Early opening attacks

As can be seen from the above examples, in the opening an unpleasant and very strong attack can arise, in particular on the king. Confirmation of this was provided by instances of the enemy queen being shut out, and of Morphy's mate. In the opening stage, when mobilization is not yet complete, attacks are short-lived, and sometimes it is difficult to distinguish them from complicated combinations. And yet here it is always possible to disclose the strategic state of affairs.

We will consider several characteristic instances.

In the initial position the most vulnerable points are the respective squares on the K-side, f2 and f7, which are protected only by the king. Attacks on these arise in many variations, which may be strategically very varied.

An example is provided by the Greco Attack in the Italian Game: 1 e4 e5 2 ♘f3 ♘c6 3 ♗c4 ♗c5 4 c3 ♘f6 5 d4 ed 6 cd ♗b4+ 7 ♘c3 ♘xe4 8 0-0 ♘xc3 9 bc ♗xc3? 10 ♕b3! ♗xa1 (saving chances are offered by 10...d5! 11 ♗xd5 0-0) 11 ♗xf7+ ♔f8 12 ♗g5 ♘e7 13 ♘e5!, and White's attack is irresistible. Here the attack on f7 stems as though from the very nature of the opening set-up. But in the Queen's Gambit Accepted too, where initially the struggle develops on the Q-side, the f7 square very often comes under attack, e.g. 1 d4 d5 2 c4 dc 3 e4 c5?! 4 d5 e6 5 ♘c3 ♘f6 6 ♗xc4 ed 7 ♘xd5 ♘xd5 8 ♗xd5, with the unequivocal threat of 9 ♗xf7+!

We will consider some further examples on this theme.

No. 72 N. N. -Richter
Berlin, 1952
Irregular Opening

1 d4 e5? 2 de ♘c6 3 ♘f3 f6?! 4 ef ♘xf6 5 ♘c3 ♗c5 6 ♗g5 ♘g4!? 7 ♗xd8? ♗xf2+ 8 ♔d2 ♗e3+ 9 ♔d3? d5 10 ♘xd5 ♗f5+ 11 ♔c3 ♖xd8 12 ♘xc7+ ♔e7 13 ♘d5+ ♔e6 14 ♘g5+ ♗xg5 15 e4 ♔e5 16 ef ♘f2 17 ♕e1+ ♘e4+ 18 ♔b3 ♘d4+ 19 ♔c4 b5+ 20 ♔b4 a5+ 21 ♔xa5 ♖a8+ 22 ♔b6 ♖hb8+ 23 ♔c7 ♗d8+ 24 ♔d7 ♖a7+ 25 ♔e8 ♗f6 mate!

An almost fantastic game, which, however, has more than a hint of a composed idea about it.

No. 73 Hofman-Petrov
Warsaw, 1844
Italian Game

1 e4 e5 2 ♘f3 ♘c6 3 ♗c4 ♗c5 4 c3 ♘f6 5 d4 ed 6 e5 ♘e4 7 ♗d5 ♘xf2! *(23)*

8 ♔xf2 dc+ 9 ♔g3 cb 10 ♗xb2 ♘e7 11 ♘g5? ♘xd5 12 ♘xf7 0-0!! 13 ♘xd8 ♗f2+ 14 ♔h3 d6+ 15 e6 ♘f4+ 16 ♔g4 ♘xe6 17 ♘xe6 ♗xe6+ 18 ♔g5 ♖f5+ 19 ♔g4 h5+ 20 ♔h3 ♖f3 mate

No. 74 Maryasin-Epstein
USSR, 1967
Danish Gambit

1 e4 e5 2 ♘f3 ♘c6 3 d4 ed 4 c3

dc 5 ♗c4 cb 6 ♗×b2 d5 7 ♗×d5 ♘f6 8 0-0 ♗e7 9 ♕b3 0-0 10 ♖d1 ♕e8? (it was essential to exchange off White's strong bishop by 10... ♘×d5; by the irony of fate it is this bishop that strikes the decisive blow) 11 ♘a3 a6 12 ♖ac1 ♗d8 13 ♘c4 ♘e7

Now 13...♘×d5 14 ed ♘b8 15 ♗a3 ♗e7 16 ♖e1 favours White.

14 ♗×f7+!

A splendid combinational blow. The bishop places itself under a three-fold attack.

14... ♖×f7

14...♔×f7 15 ♘ce5 mate! is bad, as is 14...♕×f7 15 ♘g5!

15 ♘ce5 ♘c6 16 ♖×c6 bc ♘g5!

But not 17 ♖×d8? ♕×d8 18 ♘×f7 ♗e6!, when it is Black who wins.

17... ♗e7 18 ♘e×f7 ♔f8 19 e5 ♘d5 20 ♕f3 ♔g8 21 ♖×d5! ♗g4 (21...cd 22 ♕×d5 ♗×g5 23 ♘×g5+ ♗e6 24 ♘×e6 etc. is equally bad) **22 ♕e4 ♗×g5 23 ♘×g5 ♕h5 24 ♖d4 1-0**

Sometimes these attacks are combined with threats against other weak points on the K-side.

No. 75
Ciocaltea-Nezhmetdinov
Bucharest, 1954
Two Knights Defence

1 e4 e5 2 ♘f3 ♘c6 3 ♗c4 ♘f6 4 ♘g5 d5 5 ed ♘a5 6 ♗b5+ c6 7 dc bc 8 ♗e2 h6 9 ♘f3 e4 10 ♘e5 ♕c7

11 ♘g4?! ♗×g4 12 ♗×g4 ♗c5 13 ♗e2 ♖d8 14 c3 ♘b7 15 0-0 h5 16 d4 ed 17 ♗×d3 ♘g4 18 ♕e2+ ♔f8! 19 g3 ♕d7 20 ♗e4 h4 21 ♗f4 ♘×h2

The outcome of Black's combined attack.

22 ♖e1 ♘g4 23 ♗f3 ♗×f2 24 ♗e3 hg 25 ♗×c5+ ♘×c5 26 ♗×c6 ♘h3+ 27 ♔f1 ♕f5+ 1-0

Analogous attacks on f2 and f7 sometimes comprise the tactical 'seed' in a number of variations of the Semi-Open or Closed Openings.

A variation of the Caro-Kann Defence: 1 e4 c6 2 ♘c3 d5 3 ♘f3 de 4 ♘×e4 ♘d7 5 ♗c4 ♘gf6 6 ♘eg5 e6 7 ♕e2 h6? 8 ♘×f7! ♔×f7 9 ♕×e6+ etc., or here 4...♘f6 5 ♘×f6+ gf 6 ♗c4 ♗g4? 7 ♘e5! ♗×d1? 8 ♗×f7 mate!

A variation of the Sozin Attack in the Sicilian Defence: 1 e4 c5 2 ♘f3 ♘c6 3 d4 cd 4 ♘×d4 ♘f6 5 ♘c3 d6 6 ♗c4 g6? 7 ♘×c6 bc 8 e5! de? 9 ♗×f7+, and White wins the queen.

A variation of the Albin Counter-Gambit: 1 d4 d5 2 c4 e5 3 de d4 4 e3? ♗b4+ 5 ♗d2 de 6 ♗×b4? ef+! 7 ♔e2 fg♘+!, and Black's advantage is obvious.

The castled position as a target for attack in the opening

In general, castling is a necessary ritual, but it does not always guarantee 'peace' for the king! Moreover, in a number of cases castling may prove premature and may merely assist the development of the opponent's attack.

No. 76 Steinitz-Mongredien
London, 1863
Irregular Defence

1 e4 g6 2 d4 ♗g7 3 c3 b6 4 ♗e3 ♗b7 5 ♘d2 d6 6 ♘gf3 e5?! 7 de! de 8 ♗c4 ♘e7 9 ♕e2! 0-0? 10 h4! ♘d7 11 h5 c5 12 hg ♘xg6 13 0-0-0 a6 14 ♘g5 ♘f6 15 ♘xh7! ♘xh7 16 ♖xh7! ♔xh7 (16...b5 17 ♕h5! bc 18 ♖xg7+ ♔xg7 19 ♕h6+! favours White) 17 ♕h5+ ♔g8 18 ♖h1 ♖e8 19 ♕xg6 ♕g6 20 ♗xf7+ ♕xf7 21 ♖h8+! 1-0

No. 77 Euwe-Maroczy
Amsterdam, 1921
French Defence

1 e4 e6 2 d4 d5 3 ♘c3 ♘f6 4 ♗g5 ♗e7 5 e5 ♘fd7 6 h4 0-0? 7 ♗d3 c5 8 ♕h5 g6 9 ♕h6 ♖e8 10 ♗xe7 ♕xe7 11 h5 *(24)* 11...♘f8 12 ♘f3 cd 13 ♘g5! ♘bd7 14 ♘xh7! ♘xe5 15 hg ♘fxg6 16 ♗xg6 ♘xg6 17 g4! dc 18 0-0-0 1-0

No. 78 Kmoch-Alekhine
Vienna, 1922
Queen's Gambit

1 d4 ♘f6 2 ♘f3 d5 3 c4 c6 4 e3 ♗f5 5 ♘bd2 e6 6 ♗e2 ♘bd7 7 0-0? ♗d6 8 c5 ♗c7 9 b4 ♘e4 10 ♘xe4 de! 11 ♘d2 h5! 12 f4 g5! 13 g3? ♘f6! 14 ♗b2 gf 15 ef h4 16 ♕b3 hg 17 hg ♘d5 18 ♘c4 ♘xf4! 19 ♖ae1 (19 gf ♕h4!) 19...♕g5 20 d5 ♘d3! 0-1

No. 79 Fischer-Robatsch
Varna OL, 1962
Centre Counter Game

1 e4 d5 2 ed ♕xd5 3 ♘c3 ♕d8 4 d4 g6 5 ♗f4! ♗g7 6 ♕d2! ♘f6 (6...♗xd4 7 0-0-0 or 6...♕xd4 7 ♕xd4 ♗xd4 8 ♘b5 favours White) 7 0-0-0 c6?! (better 7...♘d5) 8 ♗h6 0-0? 9 h4 ♕a5 10 h5 gh 11 ♗d3 ♘bd7 12 ♘ge2 ♖d8 13 g4! ♘f8 (13...♘xg4 14 ♖dg1!!) 14 gh ♘e6 15 ♖dg1 ♔h8 16 ♗xg7+ ♘xg7 17 ♕h6 ♖g8 18 ♖g5 ♕d8 19 ♖hg1! ♘f5? 20 ♗xf5 1-0

No. 80 Bilek-Gheorghiu
Hungary, 1968
Sicilian Defence

1 e4 c5 2 ♘c3 ♘c6 3 g3 g6 4 ♗g2 ♗g7 5 d3 d6 6 f4 e5 7 ♘h3 ♘ge7 8 0-0 0-0? (8...♘d4) 9 f5! gf 10 ef ♗xf5 (10...♘xf5 11 ♕h5!) *(25)*

11 ♖xf5! ♘xf5 12 ♗e4 ♘fd4 13 ♕h5 ♖e8 14 ♕xh7+ ♔f8 15 ♗g5 ♕d7 16 ♘d5 ♖e6 17 ♖f1 ♘xc2 18 ♗g6 ♘2d4 19 ♗h6! 1-0

Pawn storms early in the game

A pawn storm of the opponent's castled position is one of the common strategic procedures in the middle of the game, and often this becomes the main plan in the transition from opening to middlegame. Sometimes such an offensive develops before the completion of mobilization and can be very dangerous, even if initially it is of a problematic nature.

The offensive on the K-side castled position is most often conducted by the hand gpawns, but the f-pawn is also sometimes involved.

We give some examples, the analysis of which will help in the mastering of such procedures.

No. 81 Marshall-Burn
Paris, 1900
Queen's Gambit

1 d4 d5 2 c4 e6 3 ♘c3 ♘f6 4 ♗g5 ♗e7 5 e3 0-0 6 ♘f3 b6 7 ♗d3 ♗b7 8 cd ed 9 ♗xf6 ♗xf6 10 h4 g6? (10...c5!?) 11 h5 ♖e8 12 hg hg 13 ♕c2 ♗g7 *(26)*

14 ♗xg6 fg 15 ♕xg6 ♘d7 16 ♘g5 ♕f6 17 ♖h8+! 1-0

No. 82 Pillsbury-Marco
Paris, 1900
Queen's Gambit

1 d4 d5 2 c4 e6 3 ♘c3 ♘f6 4 ♗g5 ♗e7 5 e3 0-0 6 ♘f3 b6 7 ♗d3 ♗b7

8 cd ed 9 ♘e5 ♘bd7 10 f4 c5?
(10...♘e8) 11 0-0 c4 12 ♗c2 a6
13 ♕f3 b5 14 ♕h3 g6 15 f5! b4 16
fg hg 17 ♕h4! bc 18 ♘xd7 ♕xd7
19 ♖xf6! a5 20 ♖af1 ♖a6 21
♗xg6! fg 22 ♖xf8+ ♗xf8 23
♖xf8+ ♔xf8 24 ♕h8+ ♔f7 25
♕h7+ 1-0

No. 83 Suetin-Fedosov
Tula, 1948
Four Knights Game

1 e4 e5 2 ♘f3 ♘f6 3 ♘c3 ♘c6 4
♗b5 ♗b4 5 0-0 0-0 6 d3 d6 7 ♗g5
♗xc3 8 bc ♘e7 9 ♘h4 ♗g4?
(9...♘e8) 10 ♗c4 ♔h8 11 ♕f3! f6
12 ♗d2 g5?! 13 ♘f5 ♗xf5 14 ef
♘h6 15 g4 c6 16 ♔g2 d5 17 ♗b3 b5
18 h4 ♗b7 (better 18...♔g7,
although here too White has the
advantage after 19 c4!) 19 hg fg 20
♖h1 ♘f7 21 ♖h5 h6 22 f6! ♖g8 23
♖ah1 ♖g6 24 ♗xg5! ♘xg5 25
♖xh6+ ♖xh6 26 ♖xh6+ ♘h7 27
♖xh7+! 1-0

No. 84 Kopylov-Dommes
Leningrad, 1954
King's Indian Defence

1 c4 ♘f6 2 ♘c3 g6 3 d4 ♗g7 4 e4
d6 5 f3 0-0 6 ♗e3 e5 7 d5 c5 8 g4!
♘e8 9 ♕d2 a6 10 ♘ge2 ♘c7 11
♘g3 b5 12 h4! f6 13 h5 ♖f7 14 hg
hg 15 ♕h2 ♖e7 16 ♕h7+ ♔f7 17
♖h6! g5 18 ♖xf6+! 1-0

No. 85 Spassky-Evans
Varna OL, 1962
King's Indian Defence

1 d4 ♘f6 2 c4 g6 3 ♘c3 ♗g7 4 e4
d6 5 f3 c6 6 ♗e3 a6 7 ♕d2 b5 8
0-0-0 bc? (better 8...♕a5) 9
♗xc4 0-0 10 h4 d5 11 ♗b3 de 12
h5! *(27)*

27

An early, but highly effective
offensive, which White conducts
with great vigour.

12...ef 13 hg hg 14 ♗h6! fg 15
♖h4! ♘g4 16 ♗xg7 ♔xg7 17
♕xg2 ♘h6 18 ♘f3 ♘f5 19 ♖h2
♕d6 20 ♘e5 ♘d7 21 ♘e4 ♕c7 22
♖dh1 ♖g8 23 ♖h7+ ♔f8 24
♖xf7+ ♔e8 25 ♕xg6!

And in conclusion a piquant
finish.

25...♘xe5 26 ♖f8++! 1-0

No. 86 Tal-R. Byrne
Biel IZ, 1976
Sicilian Defence

1 e4 c5 2 ♘f3 d6 3 d4 cd 4 ♕xd4
♘c6 5 ♗b5 ♗d7 6 ♗xc6 ♗xc6 7

♘c3 ♘f6 8 ♗g5 e6 9 0-0-0 ♗e7
10 ♖he1 0-0 11 ♕d2 ♕a5 12 ♘d4
♖ac8 13 ♔b1 ♔h8 14 f4 h6 (14...
♖fd8 is better, and if 15 e5 de 16
fe ♘g8 with a defensible
position) 15 h4! hg? (15...♖fd8
was the lesser evil) 16 hg ♘xe4 17
♕d3! ♗xg5

Black would have been
crushed after 17...♘xc3+ 18 bc
g6 19 ♕h3+ or 17...f5 18 ♕h3+
♔g8 19 ♘xe4 ♗xe4 20 g6 ♗h4 21
♕xh4 ♖fe8 22 ♘xf5!

18 ♘xe4 ♗xe4 19 ♖xe4 ♗h6
20 g4 f5 21 ♖xe6 ♗xf4 22 ♘xf5
1-0

No. 87 Sax-Donner
Amsterdam, 1976
French Defence

1 e4 e6 2 d4 d5 3 ♘c3 ♘f6 4
♗g5 ♗e7 5 e5 ♘fd7 6 h4! 0-0 7
♗d3 f5 8 g4! c5 9 gf cd 10 f6! ♘xf6
(10...gf 11 ♗xh7+ ♔xh7 12
♕h5+ ♔g8 13 ♕g6+ ♔h8 14
♘h3! gives White a decisive
attack; 10...♗xf6!? was the
lesser evil) 11 ef ♗xf6 12 ♕h5 g6
13 ♗xg6 ♕e7 14 ♘b5! ♘c6 15
♗d3 e5 16 ♘e2 ♔h8 17 ♘c7!
♕xc7 18 ♗xf6+ 1-0

No. 88 Pokojowczyk-Schmidt
Poland, 1976
Alekhine's Defence

1 e4 ♘f6 2 e5 ♘d5 3 d4 d6 4 ♘f3
♗g4 5 ♗e2 e6 6 0-0 ♗e7 7 c4 ♘b6

8 ♘c3 0-0 9 ♗e3 d5?! 10 c5 ♗xf3
11 gf! ♘c8 12 f4 ♗h4?! 13 ♗d3 g6
14 f5! ef 15 ♕f3 c6 16 ♔h1 ♔h8 17
♖g1 ♘e7 18 ♕h3 ♘g8 19 ♗xf5!
♗e7 20 ♘e2 ♘a6 21 ♘f4 ♔g7 22
♗xg6! 1-0

No. 89 Veresov-Pokhla
Training tournament
USSR, 1972
Dutch Defence

1 d4 f5 2 ♘c3 ♘f6 3 ♗g5 e6 4 e4
fe 5 ♘xe4 ♗e7 6 ♘xf6+!? ♗xf6 7
h4! *(28)*

This move signals the start of
White's attack on the K-side.

7...0-0 8 ♗d3 ♕e7 9 ♕e2 ♘c6
10 c3 d5 11 f4 ♗d7 12 0-0-0 a6 13
♘f3 b5 14 ♘e5 ♕e8 15 ♕c2! g6 16
♗xf6 ♖xf6 17 h5 gh 18 ♗xh7+
♔g7 19 ♘xd7 ♕xd7 20 ♖xh5
♖h8 21 ♖dh1

Strategically, Black's position
is clearly lost, and the finish follows quickly.

21...♕d6 22 g3 b4 23 ♗d3
♖xh5 24 ♖xh5 bc 25 bc ♔f8 26

♕a4 a5 27 ♔b2 1-0

No. 90   Agababian-Archakova
USSR Internal OL, 1972
King's Indian Defence

1 d4 ♞f6 2 c4 g6 3 ♞c3 ♝g7 4 e4
d6 5 f3 0-0 6 ♝e3 c6 7 ♝d3 e5 8 d5
cd 9 cd ♞e8 10 ♕d2 f5 11 ♞ge2?
(11 ef!) 11...♞d7 12 0-0(?) f4 13
♝f2 g5 14 ♖fc1 ♞df6 15 h3 h5 16
♔f1

Black has created the necessary preconditions for a storming of the opponent's castled
position, and a clear-cut realization of his plan now follows.

16...g4! 17 hg hg 18 ♞g1 ♞h5
19 fg ♞g3+ 20 ♔e1 ♕h4 21 ♝e2
♞f6 22 ♞b5 ♞fxe4 23 ♕b4 ♞xf2
24 ♞f3 ♞xe2 25 ♔xe2 ♕g3 26
♞xd6 ♞xg4 27 ♖g1 ♕f2+ 28 ♔d3
♕e3+ 29 ♔c2 ♝f5+! 30 ♞xf5
♖ac8+ 0-1

The attack on h7

Among the various attacks on
the K-side castled position, including those early in the opening, one that is very dangerous is
the threat to h7. After castling
the squares h7 and h2 are the
most vulnerable, similar to f7
and f2 in the initial position. In
many cases there is the possibility of a sacrifice (most often of
a bishop), followed by the drawing of the opponent's king out of

its shelter and a vigorous attack
on it.

A model example of such an
eventuality has for many years
been provided by the following
game.

No. 91   Edward Lasker-Thomas
London, 1912
Dutch Defence

1 d4 e6 2 ♞f3 f5 3 ♞c3 ♞f6 4
♝g5 ♝e7 5 ♝xf6 ♝xf6 6 e4 fe 7
♞xe4 b6 8 ♝d3 ♝b7 9 ♞e5 0-0 10
♕h5 ♕e7!

White now carried out a brilliant combination involving a sacrifice on h7.

11 ♕xh7+! ♔xh7 12 ♞xf6++
♔h6 13 ♞eg4+ ♔g5 14 h4+ ♔f4
15 g3+ ♔f3 16 ♝e2+ ♔g2 17
♖h2+ ♔g1 18 0-0-0 mate.

Returning to the main combinational theme, we should point
out that in certain cases the
attack on h7 is then combined
with a sacrifice on g7, as is confirmed by the following
examples.

No. 92   Emanuel Lasker-Bauer
Amsterdam, 1889
Bird's Opening

1 f4 d5 2 e3 ♞f6 3 b3 e6 4 ♝b2
♝e7 5 ♝d3 b6 6 ♞f3 ♝b7 7 ♞c3
♞bd7 8 0-0 0-0 9 ♞e2 c5 10 ♞g3
♕c7 11 ♞e5 ♞xe5 12 ♝xe5 ♕c6
13 ♕e2 a6 (better 13...♞e4) 14

♘h5 ♘xh5? 15 ♗xh7+! ♔xh7
16 ♕xh5+ ♔g8 17 ♗g7! ♔xg7
18 ♕g4+ ♔h7 (18...♔f6 19 ♕g5
mate!) 19 ♖f3 e5 20 ♖h3+ ♔h6
21 ♖xh6+♔xh6 22 ♕d7! 1-0

No. 93 Prins-Angles
Leipzig OL, 1960
French Defence

1 d4 ♘f6 2 ♘c3 d5 3 ♗g5 e6 4
e4 ♗e7 5 e5 ♘fd7 6 h4! c5 7 ♘b5?!
0-0? (after 7...f6! 8 ♗d3 a6!
Black would have seized the initiative) 8 ♗d3 c4? *(29)*

9 ♗xh7+!
This piece sacrifice is typical
of such positions, but each instance has its own special
features.
9...♔xh7 10 ♕h5+ ♔g8 11
♗xe7 ♕xe7 12 ♘f3 f6 13 ♘g5!
This is the point of White's
plan. The knight sacrifices itself
for the sake of opening the h-file,
and suddenly the white g-pawn
takes on the role of battering-ram.
13...fg 14 hg ♕b4+ 15 ♔e2

♕xb5 16 g6 ♖xf2+ 17 ♔xf2 ♕f8
18 ♕f3+ ♔e7 19 ♖h8 ♘f6 20
♕a3+! 1-0

No. 94 Chigorin-Alapin
St. Petersburg, 1883
Evans Gambit

1 e4 e5 2 ♘f3 ♘c6 3 ♗c4 ♗c5 4
b4 ♗xb4 5 c3 ♗a5 6 0-0 ♘f6 7 d4
0-0 8 de ♘xe4 9 ♗d5! ♗xc3 10
♗xe4 ♗xa1 *(30)*

11 ♗xh7+! ♔h8
Chigorin-Rosenkrantz (St.
Petersburg, 1897) went 11...
♔xh7 12 ♘g5+ ♔g6 13 ♕g4 f5 14
ef ♘e5 15 ♕g3! ♔xf6 16 f4 ♔e7
17 ♖e1 d6 18 ♘c3!, and White
won.
12 ♘g5 g6 13 ♕g4 ♗xe5 14
♕h4 ♔g7 15 ♘e6+!! fe 16 ♕h6+
♔f7 17 ♗xg6+ ♔e7 18 ♕h4+!
♖f6 19 ♗a3+! d6 20 ♕h7+ ♔f8 21
♕h8+ ♔e7 22 ♕g7+ ♖f7 23 ♕xf7
mate!

Pawn weaknesses in the castled position

It has already been mentioned that weakening pawn moves in the opening on the Kside (e.g. ...h7-h6 or h2-h3) will often significantly assist the opponent in carrying out an attack on the king. Of course, for this conditions are necessary, such as a superiority in force on this part of the board, the possibility of a pawn storm, and so on. In this respect pawn weaknesses are a subsidiary, but by no means minor factor.

Let us examine a few games.

No. 95 Tal-Averbakh
USSR Ch, Moscow, 1961
Spanish Game

1 e4 e5 2 ♘f3 ♘c6 3 ♗b5 a6 4 ♗a4 ♘f6 5 0-0 ♗e7 6 ♖e1 b5 7 ♗b3 d6 8 c3 0-0 9 h3 ♘a5 10 ♗c2 c5 11 d4 ♕c7 12 ♘bd2 ♘c6 13 dc dc 14 ♘f1 ♖d8?!

The opening stage here is rather protracted. Black's last move can hardly be good, since it leaves his K-side weakened. In completing his development he should have preferred the flexible 14...♗e6.

15 ♕e2 g6 16 ♘e3 ♖b8 17 ♘g5!

Tal subtly senses the attacking motifs: the f7 square, Black's rather weakened K-side

pawn formation, and so on. The storm clouds are gathering over Black's position.

17...♗f8

This aggravates Black's difficulties in defending his K-side. But also after 17...♗b7, as in Suetin-Aberbakh (32nd USSR Ch., 1965) White gained a powerful initiative: 18 ♗b3! ♖f8 (18...c4? fails to 19 ♘×c4!) 19 ♘d5! etc.

18 ♕f3 ♗g7 19 ♘d5! ♕d6 20 ♗e3 h6 *(31)*

31

Black has to try and drive away the menacing knight at g5, but in doing do he makes a further pawn weakening, which proves fatal.

21 ♘×f6+ ♗×f6 22 ♖ad1 ♕e7 23 ♗×c5!

This combination, which concludes the struggle, was essentially begun by White on his 21st move.

23...♖×d1 (23...♕×c5 loses immediately to 24 ♕×f6) 24 ♖×d1! ♕×c5 25 ♕×f6 hg 26 ♗b3!

The point of the combination: against the threats of 27 ♕xf7+ and 27 ♕xg6+ (this is where the move . . .h7-h6 tells!) Black has no defence.

26. . .♖b7 27 ♕xg6+ ♔f8 28 ♕h6+ 1-0

No. 96 Foguelman-Bronstein
Amsterdam, 1954
Queen's Gambit Accepted

1 d4 d5 2 c4 dc 3 ♘f3 ♘f6 4 e3 ♗g4 5 ♗xc4 e6 6 ♕b3 ♗xf3 7 gf c5 8 ♕xb7 ♘bd7 9 dc(?) ♗xc5 10 f4 0-0 11 0-0 ♘d5

The start of an interesting and highly effective plan, which has the aim of exploiting the slight weakness of White's castled pawn formation.

12 ♖d1

After 12 ♗xd5 ♖b8 13 ♕c6 ♖b6 14 ♕a4 ed there appears to be no defence against . . .♖g6+ and . . .♕h4. But 12 ♖e1 would have been rather better, since now White is crushed by force.

12. . .♖b8 13 ♕c6 ♕h4! 14 ♘c3 ♖b6! 15 ♕xd7 ♘xf4! 16 ♘e2

There is a pretty finish after 16 ef ♕xf2+ 17 ♔h1 ♕f3 mate!

16. . .♘h3+ 17 ♔g2 ♘xf2 18 ♖d4 ♘g4! 19 ♖f4 ♕xh2+ 20 ♔f1 ♗xe3 21 ♗d5 ♗xf4! 0-1

No. 97 Botvinnik-Tartakower
Nottingham, 1936
Old Indian Defence

1 ♘f3 ♘f6 2 c4 d6 3 d4 ♘bd7 4 g3 e5 5 ♗g2 ♗e7 6 0-0 0-0 7 ♘c3 c6 8 e4 ♕c7 9 h3 ♖e8 10 ♗e3 ♘f8? (10. . .ed 11 ♘xd4 ♗c5 12 ♕c2 a5 was in the spirit of the position) **11 ♖c1 h6? 12 d5 ♗d7 13 ♘d2 g5?** *(32)*

A fatal weakening. 13. . .♘g6 was better, although here too after 14 b4! White has pressure on the Q-side. Now White decisively opens up the game on the K-side.

14 f4 gf 15 gf ♔g7 16 fe de 17 c5! cd 18 ♘xd5 ♕c6 19 ♘c4 ♘g6 20 ♘d6! ♗e6

Black's position is already indefensible, e.g. 20. . .♗xd6 21 ♖xf6!, or 20. . .♖f8 21 ♘xe7 ♘xe7 22 ♖xf6! ♔xf6 23 ♕h5! etc.

21 ♘xe7! ♘xe7 22 ♖xf6! ♔xf6 23 ♕h5 ♘g6 24 ♘f5! ♖g8 25 ♕xh6 ♗xa2 26 ♖d1 ♖ad8 27

♕g5+ ♔e6 28 ♖×d8 f6 29 ♖×g8 ♘f4 30 ♕g7 1-0

Those given above have been characteristic examples of piece attacks against weak points in the castled position. The following game shows a typical instance, where the weakened pawn formation of a castled position assists the mounting of a pawn storm.

No. 98 Suetin-Zilberstein
Kislovodsk, 1972
English Opening

1 c4 e5 2 ♘c3 ♘f6 3 ♘f3 ♘c6 4 g3 ♗b4 5 ♗g2 0-0 6 0-0 d6 7 d3 h6(?) 8 ♘d2!? ♗×c3 9 bc ♗d7 10 e4 ♔h8 11 ♘b3 b6 12 f4 ♘g8 13 f5 g5?! 14 ♗e3 f6 15 h4 ♗e8 16 ♗f3 ♖f7 17 ♔f2 ♔g7 18 ♖h1 *(33)*

18...♔f8 19 ♕e2 ♕c8 20 ♖h2

Exploiting the weakening of Black's K-side pawns, White mounts there a decisive offensive.

20...♖g7 21 ♖ah1 ♗f7 22 hg

fg 23 ♕d2 ♕d8 24 ♖×h6! (the decisive tactical blow) 24... ♘×h6 25 ♖×h6 ♔g8 26 ♔g1! ♖h7 27 ♗×g5 ♕f8 28 ♖×h7 ♔×h7 29 ♕h2+ ♔g8 30 ♕h4 ♕g7 31 ♗h6 ♕h7 32 ♘d2 ♘d8 33 ♕g4+ ♔h8 34 ♗g5 1-0

Counterattack in the opening

In the above examples, combinations and attacks were successful and decided the outcome at an early stage, but this is by no means always the case. It can happen that active operations will fairly quickly lead to the opposite result and meet with a decisive counteraction by the opponent.

Often active operations in the opening appear very tempting from the tactical viewpoint, but if they are analyzed, it transpires that their tactical side is not supported by a sound strategic basis. In such cases a counterattack is often employed. It is an effective measure, but at the same time it requires no less ingenuity than the organization of swift opening attacks.

This is shown by the following example, in which the Belorussian master's conduct of a brilliant counterattack was truly inspired.

No. 99   Rauzer-Veresov
Tbilisi, 1934
Caro-Kann Defence

1 e4 c6 2 d4 d5 3 ♘c3 de 4 ♘xe4 ♘d7 5 ♘f3 ♘gf6 6 ♘xf6+ ♘xf6 7 ♘e5 ♗f5 (better 7...♗e6) 8 ♗c4 (8 c3 is stronger, and if 8...e6 9 g4 ♗g6 10 h4, when Black stands badly, Karpov-Hort, Bugojno, 1978) 8...e6 9 g4? ♗e4! 10 f3 ♗d5 11 ♗d3 ♗d6! 12 c4 ♗xe5 13 de ♘xg4! 14 ♗f4 *(34)*

34

14...g5! 15 cd (bad is 15 ♗g3 ♘e3 16 ♕e2 ♕a5+ 17 ♔f2 ♘xc4 18 ♗xc4 ♕c5+ etc) 15...gf 16 fg ♕xd5 17 0-0 0-0-0 18 ♖f3 ♖g8 19 ♖h3 h5 20 ♖xh5 ♕xd3 21 ♕xd3 ♖xg4+! 0-1

Here are some further characteristic examples of this type of situation.

No. 100   Anderssen-Lange
Berlin, 1858
Spanish Game

1 e4 e5 2 ♘f3 ♘c6 3 ♗b5 ♘d4 4

♘xd4 ed 5 ♗c4 ♘f6 6 e5? d5 7 ♗b3 ♗g4 8 f3 ♘e4? 9 0-0? (9 g3!) 9...d3 10 fg? (10 ♕e1!) 10...♗c5+ 11 ♔h1 ♘g3+ 12 hg ♕g5 13 ♖f5 h5!! 14 gh ♕xf5 15 g4 ♕f2 16 g3 ♕xg3 17 ♕f1 ♕xg4 0-1

No. 101
A. Rabinovich v Ilyin-Genevsky
Moscow, 1922
Philidor's Defence

1 e4 e5 2 ♘f3 d6 3 d4 ♘f6 4 ♘c3 ♘bd7 5 ♗c4 ♗e7 6 ♗xf7+? ♔xf7 7 ♘g5+ ♔g8 8 ♘e6 ♕e8 9 ♘xc7 ♕g6 10 ♘xa8 ♕xg2 11 ♖f1 ed! 12 ♕e2 dc! 13 ♕c4+ d5 14 ♕xc8+ ♔f7 15 ♕xb7 ♕xe4+ 16 ♗e3 ♖b8 17 ♕xa7 cb 18 ♔d2 ♕b4+, and Black won.

No. 102
Semenenko-Perfiliev
Corr., 1947
Two Knights Defence

1 e4 e5 2 ♘f3 ♘c6 3 ♗c4 ♘f6 4 ♘g5 d5 5 ed ♘d4 6 c3 b5 7 ♗f1 ♘xd5 8 ♘xf7 ♔xf7 9 cd ed 10 ♕f3+? ♘f6! 11 ♕xa8

Or 11 ♗xb5 ♗e6 12 0-0 ♖b8 13 ♗c6 ♕d6 14 h3 g5! 15 ♗e4 g4! with advantage to Black.

11...♗c5! 12 ♗xb5 ♖e8+! 13 ♔f1 ♗a6!! 14 ♕c6 ♕e7! 15 g3 ♗xb5+ 16 ♕xb5 ♘e4 17 ♕c4+ ♔g6 18 ♔g1 ♕f3 19 ♕f1 d3 0-1

No. 103 Nilsson-Geller
Sweden-USSR, 1954
Sicilian Defence

1 e4 c5 2 ♘f3 ♘c6 3 d4 cd 4
♘xd4 ♘f6 5 ♘c3 d6 6 ♗g5 e6 7
♘xc6 bc 8 e5 ♕a5! 9 ♗b5? (better
9 ♗×f6 gf 10 ed) 9...cb 10 ef b4
11 ♘e4 ♕e5 12 f3 d5 13 ♕d2 h6 14
♗h4 g5! 15 ♗g3 ♕×b2! 16 ♖d1
♗a6 17 ♘d6+ ♗×d6 18 ♗×d6
♖c8 *(35)*

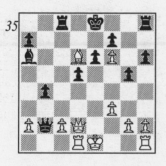

35

After great tactical complications in the opening, Black has
attained a strategically won
position. White has been aiming
for an attack on the dark squares,
but although he appears to have
achieved the desired opposite-
colour bishops, in the given
situation his dark-square bishop
is ineffective. And the pawn at
f6 essentially merely blocks
White's initiative on the K-side.

19 ♖c1 ♖c4 20 0-0 ♔d7 21 ♗e7
♖hc8 22 ♖f2 ♖×c2! 23 ♕×c2 (23
♖×c2 ♕b1+!) 23...♕×c1+!! 0-1

No. 104 Kovčić-Kažić
Yugoslavia, 1954
Sicilian Defence

1 e4 c5 2 ♘f3 ♘c6 3 d4 cd 4
♘xd4 ♘f6 5 ♘c3 d6 6 ♗g5 e6 7
♕d2 ♗e7 8 0-0-0 0-0 9 f4 e5 10
♘f3 ♗g4 11 h3 ♗×f3 12 gf ♘d4 13
fe de 14 ♖g1 ♖c8! 15 ♗h6 g6! *(36)*

36

A highly attractive strategic
plan. For the sake of the rapid
development of his counterattack on the Q-side, Black goes
in for an exchange sacrifice,
which creates a secure fortress
for his king.

After 15...♘e8? 16 ♕g2 ♗f6
17 ♗b5! White's attack would
have been very dangerous.

16 f4 (after 16 ♗×f8 ♗×f8 17
♘b5 ♗c5 18 ♘xd4 ♗×d4 19 ♖g2
♕b6! Black has irresistible
threats: 20...♗e3 or 20...
♕×b2!) 16...♕a5! 17 ♗×f8 (or
17 fe ♖fd8 18 ef ♗×f6!)
17...♗×f8 18 fe ♘f3 19 ♕d3
♖×c3! 0-1

No. 105 Buljovčić-Hort
Novi Sad, 1976
Pirc Defence

1 e4 d6 2 d4 ♞f6 3 ♞c3 g6 4 ♞ge2 h5?! 5 h3 ♞c6 6 ♞e3 ♝g7 7 ♛d2 b5!? 8 e5?! (premature activity; 8 a3 was more circumspect) 8...de 9 de ♞xe5 10 ♛xd8+ ♚xd8 11 ♞xb5 ♞c4! 12 0-0-0+?! ♝d7 13 ♝f4 ♞e4! 14 ♞ed4 ♞cd6 15 ♝e3 ♝h6! 16 ♝xh6 ♜xh6 17 ♜e1 ♞xf2 18 ♞xd6 cd 19 ♜g1 g5! 20 ♜e2 ♜f6 21 ♞f3 ♞xh3!

The decisive blow. Black's counterattack has achieved its aim.

22 gh ♜xf3 23 ♝g2 ♜g3 24 ♜f1 ♝b5 0-1

In the majority of the above examples, tactical methods of defence triumphed, but in the following example a purely tactical defence proved unreliable.

No. 106 Kupreichik-Tseshkovsky
USSR Ch., 1976
Sicilian Defence

1 e4 c5 2 ♞f3 d6 3 d4 cd 4 ♞xd4 ♞f6 5 ♞c3 a6 6 ♝g5 ♞c6 7 ♛d2 e6 8 0-0-0 h6 9 ♝e3 ♝d7 10 f3 b5 11 g4 ♞e5 12 ♝d3 b4 13 ♞ce2 d5?! 14 ♞g3 ♞xd3+?! (better 14... ♝e7) 15 ♛xd3 e5? 16 ♜he1! ed 17 ed!? de 18 ♛xe3+ ♝e7 19 d6 ♝e6 de ♛c7? (20...♛xe7 was the lesser evil) 21 ♛d4 (21 ♞f5! was even stronger) 21...h5 (21... ♜c8 was more tenacious) 22 ♞f5 ♜g8 23 ♞d6+ ♚xe7 24 ♛xb4 ♚f8 25 g5 ♜b8 26 ♛a3 ♞d7 27 ♞c8+! 1-0

three
BASIC SPATIAL FACTORS

Occupation of the centre

In earlier times the problem of the central squares was regarded in a somewhat functional sense — as applied to the expedient development of the pieces in the opening. But the centre is first and foremost an independent, base factor. In the end it serves as the main arena of struggle in any opening variation. It is a typical mistake, for example, to be diverted into playing on one of the wings, to the detriment of centralization.

The classical concept of the centre was mainly the creation of an ideal pawn pair (pawns at d4 and e4, or correspondingly at d5 and e5), or at least a single fighting unit (e.g. a mobile pawn at e4). In the latter case the adjacent wing pawn could be included (e.g., pawns at e4 and f4). In both instances the pawn pair would be expected to assist the seizure of space or the dynamic advance of the centre supported by the pieces, with the possibility of

creating an attack on one of the wings.

In this respect the following game is instructive.

No. 107 Alekhine-Marshall
Baden-Baden, 1925
Queen's Gambit

1 d4 ♞f6 2 c4 d5?! 3 cd ♞×d5 4 e4 ♞f6 5 ♗d3 e5 6 de ♞g4 7 ♞f3 ♞c6 8 ♗g5! ♗e7 9 ♗×e7 ♕×e7 10 ♞c3 ♞c×e5 11 ♞×e5 ♕×e5?! 12 h3 ♞f6 13 ♕d2 ♗d7 14 ♕e3 ♗c6 15 0-0-0 0-0?! 16 f4 ♕e6 17 e5! ♖fe8 18 ♖he1 ♖ad8?! 19 f5! ♕e7 20 ♕g5 ♞d5 f6 ♕f8 22 ♗c4! ♞×c3 23 ♖×d8 ♖×d8 24 fg! ♞×a2+ 25 ♔b1 ♕e8 26 e6! ♗e4+ 27 ♔a1 f6 28 e7+ ♖d5 29 ♕×f6 ♕f7 30 e8♕+ 1-0

Many of the strengths of the pawn centre, put forward by the classics, have not only retained their significance, but have also been significantly improved.

A wealth of practical experience has shown that a pawn centre is a very strong feature, but at the same time it can be very brittle.

Let us make a short excursion into history. Until the establishment of Steinitz's theories, central strategy was very straightforward. Sacrificing flank pawns if necessary, the active side would often endeavour to obtain a numerical pawn superiority in the centre (e.g., in the King's Gambit or Evans Gambit). Since both sides normally had the same aim, a closed formation in the centre rarely arose. Under the influence of the constant attacks on it, the centre would sometimes fairly quickly collapse.

In the middlegame, after a heated skirmish of this type, in place of a pawn centre a corresponding open space would very often arise, which increased the sharpness of the tactical play, but restricted the strategic complexity of the two sides' plans.

Such a tendency is clearly seen in many openings which are now rarely employed: Centre Game, Two Knights Defence, Vienna Game, Hungarian Defence, Italian Game, Scotch Game, and so on.

In opening systems such as these, White intends quickly and directly to seize the central squares, and, using the fact that the d4 square is 'naturally' defended, along with his development he undermines the e5 pawn by d2-d4 (or first f2-f4). But in the process Black gains the opportunity of quickly and easily mobilizing his forces, and sometimes of preparing the freeing central counterblow . . .d7-d5.

Typical, for example, is the 'fierce' opening struggle in the well-studied Moller Attack in the Italian Game: 1 e4 e5 2 ♘f3 ♘c6 3 ♗c4 ♗c5 4 c3 ♘f6! 5 d4 ed 6 cd ♗b4+ 7 ♘c3 (if 7 ♗d2 Black equalizes by 7. . .♗×d2+ 8 ♘b×d2 d5!) 7. . .♘×e4 8 0-0 ♗×c3 9 d5! ♗f6! 10 ♖e1 ♘e7 11 ♖×e4 0-0 12 d6 cd 13 ♕×d6 ♘f5 14 ♕d5 ♘e7 etc., or 11. . .d6 12 ♗g5 ♗×g5 13 ♘×g5 0-0 14 ♘×h7 etc., in both cases with a forced draw.

As we see, against correct and energetic play by Black, such an attempt by White to obtain predominance in the centre usually ends in the opening of the pawn position in the centre, which leads to complete equality, and after the slightest inaccuracy by White the initiative may pass to Black. The point is that, with the centre open a 'calculating' piece battle results, in which exceptional accuracy is demanded of both sides.

In connection with this we give the following example.

No. 108
Konstantinopolsky-Keres
USSR Ch., 1940
Vienna Game

1 e4 e5 2 ♘c3 ♘f6 3 f4 d5

Against White's undermining of the centre Black replies with a counterattack, which leads to the forced opening of the centre.

4 fe ♘xe4 5 ♘f3 ♗e7 6 d4 0-0 7 ♗d3 f5 8 ef ♗xf6 9 0-0 ♘c6

By the most natural and energetic moves Black parries White's aggressive intentions.

10 ♘xe4 de 11 ♗xe4 ♘xd4 12 ♘g5 ♗f5! 13 ♗xf5 (13 c3 is more accurate) **13...♘xf5 14 ♘e6?**

An instructive point. With the centre open, the activity of the pieces increases greatly, and the superior or poor placing of individual pieces has great significance in the assessment of the position. Every tempo acquires exceptional importance, and great accuracy and care are demanded of both sides. In the given case, in search of a non-existent advantage, White embarks on a tempting knight manœuvre, which, however, loses precious time. The correct continuation was 14 ♕xd8! ♖axd8 15 ♘e6 ♗d4+ 16 ♘xd4 ♘xd4 17 ♗g5 with subsequent full equality.

Now Black finds an elegant way to seize the initiative.

14...♕xd1 15 ♖xd1 ♖fe8! 16 ♘xc7 ♖ad8! 17 ♗f4 ♖e2 18 ♖xd8+ ♗xd8 19 ♖d1 ♗f6

As a result of the complications Black regains the sacrificed pawn and retains a positional advantage.

This unsuccessful attempt to create a pawn centre is in marked contrast to the following modern example.

No. 109 Botvinnik-Capablanca
AVRO Tournament, 1938
Nimzo-Indian Defence

1 d4 ♘f6 2 c4 e6 3 ♘c3 ♗b4 4 e3 d5 5 a3 ♗xc3+ 6 bc c5 7 cd ed 8 ♗d3 0-0 9 ♘e2 b6 10 0-0 ♗a6 11 ♗xa6 ♘xa6 12 ♗b2 ♕d7 13 a4 ♖fe8 (better 13...cd 14 cd ♖fc8 with counterplay along the c-file) **14 ♕d3 c4 15 ♕c2 ♘b8 16 ♖ae1 ♘c6 17 ♘g3 ♘a5 18 f3! ♘b3 19 e4 ♕xa4 20 e5 ♘d7 21 ♕f2 g6 22 f4** *(37)*

22...f5 23 ef ♘xf6 24 f5 ♖xe1 25 ♖xe1 ♖e8 26 ♖e6! ♖xe6 27 fe

♔g7 28 ♕f4 ♕e8 29 ♕e5 ♕e7 30 ♗a3! ♕xa3 31 ♘h5+! gh 32 ♕g5+ ♔f8 33 ♕xf6+ ♔g8 34 e7 ♕c1+ 35 ♔f2 ♕c2+ 36 ♔g3 ♕d3+ 37 ♔h4 ♕e4+ 38 ♔xh5 ♕e2+ 39 ♔h4 ♕e4+ 40 g4! ♕e1+ 41 ♔h5 1-0

No. 110 Taimanov-Petrosian
Zurich C, 1953
Nimzo-Indian Defence

1 d4 ♘f6 2 c4 e6 3 ♘c3 ♗b4 4 e3 c5 5 ♗d3 0-0 6 ♘f3 d5 7 0-0 ♘c6 8 a3 ♗xc3 9 bc b6 10 cd ed 11 ♘e5 ♕c7 12 ♘xc6 ♕xc6 13 f3! ♗e6 14 ♕e1 ♘d7 15 e4 c4(?)

Black should have played 15... f5!?, with counterplay in the centre.

16 ♗c2 f5 17 e5 ♖f7 18 a4 a5 19 f4 b5 20 ab ♕xb5 21 ♗a3 ♘b6 22 ♕h4 ♕e8 23 ♖f3 ♘c8 24 ♗a4! ♖d7 (24...♗d7 25 e6!) 25 ♖b1 ♕f7 26 ♗xd7 ♕xd7 27 ♖g3 ♘a7 28 ♗e7 ♗f7 29 ♕g6 ♗g6 30 h4 ♘c6 31 ♗a3 ♘d8 32 h5 ♘e6 33 ♕h4 ♗f7 34 h6 g6 35 ♕f6 ♕d8 36 ♗e7 ♕c7 37 ♖xg6+! hg 38 h7+ ♔xh7 39 ♕xf7+ ♘g7 40 ♔f2! 1-0

No. 111 Taimanov-Botvinnik
Match, 1953
Nimzo-Indian Defence

1 d4 ♘g6 2 c4 e6 3 ♘c3 ♗d4 4 ♘f3 c5 5 e3 0-0 6 ♗d3 d5 7 0-0 ♘c6 8 a3 ♗xc3 9 bc b6 10 cd ed 11 a4 c4(?) 12 ♗c2 ♗g4 13 ♕e1

♖e8(?) *(38)*

13...♗xf3 would have given Black a satisfactory game. Now White erects a strong centre with great 'architectural' skill.

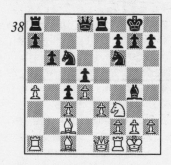

14 ♘h4! ♗h5 15 f3 ♗g6 16 ♘xg6 hg 17 e4 de 18 fe ♕d7

18...♘xe4 19 ♗xe4 ♘xd4 20 ♕e3 ♘c2 21 ♕f3 ♖xe4 22 ♕xe4 ♘xa1 23 ♗g5! favours White. In general Black's position is already difficult.

19 ♗g5 ♘h7 20 ♗e3 ♘e7 21 ♖f3 f5 22 e5 ♘f8 23 h4 ♘e6 24 ♖d1 ♕d5 25 ♗c1 ♖f8 26 ♗a3 ♖ae8 27 ♕g3 g5 (27...♔h7 28 h5!) 28 ♗xe7! ♖xe7 29 ♖xf5 ♖xf5 30 ♗xf5 ♘f4 31 ♕xg5 ♖xe5 32 de ♕xd1+ 33 ♔h2 ♕d2 34 ♗e6+ ♔h7 35 ♗xc4 g6 36 ♗e6 1-0

No. 112 Botvinnik-Keres
USSR Ch., 1952
Queen's Gambit

1 d4 ♘f6 2 c4 e6 3 ♘c3 d5 4 cd ed 5 ♗g5 ♗e7 6 e3 0-0 7 ♗d3

♘bd7 8 ♕c2 ♖e8 9 ♘ge2 ♘f8 10 0-0 c6 11 ♖ab1 ♗d6? (11...♘e4 or 11...♘h5 was in the spirit of the position) 12 ♔h1 ♘g6 13 f3! ♗e7 14 ♖be1! ♘d7 15 ♗xe7 ♖xe7 16 ♘g3 ♘f6 17 ♕f2 ♗e6 18 ♘f5 ♗xf5 19 ♗xf5 ♕b6 20 e4! de 21 fe ♖d8 22 e5 ♘d5 23 ♘e4 ♘f8 24 ♘d6 ♕c7 25 ♗e4 ♘e6 26 ♕h4 g6 27 ♗xd5 cd 28 ♖c1 ♕d7 29 ♖c3 ♖f8 30 ♘f5! ♖fe8 31 ♘h6+ ♔f8 32 ♕f6 ♘g7 33 ♖cf3 ♖c8 34 ♘xf7 ♖e6 35 ♕g5 ♘f5 36 ♘h6 ♕g7 37 g4 1-0

In the above examples White's central pawns were harmoniously supported by his pieces. But often, when there is not the necessary piece support, a pawn centre can become weak and may be destroyed at an early stage of the game.

This is illustrated by the following example (Bronstein-Evans, USSR-USA, 1955, Slav Defence): 1 d4 ♘f6 2 c4 e6 3 ♘f3 d5 4 ♘c3 c6 5 e3 ♘bd7 6 ♗d3 ♗b4 7 a3 ♗a5 8 ♕c2 0-0 9 0-0 ♗c7 10 ♗d2 dc! 11 ♗xc4 e5 12 ♗a2 h6 13 ♖ae1 ♖e8 14 de ♘xe5 15 ♘xe5 ♖xe5 16 f4? ♗f5 17 e4 ♗b6+ 18 ♔h1 ♖xe4!

This emphasizes the actual weakness of White's centre, which collapses under the powerful pressure of the black pieces.

19 ♘xe4 ♘xe4 20 ♖xe4 (forced in view of the threats of 20...♘f2+ and 20...♘g3+)

20...♗xe4 21 ♕xe4 ♕xd2. Black has an obvious advantage.

Thus whether a pawn centre is weak or strong, the conceding to the opponent of a numerical pawn superiority is acceptable only if sufficient piece pressure on it can be developed.

In our time this problem has acquired much wider significance, since our understanding of the centre has become much more complicated. In a number of cases piece pressure on the centre proves more effective than the mechanical occupation of it with pawns. The modern forms of piece pressure on the centre are highly varied. We will examine what is for the moment the most obvious of these, the effective occupation of a piece outpost in the centre, which creates here a favourable structure for a considerable part of the game.

No. 113 Petrosian-Kozma
Munich OL, 1958
Queen's Pawn Opening

1 ♘f3 ♘f6 2 d4 e6 3 ♗g5 c5 4 e3 b6?

This imperceptible slip allows White, by the following energetic move, to obtain a strong piece outpost in the centre.

5 d5! ed 6 ♘c3 ♗b7 7 ♘xd5 ♗xd5 8 ♗xf6 ♕xf6 9 ♕xd5 (39)

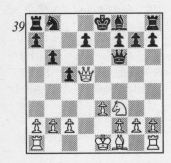

White has securely occupied the d5 square. At this post the queen cannot be successfully attacked by the black pieces, and it exerts very strong pressure. The main factor in the subsequent play is Black's weakness on the d-file.

9...♘c6

Bad is 9...♛xb2 10 ♖d1 ♛b4+ 11 c3 ♛xc3+ 12 ♖d2 ♛c1+ 13 ♔e2!, when Black loses a rook.

10 ♗c4 ♗e7 11 0-0-0 ♖d8 12 ♖d2 0-0 13 c3 ♘a5 14 ♗e2

The domination of the white pieces in the centre is quite striking! Black tries to weaken the pressure by the exchange of queens, but merely finishes up in a cheerless ending.

14...♛e6 15 ♖hd1 ♛xd5 16 ♖xd5 d6 17 ♘d2 f5 18 f4! g6 19 g3 ♖f6 20 e4 fe 21 ♘xe4 ♖e6 22 ♗f3 ♔g7 23 b3 ♘c6 24 ♖5d3

White intends to establish his bishop at d5, where it will operate with maximum force.

24...♘b8 25 ♘f2 h5 26 ♔d2!

The time has come for the king to become active. Exploiting the fact that the black forces are restricted, the leader of White's army takes up a secure post at f3, and prepares if necessary to take an active part in the battle.

26...♗f8 27 ♗d5 ♖e7 28 ♘e4 ♘a6 29 ♔e3 ♘c7 30 ♔f3 ♘xd5(?) 31 ♖xd5 ♖de8 32 ♖e1 ♖e6 33 ♖e2 b5 34 h3 a5 35 g4 hg 36 hg ♗e7 37 f5!, and White attains a strategically won position.

Thus the modern understanding of centralization considers not the formal occupation of the centre by pawns, but rather the real control of it. As Aron Nimzowitsch pointed out, what is important is not just the occupation of the centre by pawns — of much greater importance is the balance of the two sides' forces in the centre!

And here is another of the points he makes: "Here we have simply to abide by the meaning of the word. The 'centre' consists of the squares in the middle of the board, squares: not pawns. This is fundamental and must never under any circumstances be lost sight of."

The examples given above largely demonstrate the importance of a real advantage in the centre.

In practice, however, monopoly in the centre does not often occur, and is possible only as a result of serious mistakes by the opponent. The creation of such a situation, as has already been seen, is equivalent to a strategic victory. But in the struggle for the centre one normally has to be satisfied with very modest achievements. The gaining of an outpost in the centre or the obtaining of a strong mobile pawn is already considered a definite success.

Naturally, White has more chance of obtaining such advantages. For Black a quite optimal solution is to become established on one of the central squares d5 or e5, which promises him equal chances.

Thus in the struggle for the centre in modern strategy it is very important to have a critical approach to its mechanical occupation by pawns, which in the past seemed to be an almost obligatory condition for the achievement of an advantage. However, conceding a numerical pawn superiority to the opponent is admissible only if sufficient piece pressure on the centre can be created.

One cannot go to extremes and disclaim foundations which have developed from centuries of experience. In this sense

another point put forward by Nimzowitsch is very apt: "Certainly, pawns, as being the most stable, are best suited to building a centre; nevertheless centrally posted pieces can perfectly well take their place."

Springing from this, incidentally, is the modern concept of dynamic equilibrium, where the positional advantages of one side (for example, the possession of a pawn centre) are as though balanced by the harmonious pressure of the opponent's pieces on the centre.

Opening up of the centre

It is customarily thought that the rapid opening up of the centre at the start of the game contains a serious drawing 'disease' (as was seen in the examples of ancient openings given above), but on the whole this is a superficial and deceptive impression.

Practice confirms more and more that, in a number of instances in modern opening systems, freeing the centre of pawns opens scope for piece play and for all kinds of tactical operations.

This is shown by the examples given below.

No. 114 Suetin-Petrosian
18th USSR Ch., 1950
Spanish Game

1 e4 e5 2 ♘f3 ♘c6 3 ♗b5 a6 4 ♗a4 ♘f6 5 0-0 ♗e7 6 d4 ed 7 ♖e1 0-0 8 e5 ♘d5? (8...♘e8 is correct, not allowing White an important gain of tempo for the development of his initiative) 9 ♘xd4 ♘xd4 10 ♕xd4 ♘b6 11 ♗b3 d5 12 ed ♕xd6

12...♗xd6 is somewhat better, although here too after 13 ♗f4 ♕h4 14 g3 ♕g4 15 h3 ♕f3 16 ♖e3! ♕c6 17 ♖c3 ♕d7 18 ♖d3 ♗xf4 19 ♕xf4 ♕e7 20 ♘c3 ♕c5 21 ♘e4 ♕f5 22 ♕xc7 White has the advantage.

13 ♕e4!
Despite the fact that the centre has been cleared of pawns, due to the strong position of the white queen it is far from easy for Black to complete his Q-side development. White has powerful piece pressure on the centre.

13...♗f6 14 ♘c3 ♖b8
Perhaps the lesser evil was 14...♕d4 15 ♗f4 ♕xe4 16 ♘xe4 ♗d8 17 ♖ad1 ♗d7 18 ♘c5 ♗c6 19 h3, when although Black's pieces are thoroughly tied up, for the moment he manages to avoid loss of material

15 ♗f4 ♕c5 16 ♕e3!
A difficult move to find — after all, when you have the initiative you do not want to exchange queens! But there appears to be no other way for White to realize his opening advantage. If now Black simplifies with 16...♕xe3 17 ♖xe3 he loses his c-pawn, since after 17...♗d8 18 ♖d1 ♗d7 19 h3 there is no defence against 20 ♖ed3 followed by a double attack on d8 and ♗xc7. Black must therefore avoid the exchange of queens in an unfavourable situation.

16...♕c6 17 ♕g3 ♗e6
Black is obliged to give up the pawn, since 17...♗d8 18 ♗e5 g6 19 ♖ad1 ♗d7 20 ♕f4! is too unattractive, when White's attack can hardly be parried.

18 ♗xc7 ♖bc8 19 ♗e5 ♗xb3 20 ab ♘d7 21 ♗xf6 ♘xf6 22 ♖ad1
White has emerged with an extra pawn, which he successfully converted into a win.

No. 115 Lipnitsky-Petrosian
USSR Ch., 1951
Hungarian Defence

1 e4 e5 2 ♘f3 ♘c6 3 ♗c4 ♗e7 4 d4 d6 5 ♘c3 ♘f6 6 h3 0-0 7 0-0
Here a typical situation has arisen. Black has the possibility of the exchanging combination 7...♘xe4 8 ♘xe4 d5. Such simplification often leads to the removal of the pawn tension in the centre and to seemingly

harmless symmetry. But the outward simplicity conceals the difficulties of the defence, since after 9 ♗×d5 ♛×d5 10 ♘c3 ♛a5 11 ♘×e5 ♘×e5 12 de ♛×e5 13 ♖e1 ♛d6 14 ♛f3 it is very difficult for Black to complete his Q-side development, whereas White is threatening to 'open fire' on the central files.

It is interesting that at the board Tigran Petrosian remembered the lesson of the previous game. Although in the concrete opening development of these games there is not even a distant similarity, the essential point is that, after the opening of the centre, on each occasion the white queen ties down Black's forces.

7. . .a6 8 a4 ed 9 ♘×d4 ♘b4!

Now Black is threatening advantageously to release the tension, both by 10. . .♘×e4 11 ♘×e4 d5, and in some cases by . . .d5.

The game went **10 ♘d5 ♘b×d5 11 ed ♘d7 12 a5 ♗f6 13 c3** (13 ♘e6!? was possibly better, forcing simplification) **13. . .♘e5 14 ♗b3 ♖e8 15 ♗c2 ♗d7 16 f4 ♘g6 17 ♛f3 c5?! 18 dc bc 19 f5 ♗×f5 20 ♗×f5 d5 21 ♗d2 ♘f8 22 ♛d3 c5,** with a good position for Black.

In these examples the strength of the most powerful piece was very apparent.

In passing we would like to draw attention to one particular problem — the strength of a centralized queen, when it is difficult to drive it away by attacking it with minor pieces.

A frequent characteristic of modern dynamics is the sudden freeing of the centre of pawns, even sometimes in the most blocked set-ups. Such an operation is often accompanied by a sacrifice of material for the sake of active piece play, and invariably changes the picture sharply, giving the game a combinational trend.

Of course, such an opening up of the centre demands deep and accurate calculation, with the position of the king assuming considerable importance.

Piece attacks after the opening of the centre are especially dangerous, when the object of the attack becomes the enemy king. In addition to earlier examples of this type (cf. Nos. 15-17) we will consider one further game.

No. 116 Kotov-Boleslavsky
USSR Ch., 1945
Queens's Pawn Opening

1 d4 ♘f6 2 ♗g5 ♘e4 3 ♗f4 d6 4 f3 ♘f6 5 e4 g6 6 ♛d2 ♘bd7 7 ♗h6? ♗×h6 8 ♛×h6 c5 9 c3 ♛b6 10 ♛d2 cd 11 cd e5 12 ♘a3 d5! *(40)*

40

Exploiting White's poor development and the harmonious placing of his own forces, Black advantageously opens the centre and commences a very strong attack on the opponent's king.

13 de ♘xe5 14 ♗b5+ ♔f8 15 ed ♔g7 16 ♘e2 a6 17 ♗c4 ♖e8 18 ♖d1 ♗h3!

A brilliant stroke, emphasizing the scattered nature of White's forces and setting him insoluble problems.

19 ♔f1 ♘xf3 20 ♕d3 ♘g4! 21 ♕xf3 ♘e3+ 22 ♔e1 ♗xg2 (Black has a won position). **23 ♕f2 ♗xh1 24 ♖d3 ♕b4+ 25 ♖d2 ♖ac8 26 ♗b3 ♗xd5 27 ♗xd5 ♘xd5 28 ♕d4+ ♕xd4 29 ♖xd4 ♘f6 0-1**

Here we cannot avoid touching on the other side of the 'coin' – the premature opening of the centre (one of the instances of premature activity, about which we have already spoken). Practice shows that the 'sinner' in this case is usually Black, aiming as soon as possible for active play

in the centre.

We will first examine a highly primitive example, which nevertheless shows clearly that such an approach is doomed to failure.

No. 117 Boleslavsky-Gurgenidze
Rostov-on-Don, 1960
Sicilian Defence

1 e4 c5 2 ♘f3 ♘c6 3 d4 d5?

A ridiculous experiment, which is energetically refuted by White. Due to Black's lag in development, it is he who suffers from the opening of the centre.

4 ed ♕xd5 5 ♘c3 ♕e6+ 6 ♗e3 cd 7 ♘xd4 ♕d7 8 ♘db5! ♖b8 9 ♕e2! f6 10 ♖d1 ♕g4 11 f3 ♕h5 12 ♗xa7 ♘xa7 13 ♘d6+ 1-0

Below we give some more complicated examples, in which the drawbacks of opening the centre are disclosed by the purposeful actions of the opponent.

No. 118 Alekhine-Eliskases
Podebrady, 1936
Spanish Game

1 e4 e5 2 ♘f3 ♘c6 3 ♗b5 a6 4 ♗a4 ♘f6 5 0-0 ♗e7 6 ♖e1 b5 7 ♗b3 d6 8 c3 ♘a5 9 ♗c2 c5 10 d3 ♘c6 11 ♘bd2 0-0 12 ♘f1 ♖e8 13 ♘e3 d5? *(41)*

A premature opening of the centre. Here too there follows an immediate and very energetic rejoinder by White.

14 ed ♘xd5 15 ♘xd5 ♕xd5 16
d4! ed 17 ♗e4 ♕d7 (17...♕d6 18
♗f4! 18 cd ♗f6 19 ♗g5!! ♖xe4
(19...♗xg5 20 ♘xg5 g6 21 dc! or
19...♗xd4 20 ♗f5!! obviously
favours White) 20 ♖xe4 ♗xd4 21
♘xd4 ♘xd4 22 ♕h5! ♗b7 23 ♖h4
♕f5 24 ♗e3! ♖d8? 25 ♖xd4! 1-0

No. 119 Suetin-Malich
Byelorussia-East Germany
1965
Spanish Game

1 e4 e5 2 ♘f3 ♘c6 3 ♗b5 a6 4
♗a4 ♘f6 5 0-0 b5 6 ♗b3 ♗b7 7
♖e1 ♗c5 8 c3 d6 9 d4 ♗b6 10 a3!?
0-0 11 ♗c2 ♘d7 12 ♕d3 ♖e8 13

♘bd2 ♘f8 14 b4 ♘g6 15 ♘f1 d5?
(42) 16 ed ♕xd5 17 ♕f5!

It transpires that against the
threats of ♕h5, ♗e4 and ♘g5
Black has no defence.

17...♕d6 18 ♘g5 ♕f6
(18...♖f8 19 ♗b3!) 19 ♕xf6 gf 20
♘e4 ♔g7 21 ♘fg3 ed 22 ♗h6+!
♔h8 23 ♘xf6 ♖g8 24 ♘xg8 ♖xg8
25 ♗g5!, and White won.

Thus at the start of the game,
opening up the centre must be
approached with great care,
adapting to specific circumstances. At the same time, as the
given examples show, when playing Black in the opening one
must exercise due caution and
sense of measure.

The art of centralization

The art of centralization is a
very important feature of
strategy, as is confirmed by the
following instructive games, in
which step by step White was
able to gain a monopoly in the
opening.

No. 120 Alekhine-Bogoljubow
Budapest, 1921
Bogo-Indian Defence

1 d4 ♘f6 2 c4 e6 3 ♘f3 ♗b4+
4 ♗d2 ♗xd2+ 5 ♕xd2 0-0 6 ♘c3
d5 7 e3 ♘bd7 8 ♗d3 c6 9 0-0 dc 10
♗xc4 e5 11 ♗b3! ♕e7 12 e4! ed 13
♘xd4 ♘c5 14 ♗c2 ♖d8 15 ♖ad1

♗g4 16 f3 ♘e6 17 ♕f2 ♘xd4 18 ♖xd4 ♗e6 19 ♖fd1 b6 *(43)*

A situation has arisen in which White's piece formation gives him real prospects of an attack in the centre and on the Kside. Black's pawn majority on the Q-side, on the other hand, does not play any significant role, and the advance of the black pawns may merely create new weaknesses.

20 h3!

After defending the g4 square, White can begin the advance of his f- and e-pawns.

20...c5 21 ♖4d2 ♖xd2 22 ♕xd2 c4 23 f4 g6

After 23...♕c5+ White could have offered the exchange of queens by 24 ♕d4, which would have guaranteed him a clear endgame advantage.

24 ♕d4 ♖c8 25 g4!

White's mass pawn offensive on the K-side continues. It is difficult for Black to find a

defence against 26 f5 or 26 e5 followed by f4-f5.

25...♗xg4 26 hg ♘xg4 27 ♔g2 h5 28 ♘d5 ♕h4 29 ♖h1 ♕d8 30 ♗d1 1-0

No. 121 Keres-Lipnitsky
USSR Ch., 1951
Nimzo-Indian Defence

1 d4 ♘f6 2 c4 e6 3 ♘c3 ♗b4 4 e3 0-0 5 ♗d3 d5 6 ♘f3 ♘c6 7 0-0 h6 8 h3 dc 9 ♗xc4 ♗d6 10 e4 e5 11 ♗e3 a6 12 ♖e1 ♗d7 13 ♕c2 ♖e8 14 a3 ed 15 ♘xd4 ♘e5 16 ♗f1 *(44)*

The central e4 pawn restricts Black's manœuvring, and the white pieces are operating harmoniously.

16...♘g6 (the threat was 17 f4! and 18 e5) 17 ♖ad1 ♕e7 18 g3!

A characteristic situation. White sacrifices his e4 pawn — the pride of his position — for the sake of opening up the centre. Black is obliged to accept the challenge, since the threat of 19 ♗g2 and f2-f4 with further gain of space is highly unpleasant.

18...♘**xe4 19** ♗**c1 f5 20** ♗**g2**
♘**e5 21** ♘**xf5!**

Decisively breaking up
Black's fortifications, White increases his initiative with every
move.

21...♗**xf5 22** ♘**xe4** ♘**f7 23**
♕**b3** ♖**ab8 24** ♗**d2** ♕**e6 25** ♕**xe6**
♖**xe6 26** ♘**xd6 cd 27** ♗**d5!**, with a
great advantage to White.

In this game too the struggle
developed in the centre. Black's
pieces were lacking in support
and were driven back to less
favourable positions.

Let us consider some further
examples.

No. 122
Kapengut-Mikhalchishin
Lvov, 1973
Sicilian Defence

1 e4 c5 2 ♘**f3 d6 3 d4 cd 4** ♘**xd4**
♘**f6 5** ♘**c3 e6 6 f4** ♗**e7 7** ♗**e2 0-0 8**
0-0 ♘**c6 9** ♗**e3** ♗**d7 10** ♘**b3 a6 11**
a4 ♘**a5 (45) 12 e5** ♘**e8 13** ♘**xa5**
♕**xa5 14** ♕**d2** ♕**c7 15** ♗**d4 f6**

An unjustified weakening, instead of which 15...♗c6
followed by ...♖d8 came into
consideration. Now step by step
White intensifies the pressure in
the centre.

16 ♕**e3 de 17 fe fe**

17...f5! is somewhat better.

18 ♗**b6** (stronger than 18
♗xe5 ♕c5) **18...**♕**c8 19** ♖**xf8+**
♗**xf8 20** ♖**d1** ♘**d6 21** ♕**xe5** ♘**f5**
22 a5

As a result of the struggle for
the centre White has regained
his pawn and has successfully
centralized his pieces. In Black's
position persistent pawn weaknesses have been exposed at b7
and e6. White has a strategically
won game.

22...♗**e7(?) 23** ♖**xd7!** ♕**xd7**
24 ♗**c4**

White regains with interest
the sacrificed material and
achieves a decisive advantage.

24...♔**h8 25** ♗**xe6** ♕**d2 26**
♗**xf5** ♕**c1+ 27** ♔**f2** ♖**e8 28** ♔**e2**
♕**g5 29 g4!** ♖**f8 30** ♘**e4** ♕**h4 31**
♗**f2 1-0**

No. 123 Kapengut-Pytel
Ljubljana, 1973

In this game *(46)*, as in the previous one, Black has played the
opening badly and has fallen
behind in development. White
finds an effective plan of active
play.

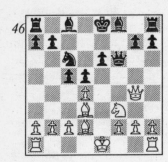

46

10 ♕g3!

It transpires that in the event 10...♘×d4 11 ♘×d4 ♕×d4 12 0-0-0 c4 13 ♗×h7! Black's position is unsatisfactory. The lesser evil was probably 10...cd.

10...c4? 11 ♗g5 ♕f7 12 ♗e2 ♗b4+ 13 c3 ♗a5 14 ♗f4 0-0 15 ♗d6 ♖d8 16 0-0 b5? 17 b4! cb

17...♗b6 18 a4! ba 19 ♖×a4 is unpromising: Black is condemned to a slow but sure loss.

18 ♗×b5! ♕b7 19 ♗×c6 ♕×c6 20 ab ♗×c3

Of course, not 20...♕×c3 21 ♖×a5 ♕×a5 22 ♗c7! etc.

21 ♗e5 ♖d7 22 ♖fc1 ♗b7 23 ♖a2 ♖c8 24 ♘g5!

Avoiding the trap 24 ♖ac2? ♕a6!, when Black can successfully defend.

24...h6 25 ♘h3 ♖f7 26 ♖ac2! 1-0

No. 124 Yuferov-Kupreichik
Minsk, 1972
Albin Counter-Gambit

1 d4 d5 2 c4 e5 3 de d4 4 ♘f3 ♘c6 5 g3 ♗g4 6 ♗g2 ♕d7 7 0-0 ♗h3 8 ♕d3 0-0-0 9 ♗×h3 ♕×h3 10 ♘bd2 ♘ge7 11 ♖d1?

This delay is fatal. 11 ♘g5! ♕h5 12 f4 was correct, with the initiative. Now Black obtains a powerful striking force in the centre.

11...♘g6 12 ♕e4 ♗e7 13 ♘b3 f5 14 ef ♗×f6 15 ♗g5 ♖he8 16 ♕c2 ♗×g5 17 ♘×g5 ♕g4 18 ♕d2 h6 19 ♘f3 d3! 20 h3 ♕f5 21 ♖e1 de 22 ♕c3 ♘ge5 23 ♘h4 ♕×h3 24 ♘c5 ♘d4 0-1

Thus modern opening strategy is notable for its rich content and for its diverse forms of struggle for the centre. This will be considered in more detail in Part II of the book. But for the moment we will dwell on some other basic spatial factors in the opening, which for all their specific nature are also closely linked with the centre.

The demarcation line of the board

The line dividing the board into two equal parts between the fourth and fifth ranks can be called the 'demarcation' line.

The side which controls more space also normally has greater manœuvring freedom. Therefore the acquisition of a spatial advantage (the crossing of the demarcation line by the pieces and pawns of one of the sides, and the subsequent consolidation of the success achieved) may give a definite advantage. In turn, the conceding of a significant amount of space may have unpleasant consequences.

A spatial advantage cannot, of course, be considered in isolation from the position on the board. Its persistence will closely depend on the deployment of the forces, and therefore the hasty seizure of space often has undesirable results.

This is shown in the following line of Alekhine's Defence: 1 e4 ♘f6 2 e5 ♘d5 3 c4 ♘b6 4 d4 d6 5 f4 (the Four Pawns Attack) 5...♗f5

This move involves a little trap. If now White carelessly plays to exchange the opponent's active light-square bishop with 6 ♗d3? (6 ♗e3! is correct), then after 6...♗×d3 7 ♕×d3 Black exploits the weakly defended state of White's advanced central pawns: 7...de 8 fe c5 9 d5 e6! 10 ♘c3 ♕h4+ 11 g3 ♕×c4, winning a pawn for no compensation at all.

The occupation of space is of significant importance from the very first moves of the game, and is linked in particular with the specific situation in the centre. The occupation of greater space is effective if its seizure is secured by the harmonious coordination of pieces and pawns.

Earlier we illustrated in some detail the structure with a strong pawn pair at d4 and e4 (Nos. 109-112), where Black's piece pressure was clearly insufficient.

The position for the defending side is even worse if the pawns can be established on the fifth rank (e.g. at d5 and e5), when a crisis situation normally arises.

This is confirmed by the following examples.

No. 125 Gligorić - Schmidt
European Team Ch, Bath, 1973
Grünfeld Defence

1 d4 ♘f6 2 c4 g6 3 ♘c3 d5 4 cd ♘×d5 5 e4 ♘×c3 6 bc ♗g7 7 ♗c4 c5 8 ♘e2 0-0 9 0-0 ♘c6 10 ♗e3 cd

11 cd ♘a5 12 ♗d3 ♘c6 13 ♗b5
♗g4 14 f3 ♗d7 15 ♖b1! ♘a5 16
♗d3 ♖c8 *(47)*

Black's uncertain play has allowed White to deploy his pieces favourably and to prepare the effective advance of his pawn centre.

17 d5! b6 18 ♗a6 ♖c7 19 ♕d3 ♘b7 20 ♗f4 ♘d6 21 e5!

White's advantage becomes clearly apparent. His central pawn avalanche (and a spatial advantage in the opening is normally associated with the problem of the centre!) inexorably bursts through the defences.

Black therefore took the play along tactical lines, but after 21...♗f5 22 ed ♗xd3 23 dc ♕xd5 24 ♗xd3 ♕xd3 25 ♖bd1! ♕xe2 26 ♖d8! e5 27 ♗d2 ♕a6 28 ♗b4 ♕c4 29 ♗xf8 ♕xc7 30 ♗e7+! he ended up in a hopeless position.

Tarrasch in his time commented that two connected passed pawns on the sixth rank were worth a rook. Practice shows that, for the sake of creating a connected pair of pawns at d5 and e5, a sacrifice of material is often fully justified.

No. 126 Tal-Ghitescu
Miskolc, 1963
Spanish Game

1 e4 e5 2 ♘f3 ♘c6 3 ♗b5 a6 4 ♗a4 ♘f6 5 0-0 ♗e7 6 ♖e1 b5 7

♗b3 d6 8 c3 0-0 9 h3 h6 10 d4 ♖e8 11 ♘bd2 ♗f8 12 ♘f1 ♗d7 13 ♘g3 ♘a5 14 ♗c2 c5 15 b3 g6 16 ♗e3 ♘c6 17 d5 ♘e7 18 ♕d2 ♔h7

Here White took the profoundly correct decision to make a positional sacrifice of a piece for two pawns, for the sake of creating a powerful pawn centre.

19 ♗xc5! dc 20 ♘xe5 ♘c8 21 f4 ♕e7 22 c4! ♗g7 23 ♘f3 bc 24 bc ♘d6 25 e5! ♘xc4 26 ♕c3 ♗b5 27 ♖ad1

It is important not to 'sell too cheaply'. After 27 ef ♕xf6 Black would have had sufficient counterplay. For the moment White's pawn centre is worth more than a piece.

27...♖ad8 28 d6 ♘xd6 (the least evil!) 29 ed ♕b7 30 ♘e5! ♘d7 31 ♘h5 ♗h8 32 ♕g3 ♘xe5 33 fe ♕d7 34 ♘f4! ♗xe5 35 ♗xg6+ ♔h8 36 ♗xf7! ♖xd4+ 37 ♖xd4! (the decisive combination) 37...♖xe1+ 38 ♕xe1 ♕xf7 39 ♕e5+ ♕g7 40 ♕xc5 ♗c6 41 ♖d2 1-0

At the same time, as has already been mentioned, the hasty and unjustified seizure of space at the start of the game will often have unsatisfactory results.

No. 127 Letelier-Fischer
Leipzig OL, 1960
King's Indian Defence

1 d4 ♘f6 2 c4 g6 3 ♘c3 ♗g7 4 e4

0-0

Here White was tempted into seizing space in the centre with gain of tempo.

5 e5 ♘e8 6 f4(?) d6 7 ♗e3 c5!

Black acts like a powerful spring. White himself has created an excellent target for his opponent to attack — his advanced pawns, which lack support by their pieces.

8 dc ♘c6 9 cd ed 10 ♘e4 ♗f5 11 ♘g3 ♗e6 12 ♘f3 ♕c7 13 ♕b1 de 14 f5? e4! (the decisive counterattack in the centre) **15 fe ef 16 gf f5! 17 f4 ♘f6 18 ♗e2 ♖fe8 19 ♔f2 ♖xe6 20 ♖e1 ♖ae8 21 ♗f3 ♖xe3 22 ♖xe3 ♖xe3 23 ♔xe3 ♕xf4+!! 0-1**

The problem of both secured, and unsecured seizure of space is typical of many modern opening systems, and determines the development of the corresponding middlegame ideas in Alekhine's Defence, the Grünfeld Defence, Benoni Defence, and so on.

Consider the following variation of the Modern Benoni:

1 d4 ♘f6 2 c4 c5 3 d5 e6 4 ♘c3 ed 5 cd d6 6 e4 g6 7 f4 ♗g7. What is more advisable for White: to continue his mobilization by 8 ♗d3 (or first 8 ♗b5+ ♘fd7 9 ♗d3) and then 0-0 etc., or to go in for the immediate seizure of space by 8 e5!? The latter way is as tempting as it is outwardly

energetic, and it naturally touches directly on the problem of secured (or unsecured?!) space.

An answer is given by the following sample variation: 8... ♘fd7 (8...de 9 fe ♘fd7 10 e6! is weaker) 9 ♘b5!? (White does not achieve anything by 9 ed 0-0 10 ♘f3 ♘f6 followed by ...♘e8) 9...de 10 ♘d6+ ♔e7 11 ♘xc8+ ♕xc8 12 ♘f3 ♖e8 13 ♗c4 ♘b6! 14 d6+ ♔f8 15 ♗b5 ♘c6 16 0-0 ♔g8 17 fe ♗xe5, and Black has a good game.

Thus the seizure of space by 8 e5?!, although not refutable, appears rather debatable. For this reason the flexible 8 ♗b5+ ♘fd7 9 ♗d3 is more advisable.

Space and blockade

Above we have mainly considered situations where the mobility of the central pawns was not restricted, but often in the opening the position in the centre fairly quickly stabilizes, with one of the sides obtaining a pawn outpost on the fifth rank. In a closed position of this type great importance is assumed by the principle of blockade.

Pawns deployed in the centre have a dual significance. On the one hand, a pawn is a good building material. On the other hand, often it simultaneously blocks important lines and becomes a serious hindrance to its own pieces. It is here that a blockade situation can arise.

No. 128 Spassky-Fischer
World Championship, 1972
Nimzo-Indian Defence

1 d4 ♘f6 2 c4 e6 3 ♘c3 ♗b4 4 e3 c5 5 ♗d3 ♘c6 6 ♘f3 ♗xc3+ 7 bc d6 8 e4 e5 9 d6 ♘e7 10 ♘h4 h6

Here there followed 11 f4?! ♘g6! 12 ♘xg6 fg 12 fe(?)

White wrongly forces matters, after which he has an unpromising game. 13 0-0 was better, maintaining the tension on e5 and not allowing Black the important d6 square.

13...de 14 ♗e3 b6 15 0-0 0-0 16 a4? *(48)*

White fails to sense the danger, and creates a further weakness in his position, taking away an important square from his bishop.

The position becomes com-

pletely blocked, which favours Black, who under the 'cover' of the white pawns is able to develop his initiative on the K-side.

16...a5 17 ♖b1 ♗d7 18 ♖b2 ♖b8 19 ♖bf2 ♕e7 20 ♗c2 g5! 21 ♗d2 ♕e8 22 ♗e1 ♕g6 23 ♕d3 ♘h5 24 ♖xf8+ ♖xf8 25 ♖xf8+ ♔xf8 26 ♗d1 ♘f4 27 ♕c2 ♗xa4! 0-1

The distinction between the two flanks

Apart from the centre and its periphery there are also two flanks on the chess board — the K-side and Q-side. The character of the play on the two flanks is rather different, and this is clearly felt in the opening stage of the game.

It will have been readily apparent that, in the majority of the examples given, the battle arena quickly became the K-side. Here a role was played both by the 'fatal' points f2 and f7, and by the possibility of more rapidly opening up the game.

Let us compare the moves 1 e4 and 1 d4. In openings beginning with 1 e4 it is possible to castle early, and hence one's mobilization can usually be completed more quickly than after 1 d4. On the other hand, the move 1 d4 immediately gives the game a solid, positional character, when (as a rule) all the opening problems are solved thoroughly, if more slowly.

There is also a difference in the struggle for the central squares, especially after 1 e4 e5 and 1 d4 d5, with which Black aims to maintain the balance of seizing space in the centre.

However, the further struggle for the centre takes on different forms. It is natural that both sides (and in particular White, as the active side) will try to remove the opponent's central pawn, in order to obtain some advantage in the centre.

In openings with 1 e4 e5 it is comparatively easy to open up the game by d2-d4, since this square is guarded by the queen. But Black too, in turn, has the real possibility of making the central counterblow . . .d7-d5.

Incidentally, this rather simple strategy is virtually the main one in a number of classical Open Games, such as: the Scotch Game, Ponziani Opening, Italian Game, Two Knights Defence, and so on.

This is why in these and other Open Games the centre is often very quickly cleared of pawns.

By contrast, after 1 d4 d5 the move e2-e4 (and especially . . .e7 -e5) is much more difficult to achieve. This explains why in very many variations the centre

remains closed for a fairly long time.

After 1 d4 d5 it is much more effective to undermine the centre by c2-c4 (for White) and . . .c7-c5 (for Black). For comparison it should be noted that the analogous undermining moves in the 1 e4 e5 openings — f2-f4 (or . . .f7-f5) involve much greater difficulties and are normally double-edged. After all, here pawns are advanced in front of the king, which always involves a considerable risk.

It can be concluded that in the opening it is easier to initiate active, and sometimes forcing play on the K-side, whereas the struggle on the Q-side is of a slower, preparatory nature. It would seem to be this that influenced the historical process of opening theory development. Not only the Closed Games, but also systems of this type in the Open Games (with the accent on the Q-side!) began to be investigated much later.

Of course, there is a limit to the logic of these reasonings, and in the Closed Games too there is enormous scope for conducting sharp play, with attacks on the king.

The procedures of play on the K-side have already been shown in a number of examples. Below we will examine certain characteristic methods in the opening stage of conducting the struggle on the Q-side.

The Q-side as the arena of opening play

At an early stage the fate of a game is comparatively rarely decided by an attack on the Q-side, but at the same time the Q-side often becomes the arena of battle. And quite often one of the sides fairly quickly, when the mobilization of the pieces is far from complete, gains a significant advantage, which later determines the course, and perhaps even the outcome of the game.

This is shown in the following thematic examples.

No. 129 Capablanca-Spielmann
New York, 1927
Queen's Gambit

1 d4 d5 2 ♘f3 e6 3 c4 ♘d7 4 ♘c3 ♘gf6 5 ♗g5 ♗b4 6 cd ed 7 ♕a4 ♗xc3+? 8 bc 0-0 9 e3 c5 10 ♗d3 c4 11 ♗c2 ♕e7 12 0-0 a6 13 ♖fe1 ♕e6 14 ♘d2! b5 15 ♕a5! ♘e4? 16 ♘xe4 de 17 a4 ♕d5 *(49)* 18 ab!! ♕xg5 (18...♗b7 19 ba!) 19 ♗xe4 ♖b8 (19...♖a7 20 b6! ♕xa5 21 ba! ♕xa1 22 ♖xa1 ♘b6 23 a8♕ ♘xa8 24 ♗xa8 leads to a win for White) 20 ba! ♖b5 21 ♕c7 ♘b6 22 a7 ♗h3 23 ♖eb1 ♖xb1+

24 ♖xb1 f5 25 ♗f3 f4 26 ef 1-0

49

No. 130 Alekhine-Nimzowitsch
San Remo, 1930
French Defence

1 e4 e6 2 d4 d5 3 ♘c3 ♗b4 4 e5 c5 5 ♗d2 ♘e7 6 ♘b5 ♗xd2+ 7 ♕xd2 0-0 8 c3 b6?

A slow plan, allowing White to obtain a solid positional advantage on the Q-side. 8...♘c6 or 8...♘f5 was better.

9 f4 ♗a6 10 ♘f3 ♕d7 11 a4 ♘bc6 12 b4! cb 13 cb ♗b7 14 ♘d6 f5? *(50)*

50

This conclusively kills off the

possibility of any active play for Black and leads to positional zugzwang. 14...a5 was comparatively best.

15 a5! ♘c8 16 ♘×b7 ♕×b7 17 a6! ♕f7 18 ♗b5 ♘8e7 19 0-0 h6 20 ♖fc1 ♖fc8 21 ♖c2 ♕e8 22 ♖ac1

Black has ended up in a deadly pin, which in the given case is not only tactical, but also strategical.

22...♖ab8 23 ♕e3 ♖c7 24 ♖c3 ♕d7 25 ♖1c2 ♔f8 26 ♕c1 ♖bc8 27 ♗a4! b5 28 ♗×b5 ♔e8 29 ♗a4 ♔d8 30 h4! 1-0

No. 131 Gheorghiu-Bellon
Las Palmas, 1976
Sicilian Defence

1 e4 e5 2 ♘f3 g6 3 d4 cd 4 ♘×d4 ♘c6 5 c4 ♗g7 6 ♗e3 ♘f6 7 ♘c3 0-0 8 ♗e2 b6 9 0-0 ♗b7 10 f3! d6 11 ♕d2 ♕d7 12 a4! e6 13 ♖fd1 ♖fd8 14 ♘×c6 ♕×c6 15 a5! ba 16 ♘b5! a6 17 ♘×d6 ♘e8 18 c5 ♖d7 19 ♕×a5 ♗×b2? (19...♘×d6 20 cd ♖×d6 was the lesser evil) **20 ♖ab1 ♘×d6 21 ♖×d6 ♖×d6 22 cd ♗f6 23 ♕c7! 1-0**

No. 132 Lombard-Rogoff
Biel IZ, 1976
English Opening

1 d4 ♘f6 2 c4 e6 3 ♘c3 c5 4 ♘f3 cd 5 ♘×d4 ♗b4 6 g3 ♘e4 7 ♕d3 ♕a5 8 ♘c2 ♗×c3+9 bc ♘c5! 10 ♕d2 b6 11 ♗g2 ♗b7 12 ♗×b7

♘×b7 13 ♗a3 ♘c6 14 0-0 d6! 15 ♖ab1 (15 ♗×d6 0-0-0! is bad for White; the lesser evil was 15 f4, although here too Black's chances are better) **15...♕a4 16 ♖fd1 0-0 17 ♖b5 ♕×c4!**

It will be apparent that White's position is already lost.

18 ♖g5 f6 19 ♖h5 ♕×a2! 20 ♖h4 ♖fd8 21 ♕d3 f5 22 c4 ♘c5 23 ♕c3 ♕b3! 24 ♕×b3 ♘×b3 25 ♖×d6 ♖×d6 26 ♗×d6 ♖d8 0-1

Premature flank operations

In certain cases one of the players aims at an early stage to place the chief emphasis of his strategic action on a flank offensive. In the Closed Games, with a blocked structure in the centre, such plans are possible, especially if the offensive is mounted on the Q-side. But in the majority of cases such strategy meets with a strong counteraction, in the form of an energetic counterblow in the centre.

We will examine several examples which are characteristic in this respect. Thus a typical mistake in this type of situation is the premature release of the central tension, with the ephemeral aim of developing flank operations with the centre unsecured.

No. 133 Lyublinsky-Averbakh
Gorky, 1940
Vienna Game

1 e4 e5 2 ♘c3 ♘c6 3 ♗c4 ♘f6 4
d3 ♗c5 5 f4 d6 6 ♘f3 ♕e7, after
which White committed a typical mistake by playing 7 f5?

White's intention is to transfer the weight of the struggle to
the K-side, but things do not
come to that. Exploiting White's
premature diversion of his attention from the centre in favour of
flank operations, Black is the
first to begin active play in the
centre and on the Q-side.

7...♘d4! 8 ♗g5 c6 9 ♖f1 b5 10
♗b3 ♗b7 (10...a5 is more energetic) 11 ♘xd4 ♗xd4 12 ♕e2 h6
13 ♗h4 a6 14 ♘d1 d5! 15 c3 ♗b6
16 ♘e3 ♕d6 17 0-0-0 0-0-0 18
♔b1 ♖d7 19 ed cd 20 ♗g3 ♕e7 21
♘c2 ♖e8 22 ♖de1 ♗c7 23 d4 e4 24
a4 ♗xg3 25 hg ♗c6 26 ♘b4 ♕d6!
27 ♔c2 ♖b7 28 ♖a1 ♗d7!

Black's advantage has assured
real proportions. He threatens
...a5, and 29 ab fails to 29...
♗xb5, winning the exchange.

29 a5 ♖c7 30 ♔b1 ♔b7 31 ♖f4
♔a7 32 ♔a2 ♗c8 23 ♖af1 ♗b7,
and Black obtained a strategically won position.

This example confirms a well
known pronouncement by Emanuel Lasker: "White did not
stand well enough in the centre
to be able to conduct operations

on the flanks". Even more
categorical, but perfectly justified here, is Nimzowitsch's
aphorism: "The centre is the
dominant principle, the flank the
subsidiary one".

In the following game it was
Black who tried at an early stage
to attack the enemy king, and by
very risky means.

No. 134 Suetin-Bondarevsky
USSR Ch., 1963
Spanish Game

1 e4 e5 2 ♘f3 ♘c6 3 ♗b5 a6 4
♗a4 d6 5 0-0 g5?!

A clever, but hardly justified
diversion on the K-side. It is possible that in the event of slow
play by White such as 6 c3 g4 7
♘e1 ♗g7 followed by ...h5
Black would have succeeded in
obtaining real counterplay. But
White finds a strong counter,
consisting in energetic action in
the centre.

6 d4! g4 (after 6...b5 7 ♗b3 g4
8 ♘g5 ♘h6 9 ♗d5! Black's position is very difficult) 7 ♗xc6+ bc
8 ♘e1 ed 9 ♕xd4 ♕f6 10 ♕a4!

This queen manœuvre, to-
gether with White's 12th move,
emphasizes Black's opening
difficulties.

10...♘e7 11 ♘c3 ♗d7 12 ♕a5!

Completing the queen ma-
nœuvre; to avoid loss of material
Black has to give up the right to

castle.

12... &d8 13 ∅d3 ∆g7 14 e5!

And now the time is ripe for this breakthrough in the centre. Bad is 14...de 15 ∅c5, when the threat of ∃d1 cannot be parried.

14...♕f5 15 ∃e1 d5

15...∅g6 was comparatively best, when I was intending 16 ∅e4! ∆×e5 17 ∅×e5 ♕×e5 18 ♕b4!, and White's attack is very dangerous.

16 ∅e2 ∅g6 17 ∅g3 ♕e6 18 ∆g5+ ♚c8 19 ∅c5 ♕e8 20 ∅h5!

Let us dwell here on the following feature. It is clear that White has a completely won position, and yet, out of the 20 moves made by him, 11 have been by his queen and knights! The point is that Black chose a fanciful plan with 5...g5, and the only way to refute this was by unusual, very determined means. In the given case the only way to punish the opponent for his dubious experiment was by energetic queen and knight manœuvres.

20...∃g8 21 ∅×g7 ∃×g7 22 ∅×a6 ∃a7 23 ∆e3 ∃×a6 24 ♕×a6+ ♚d8 25 ∆g5+ ∅e7 26 ∆f6 ∃g6 27 a4 ∆c8 28 ♕d3 ♚d7 29 a5 ∆b7 30 b4 ∅g8 31 c4 ♕e6 32 ♕d4 ♚e8 33 b5 cb 34 cb ∅e7 35 ♕c5 ♕d7 36 ∃ec1 1-0

Against a flank diversion — a counterblow in the centre

In reply to a flank diversion at an early stage of the game it is often expedient to make an effective counterblow in the centre. It will sometimes be sharp and tactical, demanding deep calculation, imagination and great energy. This classical procedure of a pawn counterblow in the centre in reply to a flank attack remains unshakeable and is constantly being enriched by new forms.

We give a game in which this procedure was employed at an early stage.

No. 135 Neegard-Simagin
Corr., 1964

51

White has begun a pawn offensive on the K-side, relying on the solidity of his central formation. And yet Black finds an effective way of opening up the game.

16...b5! 17 cb d5!! 18 ed e4!

Black sacrifices three pawns, but gains the chance to mount a very strong attack on the white king.

19 ♕xe4 (19 fe ♘e5!) **19... ♗xg4 20 ♕f4**

Black also has dangerous threats after 20 ♕xg4 ♖xe3 21 ♔f2 ♗c5

20...♗h5 21 ♔f2 ♘e5 22 ♗g2 ♗d6 23 ♕a4 ♖c8 24 ♖d2 ♕f6

All the black pieces are participating in the attack. White's position is hopeless.

25 ♗g5 ♕f5 26 ♘f4 ♗xf3 27 ♗h3 ♗g4 28 ♔g2 ♖c2! 0-1

No. 136 Botvinnik-Schmid
Leipzig OL, 1960
Benoni Defence

1 d4 c5 2 d5 d6 3 e4 g6 4 ♘f3 ♗g7 5 ♗e2 ♘f6 6 ♘c3 ♘a6 7 0-0 ♘c7 8 a4 a6 9 ♘d2! ♗d7 10 ♘c4 b5 (52)

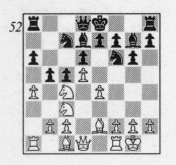

Black appears to have a good position in view of his healthy Q-side pawn phalanx, but the following pawn thrust in the centre clarifies the situation.

11 e5!

An essential, and at the same time highly effective plan. White begins a swift attack in the centre, taking into account the insecure position of the black king.

11...de (White's advantage is also obvious after 11...bc 12 ef ♗xf6 13 ♗h6!) **12 ab ab** (12... ♘xb5 is slightly better) **13 ♖xa8 ♕xa8 14 ♘xe5 b4 15 d6!**

Black's centre is on the point of collapse, and it is to here that the main weight of the struggle transfers. Black's successes on the Q-side prove short-lived.

15...bc

15...ed 15 ♕xd6 bc 17 ♗f3 ♕a6 18 ♗c6! etc. is also bad.

16 dc ♕c8 17 ♗f4 cb 18 ♘xd7 ♘xd7 19 ♗b5 ♗d4 20 c3 e5 21 cd ef 22 ♗xd7+ ♕xd7 23 ♕e2+ ♔f8 24 ♕e5 ♔g8 25 ♖b1, and White soon won.

Here are some further examples.

No. 137 Spassky-Schmid
Varna OL, 1962
Benoni Defence

1 d4 c5 2 d5 d6 3 e4 g6 4 ♘f3 ♗g7 5 ♗e2 ♘f6 6 ♘c3 ♘a6 7 0-0 ♘c7 8 ♖e1 0-0 9 a4 a6 10 ♗g5 h6 11 ♗f4 ♗d7 12 ♕d2 b5? 13 e5! de

14 ♗xe5 b4 15 ♗xf6 ♗xf6 16 ♘e4 ♗g7 17 ♘xc5 ♗xb2 18 ♖ad1 ♗f5 (18...♗c3 19 ♕xh6, with the strong threat of ♘g5) 19 ♕xh6 ♗g7 20 ♕h4! ♗d6 21 ♘g5 ♖fe8 22 ♗d3! ♕xc5 23 ♗xf5 ♘xd5 24 ♗e6! 1-0

No. 138 Spassky-Mikenas
USSR Ch, Riga, 1959
Albin Counter-Gambit

1 d4 d5 2 c4 e5 3 de d4 4 e4 ♘c6 5 f4 g5? 6 f5 ♘xe5 7 ♘f3 ♗b4+? 8 ♘bd2 ♘c6 9 ♗d3 g4 10 0-0! gf 11 ♘xf3 ♗d6 12 e5 ♘xe5 13 ♖e1 f6 14 c5! ♗e7

After 14...♗xc5 15 ♘xe5 fe 16 ♖xe5+ ♗e7 17 ♕h5+ ♔d7 18 ♗b5+ c6 19 ♖d5+! ♗d6 20 ♗f4 White wins by force.

15 ♘xe5 fe 16 ♖xe5 ♘f6 17 ♗g5 0-0 18 ♕b3+ ♔h8 19 ♖ae1 ♗xc5 20 ♖xc5 ♕d6 21 ♖ce5 ♘g4 22 ♗f4 ♗d7 23 ♗g3 ♗c6 24 ♖5e4 1-0

No. 139 Averbakh-Aronin
Riga, 1954
King's Indian Defence

1 d4 ♘f6 2 c4 g6 3 ♘c3 ♗g7 4 e4 d6 5 ♗e2 0-0 6 ♗g5 c5 7 d5 h6 8 ♗f4 ♘bd7? (8...e6! is correct, and if 9 de ♗xe6 10 ♗xd6 ♖e8 11 ♗xc5 ♕a5, when Black has a strong counterattack) 9 ♘f3 ♘g4 10 ♕d2 ♔h7 11 ♗g3 ♘ge5 12 ♘xe5 ♗xe5 13 f4 ♗d4 14 ♘b5

♗f6 15 0-0 g5?

Black has played the opening badly, and now, in trying forcibly to create active play on the K-side, he quickly ends up in a lost position. The lesser evil was 15...a6 16 ♘c3 ♗d4+ 17 ♔h1 e5!?

16 e5! de (16...gf 17 ef fg 18 ♗d3+ is bad for Black) 17 fg ♗xg5 18 ♗d3+ ♔g7 19 ♕e2 ♖h8 20 d6 e6 21 ♘c7 ♖b8 22 ♖xf7+! 1-0

Often, if the opponent's king is in the centre and he engages in early flank operations, there follows an explosive, sacrificial attack in the centre, aimed at the king. Here are two characteristic games, which are similar not only outwardly.

No. 140 Alekhine-Böök
Margate, 1938
Queen's Gambit Accepted

1 d4 d5 2 c4 dc 3 ♘f3 ♘f6 4 e3 e6 5 ♗xc4 c5 6 0-0 ♘c6 7 ♕e2 a6 8 ♘c3 b5 9 ♗b3 b4? 10 d5! ♘a5 (10...ed 11 ♘xd5 ♘xd5 12 ♖d1! ♗e6 13 e4 or 10...bc 11 ♗a4 ♕xd5 12 e4! also favours White) 11 ♗a4+ ♗d7 12 de fe 13 ♖d1! bc 14 ♖xd7! ♘xd7 15 ♘e5 ♖a7 16 bc ♔e7 17 e4! ♘f6 18 ♗g5 ♕c7 19 ♗f4 ♕b6

A pretty variation would have resulted after 19...♕b7 20 ♕e3! ♔d8 21 ♕d3+ ♔c8 22 ♖b1 ♕xe4

23 ♘f7!! etc.

20 ♖d1! g6 21 ♗g5 ♗g7 22 ♘d7 ♖xd7 23 ♖xd7+ ♔f8 24 ♗xf6! ♗xf6 25 e5 1-0

No. 141
Taimanov-Polugayevsky
USSR Ch., 1960
Queen's Gambit Accepted

1 d4 d5 2 c4 dc 3 ♘f3 ♘f6 4 ♕a4+ ♘bd7 5 ♘c3 e6 6 e4 c5 7 d5! ed 8 e5! d4 9 ♗xc4 dc 10 ef ♕xf6 11 ♗g5 ♕c6 12 0-0-0! *(53)*

12...cb+ (after 12...♕xa4 13 ♖he1+ ♗e7 14 ♖xe7+ ♔f8 15 ♖xf7+ ♔e8 16 ♖e1+ ♘e5 17 ♘xe5 or 15...♔g8 16 ♖fxd7+ ♕xc4 17 ♖d8+ ♔f7 18 ♘e5+ White wins prettily) 13 ♔xb2 ♗e7 14 ♖he1! f6 15 ♗b5 ♕b6 16 ♔c1 fg 17 ♗xd7+ ♔f8 18 ♖xe7! ♔xe7 19 ♕e4+ ♔d8

Or 19...♔f6 20 ♕f5+ ♔e7 21

♕e5+ ♔f7 22 ♘xg5+!, and wins.

20 ♗f5+ ♔c7 21 ♕e5+ ♔c6 22 ♖d6+ ♔b5 23 ♕b2+ 1-0

These are certainly striking examples, but in general a rapid attack in the centre in reply to a flank offensive may not always prove successful, as the following game demonstrates.

No. 142 Spassky-Suetin
USSR Spartakiad, 1963
Queen's Gambit Accepted

1 d4 d5 2 c4 dc 3 ♘f3 ♘f6 4 e3 e6 5 ♗xc4 c5 6 0-0 a6 7 ♕e2 b5 8 ♗b3 ♗b7 9 ♖d1 ♘bd7 10 ♘c3 ♕c7!? 11 e4 cd 12 e5? (a mistake; 12 ♘d5!? or 12 ♘xd4 is better) 12...dc 13 ef ♘xf6 14 ♘e5 ♗c5! 15 ♗f4 ♕b6 16 ♘xf7?! 0-0 (16...♔xf7? 17 ♖d6!! wins for White) 17 ♘g5 (17 ♘d6 was the lesser evil) 17...cb 18 ♖ab1 ♖ae8 19 ♖xb2 ♕c6 20 ♘f3 ♘e4 21 ♗g3 ♘c3 22 ♕d3 ♘xd1 23 ♕xd1 ♖d8 24 ♕e2 ♕e4!, and Black soon won.

Thus a strong and solid centre is a secure guarantee against flank diversions. At the same time, control of the centre assists the mounting of an attack on the flank (examples Nos. 109-112).

four
GENERAL OPENING PROBLEMS

Pawn Weaknesses

The pawn formation determines the course of play to a considerable degree. Many opening positions, where organic defects occur in the pawn formation (isolated, doubled or backward pawns), are considered unsatisfactory, and the variations leading to them have been rejected by theory.

In such situations it is not only the pawns which are weak, but also the squares in front of them, the latter providing excellent invasion points for the opponent's pieces.

Organic pawn weaknesses in the opponent's position are a considerable assistance to the long-term active deployment of the forces. In this respect the following variation of the English Opening is instructive: 1 c4 ♘f6 2 ♘c3 c5 3 g3 d5 4 cd ♘xd5 5 ♗g2 ♘c7 6 d3 ♘c6? 7 ♗xc6+ bc 8 ♕a4.

Black has doubled pawns on the half open c-file, and as a re-sult they are a convenient target for attack. Given the opportunity, White will establish one of his knights on the strong square c4. Of course, it cannot be categorically stated that Black's position is totally unsatisfactory, but his difficulties on the Q-side are great.

This variation of the Spanish Game is no less significant: 1 e4 e5 2 ♘f3 ♘c6 3 ♗b5 a6 4 ♗a4 d6 5 0-0 ♗g4 6 h3 h5 7 d4 ♕f6 8 hg hg 9 de de 10 ♗g5 ♕g6 11 ♕d7+! ♔xd7 12 ♘xe5+ ♔e6 13 ♘xg6 fg 14 ♗xc6 bc *(54)*, where Black's pawn formation is completely unsatisfactory.

In the above examples the

weakness of one side's pawn formation had a significant influence on the course and the assessment of the opening struggle. However, it should be mentioned that, in modern times, pawn weaknesses in the opening are assessed only taking account of the overall coordination of the forces.

If they are compensated by an active or harmonious deployment of the pieces, pawn weaknesses are admissible in many topical opening systems.

Let us return to the structure with double pawns. As was seen, if in addition they form a separate pawn island, these pawns constitute a significant positional weakness. But in a number of modern opening systems one of the players allows the doubling of his pawns in the centre or on the flank (most often on the c-file), with the aim of controlling important squares in the centre, which in certain cases assists their occupation by pieces (and no less often facilitates the setting-up of a pawn centre, cf. No. 109, for example).

In this respect the following example is instructive.

No. 143 Botvinnik-Kan
USSR Ch., 1939
Nimzo-Indian Defence

1 d4 ♘f6 2 c4 e6 3 ♘c3 ♗b4 4 ♘f3 c5 5 a3 ♗xc3+ 6 bc ♕a5 7 ♗d2 ♘e4 8 ♕c2 ♘xd2 9 ♘xd2 d6 10 e3 e5 11 de de

A highly noteworthy structure in the centre has resulted, where in the given instance White's doubled pawns on the c-file constitute not a weakness, but a real strength. The point is that in Black's position there is a serious weakness at d5, and for White to occupy it securely he will have to advance his pawn from e3 to e4. In this case the doubled c3 pawn, preventing Black in turn from becoming established at d4, will be a reliable guard of this square.

12 ♗d3 h6 13 0-0 0-0 14 f4! *(55)*

What, one might ask, could have been simpler and more natural than the immediate transfer of the knight to d5: 14 e4 ♘c6

15 ♖fd1 ♗e6 16 ♘f1 ♖ad8 17
♘e3. But after 17...♘e7! 18
♘d5(?) ♗×d5! followed by the
transfer of the knight to d6, the
advantage could even have
passed to Black. Therefore
White, for the moment keeping
his main strategic idea a secret,
makes use of another trump —
his lead in development. To exploit this factor it is favourable
for him to open up the game, and
this is assisted by his last move.

14...♘d7 (14...ef 15 ef would
have merely assisted White's
plan) **15 f5 ♘f6(?)** (15...f6 was
better) **16 ♘e4!**

The exchange of knights
favours White, since after it his
bishop establishes itself on the
critical d5 square.

**16...♕d8 17 ♘×f6+ ♕×f6 18
♗e4 ♖b8 19 ♖ad1 b6 20 h3 ♗a6
21 ♗d5 b5 22 cb ♖×b5 23 c4** with
an obvious advantage to White.

The following example is also
of interest.

No. 144 Aronin–Suetin
RSFSR Ch., 1953
Spanish Game

**1 e4 e5 2 ♘f3 ♘c6 3 ♗b5 a6 4
♗a4 d6 5 ♗×c6+ bc 6 d4 ♘f6 7
♘c3 ♘d7 8 ♗e3 ♗e7 9 de de 10
0-0 0-0 11 ♕d3 ♗d6 12 ♖fd1 ♕e7
13 ♕c4 ♗b7 14 ♘a4 c5 15 ♗g5
♕e8 16 ♘h4 ♕e6!?** (56)

At first sight this seems anti-

positional, since to go with his
pawn weaknesses on the Q-side
Black allows a serious worsening
of his central pawn formation.
But in doing so he has taken account of the specific possibilities
of piece play, and in particular
the establishment of his knight
on the strong outpost at d4.

56

17 ♕×e6 fe 18 ♘c3 ♘b8! (an
essential part of an important manœuvre, aimed at invading with
the knight at d4) **19 ♘f3 ♘c6 20
♘d2 ♘d4 21 ♖ac1 ♖f7 22 ♘c4 a5
23 ♖d2 a4 24 b3 ♗a6 25 ♗e3 ab 26
cb ♗×c4 27 bc c6!**

A remarkable position. If all
the pieces were to be removed
from the board, Black's formation would be hopeless, but
in this complex 'semi-middle-
game' the pawn defects are of secondary importance, and even
help Black to occupy important
points in the centre.

**28 ♖b2 ♖fa7 29 a4 ♗c7 30 ♖a1
♗a5 31 ♘d1 ♗b4 32 ♗×d4 ed 33
♖ba2 d3!** (otherwise ♘d1-b2-d3)

34 a5 ♖d8 35 f3 ♖d4 36 ♘e3 ♗c3 37 ♖b1 ♖xa5, and Black achieved an obvious superiority in the ending.

Thus the modern interpretation of pawn weaknesses in the centre is basically dialetical, i.e. they are admissible if they are compensated by the dynamics of the position.

Pawn chains and their mobility

Both in the opening and in the middlegame, pawn phalanxes are a very important offensive force in the seizure of space. Their advance creates scope for the pieces, and at the same time restricts the mobility of the opponent's forces. In the majority of closed set-ups there is no other way of breaking up the opponent's defences.

We give one of the typical plans of a Q-side pawn offensive.

No. 145 Geller-Bondarevsky
USSR Ch., 1963
Spanish Game

1 e4 e5 2 ♘f3 ♘c6 3 ♗b5 a6 4 ♗a4 d6 5 0-0 ♗d7 6 d4 ♘ge7 7 d5 ♘b8 8 c4 ♘g6 9 ♗e3 ♗e7 10 ♘bd2 0-0

Exploiting his spatial advantage on the Q-side, White begins a purposeful offensive on that part of the board.

11 b4 c5

Black does not wish to remain passive in anticipation of the c4-c5-c6 breakthrough. But now he is saddled with a weakness on the half open b-file, and the d5 pawn gains in strength.

12 bc! dc 13 ♗xd7 ♘xd7 14 a4 a5 15 ♖b1 b6 16 ♖b3 ♘f6 17 ♕b1 ♖b8 18 ♕b2 ♕c7 19 ♖b1 ♘d7 20 ♕c2 ♖b8 h6 21 ♘f1 ♘f4 22 ♖d1 ♕d6 23 ♗c1 g6 24 ♘e3 ♔h7 25 g3 ♘h5 26 ♘g4

White has achieved an obvious superiority on both wings.

26. . .f5?! 27 ♘xh6 f4 28 ♘g4 ♖be8 29 ♔g2 ♗d8 30 ♗b2 g5 31 ♖bd3 ♔g6 32 ♗c3 ♘hf6 33 ♘xf6 ♗xf6 34 h3 ♖h8 35 ♘h2 ♗e7 36 ♖g1 fg 37 fg ♘f6 38 ♖f1, and White confidently realized his advantage.

In modern opening strategy the mobility of pawn chains has broad significance and takes on a rich variety of forms. To a great extent this determines the promise (or lack of promise) of this or that opening system. It is no accident that variations such as the following have disappeared from the scene: 1 e4 e5 2 ♘f3 ♘c6 3 ♗c4 ♗c5 4 d3 d6 5 ♘c3 ♘f6 6 ♗e3 ♗b6 7 h3 ♗e6 8 ♗b3 0-0, or 1 e4 e5 2 ♘f3 ♘c6 3 ♘c3 ♘f6 4 ♗b5 ♗b4 6 0-0 0-0 d3 d6 8 ♘e2 ♘e7. For the creation of active plans there is scope in them neither in the centre, nor on the flanks, mainly because the pawn phalanxes of both sides are frozen.

For comparison, we give a relatively new system in the English Opening: 1 c4 ♘f6 2 ♘c3 g6 3 g3 ♗g7 4 ♗g2 0-0 5 e4 d6 6 ♘ge2 c5 7 d3 ♘c6.

Although White's formation in the centre looks rather modest, and he has even allowed the creation of a weak square at d4, his position is promising, since he has a highly mobile pawn phalanx both on the Q-side, and on the K-side, where depending on circumstances he can begin a pawn storm, e.g. by a2-a3 and b4-b4, or by h2-h3, f2-f4-f5 and g3-g4 etc.

Also typical is the following example, where by purely strategic methods White quickly punished his opponent for routine play.

No. 146
Botvinnik-Shcherbakov
USSR Ch., 1955
English Opening

1 c4 ♘f6 2 ♘c3 g6 3 g3 ♗g7 4 ♗g2 0-0 5 e4 d6 6 ♘ge2 e5(?) (6...c5) 7 0-0 ♘bd7 8 d3! ♘c5 9 f4! c6 10 h3 ♘e6 11 f5 ♘d4 12 g4 ♘e8 13 ♗e3 a6 14 ♕d2 b5 15 ♗g5 ♗f6? *(57)*

15...f6 was more tenacious.

16 ♗xf6 ♘xf6 17 ♘xd4 ed 18 ♘e2 ♕b6 19 cb ab 20 ♕h6! ♗d7 21 g5 ♘h5 22 ♘f4 ♘g7 23 f6! 1-0

It has been repeatedly stated that in the opening one should avoid superfluous pawn moves. But the modern forms of opening struggle are so diverse that they cannot be encompassed by a single set of rules, however specific!

In certain variations, where the central structure is blocked, truly paradoxical situations are possible, in which practically pawns alone are moved in the opening.

Instructive in this respect is a variation of the Caro-Kann Defence — 1 e4 c6 2 d4 d5 3 e5 ♗f5! 4 h4!?, which was introduced by Tal and successfully employed by him in a number of games, including some from his 1961 match with Botvinnik.

The following game is also of interest.

No. 147 Tal-Bagirov
29th USSR Ch., 1961
Caro-Kann Defence

1 e4 c6 2 d4 d5 3 e5 ♗f5 4 h4 h6

Bad, of course, is 4...e6? 5 g4 when Black loses a piece, but 4...h5 comes into consideration, blocking White's imminent pawn offensive.

5 g4! ♗d7 (5...♗h7? 6 e6!) 6 h5

The advance of the white pawns is by no means a consequence of recklessness or impulse, but is a well thought-out plan. White takes control of the important squares f5 and g6, hindering Black's expedient mobilization. Thus the knight at g8 can no longer be manœuvred to f5 or g6 via e7.

6...c5 7 c3 e6 8 f4! ♕b6

As can be seen, up till now White has moved only pawns, and despite this he has obtained the more promising position. It unexpectedly transpires that Black has been squeezed into a smaller amount of space and is obliged to defend for a long time.

9 ♘f3 ♘c6 10 ♗h3 *(58)*

The pawns have done their important work, and now White's pieces come into play. Under cover of the powerful pawn screen they can immediately choose for themselves the

most active posts. Thus at h3 the bishop is best placed to support the preparation of the f4-f5 breakthrough.

10...cd

Releasing the tension in the centre favours White (for the umpteenth time!). 10...♘ge7 was preferable.

11 cd f6 12 ♘c3 0-0-0 13 0-0 ♘ge7 14 ♘a4 ♕c7 15 ♘c5 b6

15...♘xd4 16 ♕xd4 ♘f5 17 gf! ♗xc5 18 fe ♗xd4+ 19 ♘xd4 favours White.

16 ♘d3 f5 17 ♗e3 ♔b8 18 ♘h4 fg 19 ♗xg4 ♘f5 20 ♗xf5 ef 21 ♖c1

The outcome of the opening is clearly favourable to White.

The blocking of pawn chains

In principle, every active pawn unit of the opponent's should be opposed by one of your own, to prevent him from setting up a powerful pawn phalanx. This was shown in the examples of various mobile pawn centres, where, in a narrower and at the same time specific sense, it was essentially the same logic which applied.

In a number of cases the blocking of pawn chains is initially carried out in the most natural way, using the simplest 'building material' – pawns.

We give a simple example to confirm this: 1 e4 e5 2 ♘f3 ♘c6 3 ♗c4 ♗c5 4 c3 ♘f6 5 d4 ed 6 cd ♗b4+ 7 ♗d2 ♗×d2+ 8 ♘b×d2 d5! etc. By this timely advance Black breaks up the 'ideal' white centre. After 9 ed ♘×d5 he continues ... ♘ce7 and ...c6, securely fixing White's central pawn and creating strong piece pressure on the centre.

And now let us consider a more modern system in the English Opening:

No. 148 Holmov-Boleslavsky
USSR Ch., 1957
English Opening

1 c4 ♘f6 2 ♘c3 g6 3 g3 ♗g7 4 ♗g2 0-0 5 e4 d6 6 ♘ge2 c5 7 0-0 ♘c6 (59)

As has already been mentioned, in this system White has available the strategic threat of a pawn storm both on the Q-side, and in some cases on the K-side.

8 ♖b1 ♘e8 9 a3 ♘c7 10 b4 ♘e6

11 d3 ♖b8 12 ♘d5! ♘ed4 13 ♘×d4 ♘×d4 14 ♗g5 ♖e8 15 ♕d2 b6 16 ♖fe1 f6 17 ♗e3 ♗d7 18 b5 e6 19 ♘c3 f5 20 f4! ♕f6 21 a4 ♘f3+ 22 ♗×f3 ♕×c3 23 e5!, and White retained a persistent initiative.

In this example Black based his counterplay on exploiting the slight weakness of the d4 square, but this plan is not altogether correct. In the given situation Black should first and foremost neutralize White's offensive on the Q-side, and with this aim after 8 ♖b1 he should have already been thinking of how to put a timely check on the advance of the white pawns. For this he should have continued 8...a6! 9 a3 ♖b8 10 b4 cb 11 ab b5! 12 cb ab, halting White's Q-side offensive and gaining equal chances.

In many cases, especially in modern games, the problem of blocking a pawn chain is closely linked with timely prophylactic measures. After all, often a pawn phalanx arises (or a pawn phalanx of the opponent's is destroyed) suddenly, by tactical means.

Thus after 1 e4 g6 2 d4 ♗g7 3 f4 c5 4 d5 d6 5 ♘c3 ♘f6 6 ♗e2 0-0 the natural move 7 ♘f3? allows a sharp counter on the Q-side — 7...b5, when unexpectedly the black Q-side pawns become active and advance energetically. It transpires that the variations 8 ♘xb5 ♘xe4 or 8 ♗xb5 ♘xe4! 9 ♘xe4 ♕a5+ 10 ♘c3 ♗xc3+ 11 bc ♕xb5 are favourable to Black, who has destroyed White's centre. And the alternative of gaining a pawn phalanx on the Q-side, if White does not force matters, is also advantageous to Black.

White's mistake was that he failed to take prophylactic measures against this counteroffensive. Instead of 7 ♘f3 he should have played 7 a4!, radically preventing...b5.

Such an 'explosive' pawn wave occurs more rarely on the K-side.

In this respect the following example appears paradoxical, but I fancy that this will help the reader to remember it.

No. 149 Sakharov-Petrosian
Kiev, 1957
French Defence

1 e4 e6 2 d4 d5 3 ♘c3 ♗b4 4 e5 c5 5 ♗d2 ♘e7 6 a3 ♗xc3 7 ♗xc3 cd 8 ♕xd4 ♘f5 9 ♕g4

There seemed to be no portent of danger for White after this natural move, since if 9...h5 10 ♕f4. But suddenly there followed:

9...g5! 10 ♗b5+ ♘c6 12 ♕d2 d4 13 ♗b4 ♕d5

Black's pawn offensive has enabled him to assume a dominating position in the centre and to gain a clear lead in development, whereas here the 'weakening' of his pawn phalanx is not at all a reality.

14 ♕e2 ♕xg2 15 ♕f3 ♕xf3 16 ♘xf3 ♗d7 17 ♘xg5 ♘xe5 18 ♗xd7+ ♘xd7 19 0-0-0 a5 20 ♗d2 ♖d8, and Black already has a winning position.

Since that time 9 ♕g4 has not been played. White prudently prefers to play 9 ♕f4, avoiding such a plan by Black.

Modern methods of halting pawn offensives are very diverse. But this is rather a middlegame theme, and will be mentioned in Part II of the book, where certain positional elements will be examined, in particular the mounting of breakthroughs at important points, flank pawn storms, pawn 'wedges' and so on.

The coordination of pieces and pawns at the start of the game

In the initial stage of the game the coordination of the forces merely begins to take shape, there being a large number of pieces and pawns on the board. At this stage the connection between pawn chains and the pieces acquires considerable importance. Pawn chains can both complement the actions of the pieces, and also restrict them.

In cases where the pawns of one player restrict the actions of his pieces, the coordination of his forces is destroyed. This happens if a pawn chain is fixed on squares of one colour and restrict the mobility of his bishop. Especially if it is deployed behind his pawns, as in the following example.

No. 150 Schlechter-John
Barmen, 1905
Dutch Defence

1 d4 d5 2 c4 e6 3 ♘c3 f5 4 ♘f3 c6 5 ♗f4 ♗d6 6 e3 ♘f6 7 ♗d3 ♕c7

Taking account of the fact that Black's c6-d5-e6-f5 pawn chain is fixed on light squares, Schlechter consistently plays for the 'suffocation' of the c8 bishop.

8 g3! 0-0 9 0-0 ♘e4 10 ♕b3 ♔h8 11 ♖ac1 ♗xf4 12 ef ♕f7 13 ♘e5 ♕e7 14 ♗xe4! fe 15 f3! ef 16 ♖ce1 ♕c7 17 ♕a3

White has successfully carried out his opening plan, exchanging the dark-square bishops and establishing control of the dark squares. As a result Black's light-square bishop is without prospects, and this soon leads to a general 'paralysis' in the coordination of his forces.

17...♔g8 18 ♖xf3 ♘a6 19 b3 ♕d8 20 c5 ♘c7 21 ♕b2 ♗d7 22 ♕c2 ♕e7 23 ♖ef1 ♖ae8 24 g4 ♗c8 25 ♖h3!

An instructive point. White provokes...g6, which conclusively weakens the dark squares in Black's position.

25...g6 26 b4! ♕f6 27 ♖hf3 ♖e7 28 a4 a6 29 ♘d1 ♖g7 30 ♘e3 ♕e7 31 g5 ♗d7 32 ♘3g4 ♗e8 33 ♘h6+ ♔h8 34 ♕e2 ♕d8 35 ♘eg4 ♗d7 36 ♕e5 ♘e8 37 ♖h3 ♕c7 38 ♘f6! ♕xe5 39 fe ♖e7 40 ♖hf3 ♘xf6 41 ♖xf6 ♖xf6 42 ef ♖e8 43 ♘f7+ ♔g8 44 ♘e5 ♖d8 45 ♔g2 ♔f8 46 h4 ♗e8 47 ♔f3 ♗f7 48 ♔f4 ♔e8 49 ♖b1 ♔f8 50 b5! 1-0

On the other hand, the pieces should on no account restrict pawn advances, which are very important in the struggle for control of space, provided of course that they are supported by pieces. Therefore an attempt in the opening to retain without fail an unweakened pawn formation is often incorrect.

To illustrate this we give an instructive game.

No. 151 Smyslov-Suetin
USSR Ch., 1952
Catalan Opening

1 c4 e6 2 g3 d5 3 ♗g2 ♘f6 4 ♘f3 dc 5 ♕a4+ ♗d7 6 ♕xc4 ♗c6 7 ♕c2 ♘bd7 8 0-0 e5 9 ♘c3 ♗c5 10 d3 0-0 11 e4!?

This move shows that White is planning a pawn offensive in the centre.

Although Black's pieces are well developed, he is clearly short of pawn material in the battle for the central squares, and his bishops are restricting the mobility of his important c-pawn.

11. . .♖e8 12 ♗e3 ♕e7 13 ♖ac1 ♖ad8!

Black fails to sense the danger. He should have relieved the tension by 13. . .♗xe3 14 fe ♘g4 15 ♕e2 ♖ad8, maintaining a defensible position.

14 ♘h4 ♕f8 15 ♘f5 ♗b6 16 a3 ♘g4 (now after 16. . .♗xe3 17 ♘xe3 ♘c5 White has the unpleasant 18 ♘cd5) 17 ♗xb6 ♘xb6 18 h3 ♘f6 19 f4!

And now comes the second stage of the pawn offensive. The avalanche of white pawns advances inexorably.

19. . .ef 20 gf g6 21 ♘g3 ♕c5+ 22 ♔h2 ♔g7 23 b4 ♕d4 24 ♖f3 a6 25 ♘ce2 ♕d7 26 ♔b2 ♕e7 27 ♘d4 ♔g8 28 ♘xc6 bc 29 ♖xc6 ♖d6 30 ♖c2 ♖d7 31 ♗f1 h5 32 ♖g2 ♔h7 33 e5 ♘fd5 34 ♘e4 ♕h4 35 ♕f2 ♕xf2 36 ♖gxf2 ♔g7 37 d4 ♖a8 38 ♘c5 ♖dd8 39 f5! g5 40 f6+ ♔h6 41 ♘xa6 c6 42 ♖c2 ♖ac8 43 ♘c5 ♘f4 44 ♖d2 ♘d7 45 ♘e4 ♘f8 46 h4

White has a won position, and he confidently realizes his advantage.

46. . .♘8e6 47 ♘xg5 ♘xg5 48 ♖xf4 ♘e6 49 ♖e4 ♖a8 50 ♖d3 ♖a7 51 ♗h3 ♘c7 52 e6 fe 53 ♗xe6 ♘b5 54 f7 ♖f8 55 ♖g3 ♖xa3 56 ♖g8 ♖aa8 57 ♗c4 ♘c7 58 ♖e7 ♘d5 59 ♖e6+ 1-0

Coordination problems of this type often coincide with problems of the centre and of pawn chains, which were examined above. For example, central pawns which are far advanced but are not supported by the pieces constitute a serious weakness.

The examples given indicate the importance of harmonious coordination between the pieces and pawn chains or groups. Often this will compensate (even with interest!) for the creation of pawn weaknesses or a lack of space, as has already been mentioned.

In this respect the following variation of the Spanish Game is typical: 1 e4 e5 2 ♘f3 ♘c6 3 ♗b5 a6 4 ♗a4 d6 5 ♗×c6+ bc 6 d4 f6 *(60)*

Black's Q-side pawns are weakened, and his position is markedly cramped, but nevertheless it is fully viable. A highly important role is played by his light-square bishop, which compliments the action of his pawn chain in the centre. Subsequently Black's centre may advance with great power (...d5 or ...f5!)

The development of the following game is instructive.

No. 152 Bannik-Sakharov
Kiev, 1948

7 ♗e3 ♘e7 8 c4?! ♘g6 9 ♘c3 ♗e7 10 c5 0-0 11 d5 ♖b8 12 ♕c2 f5! 13 cd ♕×d6 14 0-0 f4 15 ♗c1 ♗g4 16 ♕d3 c5 17 b3 ♕d7 18 ♔h1

♗×f3 19 ♕×f3 ♘h4 20 ♕d3 f3 21 g3 ♕h3! 22 ♖g1 ♕g2+! 23 ♖×g2 fg+ 24 ♔g1 ♘f3+, and Black gained a decisive advantage.

Very often in the Open Games the centre is quickly cleared of pawns, and a sharp piece battle commences. Here, as has already been mentioned, it is very important to have good development and well coordinated pieces.

It is in open positions that the connection between material and time (tempi) becomes very clear. An extra pawn is approximately equivalent to three tempi. This rule does not always apply, by any means, but it does no harm to remember it during gambit play in the opening.

The employment of this rule in practice means giving up material gained (if, of course, the opponent has a growing initiative) in order to neutralize the opponent's dangerous threats and to solve one's development problems.

In this respect a variation of the Italian Game is instructive: 1 e4 e5 2 ♘f3 ♘c6 3 ♗c4 ♗c5 4 c3 ♘f6 5 d4 ed 6 cd ♗b4+ 7 ♘c3 ♘×e4 8 0-0 ♘×c3 9 bc.

Here, instead of the 'draughts-like' pursuit of material (after all, in chess it is not obligatory to capture!) 9... ♗×c3? 10 ♕b3! ♗×a1 11 ♗×f7+

etc., the correct continuation for Black is 9...d5! 10 cb dc 11 b5 ♘e7 12 ♗a3 0-0 13 ♕e2 ♖e8, returning the pawn, but successfully completing his mobilization and achieving approximate equality.

Coordination of the forces in the opening

It is very important that from the start of the game the coordination of the forces should be harmonious. Along with active development, the occupation of space and the creation of a favourable structure in the centre, this presupposes the harmonious and purposeful coordination of pieces and pawns.

As is shown by some of the examples from the chapter 'Active operations in the opening', often the cause of failure is a disruption in the harmony of the forces. Here we give several such examples.

No. 153 Alekhine-Bogoljubow
Triberg, 1921
Queen's Indian Defence

1 d4 ♘f6 2 ♘f3 e6 3 c4 b6 4 g3 ♗b7 5 ♗g2 c5 6 dc ♗xc5 (better 6...bc) 7 0-0 0-0 8 ♘c3 d5 *(61)*
After this White begins an

interesting plan of active play in the centre, which has the aim of disrupting the coordination of Black's forces.

9 ♘d4! ♗xd4 (it was hardly correct to hurry over this exchange) 10 ♕xd4 ♘c6 11 ♕h4 dc 13 ♖d1 ♕c8 14 ♗g5! ♘d5 14 ♘xd5 ed 15 ♖xd5 ♘b4? 16 ♗e4!!
This move signifies the achievement of White's goal. Although Black has not made any direct mistake, he has played superficially, and his pieces are now scattered and driven away from the K-side — here the most important part of the board. Black has no way of opposing the unusually active force of white pieces which now assails his K-side.

16...f5
White also has a winning position after 16...h6 17 ♗xh6 f5 18 ♕g5 ♕c7 19 ♗xg7 ♕xg7 20 ♕xg7+ ♔xg7 21 ♖d7+, or 16...g6 17 ♗f6 ♘xd5 18 ♗xd5

17 ♗xf5 ♖xf5 18 ♖d8+ ♕xd8

19 ♗xd8 ♖c8 20 ♖d1 ♖f7 21 ♕g4 ♘d3 22 ed ♖xd8 23 dc, and White soon won.

In the following example Alekhine exploits an inaccuracy by Black in the opening, and skilfully unites his pieces for a purposeful attack on f7.

No. 154 Alekhine-Duras
St. Petersburg, 1913
Spanish Game

1 e4 e5 2 ♘f3 ♘c6 3 ♗c5 a6 4 ♗a4 ♘f6 5 ♕e2 b5 6 ♗b3 ♗c5 7 a4 ♖b8 8 ab ab 9 d3 d6 10 ♗e3 ♗g4?! 11 h3 ♗h5 12 ♘bd2 0-0 13 0-0 ♘d4? 14 ♗xd4 ♗xf3 15 ♘xf3 ed
(62)

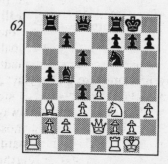

16 e5 ♕e7 17 ♖ef1 ♖be8 18 ♕d2 de 19 ♖xe5 ♕d6 20 ♕g5! ♖xe5 21 ♘xe5 ♕b6 22 g4! ♗d6? (22...♗e7 is slightly better) **23 ♘xf7! ♖xf7 24 ♕f5! g6 25 ♕e6 ♔g7 26 ♕xf7+ ♔h6 27 ♗e6 1-0**

Harmony of the forces can also prove highly effective in defence.

No. 155 Haag-Suetin
Debrecen, 1961
Sicilian Defence

1 e4 c5 2 ♘f3 e6 3 d4 cd 4 ♘xd4 ♘c6 5 ♘c3 ♕c7 6 ♗e3 a6 7 a3 b5 8 ♗d3 ♗b7 9 ♘b3 ♗e5 10 0-0 ♘f6 11 f4 ♘c4 12 ♗d4?! ♘xb2! 13 ♘xb5 ab 14 ♗xb2 ♘xe4 15 ♕h5 *(63)*

Strangely enough, this sortie leads to a loss virtually by force. White should have played 15 f5 ♗c5+ 16 ♔h1 ♘f2+ 17 ♖xf2 ♗xf2 18 fe de 19 ♗xb5+ with a double-edged game. Now White encounters a harmonious and active tactical defence by Black.

15...♘c5! 16 ♗xb5 ♕b6! 17 ♘d4 ♘a4! 18 ♖ae1 ♗c5! 19 ♗xd7+ ♔xd7 20 ♕xf7+ ♔c8 21 ♖xe6 ♗xd4+ 22 ♗xd4 ♕xd4+ 23 ♔h1 ♖d8!

White's position is quite hopeless, and he could have calmly resigned. From inertia there followed:

24 ♖b1 ♕d1+ 25 ♖e1 ♕d5 26

♛xg7 ♜g8 27 ♜xb7 ♜xg7 28
♜xg7 ♚d8 29 f5 ♜a6 0-1

Thus the role of tactics in the
opening is diverse and highly important. A mastery of tactical
coordination is one of the most
important conditions for the
genuine improvement of a
player.

We will examine some
further examples which contain
certain significant methodological features.

No. 156 Toran-Tal
European Team Ch.,
Oberhausen, 1961
English Opening

1 c4 e5 2 ♞c3 d6 3 g3 f5 4 d4 e4
5 f3 ♞f6 6 ♝g2 ef 7 ♞xf3 g6 8 0-0
♝g7 9 e4(?) fe 10 ♞g5 0-0 11
♞gxe4 ♞xe4 12 ♜xf8+ ♛xf8 13
♞xe4 ♞c6 14 ♝e3

White has played the opening
routinely, and his pieces are
awkwardly placed.

Black's next move emphasizes the lack of harmony in
his opponent's forces.

14...♝f5 15 ♛d2 ♜e8 16 ♞g5
♜xe3!

And here comes a tactical
blow based on the disharmony
of White's forces.

17 ♝d5+

After 17 ♝xc6 ♛e7! 18 ♝d5+
♚f8 19 ♞xh7+ ♚e8! Black has a
big advantage.

17...♚h8 18 ♞f7+ ♛xf7!! 19
♝xf7 ♜d3 20 ♛e2 ♝xd4+ 21 ♚g2
♞e5 22 ♜d1 ♜e3! 23 ♛f1

This leads to an immediate
loss, but White's position was
already unsatisfactory: 23 ♛f2
♝b6! 24 ♝d5 c6 25 c5 ♞xc5 26
♝b3 ♜xb3!, and Black wins.

23...♞e4+ 24 ♚h3 ♜f3 25
♛e2 ♝f5+ 0-1

No. 157 Suetin-Rabar
USSR v Yugoslavia, 1958
Spanish Game

1 e4 e5 2 ♞f3 ♞c6 3 ♝b5 a6 4
♝a4 ♞f6 5 0-0 ♝e7 6 ♜e1 b5 7
♝b3 d6 8 c3 0-0 9 h3 ♞a5 10 ♝c2
c5 11 d4 ♛c7 12 b4!? cb 13 cb ♞c4
14 ♞bd2 ♝d7 (better 14...♝b7)
15 ♞xc4 bc 16 ♜e3 a5? *(64)*
(16...♜ab8 is correct)

Just before this match, interestingly enough, an extensive
monograph by Rabar on the
Spanish Game had been published. However, the 12 b4!? variation was then little known, and

on encountering this line for the first time Rabar was not able to work things out, despite a great deal of thought. After the game he admitted that he had played ...a5 in analogy with Keres - Matanovic (Belgrade, 1956), a game which was well known at that time.

That game went 1 e4 e5 2 ♘f3 ♘c6 3 ♗b5 a6 4 ♗a4 ♘f6 5 0-0 ♗e7 6 ♖e1 b5 7 ♗b3 d6 8 c3 0-0 9 h3 ♘a5 10 ♗c2 c5 11 d4 ♕c7 12 ♘bd2 ♗d7 13 ♘f1 ♖fe8 14 ♘e3 g6 15 b4!? cb 16 cb ♘c4! 17 ♘xc4 bc 18 ♖b1 ♖ab8 19 ♗d2 c3 20 ♗h6, when 20...a5! proved very timely.

But here on 16...a5? there followed

17 ba c3 18 ♗a3!

After this move Black's tactical weakness on the a3-f8 diagonal is keenly felt, which emphasizes the lack of harmony in his game.

18...♕xa5 19 de ♕xa3 20 ef ♗xf6 21 e5! ♗e7 22 ed ♗xd6 23 ♘g5, and Black came under a crushing attack.

No. 158 Fischer-Benko
US Ch., 1963-64
Pirc Defence

1 e4 g6 2 d4 ♗g7 3 ♘c3 d6 4 f4 ♘f6 5 ♘f3 0-0 6 ♗d3 ♗g4 7 h3 ♗xf3 8 ♕xf3 ♘c6 9 ♗e3! e5 10 de de 11 f5! gf 12 ♕xf5 ♘d4 13 ♕f2!

♘e8 14 0-0 ♘d6 15 ♕g3! ♔h8 16 ♕g4 c6?! 17 ♕h5 ♕e8?

Black was evidently pinning great hopes on this move, intending to include his queen in the defence of his K-side. But he overlooked the following combinational possibility for White, which reveals the harmony of his attacking position.

18 ♗xd4 ed 19 ♖f6!! (the point of White's play; his rook blocks the key f6 square, and the threat of e4-e5! becomes irresistible) **19 ...♔g8 20 e5 h6 21 ♘e2 1-0**

Of no less importance than the tactical disruption of the forces' coordination in the opening are certain strategic features, which will now be described.

Isolation of part of the forces

Often the coordination of the forces is strongly influenced by the poor placing of certain pieces, which are restricted in their movements, etc. If part of the forces are poorly defended or isolated, this often becomes a serious obstruction on the path to achieving harmonious coordination.

For example, the following variation of the Spanish Game is rightly considered unfavourable for Black: 1 e4 e5 2 ♘f3 ♘c6

3 ♗b5 a6 4 ♗a4 ♘f6 5 0-0 ♗e7 6 ♖e1 b5 7 ♗b3 d6 8 c3 ♘a5 9 ♗c2 c5 10 d3 ♗g4(?) 11 h3 ♗h5 12 ♘bd2 0-0 13 g4! etc.

Here White shuts the light-square bishop out of play for a long time, and gains an obvious positional advantage.

This idea belongs to Capablanca. Both in his games and in his writings, Capablanca rejected the routine development of pieces in the opening, and reckoned that it should be subordinate to a definite plan for achieving harmonious piece coordination. One specific expression of this was the procedure, worked out by him, of isolating one of the opponent's bishops from the main theatre of operations at an early stage of the game.

In this respect the following games are characteristic.

No. 159 Capablanca-Black
New York, 1915
Spanish Game

1 e4 e5 2 ♘f3 ♘c6 3 ♗b5 a6 4 ♗a4 ♘f6 5 0-0 ♗e7 6 ♖e1 d6 7 c3 0-0 8 d4 b5 9 ♗c2 ♗g4 10 d5! ♘b8 11 h3 ♗h5(?) 12 ♘bd2 ♘bd7 13 ♘f1 ♖e8 14 g4!

The point of White's strategic plan: the black bishop is driven back to g6, where for a long time it is shut out of play. In our time

such a plan has become typical.

14...♗g6 15 ♘g3 h6 16 a4 ♘h7 17 ♕e2 ♖b8 18 ab ab 19 b4!

Having achieved an advantage on the K-side, White switches the offensive to the Q-side, taking account of the isolation of the bishop at g6.

19...♕c8 20 ♗d3 c6 21 dc ♕xc6 22 ♖a5! ♕xc3 23 ♗xb5 ♕c7 24 ♗e3 ♖ed8 25 ♖c1!

White has an overwhelming advantage.

No. 160 Winter-Capablanca
Hastings, 1919
Four Knights Game

1 e4 e5 2 ♘f3 ♘c6 3 ♘c3 ♘f6 4 ♗b5 ♗b4 5 0-0 0-0 6 ♗xc6 dc 7 d3 ♗d6 8 ♗g5 h6 9 ♗h4 c5 10 ♘d5 g5! 11 ♘xf6+ ♕xf6 12 ♗g3 ♗g4 13 h3 ♗xf3 14 ♕xf3 ♕xf3 15 gf f6 *(65)*

A remarkable position. White has a bishop, and yet he has not! Black wins by an attack on the opposite flank.

16 ♔g2 a5 17 a4 ♔f7 18 ♖h1
♔e6 19 h4 ♖fb8 20 hg hg 21 b3 c6
22 ♖a2 b5 23 ♖ha1 c4! 24 ab cb3
25 cb ♖xb5 26 ♖a4 ♖xb3 27 d4
♖b5 28 ♖c4 ♖b4 29 ♖xc6 ♖xd4
0-1

At the present time the isolation of part of the forces is understood in a broader sense. A splendid example of this type, which as though anticipates the modern interpretation, is provided by a game played more than 80 years ago.

No. 161 Teichmann-Chigorin
Cambridge Springs, 1904
Chigorin Defence

1 d4 d5 2 c4 ♘c6 3 ♘f3 ♗g4 4 cd
♗xf3 5 dc ♗xc6 6 ♘c3 e6 7 ♗f4?
♘f6 8 e3 ♗b4 9 ♕b3 ♘d5 10 ♗g3
0-0 11 ♗d3 ♕g5! 12 ♕c2 (12 0-0
♗xc3 13 bc ♘xe3! etc) 12...f5 13
♗e5 ♖f7 14 0-0-0 ♗xc3 15 bc b5!
(66)

66

From an early stage of the opening Black was aiming for

this position. He has a powerful positional superiority over a whole complex of light squares.

It may seem paradoxical, but the outwardly active white bishop at e5 is essentially shut out from the main battle.

16 ♖hg1 ♕e7! 17 ♖df1 ♕a3+
18 ♔d2 b4! 19 c4 ♗a4! 20 ♕b1
♘c3! 21 ♕a1 ♖d8! 22 g3 ♘e4+ 23
♔e2 ♘c5 24 ♕b1 (24 dc ♕xd3+
25 ♔f3 ♗c6+ etc. is also bad)
24...♘xd3 25 ♕xd3 ♕xa2+ 26
♔f3 ♗c2! 0-1

Coordination and basic opening principles

The aim of achieving harmony of the forces in the opening is closely linked with a correct and skilful mastery of opening principles. Connections between pieces which are far-fetched and cut off from the real live situation on the board prove to be short-lived.

It is another matter to demonstrate this. It sometimes demands a maximum penetration into the true essence of the position. This is confirmed by the following examples.

No. 162 Castaldi-Tartakower
Stockholm OL., 1937
Philidor's Defence

1 e4 e5 2 ♘f3 d6 3 d4 ♘f6 4 ♘c3♘bd7 5 ♗e2 ♗e7 6 0-0 h6?! 7 b3 c6 8 ♗b2 ♕c7 9 ♕d2 g5?! 10 ♖fd1 ♘f8? *(67)*

Black outlined his plan back on the 6th move. He was anticipating a massed offensive on the K-side after ...♘g6 followed by ...♘f4 or ...g4 etc.

But while the knight has moved from d7 and has not yet reached g6, Black's control over e5 has been markedly weakened, and White notices a disruption in the tactical coordination of the black pieces.

11 de de 12 ♘xe5!

Here is the solution to the question. The knight is taboo: 12...♕xe5 13 ♘d5! ♕xb2 14 ♘c7 mate, or 13...♕d6 14 ♘xf6+, while on 13...♘xe4 there followes 14 ♗xe5 etc. In the refutation of Black's play the

major role was played by the good development of the white pieces, which created all the preconditions for their harmonious coordination.

12...♗e6 13 ♘b5!

A further combinational blow. Black cannot play 13...cb because of 14 ♗xb5+, and he is bound to lose more material.

13...♕b8 14 ♕a5 ♗d8 (or 14...b6 15 ♘xc6 ba 16 ♘xb8 ♗d8 17 ♗xf6 ♗xf6 18 ♘c7+ ♔e7 19 ♘c6 mate) **15 ♖xd8+ ♕xd8 16 ♘c7+ ♔e7 17 ♗a3+ 1-0**

As we see, it is unpleasant to have to deal with an early attack, especially in an open position. But if the opening principles have been precisely observed and no mistakes have been made, an inner harmony of the forces can be found, which will not only allow the onslaught to be parried, but also in many cases an advantage to be achieved. The following example illustrates this.

No. 163 Padevsky-Botvinnik
Moscow, 1956
Sicilian Defence

1 e4 c5 2 ♘f3 ♘c6 3 d4 cd 4 ♘xd4 ♘f6 5 ♘c3 d6 6 ♗c4 e6 7 0-0 ♗e7 8 ♗e3 0-0 9 ♗b3 ♘a5 10 f4 b6?! 11 ♕f3? (11 e5! is correct) 11...♗b7 12 g4?

White begins a seemingly

very dangerous pawn storm (here 12 f5 is objectively better), which Black meets with energetic and accurately calculated counterplay on the Q-side and in the centre.

12. . .♖c8! 13 g5 ♖xc3!

An excellent tactical blow, which disrupts White's communications in the centre.

14 bc?

The lesser evil was 14 gf ♖xe3 15 ♕xe3 ♗xf6 16 c3 with a tolerable game for White.

14. . .♘xe4! 15 ♕g4 ♕c8! 16 ♖f3 ♘xb3 17 ab f5 18 ♕h4 (18 gf ♖xf6! 19 f5 ef 20 ♘xf5 ♗f8 favours Black) **18. . .e5!**

Black's play develops very harmoniously.

19 ♖h3 h6 20 ♕h5 ♕xc3 21 ♖d1 ed 22 ♗xd4 ♕c6 23 gh ♘g5! 24 ♖g3 ♕h1+ 24 ♔f2 ♘e4+ 0-1

No. 164 Klovan-Suetin
Byelorussia-Latvia, 1962
Göring Gambit

1 e4 e5 2 ♘f3 ♘c6 3 d4 ed 4 c3 dc 5 ♗c4 cb 6 ♗xb2 ♗b4+ 7 ♘c3 ♘f6 8 ♕c2

Here it appears that White can develop a strong initiative by 8 e5!?, but Black has the strong counter 8. . .d5!, and if 9 ef ♕xf6!, when the advantage passes to him, as in Stein-Spassky (Tallinn 1959). A good illustration of the inner resources of well coordinated forces!

8. . .d6 9 0-0-0 0-0 10 e5!?

It cannot be denied that White's initiative looks very dangerous. But Black has not made any fundamental mistakes, and this allows him to look to the future with confidence. Under the influence of White's onslaught Black quickly sets up harmonious connections between his pieces, which disrupt White's plans.

10. . .♘g4 11 h4 ♘cxe5 12 ♘d5 ♗c5 13 ♘g5 g6 14 ♘e4 ♗f5 15 f4 *(68)*

68

15. . .c6!

White's pieces have overstepped the mark and lack coordination, and he now suffers a decisive loss of material.

16 fe cd 17 ♗xd5 ♖c8 18 ♔b1 ♘e3 19 ♕e2 ♕b6 20 ♔a1 ♗xe4 21 ♗xe4 ♘xd1 22 ♖xd1 de 23 ♗xe5 ♖fe8 24 ♗b2 ♖cd8 25 ♖xd8 ♖xd8 0-1

We will give two further games. In the first of these

White's attacking plans were disrupted by an unexpected but thoroughly correct sacrifice of material. In the second the cause of Black's misfortune was an impulsive queen sortie, which White opposed with a harmonious attack.

No. 165 Doroshkevich-Tal
USSR Ch., 1975
King's Indian Defence

1 d4 g6 2 c4 ♗g7 3 e4 c5 4 d5 d6 5 ♘c3 ♘f6 6 ♗e2 0-0 7 f4 e6 8 ♘f3 ed 9 cd ♗g4 10 0-0 ♗xf3! 11 ♗xf3 ♘bd7 12 ♔h1 a6 13 ♗e3?! ♖e8 14 g4 h6 15 g5? hg 16 e5?! gf!

By sacrificing a piece, Black destroys the white centre and seizes the initiative on the most important part of the board.

17 ef ♖xe3 18 fg ♘e5 19 ♗g2 ♕g5 20 ♘e4 ♕h4 21 ♕d2 ♔xg7 22 ♕f2 ♕xf2 23 ♖xf2 f3! 24 ♘d6 ♖d8 25 ♘xb7 fg+ 26 ♔xg2 ♖xd5 27 b3 ♘d3 28 ♖c2 ♖e1 0-1

No. 166 Kopayev-Polyak
Kiev, 1946
Scotch Game

1 e4 e5 2 ♘f3 ♘c6 3 d4 ed 4 ♘xd4 ♘f6 5 ♘xc6 bc 6 e5!? ♘d5?
Strangely enough, this natural move is a mistake. Correct is 6...♕e7! 7 ♕e2 ♘d5 8 c4 ♗a6! with fair counterplay for Black.

7 ♗d3 ♕h4?

This violent attempt to obtain counterplay merely aggravates Black's difficulties. His queen soon finds itself trapped.

8 0-0 ♗c5 9 ♘d2 0-0 10 ♘e4! ♗e7 11 ♖e1 d6 12 c4 ♘b4 13 ♘f6+! ♗xf6 14 ♖e4! ♘xd3 15 ♖xh4 ♗xh4 16 ♕xd3 de 17 ♕e4 ♗f6 18 ♕xc6, and White won.

Disuniting the opponent's flanks

Certain opening variations are characterized by the procedure of disuniting the opponent's flanks, which destroys the coordination of his forces. In this respect the following game is instructive.

No. 167 Mikenas-Goldenov
Tbilisi, 1946
English Opening

1 c4 ♘f6 2 ♘c3 d5 3 cd ♘xd5 4 e4 ♘b4 5 ♗c4 ♗e6!? 6 ♗xe6 fe 7 ♘ge2 ♘d3+ 8 ♔f1 ♘c6 9 ♕b3 ♕d7! 10 ♕xb7 ♖b8 11 ♕a6 *(69)*

11...g6 12 h4 罩b6 13 豐a4 皇g7 14 罩h3 0-0 15 ⊘d1 罩b4! 16 罩×d3 豐×d3 17 豐×c6 罩×e4 18 ⊘e3 罩×e3! 0-1

Here Black carried out a very strong and interesting opening plan. At an early stage of the game he permitted a weakening of his central pawn structure, but in return he not only weakened the opponent's light squares, but, more importantly, he established his knight at d3, deep in enemy territory. This prevented White's flanks from uniting and led to a serious disruption in the coordination of his pieces. At an early stage White was already completely helpless and he swiftly came under a crushing attack.

Often such a disuniting of the flanks is caused by a far-advanced central pawn, supported by its pieces or pawns. Here a wedge is as though driven into the opponent's ranks, disrupting the coordination of his pieces and causing 'panic'.

We illustrate this with two typical examples.

No. 168 Bronstein–Simagin
28th USSR Ch., 1961
Nimzo-Indian Defence

1 c4 ⊘f6 2 ⊘c3 e6 3 d4 皇b4 4 a3 皇×c3+ 5 bc c5 6 f3 ⊘c6 7 e4 0-0 (better 7...b6, intending to at-

tack the c4 pawn by...⊘a5 and...皇a6) 8 e5 ⊘e8 9 f4 cd? 10 cd b6 11 ⊘f3 皇a6 12 皇d3 f5 13 d5 ⊘a5 14 d6! 罩c8 15 0-0 g6 16 c5! 皇×d3 17 豐×d3 罩×c5 18 皇e3 罩d5 19 豐a6 ⊘c6 20 罩fc1 ⊘g7 21 罩×c6!

It has already been mentioned that a strong pawn which has reached the sixth rank is sometimes more valuable than a material deficit. The exchange sacrifice merely emphasizes the power of White's central pawn wedge, disuniting Black's forces.

21...罩a5

21...dc 22 豐×a7 did not appeal to Black, but now, with the same aim, White offers his queen.

22 豐×a5! ba 23 罩c7 h6 24 罩ab1! ⊘e8 25 罩×a7 g5 26 皇b6 豐b8 27 罩×d7 豐c8 28 罩e7 豐c2 29 罩f1 豐c6 30 皇f2 ⊘g7 31 fg hg 32 ⊘×g5 豐d5 33 ⊘f3

For the queen White has gained sufficient material, but this is not the only point. The fate of the game is decided by his powerful passed pawn.

33...f4 34 罩c7 ⊘f5 35 罩b1 ⊘e3 36 h3 豐d3 37 罩bc1 ⊘d5 38 罩7c6 ⊘e3 39 罩6c3 豐b5 40 皇×e3 fe 41 罩×e3 豐b6 42 罩cc3 ⾒g7 43 ⾒h2 1-0

No. 169 Euwe-Najdorf
Zurich C, 1953
King's Indian Defence

1 d4 ♘f6 2 c4 g6 3 g3 ♗g7 4 ♗g2 0-0 5 ♘c3 c5 6 d5 e5 7 ♗g5 h6 8 ♗xf6 ♕xf6 9 d6! ♘c6 10 e3 b6 11 ♗d5 ♔h8 12 ♘e4 ♕d8 13 h4! f5 14 ♘g5 ♗b7 15 g4 e4 16 ♘e2! ♗xb2 17 ♘f4! ♕f6 18 gf! ♗xa1 19 ♘xg6+ ♔g7 20 ♘xe4 ♗c3+ 21 ♔f1 ♕xf5 22 ♘f4 ♔h8 23 ♘xc3 ♖ae8 24 ♘ce2 ♖g8 25 h5 ♖g5 26 ♘g3 ♖xg3 27 fg ♖xe3 28 ♔f2 ♖e8 29 ♖e1 ♖xe1 30 ♕xe1 ♔g7 31 ♕e8 ♕c2+ 32 ♔g1 ♕d1+ 33 ♔h2 ♕c2+ 34 ♘g2 ♕f5 35 ♕g8+ ♔f6 36 ♕h8+ ♔g5 37 ♕g7+ 1-0

An energetically conducted attack.

We must also mention the analogous procedure of driving a wedge into one of the flanks, paralyzing the latter or shutting a large part of the enemy forces out of play.

Such situations usually arise in the middlegame, but sometimes also in the opening.

No. 170 Sokolsky-Gutorev
Byelorussian Ch., 1960
English Opening

1 c4 ♘f6 2 ♘c3 g6 3 e4 d6 4 g3 ♗g7 5 ♗g2 e5 6 ♘ge2 0-0 7 d3 ♗e6 8 0-0 ♕c8 9 f4 ♗h3? 10 f5! ♗xg2 11 ♔xg2 ♘c6 12 ♘d5 ♘xd5 13 cd ♘b8 14 f6! ♗h8 15 ♘c3 c6 16

g4 a6 17 a4 ♘d7 18 g5 b6 19 h4

White is essentially a piece up. The plan for realizing his advantage consists in an attack on the black king.

19...♖a7 20 ♗e3 ♖d8 21 ♕f3 ♘f8 22 ♘d1 h5 (White was threatening ♘d1-f2-g4-h6 mate!) 23 gh ♘h7 24 ♗g5 ♖dd7 25 ♘e3 ♕d8 26 ♕g3 ♗xf6 27 ♖xf6! ♘xf6 28 ♕f3 1-0

Models of harmonious piece coordination

The basic principle of chess is harmony of the pieces, which can truly result in the creation of chess masterpieces. We give some model games of this type.

No. 171 Alatortsev-Boleslavsky
USSR Ch., 1950
King's Indian Defence

1 d4 ♘f6 2 c4 d6 3 ♘c3 e5 4 e4 ed 5 ♕xd4 ♘c6 6 ♕d2 g6 7 b3 ♗g7 8 ♗b2 0-0 9 ♗d3 ♘g4!

An illogical move from the viewpoint of normal ideas of development. It can be understood only in association with Black's overall conception, aimed at achieving specific coordination of the black pieces, which are lining up from afar against White's K-side.

10 ♘f3 ♘ge5 11 ♗e2 ♘xf3+ 12 ♗xf3 ♘d4! 13 ♗d1 f5! 14 ef ♗xf5

15 ♘e2?

White should have played 15 0-0. In trying to exchange off the annoying black knight as soon as possible, he overlooks the attack by Black on the K-side which now develops by force.

15...♘xe2 16 ♗xe2

16 ♗xg7 was somewhat better, although here too after 16...♘f4! Black has a strong initiative.

16...♗xb2 17 ♕xb2 ♕g5! 18 g3 ♖e8 19 0-0 ♗h3 20 f4 (20 ♖fe1 ♖xf2!) 20...♗xf1!!

A beautiful combinational blow, revealing the depth of Black's strategy.

Throughout the entire game the black pieces have been well coordinated, and the finale takes the form of a miraculous harmony!

21 fg ♖xe2 22 ♕c3 ♗g2! 23 ♕d3 ♗f3 24 ♖f1 ♖g2+ 25 ♔h1 ♗c6! 26 ♖xf8+ ♔xf8 27 ♕f1+ ♖f2+ 0-1

No. 172
Tseshkovsky-Lutikov
36th USSR Ch., 1969
Philidor's Defence

1 e4 e5 2 ♘f3 d6 3 d4 ♘f6 4 ♘c3 ♘bd7 5 ♗c4 ♗e7 6 0-0 0-0 7 a4 c6 8 ♕e2 ed 9 ♘xd4 ♘xe4?! 10 ♘xe4!

After 10 ♕xe4 d5 11 ♗xd5 ♘f6 12 ♗xf7+ ♖xf7 13 ♕d3 ♗d6 Black has fair counterplay.

10...d5 11 ♘f5! dc (70)

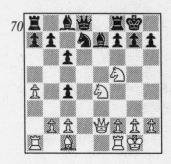

12 ♗h6!

A splendid tactical blow, destroying the castled position. At the finish the actions of White's pieces fuse into a powerful, united force.

12...♘f6

White wins prettily after 12...♗f6 13 ♗xg7! ♗xg7 14 ♕g4!, or 12...gh 13 ♕g4+ ♗g5 14 ♘xh6+ etc.

13 ♘eg3 ♗xf5 14 ♘xf5 gh 15 ♘xe7+ ♔g7 16 ♘f5+ ♔g6 17 ♘e7+ ♔g7 18 ♕e5 ♕b8 19 ♘f5+ ♔g6 20 ♘d6! ♔g7 21 ♖fe1 ♖d8 22 ♖ad1 ♖d7 23 ♖d4 ♕c7 24 ♖g4+ 1-0

No. 173 Brants-Veresov
Minsk, 1956
King's Indian Defence

1 d4 ♘f6 2 ♘f3 g6 3 g3 ♗g7 4 ♗g2 0-0 5 0-0 d6 6 c4 ♘bd7 7 ♘c3 e5 8 e4 c6 9 h3 ed 10 ♘xd4 a5 11 ♗e3 ♖e8 12 ♕c2 ♘c5 13 ♖ad1 ♘fd7 14 ♖fe1

A routine move. 14 ♘b3! is much stronger.

14...a4 15 ♘de2 ♛a5! 16 ♖xd6 ♘e5 17 b3 ab 18 ab ♗xh3! 19 b4 ♗xg2!! 20 ♖b1 ♗xe4! 21 ♘xe4 ♛a4 22 ♛xa4 ♘xa4 23 ♘f6+ ♗xf6 24 ♖xf6 ♘xc4, and Black won.

No. 174 Veresov-Bunatian
Moscow, 1965
Veresov Opening

1 d4 ♘f6 2 ♘c3 d5 3 ♗g5 ♘bd7 4 ♘f3 g6 5 e3 ♗g7 6 ♗d3 0-0 7 0-0 c5 8 ♘e5 e6 9 ♖e1 ♛a5 10 a3 a6 11 ♛d2 cd? 12 ed ♘xe5 13 de ♘g4 14 ♛f4! ♘xe5 15 ♖xe5 f6 16 ♘xd5!! ed 17 ♖xd5 ♛b6 18 ♛c4 ♗e6 19 ♗e3! 1-0

The intelligent application of opening principles

Correct play in the opening demands primarily an impeccable knowledge and application of opening principles. Along with real possibilities of fighting for the initiative, from the very first moves a player is faced with all kinds of variations, with both correct and incorrect active possibilities.

In the opening it is sometimes not easy to distinguish the correct path from the false, and it is in such situations that opening principles should come to one's aid. A basic mastery of them allows the numerous variations to be successfully 'managed'. Incidentally, it is this guide which enables an experienced player to memorize new variations and to sift out irrational continuations.

As is apparent from the examples given, the struggle in the opening is often highly specific in nature. At an early stage sharp positions arise, which require that development be combined with active play. In the handling of such situations a knowledge of principles alone is by no means sufficient. Another important factor of opening play is essential — a concrete approach to the solving of the problems arising.

A concrete approach signifies a comprehensive study of the features of the position, taking account of the prospects and individual features of this or that variation. Its basic aim is to find the most effective plan, corresponding to the demands of the position. At the same time each individual move, while corresponding to the basic plan, should solve the most urgent problem of the given position.

It is from this viewpoint, in which the concrete ideas and plans of the two sides, arising sometimes in the very first moves of the game, are taken into account, that the implementation of basic opening problems should be approached.

An important indication of a sure mastery of opening principles and a concrete approach to them is correct orientation in an unfamiliar opening situation.

Consider a variation where at an early stage a player begins unexpectedly playing sharply. His opponent is convinced that this is unfounded, but there is not time to reason in general terms. He must act, and take concrete decisions. This gives rise to a typically complex problem, where mobilization principles have to be combined with a penetration into the tactical, individual features of the position.

Of course, playing according to this method is not easy. It is much easier to be governed by general development principles in a quiet situation. From this it follows that, for the development of skill in opening play, an analysis of such situations is very useful.

Sometimes an opponent's eccentric play in the opening can be punished only by energetic manœuvres with one and the same pieces. Thus, while firmly condemning the pointless loss of tempi in the opening, Alekhine once wrote: "One can afford to lose time, only if it gives a firm

control of important squares"

A number of examples confirming this can be found in the games of Alekhine himself.

No. 175 Alekhine-Wolf
Pistyan, 1922
Queen's Gambit

1 d4 d5 2 ♘f3 c5 3 c4 cd 4 cd ♘f6 5 ♘xd4 a6 6 e4! ♘xe4 7 ♕a4+ ♗d7 8 ♕b3 ♘c5 9 ♕e3! g6 10 ♘f3 *(71)*

71

White appears to have broken the principles of economizing on tempi in the opening, since out of the ten moves made, six have been by his queen and knight. Nevertheless, White has gained control of the most important central points, and has obtained virtually a won position. How did this happen? The point is that Black played the opening passively (5. . .a6?) and his tactics could be refuted only by energetic manœuvres of this type. These manœuvres cannot be considered mechanically, but only in connection with a definite purpose, the aim of which was to disorganize Black's development and keep his king in the centre.

10...♕c7 11 ♕c3 ♖g8 12 ♗e3 b6 13 ♘bd2 ♗g7 14 ♗d4 ♗×d4 15 ♕×d4 ♗b5 16 ♗×b5 ab 17 0-0 ♖a4 18 b4 ♕d8 19 a3 ♘bd7 20 ♖fe1 ♔f8 21 d6! and White mounted a decisive attack on the opponent's king caught in the centre.

Alekhine's method in this game is by no means exceptional. Moreover, this concrete plan has become characteristic in such situations.

Here is another typical example.

No. 176 Portisch-Bronstein
Monaco, 1969
Queen's Gambit

1 d4 d5 2 c4 c5?! 3 cd ♘f6 4 e4! ♘×e4 5 dc ♘×c5 6 ♘f3 e6 7 ♘c3 ed 8 ♕×d5 ♕e7+ 9 ♗e3 ♘c6 10 ♗b5 ♗d7 11 0-0 ♘e6 12 ♘e5! ♘×e5 13 ♕×e5 ♗×b5 14 ♘×b5 a6 15 ♖ad1! ♖d8 16 ♗b6 ♖×d1

Black's position is hopeless. White also wins after 15...ab 16 ♗×d8 ♘×d8 17 ♕×b5+ ♘c6 18 ♖fe1.

17 ♖×d1 f6 18 ♕f5 g6 19 ♘c7+ ♔f7 20 ♕d5! 1-0

One should also have a concrete approach to many other opening principles and features. When playing chess in general, and in the opening in particular, it is useful to remember that there are no rules without exceptions.

Thus the main and most general task when mobilizing the forces in the opening consists in ensuring their harmonious coordination. This is assisted by a correct combining of mobilization principles with a penetration into the tactical process, and by taking account of the individual features of the opening set-up.

At the same time one should have a clear impression of the strategic contours of the impending middlegame, and aim to seize the initiative and retain it, which will hinder the opponent in carrying out his active plans.

PART II
THE DEVELOPMENT OF
OPENING THEORY

five

THE CONNECTION OF THE OPENING WITH THE LATER STAGES OF THE GAME

The opening as a sum total of knowledge about the initial position

In the first part of the book we gave a fairly detailed analysis of many typical opening mistakes. In the majority of the examples given there, the outcome was decided directly or was pre-determined in the opening stage.

However, as has repeatedly been emphasized, in many cases the 'pure' mobilization of the forces is very short-lived.

When the forces come into close contact (sometimes this happens very quickly) there commences a struggle which in many respects is characteristic of the middlegame, with all the consequences following from this. Here there are all kinds of tactical surprises, attacks on the king, the concrete nature of the play in general, and so on.

The proportion of opening variations such as those given above — with a swift crisis — is comparatively small. Opening guides are largely made up of problematic variations running many moves deep, and yet not giving any obvious advantage to either side, at the end of which rather cautious assessments are given, such as "White stands slightly better", "chances are roughly equal", and so on.

Problematic variations of this type arise if both sides observe the opening principles, tactical accuracy and strategic purposefulness (which, incidentally, is a necessary condition in master play!). In these cases the opening serves mainly as a prelude to the main struggle, although many variations extend as far as sharp clashes in the middlegame, or even deep into the endgame. And yet at the end of such variations, even if they continue to move 25 and beyond, there usually arises a problematic position, the assessment of which is possible only after serious practical testing.

In no other stage of the game is theory progressing with such intensity as in the modern opening, which has essentially long been a synthesis of the mobilization of the forces and a concrete study of the resulting middlegame.

The development of opening theory is steadily seeing the further merging of these two stages. A study of an opening also signifies research into the middlegame which logically arises from the opening set-up.

As a result the opening appears as the sum total of knowledge of the initial position, which Wilhelm Steinitz called the most complex and enigmatic of all positions on the chess board. In the initial position, chess contains an enormous, practically inexhaustible number of possibilities.

It follows that we can be talking only about individual, partial solutions. And in studying such questions one's attention is in general attracted by various strategic and tactical problems, among which an important place is occupied by the transition stage from opening to middlegame. Certain aspects of this transitional stage are expounded in the present part of the book.

The choice of strategic 'weapon'

The first criterion for the viability of a particular opening system is an abundance of possible plans in the transition from opening to middlegame. If there is only one such possibility, or if the number is limited, such systems normally hold little promise.

Popular opening systems are notable for their strategic (and, of course, tactical) diversity.

In such systems the transition from opening to middlegame, and the typical paths of this sometimes imperceptible stage, are naturally of interest.

Let us first examine a closed type of game, for example the starting position of the Chigorin Variation in the Spanish Game: 1 e4 e5 2 ♘f3 ♘c6 3 ♗b5 a6 4 ♗a4 ♘f6 5 0-0 ♗e7 6 ♖e1 b5 7 ♗b3 d6 8 c3 0-0 9 h3.

Mobilization is largely completed, but can it be considered that the transition to the middlegame has commenced? This is a complex, and to a certain extent, academic question, since the start of the main battle and the determination of the two sides' plans are still some way off. For the moment each side is left to his own devices. In almost every case White must make the obligatory moves d2-d4 and ♘bd2, at which his mobilization is by no means complete and is subsequently notable for its great diversity. In many cases (for example, in the Smyslov Variation: 9...h6 followed by 10...♖e8 and ...♗f8) White has a choice between the knight manœuvre ♘d2-f1-g3 and the set-up with ♗c2, b2-b4, ♗b2 etc., which also relates rather to development problems.

In the critical position Black has an even greater choice of the most diverse continuations: 9...♘a5, 9...h6, 9...♗b7, 9...♘d7, 9...a5, 9...♕d7, and even the paradoxical returning of his knight to its initial square 9...♘b8, which in recent times has been one of the most popular continuations.

For the moment all these, even the most serious and positionally well-founded, are only preliminary drafts of the plan to be chosen.

But suppose that we make the further moves 9...♘a5 10 ♗c2 c5 11 d4 ♕c7 12 ♘bd2 ♘c6 13 d5. White's last move largely determines the forthcoming struggle, although the concrete plans of the two sides are still not clear. The almost total completion of mobilization and the fixing of the central pawn formation signify only in the most

general terms the conclusion of the opening stage. However, the middlegame is now imminent!

No. 177 Geller-Mecking
Palma de Mallorca IZ, 1970

13...♘a5 14 b3 ♗d7 15 ♘f1 ♘b7 16 ♘g3 c4(?) 17 b4!
After this the region of the main middlegame battle is decided — it will be the Q-side, where White develops a persistent initiative.

17...♖fc8 18 ♘f5 ♗f8 19 ♘h2 a5 20 ♖e3 ab 21 cb ♗xf5? 22 ef c3 23 ♘g4! with an obvious advantage to White.

No. 178 Keres-Vidmar
Bad Nauheim, 1936

13...♘d8 14 a4 ♖b8 15 c4 b4 ♘f1 ♘e8
By contrast, here White has decided on the plan of a K-side offensive, after first provoking a complete blocking of the Q-side.

17 g4 g6 18 ♘g3 ♘g7 19 ♔h2 f6 20 ♖g1 ♘f7
The battle arena has become the K-side, and Black must play very accurately in order to maintain a flexible defence.

In the given example the transition from opening to middlegame passed almost unnoticed, concealed behind the movements of the forces within their own territory. The two sides unhurriedly embarked on a fierce battle even on unimportant parts of the board.

By contrast, in other cases, especially in gambit systems both old and new, the middlegame may 'mature' before development is complete and before a serious 'declaration' in the centre takes place.

An illustration of this is provided by the Jaenisch Variation in the Spanish Game: 1 e4 e5 2 ♘f3 ♘c6 3 ♗b5 f5 4 ♘c3 fe 5 ♘×e4 d5!? 6 ♘×e5 de 7 ♘×c6 bc 8 ♗×c6+ ♗d7 9 ♕h5+ ♔e7 10 ♕e5+ ♗e6 11 ♗×a8 ♕×a8 etc.

The greater part of both sides', forces have been completely inactive, and yet the opening stage has flashed by like a whirlwind. A typical middlegame has been reached with unbalanced material, where it is very difficult to decide who will gain a subsequent advantage.

In the given case the transition to the middlegame came very early, prompted by the move 5...d5!?, after which there followed a six-move forcing operation, leading to this strange position.

Such contrasts in the choice of plan in the transition to middlegame are not surprising, since the range of opening set-ups is immense.

A general feature of any form of transition from opening to middlegame lies in the choice of a definite strategic character of the main battle. And here the development of theory is disclosing truly enormous 'reserves' of highly valuable material.

Consider for example, this variation of the King's Indian Defence: 1 d4 ♘f6 2 c4 g6 3 g3 ♗g7 4 ♗g2 d6 5 ♘c3 0-0 6 ♘f3 *(72)*.

72

For a long time Black appeared to have virtually only one plan in this position: 6... ♘bd7 7 0-0 e5, and at an appropriate moment...ed, creating counterplay with the pieces in the centre. Then in the 1950s the variation 6...♘c6 7 0-0 a6 8 d5 ♘a5 became popular, as a result of which a greater number of problems and lines arose. Comparatively recently this line acquired a further interesting addition. Along with 7...a6 they began playing 7...♗f5!?, which also leads to distinctive variations.

In the 1950s Black began employing the variation 6...c6 7 0-0 a6, with the intention of organizing counterplay on the Q-side and of undermining the c4 pawn by...b5 etc. The given variation proved to be not very promising, but the move 6...c6 did not disappear, since it assisted in the creation of an interesting and topical variation — 7 0-0 ♕a5!? etc.

At the same time, reverting to the 6...♘bd7 7 0-0 e5 variation, it should be noted that its theory is being constantly enriched with new plans in the middlegame. This testifies to the promising nature of this opening system, which has long been regarded as durable.

Before moving on to an examination of how the struggle develops in complex modern variations we will dwell on some more obvious strategic situations.

The realization of an opening advantage in the middlegame

In a number of cases when, as a result of serious mistakes by the opponent, one side emerges from the opening with a big advantage, the outcome of the game may be settled. Very often things will be decided by a tactical

blow, a combination, a deadly attack on the king, and so on.

Examples of this type were given in Part I of the book. In many of them the retribution for the mistakes came in the opening itself, in others it came in the early middlegame, or, more precisely, comprised the transition stage from opening to middlegame.

But the exploitation of an advantage is by no means always achieved by tactical means. In practice an opening advantage is more likely to be reinforced by a further augmenting of positional advantages, as in the following examples.

No. 179 Botvinnik-Alekhine
AVRO Tournament, 1938
Queen's Gambit

1 d4 d5 2 c4 e6 3 ♘c3 ♘f6 4 ♘f3 c5 5 cd ♘xd5 6 e3 ♘c6 7 ♗c4 ♗e7 8 0-0 cd 9 ed 0-0 10 ♖e1

Here Black incautiously played **10...b6?** (10...♘xc3 was better, and only then 11...b6), which allowed White to develop immediate pressure on the Q-side.

11 ♘xd5 ed 12 ♗b5 ♗d7? *(73)*

And this is a very serious mistake, after which Black comes under severe pressure on the Q-side. 12 ♘a5 is essential, although even then White's position is the more promising.

73

13 ♕a4! ♘b8

Forced. As shown by Botvinnik, on 12...♖c8 there would have followed 13 ♗d2! a6 14 ♗×c6 ♗×c6 15 ♕×a6, when Black loses a pawn.

14 ♗f4 ♗×b5 15 ♕×b5 a6 16 ♕a4 ♗d6 17 ♗×d6 ♕×d6 16 ♖ac1 ♖a7 19 ♕c2!

White has secure control of the important open file and has practically immobilized Black's Q-side (the position of the black knight is especially pitiful). Only now does it become clear that Black's opening inaccuracies on moves 10 and 12 have led almost by force to a lost position.

In the resulting position even Alekhine was unable to display his ingenuity. The black king slowly but surely has to mount the 'scaffold'!

White accurately realized his advantage:

19...♖e7 20 ♖×e7 ♕×e7 21 ♕c7 ♕×c7 22 ♖×c7 f6 23 ♔f1 ♖f7 24 ♖c8+ ♔f8 25 ♖c3! g5 26 ♘e1 h5 27 h4!

Black can hardly move a piece, since 27...♘d7 and 27...♖e8 are both met by 28 ♖c7! Therefore, despite the small amount of material, Black loses due to positional zugzwang.

27...♘d7 28 ♖c7 ♖f7 29 ♘f3 g4 30 ♘e1 f5 31 ♘d3 f4 32 f3 gf 33 gf a5 34 a4!, and White soon won.

In the next example the cause of Black's misfortune was a serious concession in the centre, made in the opening.

No. 180 Averbakh–Aronin
USSR Ch., 1951
Queen's Gambit Accepted

1 d4 d5 2 c4 dc 3 ♘f3 ♘f6 4 e3 e6 5 ♗×c4 c5 6 0-0 a6 7 ♕e2 b5 8 ♗d3 ♗b7 9 a4 c4?

By releasing the tension, Black concedes his opponent the centre, which has the main influence on subsequent events. 9...cd 10 ed ba was correct, with a perfectly satisfactory game.

10 ♗c2 ♘bd7 11 e4 ♗e7 12 ♗g5 0-0 13 ♘bd2 ♖e8 14 ♖fd1 h6 15 ♗f4 ♘f8

As a result of the opening White has achieved an obvious advantage in the centre, and although for the moment he does not have any concrete threats, Black's position is very difficult since he is deprived of active counterplay. White consistently increases the pressure.

16 ♘e5! (not allowing 16...♘g6) **16...♗d6 17 ♘f1 ♕c7 18 ♗g3 ♘6d7 19 ♘×d7 ♘×d7?**

In a difficult position Black makes a further error. 19...♕×d7 was stronger, maintaining his knight in its important defensive position.

20 ♗×d6 ♕×d6 21 ♖a3!

This gives an important impetus to White's developing offensive. He brings his rook into play and, by switching it to g3, begins a strong K-side attack.

21...f6

Had Black's knight been at f8, he would have had 21...e5, but now he is forced to make a significant weakening of his K-side.

22 ♖g3 ♘f8 23 e5! ♕e7 24 ef ♕×f6 25 ♘e3 ♖ad8 26 ♘g4 ♕f4 27 ♕e3! ♕×e3 28 fe ♔h8 29 ♖f1 ♖e7 30 ♘e5 ♔g8 31 ♘g4 ♔h8 32 ♘e5 ♔g8 33 ♖f6

This manoeuvre allows White to force the win of a pawn, with a continuing attack.

33...♘d7 34 ♘×d7 ♖d×d7 35 ♖×h6 e5 36 ♗f5!, and White safely realized his material advantage: **36...ed 37 ♗×d7 ♖×d7 38 ed b4 39 a5 c3 40 bc bc 41 ♖h5 c2 42 ♖c5 ♗e4 43 ♔f2 ♖b7 44 ♖gc3 ♖b2 45 ♔e3 ♗h7 46 h4 ♔f7 47 ♖c7+ ♔e6 48 ♖3c6+ ♔d5 49**

♖c5+ ♔d6 50 ♖×g7 1-0

In the following example Black's defeat resulted from him weakening his Q-side pawns in the opening.

No. 181 Suetin–Furman
USSR Ch., 1963
Sicilian Defence

1 e4 c5 2 ♘f3 e6 3 d4 cd 4 ♘×d4 ♘c6 5 ♘c3 a6 6 ♗e2 ♕c7 7 0-0 ♘f6 8 ♗e3 ♗b4 9 ♘a4! b5(?) (better 9...0-0) **10 ♘×d6 dc**

10...♕×c6? is bad because of 11 ♘b6 ♖b8 12 e5 ♘g8 13 ♗f3! etc.

11 ♗c5!

This manoeuvre sets Black difficult problems, whereas after 11 ♘b6 ♖b8 12 ♘×c8 ♖×c8 13 f3 ♖d8 he would have equalized.

11...♗×c5 12 ♘×c5 0-0

12...♕e5 13 b4 a5 or 12...e5 13 ♕d2 ♘d7 was slightly better. Now White establishes his knight on the critical c5 square.

13 ♕d4 e5

In the event of 13...♘d7 14 ♖d1! Black would have faced a different threat: White would have securely occupied the only open file.

14 ♕c3 a5 15 ♖fd1 *(74)*

White's superiority has assumed real proportions, and, as the further course of the game shows, Black is unable to escape from the vice. 15...♘d7 again fails, this time to 16 ♘×d7 ♗×d7 17 ♗×b5, when White wins a pawn. Black tries to activate his bishop and reorganizes his Q-side pawns, but this creates new vulnerable points in his position.

74

15. . .b4 16 ♕e3 ♖d8 17 ♕g5 ♖×d1+ 18 ♖×d1 ♕e7 (bad is 18. . .♗e6? 19 ♘a6! ♕b6 20 ♕×e5! etc) **19 e3 h6 20 ♘a4** (aiming at b6) **20. . .♗a6 21 ♗×a6 ♖×a6 22 f3 ♖a7 23 ♘b6!**

White has selected another excellent post for his knight — c4, from where it will threaten the pawns at e5 and a5.

23. . .♖b7 24 b3 ♖b8 25 ♘c4!

Black has solved part of his defensive problems by exchanging his inactive bishop for its white opponent. But (and this is an instructive point!) this does not mean that he has solved his main, general problem. In fact, in the given case White's advantage has increased still further. His knight has occupied a

dominating post, and he has a strategically won position.

25. . .♖d8 26 ♖×d8+ ♕×d8 27 ♕d3 ♕c7 (after 27. . .♕×d3 28 cd Black loses a pawn) **28 ♕d6!**

By continuing the 'pursuit' of the black queen, White decisively strengthens his position.

28. . .♕a7+ 29 ♔f1 ♘d7 30 ♕×c6 ♘f8 31 ♕b6 ♕d7 32 ♕d6 ♕a7 33 ♕×e5, and White won.

As has been shown, even a single insignificent mistake in the opening can have far-reaching consequences, and chess logic dictates that in the subsequent middlegame it is very difficult to change a course of events predetermined in the opening.

At the same time the transition to the middlegame is often closely connected with various elements of positional play.

The plan of accumulating positional advantages

There exist a number of characteristic plans of accumulating positional advantages in the transition to the middlegame, associated, for example, with the exploitation of weak pawns and squares, arising from defects in the pawn formation.

Without great difficulty one could compile a whole series of colourful variations on exploiting weak squares in the 'extended centre' (c3-c6-f6-f3), each point on which has numerous times been the target of an offensive. Naturally, it is not possible to cover all instances of such plans.

Our problem is mainly to give players a definite system of knowledge and (more importantly) methods, which will help in the solving of both practical and theoretical opening questions.

Certain characteristic plans and examples of 'square-controling' play will be shown in the section on typical pawn structures.

Here we should once again remind the reader that, in the light of modern opening strategy, the concept of pawn weaknesses has become much broader and has been increased by new forms. Thus modern games persistently show that a pawn weakness becomes insignificant if it is compensated by active and harmoniously placed pieces. As has already been stated, a flexible pawn formation should not be an end in itself, and should certainly not be achieved contrary to the overall coordination of the forces.

At the same time, if sufficient compensation, e.g. in the form of active play, cannot be obtained, then even the most insignificant weakness in the pawn formation may carry the serious danger of eventual defeat.

New methods of creating and exploiting weak pawns and squares are constantly being found. One of these we will call the 'fixing' of a square. This can happen, in particular, in a fairly popular variation of the French Defence: 1 e4 e6 2 d4 d5 3 e5 c5 4 c3 ♘c6 5 ♘f3 ♕b6 6 a3 c4!?

In this way Black immobilizes White's Q-side pawn phalanx (b2-b4!), and in addition he fixes the b3 square, on which he may be able to build active plans. At the same time he must keep a very careful watch on the b3 square, since White may be able to open the b-file and begin an attack on Black's Q-side castled position.

No. 182 Clarke–Petrosian
Munich OL, 1958

7 g3 ♗d7 8 ♘g2 0-0-0!? 9 0-0 ♘a5 10 ♘bd2 h6

The correct decision. Black prevents ♘g5 and prepares a possible offensive by ...g5. 10...f6 11 ef gf is worse, since White gains active play in the centre.

11 ♖e1 ♘e7 12 ♘f1 ♘f5 13 ♘e3 ♘xe3 ♗e7 15 ♖e1 ♕b3!.

Reasoning that the exchange

of queens is unfavourable for White, Petrosian uses b3 as a transit square for the important switching of his queen to the K-side, where he plans in time to carry out a decisive offensive.

16 ♕e2 ♗a4! 17 ♗e3 ♔b8 18 ♖ed1 ♕c2! 19 ♖d2 ♕f5 20 ♖d1 g5 21 h3 h5 22 ♘h2 ♖dg8 23 g4 ♕g6 24 ♗f3 hg 25 ♗xg4 ♘c6!

25...♘b3 would have been a routine move. Black needs his knight to be attacking, not adopting an elegant pose!

26 f3 ♗d8 27 ♗f2 ♘e7 28 ♖e1 ♖h6 29 ♘f1 ♖gh8 30 ♗g3 ♖xh3!

The decisive positional sacrifice, destroying White's K-side defences.

31 ♗xh3 ♖xh3 32 ♕g2 ♕h7 33 ♘e3 ♘g6 34 ♘g4 ♘f4! 35 ♗xf4 gf 36 ♔f1 ♖g3 37 ♕f2 ♕h3+ 38 ♔e2 ♖g2 39 ♖g1 ♖xf2+ 40 ♘xf2 ♕h7 41 ♖h1 ♕g6 0-1

Such a plan with the fixing of a flank square on the sixth rank is by no means exceptional. For example, the following line of the King's Indian Sämisch Variation is instructive: **1 d4 ♘f6 2 c4 g6 3 ♘c3 ♗g7 4 e4 d6 5 f3 0-0 6 ♗e3 e5 7 ♘ge2 c6 8 ♕d2 ♘bd7 9 0-0-0 a6 10 ♔b1 ♕a5 11 ♘c1 ♖e8**

In the given position, where Black appears ready to begin a promising pawn offensive against White's castled position by ...b5, the timely fixing of Black's pawn phalanx is un-doubtedly correct: **12 ♘b3 ♕c7 13 de de 14 c5!** *(75)*

While paralyzing Black's counterplay on the Q-side, White at the same time creates powerful pressure on the central file.

No. 183 Geller-Boleslavsky
USSR Ch., 1952

14...♘f8 15 ♕d6 ♘e6 16 ♗c4! ♗f8 17 ♕xc7 ♘xc7 18 ♘a5 ♖b8 19 ♘a4!

White has achieved an overwhelming positional advantage, and he now takes play into a favourable endgame. Black's position is strategically lost.

19...♗e6 20 ♗xe6 ♘xe6 21 ♘c4 ♘c7 22 ♘ab6 ♘e6 23 b4 ♘f4 24 ♖d2 ♖bd8 25 ♖hd1 ♖xd2 26 ♖xd2 ♗g7 27 ♘a5 ♖b8 28 ♗xf4! ef 29 ♘d7 ♖d8 30 ♘xf6+ ♗xf6 31 ♖xd8+ ♗xd8 32 ♘xb7, and White won a pawn, and with it soon the game.

In many modern-day opening

systems the seizure of squares outside the extended centre, in particular b5(b4) or a5, is of considerable importance.

A characteristic example is provided by a variation of the Benoni Defence: 1 d4 ♘f6 2 c4 c5 3 d5 g6 4 ♘c3 d6 5 e4 ♗g7 6 ♘f3 0-0 7 h3 e6 8 ♗d3 ed 9 ed ♖e8+ 10 ♗e3 ♘a6 11 0-0 ♘c7 12 a4 ♘a6!? 13 ♖c1 ♘b4 14 ♗b1. Black has established his knight at b4, from where it controls a number of important squares on the Q-side and undoubtedly promises him definite counterplay. The knight looks fine at b4, of course, but in chess the concept of effectiveness is more significant, and it is very important that a knight there should be first and foremost an active piece, and not a passive observer, as often happens.

For this reason it is sometimes advisable to avoid establishing a knight there, as the following example confirms.

No. 184 A. Zaitsev-Gufeld
Debrecen, 1970
Modern Benoni

1 d4 ♘f6 2 c4 c5 3 d5 e6 4 ♘c3 ed 5 cd d6 6 e4 g6 7 f4 ♗g7 8 ♗b5+ ♘fd7 9 a4! 0-0 10 ♘f3 ♘a6 11 0-0 ♘b4(?)

11...♘c7 should have been preferred. Now the knight only

appears to be well placed; in reality it is cut off from the main battlefield.

12 ♗e3 a6 13 ♗c4 ♖b8 14 h3 ♖e8?! 15 ♗f2 b5? 16 ab ♘b6 17 ♗e2 ab 18 ♗h4 ♗f6 19 ♗xf6 ♕xf6 20 ♗xb5 ♗d7 21 ♗xd7 ♘xd7 22 ♕d2! c4 23 e5! de 24 fe ♘xe5 25 ♘xe5 ♕xe5 26 ♖ae1 ♕d6 27 ♖xe8+ ♖xe8 28 ♕d4! ♘c2? 29 ♕f2 1-0

Another characteristic group of plans in the transition to the middlegame is play on open files. Here too a large number of procedures has been worked out for controlling 'in turn' all the files from a- to h- (depending on the specific situation of this or that opening variation). The skilful opening of a file and the occupying of it, as well as the exploitation of the only open file, is sometimes the best plan in the transition to the middlegame.

The control of an open file by a rook is of importance strategically in the achievement of a plan. All other things being equal, in the majority of cases the domination of an open file guarantees a persistent initiative, and sometimes even a decisive advantage.

The control of central files is particularly important since operations on them are the most dangerous in the middlegame.

This is confirmed by the following examples.

No. 185 Botvinnik-Sorokin
USSR Ch., 1931
Queen's Gambit

1 d4 d5 2 ♘f3 ♘f6 3 c4 e6 4 ♘c3 ♘bd7 5 ♗g5 ♗e7 6 e3 0-0 7 ♗d3 c6 8 0-0 a6 9 a4 dc 10 ♗xc4 c5 11 dc ♗xc5 12 ♕e2 h6 13 ♗h4 ♗e7 14 ♖fd1 ♘h5 15 ♗xe7 ♕xe7 16 ♖d2! ♘b6 17 ♖ad1 ♕c5 18 ♗a2 ♘f6 19 e4 e5 20 ♕e3!

An instructive moment. After concentrating his rooks on the central file, White finds the most effective solution for further strengthening his position. This involves the exchange of queens, after which his pressure on the d-file can only increase.

20...♕xe3 21 fe ♗g4 22 a5 ♘c8 23 ♖c1 ♗xf3 24 gf ♘e7 25 ♘d5! ♘c6 (25...♘xd5 26 ♗xd5) 26 ♘xf6+ gf 27 ♖d7 ♖b8 28 ♔f2! ♘xa5 29 ♖cc7 ♖bc8 30 ♖xf7 ♖xc7 31 ♖xc7+ ♔h8 32 ♗d5 b5 33 b3 ♖d8 34 ♔g3 f5 35 ♔h4 fe 36 fe ♖d6 37 ♔h5 ♖f6 38 h3 ♖d6 39 h4 ♖b6 40 ♔g4 ♖f6 41 ♖a7 ♖b6 42 ♖e7 ♖d6 43 ♖c7 ♖f6 44 ♖a7 ♖b6 45 ♖c7 ♖f6 46 ♔h5 ♖d6 47 ♗f7! ♖f6 (47...♔g7 48 ♗d5+ and 49 b4!) 48 ♗g6 ♘xb3 49 ♔xh6 ♖f8 (or 49...♔g8 50 ♔g5 ♖f1 51 h5!, and White wins) 50 ♖h7+ ♔g8 51 ♖g7+ ♔h8 52 ♗f7

♖xf7 53 ♖xf7 ♔g8 54 ♔g6 ♘d2 55 ♖d7 1-0

No. 186 Botvinnik-Boleslavsky
USSR Ch., 1945
Spanish Game

1 e4 e5 2 ♘f3 ♘c6 3 ♗b5 a6 4 ♗a4 ♘f6 5 0-0 d6 6 c3 ♗d7 7 d4 g6 8 ♘bd2 ♕e7 9 ♖e1 ♗g7 10 ♘f1 0-0 11 ♗g5 h6 12 ♗h4 ♕e8 13 ♗c2 ♘h5 14 ♘e3 ♘e7 15 de! de 16 ♗g3! ♘xg3 17 hg ♖d8 18 ♕e2 ♘c8 19 ♖ad1 c6 20 ♖d2 ♕e7 21 ♖ed1 ♘b6 22 b4!

By subtle manœuvring White has first restricted Black's counterplay on the K-side and then concentrated his heavy pieces on the only open file. It is this that becomes the main arena of his subsequent offensive.

22...♗e6 23 ♗b3 ♖xd2 24 ♕xd2 ♗xb3 25 ab ♕e6 26 c4 ♗f6 27 c5! ♘c8 28 ♕d7! ♕xb3 (or 28...♖d8 29 ♕xe6 ♖xd1+ 30 ♘xd1 fe 31 ♘e3, winning a pawn) 29 ♕xb7 ♗g5 30 ♘xg5 hg 31 ♕xa6 ♘e7 32 ♕b7 ♖e8 33 ♕d7 ♔f8 34 ♕d6 ♕xb4 35 ♘g4! ♖a8 36 ♕xe5 ♕b3! 37 ♖d7 ♘g8 38 ♕d6+ ♔g7 39 ♕d4+!

The final subtlety. The tempting 39 ♘e5 would have encountered resistance after 39...♘f6 40 ♖d8 (40 ♖xf7+ ♕xf7! 41 ♘xf7 ♖a1+ 42 ♔h2 ♘g4+ 43 ♔h3 ♘xf2+ 44 ♔h2 ♖h1 mate!) 40...♖xd8 41 ♕xd8 ♕b1+ 42

♔h2 ♛xe4 43 ♕c7 ♕d5, with a draw.

39...♔h7 40 ♘f6+ ♘xf6 41 ♕xf6 ♔g8 42 ♔h2 ♖f8 43 ♕xc6! ♔g7 44 ♕d6 ♕b1 45 ♕d4+ ♔h7 46 c6 1-0

It often happens in practice that control of an open file fairly quickly provides the springboard for penetration into the opponent's rear, and in particular onto the 7th rank. Regarding this, Nimzowitsch stated in his customarily categorical way: "The ideal which lies at the root of every operation in a file is the ultimate penetration by way of this file into the enemy's game, that is to say to our 7th or 8th rank".

We give a convincing example of such play, taken from a modern game.

No. 187 Botvinnik-Portisch
Monaco, 1968
English Opening

1 c4 e5 2 ♘c3 ♘f6 3 g3 d5 4 cd ♘xd5 5 ♗g2 ♗e6 6 ♘f3 ♘c6 7 0-0 ♘b6 8 d3 ♗e7 9 a3 a5 10 ♗e3 0-0 11 ♘a4 ♘xa4 12 ♕xa4 ♗d5 13 ♖fc1 ♖e8 14 ♖c2! ♗f8 15 ♖ac1 ♘b8?

Black's position is already difficult. For example, 15...e4 16 de ♗xe4 17 ♖d2 ♕f6 18 ♖c4 etc. is unattractive. 15...♖b8 was probably best, intending a

possible ...b5. Now the white rook penetrates with great effect onto the 7th rank.

16 ♖xc7 ♗c6

This is what Black was counting on, but he failed to reckon with White's subsequent combination.

17 ♖1xc6! bc 18 ♖xf7!!

The point of White's plan. The white rook 'rages' along the 7th rank.

18...h6 19 ♖b7 ♕c8 20 ♕c4+ ♔h8 (20...♕e6 21 ♘xe5!) **21 ♘h4!**

Black's position is indefensible.

21...♕xb7 22 ♘g6+ ♔h7 23 ♗e4 ♗d6 24 ♘xe5+ g6 25 ♗xg6+ ♔g7 26 ♗xh6+! 1-0

A similar theme is seen in the 'Evergreen' game Anderssen-Dufresne, and in the famous game Steinitz-Bardeleben, where the invasion of the 7th rank by a rook was a powerful stimulus for a decisive and brilliant attack by White on the enemy king.

In these games the invasion of the opponent's rear at an early stage was the decisive factor in success.

No. 188 Andersson-Dufresne
Berlin, 1852
Evans Gambit

1 e4 e5 2 ♘f3 ♘c6 3 ♗c4 ♗c5 4

b4 ♗xb4 5 c3 ♗a5 6 d4! ed
7 0-0 d3 8 ♕b3 ♕f6 9 e5 ♕g6 10
♗a3 ♘ge7 11 ♖e1 b5? (better
11...d6) 12 ♗xb5 ♖b8 13 ♕a4
♗b6 14 ♘bd2 ♗b7 15 ♘e4 ♕f5 16
♗xd3 ♕h5 17 ♘f6+ gf 18 ef ♖g8
19 ♖ad1! ♕xf3 20 ♖xe7+!! ♘xe7
21 ♕xd7+!! ♔xd7 22 ♗f5++ ♔e8
23 ♗d7+ ♔d8 24 ♗xe7 mate!

No. 189 Steinitz-Bardeleben
Hastings, 1895
Italian Game

1 e4 e5 2 ♘f3 ♘c6 3 ♗c4 ♗c5
4 c3 ♘f6 5 d4 ed 6 cd ♗b4+ 7 ♘c3
d5 8 ed ♘xd5 9 0-0 ♗e6 10 ♗g5
♗e7 11 ♗xd5 ♗xd5 12 ♘xd5
♕xd5 13 ♗xe7 ♘xe7 14 ♖e1 f6
15 ♕e2 ♕d7 16 ♖c1 c6? (better
16...♔f7) 17 d5! cd 18 ♘d4 ♔f7
19 ♘e6 ♖hc8 20 ♕g4 g6 21 ♘g5+
♔e8 22 ♖xe7+ ♔f8!

Both here and later the rook is
taboo. After 20...♕xe7? 23
♖xc8+ or 22...♔xe7 23 ♖e1+
♔d6 24 ♕b4+ ♔c7 25 ♘e6+ ♔b8
26 ♕f4+ White wins.

23 ♖f7+! ♔g8 24 ♖g7+! ♔h8
25 ♖xh7+! 1-0

No. 190 Steinitz-Anderssen
Vienna, 1873
Queen's Gambit

1 d4 d5 2 c4 e6 3 ♘c3 ♘f6 4 ♗g5
♗e7 5 e3 0-0 6 ♘f3 b6 7 ♗d3 ♗b7
8 0-0 ♘bd7 (8...dc! 9 ♗xc4 c5) 9
cd ed 10 ♖c1 c5 11 dc bc 12 ♕a4

♘e4? 13 ♗xe4 de 14 ♖fd1! ♗xg5
15 ♘xg5 ♕xg5 16 ♖xd7 ♖fb8 17
♕b3! ♗c6 18 ♕xf7+ ♔h8 19 h4!
♕g4 20 ♖xa7 ♖xa7 21 ♕xa7
♖xb2 22 ♕xc5 ♕e6 23 ♖d1 h6 24
♖d6 ♕f7 25 ♘d1 ♖e2 26 ♔f1 1-0

No. 191 Alatortsev-Capablanca
Moscow, 1935
Queen's Gambit

1 d4 ♘f6 2 c4 e6 3 ♘c3 d5 4 ♗g5
♗e7 5 e3 0-0 6 cd?! ♘xd5 7 ♗xe7
♕xe7 8 ♘f3 ♘xc3 9 bc b6 10 ♗e2
♗b7 11 0-0 c5 12 ♘e5 ♘c6 13
♘xc6(?) ♗xc6 14 ♗f3 ♖ac8

Black has not only successfully overcome his opening difficulties, but has even gained
slightly the better prospects.
In trying for further simplification, subsequently White
incautiously permits the penetration of the black rooks along
the c-file into his rear.

15 a4 cd 16 cd g6 17 ♗xc6
♖xc6 18 ♕d3 ♕b7 19 ♖fb1? (19
♖ab1 is correct) 19...♖fc8 20 h3
a6! 21 ♕a3? ♖c2! 22 ♕d6? (76)

76

22...Ξxf2! 23 ♕g3 (23 ♔xf2 Ξc2+ 24 ♔e1 ♕xg2 25 ♕b8+ ♔g7 26 ♕e5+ f6, and Black wins) 23...Ξe2 0-1

No. 192 Petrosian-Matanović
Portorož IZ, 1958
Ragozin Defence

1 c4 ♘f6 2 ♘c3 e6 3 ♘f3 d5 4 d4 ♗b4 5 cd ed 6 ♗g5 h6 7 ♗h4 c5 8 e3 0-0 9 dc ♘bd7 10 ♗e2 ♕a5 11 0-0 ♗xc3 12 bc ♕xc5 13 Ξc1 b6 14 c4 ♗b7 15 ♘d4 Ξac8?! (15...dc!) 16 ♗f3 ♕b4 17 a3! ♕xa3?

This loses virtually by force. 17...♕c5 was comparatively best.

18 Ξa1 ♕c5 19 Ξxa7 ♗a8 20 ♕a1! ♔h7 21 Ξd1! ♕xc4 22 ♗e2 ♕c3 23 Ξxa8! 1-0

In a number of openings, especially modern ones with the fianchetto of the bishops at b2 and g2 (or correspondingly at b7 and g7), a plan of active play along the main diagonals becomes important. Such plans often arise at an early stage of the game, and are often associated with an attack on the king.

No. 193 Alekhine-Alexander
Nottingham, 1936
Queen's Indian Defence

1 d4 ♘f6 2 c4 e6 3 ♘f3 ♗b4+ 4 ♘bd2 b6 5 g3 ♗b7 6 ♗g2 0-0 7

0-0 ♗xd2? (7...Ξe8 8 a3 ♗f8) 8 ♕xd2! d6 9 b3 ♘bd7 10 ♗b2 Ξb8?! 11 Ξad1 ♘e4 12 ♕e3 f5 13 d5! ed (13...e5? 14 ♘h4, and the threat of ♘xf5 cannot be parried) 14 cd ♘df6 15 ♘h4 ♕d7 16 ♗h3 g6 17 f3 ♘c5 18 ♕g5 ♕g7 19 b4 ♘cd7 20 e4! ♘xe4 21 ♕c1! ♘ef6 22 ♗xf5 ♔h8 23 ♗e6 ♗a6 24 Ξfe1 ♘e5 25 f4 ♘d3 26 Ξxd3 ♗xd3 27 g4 1-0

No. 194 Rashkovsky-Filip
Sochi, 1973
Queen's Indian Defence

1 d4 ♘f6 2 c4 e6 3 ♘f3 b6 4 g3 ♗b7 5 ♗g2 ♗e7 6 0-0 0-0 7 b3 c5 8 ♗b2 cd 9 ♕xd4 ♘c6 10 ♕f4 d5 11 Ξd1 ♕b8 12 ♘c3! dc 13 ♕xc4 Ξc8? 14 ♕h4! ♘d5 15 ♘g5! h6 16 ♘xd5 (77)

77

White's piece attack has become very much a reality. The finish of the game is a triumph for the long-range bishops.

16...♗xg5 17 ♕g4 ed 18 f4 Ξe8? (18...d4 is more

tenacious) **19 ♗xd5! ♘e7 20 fg h5 21 ♗xf7+! ♔xf7 22 ♕xh5+! ♔g8 23 ♗xg7 ♗e4 24 ♗f6 ♕b7 25 ♕h8+ ♔f7 26 ♕g7+ ♔e6 27 ♗e5 ♗d5 28 ♕f6+ ♔d7 29 ♕d6+ 1-0**

And what about play against a 'bad' bishop? Such plans are typical of the French Defence, Caro-Kann Defence, Queen's Gambit, King's Indian Defence, and so on. A plan of this type was given in the game Schlechter-John (No. 150), and it will also be mentioned in the section on weak square complexes.

In many opening variations a struggle takes place between a knight and an enemy bishop. Here too everything depends on the character of the position. Thus the superiority of bishops over knights is very marked in positions with an open centre. But in closed set-ups with blocked pawn chains the role of the knight increases, especially if the bishop is restricted by its own pawns, or if the knight occupies a centralized position (e.g. blockading an isolated pawn).

These features rarely appear in pure form at an early stage of the game. There is usually a complicated 'mixture' of them, where the main components are gradually exchanged. The following example is typical in this respect.

No. 195 Karpov-Smyslov
USSR Internal OL, 1972
Petroff's Defence

1 e4 e5 2 ♘f3 ♘f6 3 ♘xe5 d6 4 ♘f3 ♘xe4 5 d4 ♗e7 6 ♗d3 ♘f6 7 h3 0-0 8 0-0 c5?! 9 ♘c3 ♘c6 10 ♖e1 a6 11 d5! *(78)*

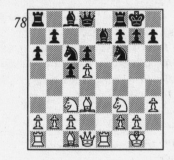

As a result of Black's passive opening play, White has gained a clear and persistent advantage, consisting in his greater freedom and his control of the only open file. Now Black should probably have reconciled himself to the necessity for a lengthy defence, and retreated his knight to b8. In trying to complicate the game, he prefers the eccentric retreat to a7, but after this he is faced with a new, more serious strategic danger — for a long time the knight at a7 cannot coordinate with his other forces, and simply fails to find a good post. From this point White's main plan becomes playing to restrict and isolate the knight at a7.

11...♘a7? 12 a4 ♗d7 13 a5! ♖e8 14 ♗f1 h6 15 ♗f4 ♗f8 16 ♖xe8 ♕xe8 17 ♗h2 ♕d8 18 ♘d2 ♕c7 19 ♘de4! ♘xe4 20 ♘xe4 ♗f5 21 ♘d2 ♖e8 22 c3

The numerous exchanges have only favoured White. Now the poor position of the black knight is especially perceptible.

22...♕d8 23 ♕b3 ♕d7 24 c4! ♘c8 25 g4! (taking away the important f5 square) 25...♗h7 26 ♗d3 ♗xd3 27 ♕xd3 g6 28 ♖b1 ♗g7 29 b4! cb 30 ♖xb4 ♕c7 31 ♘b3

How Black would like to have his knight at d7! But although only one square separates it from there, the way to it proves unattainable. For example, 31...b6? 32 ab ♘xb6 33 c5!, and Black's position is on the verge of collapse.

31...♗e5 32 ♗xe5 ♖xe5 33 ♕d4 g5 34 ♔g2! ♕e7 35 ♘d2 ♖e1 36 ♖b3 ♖e2 37 ♔f3! ♖e5 38 ♖e3 f6 39 ♘e4 ♔g7 40 ♔g2! ♕c7 41 ♖f3 b5 42 ab 1-0

Simplifying from the opening into a complex endgame

Usually the transition from opening to middlegame as though reveals the strength of the pieces, whereas when play goes into an endgame (including straight from the opening) this always leads first and foremost to a marked reappraisal of middlegame values.

Thus in the middlegame the king usually keeps itself well hidden, but in the endgame it feels much more confident and will often take an active part in the battle (and the strength of the king in a 'pure' endgame sometimes achieves the level of a rook).

Pawns, after only recently being common 'workers', or even mere 'cannon-fodder', become highly respected veterans. And in general, every unit of material, even the weakest, begins to demand careful attention. Especially passed pawns. In the middlegame they are only rarely a powerful and independent force, but in the endgame they often lead an offensive, and for their life the opponent may have to pay dearly.

The strength of the rook also increases sharply. Like mortars in old war films, they are often ready to destroy the opponent's unsupported defences.

But in many cases the importance of the minor pieces falls in comparison with the rook. There are now fewer possibilities for an attack on the king, and also their influence on the chess board is not as great as in the middlegame. What tells here is a definite geometric restriction on the actions of minor pieces, which, incidentally, in many cases (with a small number of pieces) is subject to purely mathematical analysis.

Of course, these considerations apply mainly to exclusively endgame situations, whereas, on the transition from the opening to a complex endgame, both middle game and endgame motifs are usually present simultaneously.

Nevertheless, on each occasion a player should take serious account of these factors and have a clear impression of them, when going in for considerable simplification in the opening.

In many cases the strategic procedure of simplification is associated with the gaining in the opening of certain positional advantages, which can be most effectively exploited in the endgame, such as: weaknesses in the opponent's pawn formation, possibilities of invading with the rook to the rear, and so on.

Here are a few examples of this type.

No. 196 Simagin-Keres
Moscow, 1963
Spanish Game

1 e4 e5 2 ♘f3 ♘c6 3 ♗b5 a6

4 ♗a4 ♘f6 5 0-0 d6 6 ♗×c6+ bc 7 d4 ed(?) 8 ♕×d4 ♗e7 9 e5! c5 10 ♕d3 de 11 ♕×d8+ ♗×d8 12 ♘×e5 ♗e7

Black played the opening badly, leading to the significant weakening of his Q-side pawns. White successfully grasped this feature and at the transition stage he found the effective plan of taking play into a favourable endgame.

Although Black has two bishops, the situation is nevertheless dictated by the irreparable weakness of his pawns.

13 ♖e1 ♗e6 14 ♘c3 0-0 15 ♗g5 h6(?) 16 ♘g6! fg 17 ♖×e6 ♔f7 18 ♖ae1 ♖fe8 19 ♗×f6 ♗×f6 (19...gf 20 ♘d5!) 20 ♖×e8 ♖×e8 21 ♖×e8 ♔×e8 22 ♘d1 ♔d7 23 ♔f1 ♔c6 24 ♔e2 ♗e5 25 h3 ♔d5 26 ♘e3+ ♔e4 27 c3 h5 28 ♘c4 ♗f4 29 g3 ♗g5 30 f3+ ♔d5 31 ♔d3 ♗e7 32 ♘e3+ ♔e6 33 ♔e4! g5 34 ♘c4

As early as move 21 a purely technical ending arose, and White has handled it with great mastery. We should mention that in general the transition to the endgame is closely associated with good technique required for realizing an advantage. Of course, there may be various ways of realizing an advantage, which may involve an attack and even sacrifices. And yet the realization of an advantage by simplifying is highly typical, and improvement cannot be achieved without a mastery of its technique.

34...g6 35 g4 hg 36 fg ♗f6 37 a3 ♗e7 38 a4 ♗f6 39 ♘d2 ♗e7 40 ♘f3 ♗f6 41 ♘d2 ♔d6 42 ♘c4+ ♔e6 43 ♘a5 ♔d6 44 ♔d3 ♔d5 45 ♘c4 c6 46 ♘b6+ ♔d6 47 a5 ♗d8 48 ♔c4 ♗c7 49 ♘a4 ♗xa5 50 ♘xc5 ♗b6 51 ♘xa6 ♗e3 52 ♘b4 ♗c1 53 b3 ♗f4 54 ♘c2 ♗e5 55 ♘d4 ♗f6 56 b4

White has won a pawn, which in the given situation is equivalent to winning the game.

56...♗e7 57 ♘f3 ♗f6 58 ♔d3 c5 59 b5 ♔d5 60 c4+ ♔e6 61 ♔e4 ♔d6 62 b6 ♔c6 63 ♘e5+ ♔b7 64 ♘d7 ♗d4 65 ♔d5 1-0

In the following examples the transition to the endgame is seen in a different light, the theme of the active side being an attack on the king. Yes, an attack, although there is little material left on the board.

No. 197 Karpov-Mecking
Hastings, 1971/72
Sicilian Defence

1 e4 c5 2 ♘f3 d6 3 d4 cd 4 ♘xd4 ♘f6 5 ♘c3 a6 6 ♗e2 e5 7 ♘b3 ♗e6 8 f4 ♕c7 9 a4 ♘c6?!

9...♗e7 or 9...♘bd7 is more flexible. Now White forcibly gains control of the critical square d5.

10 f5 ♗xb3 11 cb ♕b6 12 ♗g5 ♗e7 13 ♗xf6 ♗xf6 14 ♘d5 ♕a5+ 15 ♕d2! ♕xd2+ 16 ♔xd2 ♗g5+ 17 ♔d3 0-0 18 h4 ♗d8 19 ♖ac1

Despite the simplification, White has obtained a strong attacking position, whereas Black has no possibility of active counterplay. The game is finally decided by a storming of Black's castled position, a situation which in practice often occurs in the endgame.

19...a5 20 ♔d2 ♖b8 21 g4! ♘b4 22 ♗c4 ♘xd5 23 ♗xd5 (79)

A typical structure, where the opposite-colour bishops merely facilitate White's attack.

23...g5!?

Black tries to block the white pawn mass, but Karpov's offensive develops inexorably.

24 fg hg 25 ♔d3 ♔g7 26 h5 ♗b6 27 ♖h3 ♗c5 28 ♖f1 f6 29 hg ♔xg6 30 ♖fh1 ♖be8 31 ♖h7 ♔g5 32 ♔e2 ♔f4 33 ♖1h3! ♗d4 34 ♖g7! 1-0

We will also consider an

example from the Exchange Variation of the Spanish Game:
1 e4 e5 2 ♘f3 ♘c6 3 ♗b5 a6 4 ♗×c6 dc 5 d4 ed 6 ♕×d4 ♕×d4 7 ♘×d4 *(80)*

Play has gone into a complex endgame, where Black has been given doubled pawns on the c-file and White has gained a K-side pawn majority.

This factor undoubtedly plays a certain role, and it could become decisive if a pawn ending were to be reached. But this is a long way off. For the moment not only are there many pieces on the board, but also of considerable importance is the fact that Black has no difficulties with the development of his pieces: he has two strong bishops and good possibilities for piece play.

In short, for the moment the character of the pawn formation is not so important.

The development of events in the following game is instructive.

No. 198 Verlinsky-Alekhine
St. Petersburg, 1909

7...c5 8 ♘e2 ♗d7 9 b3? c4! 10 bc ♗a4 11 c3 0-0-0 12 ♘d2 ♗c2 13 f3 ♗c5 14 a4 ♘f6 15 ♗a3 ♗e3! 16 ♘f1 ♗a7 17 a5 ♖d3 18 c5 ♖hd8 19 ♔f2 ♘d7 20 ♘e3 ♘×c5! 21 ♘d4 ♗b3

In the best traditions of the middlegame Black has managed to disorganize his opponent's forces and achieve a decisive advantage. There was a highly elegant finish to the game:

22 ♔e2 ♖×c3 23 ♗b2 ♖×e3+ 24 ♔×e3 ♘e6 25 ♖a3 ♘×d4 26 ♔f4 ♗c5 27 ♖aa1 ♘e2+ 28 ♔g4 ♗e6+ 0-1

It can be considered that, in complex endgame positions arising as a result of an opening struggle, middlegame and endgame themes are very closely interwoven. Sometimes their connection is highly contradictory. After all, in spite of a certain sharpness in the tactical struggle which sometimes results, many possibilities, which are characteristic of the middlegame, markedly lose their effect as the game becomes simplified. Thus very often an attack on the king is not so sharp, it is not often that material can be sacrificed, and so on.

In this sense the development of events in the following game is instructive.

No. 199 Chistyakov-Suetin
Riga, 1954
English Opening

1 d4 ♘f6 2 c4 c5 3 ♘f3 g6 4 ♘c3 cd 5 ♘xd4 d5 6 cd ♘xd5 7 ♘db5 ♘xc3 8 ♕xd8+ ♔xd8 9 ♘xc3 *(81)*

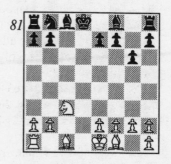

White has prevented the black king from castling, a 'small' achievement on his part. But subsequently he clearly overrates his possibilities, trying at any cost to mount an attack on the black king. It is here that the absence of the queens is felt.

9...♗g7 10 ♗f4 ♗e6 11 g3 (11 ♖c1 is more accurate) 11... ♗xc3+!

An important exchange. Of course, it was a pity to have to part with this bishop. But Black makes a timely simplification of the position, blocks the c-file for

White and weakens his Q-side pawns. In the subsequent play the white bishops are simply unable to display their great strength.

12 bc ♘c6 13 ♗g2 ♔c8 14 0-0 ♖d8 15 a4 ♗d5 16 ♗h3+ e6 17 f3 ♗c4 18 ♔f2 b6 19 ♖fd1 ♔b7 20 ♗g5 ♖d5! 21 ♖xd5 ed 22 ♖d1 ♖e8 23 ♖d2 ♘b8 24 e4? de 25 fe ♗e6

In trying to activate his pieces, White has merely weakened his pawns still further; his position is now very difficult. For example, after 26 ♗xe6 ♖xe6 27 ♖d8 f6! 28 ♗f4 ♘c6 29 ♖d7+ ♔a6 30 ♖xh7 ♖xe4 31 ♖f7 ♖e6! Black later threatens to eliminate the weak white pawns on the Q-side. It is clear that purely endgame themes have come into force, and it is they that decide the outcome of the game.

26 ♗f1 ♖c8 27 ♗f6 ♘d7 28 ♗d4 ♘c5!, and without particular difficulty Black exploited his opponent's pawn weaknesses.

In this example one can follow how inexorably White's initiative faded, and how the positional drawbacks of his set-up became more and more apparent.

In any situation the natural task for each of the two sides is to exploit the advantages of their own position while simultaneously neutralizing corresponding attempts by the opponent. As applied to a complex endgame, this often signifies that one side has some durable positional advantage which can be exploited through further simplification, whereas the other is aiming to exploit his dynamic advantages. Often the second factor plays a more important role, and may, for example, assist the mounting of an attack on the opponent's king; in other cases, on the contrary, the motifs of the impending basic endgame acquire more significance.

In such positions much depends not only on who holds the initiative, but also on how persistent it is. The following example is instructive in this respect.

No. 200 Kan-Eliazarov
Moscow, 1956
French Defence

1 e4 e6 2 d4 d5 3 ♘d2 e5?!

An objectively dubious pawn sacrifice, which, however, as though changes the roles in the opening: here it is White who finds himself as the defending side.

4 de de 5 ♘xe4 ♕xd1+ 6 ♔xd1
(82)

White's task is simple: to retain his extra pawn and exploit it in the endgame. He tries to

achieve this by further exchanges (expedient ones, of course). Black, on the other hand, must aim to exploit the activity of his pieces and if possible to build up an attack on the white king, which is caught in the centre. In short, we have a typical situation of the type under discussion.

82

6...♘c6 7 f4 f6!? 8 ef ♗g4+ 9 ♗e2 0-0-0+ 10 ♗d2 ♗xe2+ 11 ♘xe2 ♘xf6 12 ♘xf6

A natural but routine exchange, after which Black's initiative merely increases. 12 ♘f2! followed by ♘d3 would have been correct, considerably strengthening the king's defences. Then Black's initiative would have gradually faded and White's material advantage would have told.

12...gf 13 c3 ♗c5 14 ♔c2 ♖he8 15 ♘c1 h5! 16 ♖e1 ♖xe1 17 ♗xe1 ♖g8 18 g3 ♖e8 19 ♔d1 ♗g1!, and Black gained equal chances.

Often the transition into a complex endgame is associated with square-controlling play, which is assisted by favourable simplification. A splendid example of this is provided by the following game, in which, incidentally, at the decisive stage middlegame motifs are clearly apparent.

No. 201 Fischer-Petrosian
Candidates Match, 1971
Sicilian Defence

1 e4 c5 2 ♘f3 e6 3 d4 cd 4 ♘xd4 a6 5 ♗d3 ♘c6 6 ♘xc6 bc 7 0-0 d5 8 c4! ♘f6 9 cd cd 10 ed ed 11 ♘c3! ♗e7 12 ♕a4+ ♕d7 (White also retains the initiative after 12. . . ♗d7 13 ♕c2! 0-0 14 ♗g5!) **13 ♖e1!** *(83)*

A very subtle decision. White takes play into an endgame where Black's pawn weaknesses are a telling factor.

13. . .♕xa4 14 ♘xa4 ♗e6 15 ♗e3 0-0 (White's advantage is

also obvious after 15. . .♘d7 16 f4! g6 17 ♗d4 0-0 18 ♖ac1) **16 ♗c5 ♖fe8 17 ♗xe7 ♖xe7 18 b4! ♔f8 19 ♘c5 ♗c8 20 f3 ♖ea7 21 ♖e5! ♗d7 22 ♘xd7+! ♖xd7 23 ♖c1 ♖c6 24 ♖c7 ♘d7 25 ♖e2 g6 26 ♔f2 h5**

The finish takes the form of a powerful attack by White.

27 f4 h4 28 ♔f3 f5 29 ♔e3! d4+ 30 ♔d2! ♘b6 31 ♖ee7 ♘d5 32 ♖f7+ ♔e8 33 ♖b7 ♘xb4 34 ♗c4 1-0

In analyzing the various factors arising in the transition from opening to endgame, it will not be out of place to recall the following comment by Alekhine: "Every chess master is morally obliged to try as well as possible to solve the problems of a position without 'fear' of simplification. Playing for complications is an extreme measure, to which a player should resort only when he is unable to find a clear and logical plan".

These words are very colourfully confirmed by the following example, where White, with a spatial advantage in the opening, accepted without hesitation the simplification offered by his opponent at the transitional stage. His subsequent, accurately calculated attack in the centre demonstrates that simplification by no means restricts the scope for imagination.

No. 202 Razuvayev-Honfi
Cienfuegos, 1976
Sicilian Defence

1 e4 c5 2 ♘f3 ♘c6 3 d4 cd
4 ♘xd4 g6 5 c4 ♗g7 6 ♗e3 ♘f6
7 ♘c3 0-0 8 ♗e2 d6 9 0-0 ♗d7 10
♖c1 ♘xd4 11 ♗xd4 ♗c6 12 f3
♘d7 13 b4! ♗xd4+ 14 ♕xd4
♕b6? 15 ♕xb6 ♘xb6 *(84)*

16 e5! de 17 b5 ♗e8 18 c5! ♘d7
19 ♘d5 e6 20 ♘e7+ ♔g7 21 c6 bc
22 bc ♘b6 23 c7 ♗d7 24 ♖fd1 ♗a4
25 ♖d6! ♔f6 26 ♖xb6 ♔xe7 27
♖b7 ♔f6 28 ♖cb1 ♗c6 29 ♖b8
♖c8 30 ♖c1 ♖axb8 31 cb♕ ♖xb8
32 ♖xc6 ♖b2 33 ♗c4 h5 34 h4 g5
35 hg+ ♔xg5 36 ♔h2 ♖b4 37 ♗b3
a5 38 ♖a6 ♖b5 39 ♖a7 ♔f6 40
♗a4 1-0

It should be mentioned that
in certain variations play for simplification and the transition into
the endgame is the only correct
solution to the opening problems, e.g. 1 e4 e5 2 ♘f3 ♘c6
3 ♗b5 a6 4 ♗a4 ♘f6 5 0-0 ♗e7
6 ♖e1 b5 7 ♗b3 d6 8 c3 0-0 9 h3

♘b8 10 d4 ♗b7?! 11 de de 12
♕xd8 ♗xd8 13 ♘xe5 ♘xe4 14
♗e3! etc., or 1 d4 ♘f6 2 c4 g6
3 ♘c3 ♗g7 4 e4 d6 5 f3 0-0 6 ♗e3
e5 7 ♘ge2 c6 8 ♕b3 ♘bd7 9 0-0-0
♕a5 10 ♔b1 ♖b8 11 de de 12
♕a4! etc.

In other cases such a solution
is the optimal one.

No. 203 Polugayevsky-Ivkov
Belgrade, 1969
Sicilian Defence

1 ♘f3 ♘f6 2 c4 c5 3 ♘c3 ♘c6
4 d4 cd 5 ♘xd4 ♘xd4 6 ♕xd4 g6
7 e4 ♗g7 8 ♗e3 d6 9 f3 0-0 10 ♕d2
♗e6 11 ♖c1 ♕a5 12 ♘d5! ♕xd2+
(practice has shown that 12...
♕xa2 is better here) 13 ♔xd2
♗xd5 14 cd ♖fc8 15 ♗e2 a6 16 b4!
(85)

In the resulting ending White
has a number of small but significant advantages: the two bishops, greater space in the centre,
and an active plan of play on the
Q-side. All this allows him con-

sistently to strengthen his position.

**16...&f8 17 a4 &d7 18 a5!
&b2 19 &c2 &xc2+ 20 &xc2 &g7
21 &b3 &c8 22 &d2 &d4 23 g4
&g7 24 g5!**

After restricting Black's forces on the Q-side, White begins a decisive offensive on the K-side.

**24...&c7 25 &d1 &f8 26 f4
&c8 27 &g4 &e8 28 &f1 &c7 29
h4 &g7 30 h5! &d4 31 &h1 &g7
32 &h3 &f8 33 h6! &d4 34 &d3
&a7 35 &h3 &g1 36 &c3 &e8 37
e5 &h2 38 ed ed 39 &e3+ &d8 40
&e4 &g1 41 &xd7 1-0**

No. 204 Karpov-Kavalek
Nice OL, 1974
Sicilian Defence

**1 c4 c5 2 &f3 g6 3 d4 cd 4 &xd4
&c6 5 e4 &f6 6 &c3 d6 7 &e2
&xd4 8 &xd4 &g7 9 &g5 0-0 10
&d2 &e6 11 &c1 &a5 12 f3 &fc8
13 b3 a6 14 &a4! &xd2+ 15 &xd2
&c6** (better 15...&d7) **16 &c3
&ac8** (16...&e8! should probably have been preferred) **17
&d5 &f8 18 &e3 &d7 19 h4
&xd5(?)** (19...f5 offered better chances) **20 ed &c7 21 h5 &g8 22
f4 &c5 23 &g4! &e4+ 24 &d3 f5
25 &f3 b5 26 g4! bc+ 27 &xc4!
&xc4 27 bc &c5+ 29 &xc5**

As in the Karpov-Mecking game (No. 197), here the opposite-colour bishops merely make Black's defence more difficult.

**29...&xc5 30 h6! &f8 31 &c3
fg 32 &xg4 &f7 33 &e6+ &f6 34
&g8 &c7 35 &xh7 e6 36 &g8 ed
37 h7! &g7?**

The decisive mistake. Black would have retained drawing chances after 37...&xc4+ 38 &d3 &g7 etc.

**38 &xd5 &h8 39 &d3 &f5 40
&e3 &e7+ 41 &f3 a5 42 a4 &c7 43
&e4+ &f6 44 &h6 &g7 45 &g4
1-0**

In the above games the transition from the opening into a complex endgame was dictated mainly by creative considerations. Such a transition may also be motivated by purely practical or competitive reasons, for example, by a desire to avoid a complex or sharp combinational struggle. But such reasons rarely assist the creation of new procedures and methods, and for the most part are of a strictly utilitarian nature.

In general, in the modern opening one should be very watchful for sudden simplification, irrespective of the reasons for it. Objectively, such a method of play does not perhaps promise a great deal, but in practice it is often employed by players with good endgame technique if the opponent is weak in this respect.

Thus it can be said that a

player's technique and opening culture are interconnected. This question will be examined later from another viewpoint, when typical opening positions will be discussed (chapter 9).

six

ATTACK DURING THE TRANSITION TO THE MIDDLEGAME

Attack as an effective strategic means

As was mentioned in chapter 2, strong and sharp attacks, directed mainly at the opponent's king, can arise at a very early stage of the game. There are many possibilities of this type, but (and this is perfectly natural) there are even more in the transition stage from opening to middlegame. After all, by this time not only have the main forces been brought into play, but the conditions have also been created for pawn storms on the flanks, the transfer of the offensive from the centre to the flank, and so on.

Along with defence, attack is undisputably the most universal strategic procedure in chess, and like many other universal concepts it can be considered from two aspects. In the broad sense of the word, all forms of offensive operations can come under this concept. In its more concrete, authentic meaning, attack is distinguished from other offensive operations mainly by decisiveness. At this moment all the power of the blow is as though concentrated on a definite, sometimes small part of the board, to achieve which a player will often have to 'burn his boats'.

The concept of attack should on no account be restricted to cases when the king is the target, as is done in certain books. Often sharp attacks are directed at the centre, at the Q-side, at mobile targets, and so on. Such attacks sometimes demand no less determination, strategic risk and inventiveness than attacks on the king.

At the same time, in no other strategic procedure are the elements of strategy and tactics so close, as in attack. And sometimes it is difficult to decide whether a particular attack (especially on the king!) is a strategic plan or a purely tactical operation.

This relates equally to

attacks at an early stage of the game (as has already been seen in earlier examples). Certainly, an attack in the opening invariably involves the use of strong tactical measures. An outwardly similar picture is seen if, thanks to a mistake by the opponent, one side gains an advantage in the opening, which, however, can be consolidated only by tactical means.

Compare the following two examples.

No. 205 Donner-Euwe
Match, 1955/56

This position *(86)* was reached after 14 moves. At the transition to the middlegame White committed a serious mistake, choosing the incorrect plan of a pawn offensive in the centre:

15 f4?

Correct was 15 ♗f4!, which would have set Black difficult problems. Donner chooses a dif-

ferent plan, which at first sight seems active and natural, but he overlooks a latent and highly dangerous counterattack on the K-side, which tactically refutes White's idea.

15. . .♕h5 16 e5 ♗xh3!

White had reckoned only on 16. . . ♗f5, to which he had prepared 17 ♕f2 b4 18 ef bc 19 g4! etc.

17 ef

White's position would have been equally cheerless after 17 ♗xc6 b4 18 ♗xa8 bc 19 ♗g2 ♗f5!

17. . .♗xf6 18 ♘e4 ♖xe4!

The point of Black's tactical plan. Although White is now a rook up, the black pieces descend violently on his king.

19 ♗xe4 ♖e8 20 ♗e3 (also bad is 20 ♗xc6 ♗f5 21 ♕d2 ♗d4+!, or 20 ♖d2 ♗f5 21 ♗xf5 ♖e1+ 22 ♔f2 ♕h1! 23 ♗h3 ♕g1+ 24 ♔f3 ♖e3+! etc) **20. . .♗f5! 21 ♕xc5?**

This loses immediately, but White would also have been close to catastrophe after 21 ♗xf5 ♖xe3 22 ♕f2 ♗d4 23 ♖xd4 cd 24 ♗c8 ♕d5 25 ♖e1 ♕xa2! 26 ♖xe3 de 27 ♕xe3 ♕b1+.

21. . .♖xe4 22 ♖d2 ♕f3! 0-1

A possible variation is 23 ♗f2 ♗h3 24 ♗e1 ♖xe1+ 25 ♖xe1 ♕xg3+, and Black wins.

This is a typical instance of the tactical exploitation of an opening advantage, and here this was the only way of realizing it.

No. 206 Geller-Vatnikov
Kiev, 1950
Sicilian Defence

1 e4 c5 2 ♘f3 ♘c6 3 d4 cd 4 ♘×d4 ♘f6 5 ♘c3 d6 6 ♗c4 e6 7 0-0 ♗e7 8 ♗b3 0-0 9 ♗e3 ♘a5 10 f4 b6 11 e5!

White begins an energetic attack in the centre and on the K-side, using the active placing of his pieces. The alternative 11 ♕f3 ♗b7 12 g4? is less energetic (cf. Padevsky-Botvinnik, No. 163)

11...♘e8 (bad is 11...de 12 fe ♘d7 13 ♖×f7!, when White wins) 12 f5 *(87)*

The logical continuation of White's attacking plan. If now 12...♘×b3 13 ♘c6! ♕c7 14 ♘×e7+ ♕×e7 15 f6 gf 16 ef! with a decisive attack.

12...de 13 fe f6 14 ♘f5! ♘×b3 15 ♘d5!

The decisive blow. Black cannot play 15...♘×a1 because of 16 ♘d×e7+, when he loses his queen due to the tactical weakness of his back rank, where his pieces are merely interfering with one another. The game is decided.

It might be imagined that this game, in which White's attack developed quickly and unhindered, is a typical instance of the tactical exploitation of an opening advantage. But this is not altogether so.

The significant difference between the two games considered is that in the first the attack was calculated to the finish, whereas in the second the plan involved much greater risk.

Thus it is far from clear how White's attack would have concluded, if instead 13...f6 Black had played 13...♘×b3 14 ♘c6 ♕d6!

No. 207 Bilek-Petrosian
European Team Ch., Oberhausen, 1961

To the natural 15 ♘d5(?) Black replied with the unexpected 15...♗h4!, after which he had much the better chances. The game lasted only another four moves: 16 ef+ ♖×f7 17 ♖×f7 ♘×a1 18 ♕f1 ♗f6! 19 ♘×f6+ ♘×f6 0-1 (instead of 15 ♘d5, correct was 15 ♕×d6 ♗×d6 16 ab).

This indicates that, although

White's attack resulted from the assessment of the position, in the given case it was double-edged (which distinguishes it from the previous one). At times it is difficult to establish this, but in general it should be remembered that a plan of attack is by no means the same as the tactical realization of an advantage. And one of the indications of this is the fact that, in the majority of cases, at the starting point of the attack (irrespective of its form) at the transition from opening to middlegame the attacking side has no real advantage.

It is essential to distinguish a winning continuation of the attack (Donner-Euwe, No. 205) from a dangerous one, which can nevertheless be parried, albeit sometimes with great difficulty (Geller-Vatnikov, No. 206)

We will now turn to typical attacking plans which arise at the transitional stage.

Offensive in the centre

A superiority in the centre is not some constant factor. It implies a dynamic, skilful and timely transformation of this advantage for the achievement of more concrete aims. Therefore the outward virtues of a centre should never be overesti-

mated (incidentally, this can be applied more broadly — literally to all positional factors). The transformation may be a direct necessity, but more often it is dictated by a deep understanding of coming events. In connection with this we will look at the problem of the central pawn pair (d4 and e4 for White, or d5 and e5 for Black).

In this situation the transformation is comparatively rarely associated with a direct pawn offensive in the centre and the creation here of a strong passed pawn. And yet this method can be highly effective, as the following example shows.

No. 208 Spassky-Petrosian
World Ch., 1969
Queens Gambit

1 c4 ♘f6 2 ♘c3 e6 3 ♘f3 d5 4 d4 c5 5 cd ♘xd5 6 e4 ♘xc3 7 bc cd 8 cd ♗b4+ 9 ♗d2 ♗xd2+ 10 ♕xd2 0-0 11 ♗c4 ♘c6 12 0-0 b6 13 ♖ad1 ♗b7 14 ♖fe1 ♖c8 (88)

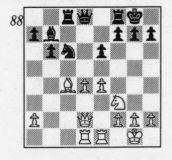

15 d5! ed? (15...♘a5) **16 ♗xd5 ♘a5 17 ♕f4 ♕c7 18 ♕f5 ♗xd5 19 ed ♕c2 20 ♕f4 ♕xa2** (better 20...♖ce8) **21 d6 ♖cd8 22 d7!**

White has achieved his strategic aim. His pawn at d7 is a powerful wedge, paralyzing Black's position.

22...♕c4 23 ♕f5 h6 24 ♖c1! ♕a6 25 ♖c7 b5 26 ♘d4 (26 ♖e8! is even stronger) **26...♕b6 27 ♖c8 ♘b7 28 ♘c6 ♘d6 29 ♘xd8! ♘xf5 30 ♘c6 1-0**

Switching the attack from the centre to the K-side

A superiority in the centre may provide the springboard for an attack on one of the flanks, where the opponent may have vulnerable points or where it will be easier to strike a blow. In such cases at the transitional stage, the target of the attack will often become the K-side.

Examples of this were given earlier, when we were investigating the setting up of a strong centre (Nos. 109-112). In each of those cases, the painstaking construction of a centre immediately became the springboard for transferring the attack to the opponent's king, and where necessary the centre was sometimes sacrificed.

We give some further examples of this type for independent study.

No. 209 Tarrasch-Alekhine
Pistyan, 1922
Blumenfeld Counter-Gambit

1 d4 ♘f6 2 ♘f3 e6 3 c4 c5 4 d5 b5 5 de? (5 ♗g5!) **5...fe 6 cb d5 7 e3?** (7 g3!) **7...♗d6 8 ♘c3 0-0 9 ♗e2 ♗b7 10 b3 ♘bd7 11 ♗b2 ♕e7 12 0-0 ♖ad8 13 ♕c2 e5** *(89)*

89

Black has set up an ideal centre, which in combination with his prospects of a K-side attack more than compensates for the sacrificed pawn.

14 ♖fe1 e4 15 ♘d2 ♘e5 16 ♘d1 ♘fg4 17 ♗xg4 ♘xg4 18 ♘f1 ♕g5! 19 h3 ♘h6 20 ♔h1 ♘f5 21 ♘h2 d4! 22 ♗c1 d3 23 ♕c4+ ♔h8 24 ♗b2 ♘g3+! 25 ♔g1 ♗d5 26 ♕a4 ♘e2+ 27 ♔h1 ♖f7 28 ♕a6 h5! 29 b6 ♘g3+! 30 ♔g1 ab 31 ♕xb6 d2 32 ♖f1 ♘xf1 33 ♘xf1 ♗e6!! 34 ♔h1 ♗xh3 35 gh ♖f3 36 ♗g3 h4 37 ♗f6 ♕xf6 38 ♘xe4 ♖xh3+ 0-1

No. 210 Botvinnik-Keres
The Hague/Moscow, 1948
Nimzo-Indian Defence

1 d4 ♘f6 2 c4 e6 3 ♘c3 ♗b4 4 e3
0-0 5 a3 ♗xc3+ 6 bc ♖e8 7 ♘e2
e5 8 ♘g3 d6 9 ♗e2 ♘bd7 10 0-0
c5? (better 10...b6 or 10...♘f8)
11 f3! cd? 12 cd ♘b6 13 ♗b2 ed 14
e4! ♗e6 15 ♖c1 ♖e7 16 ♕xd4
♕c7 17 c5! dc 18 ♖xc5 ♕f4 19
♗c1 ♕b8 20 ♖g5!

Black has no defence, e.g.
20... ♘e8 21 ♘h5 f6 22 ♘xf6+
etc.

20...♘bd7 21 ♖xg7+! ♔xg7
22 ♘h5+ ♔g6 23 ♕e3 1-0

No. 211 Boleslavsky-Moiseyev
Kharkov, 1948
Queen's Gambit

1 d4 d5 2 c4 ♘f6?! 3 cd ♘xd5 4
♘f3 e6? (4...♗f5) 5 e4 ♘f6 6 ♘c3
♗e7 7 ♗d3 c5 8 e5 ♘d5 9 0-0 ♘c6
10 dc ♘xc3 11 bc ♕a5 12 ♕c2 h6
13 ♖b1 a6 14 ♗f4 ♕xc5 15 ♖fe1
0-0 16 ♗e3 ♕a3?

16...♕d5 is better. After re-
moving his queen from the defence of the main battlefield —
the K-side, Black comes under
an irresistible attack.

17 ♖b3 ♕a4 (after 17...♕a5 18
♗b6 ♕d5 19 ♖d1 Black loses his
queen) 18 ♗xh6! f5 (18...gh 19
♖e4 ♕a5 20 ♖g4+ ♔h8 21 ♕d2!
is bad for Black) 19 ef ♗xf6 20
♗c1 ♘e7 21 ♗a3 ♖d8 22 ♗h7+

♔f8 23 ♘e5 ♗xe5 24 ♗xe7+
♔xe7 25 ♖xb7+ ♗xb7 26 ♕xa4
1-0

No. 212 Smyslov-Florian
USSR-Hungary, Budapest 1949
Grünfeld Defence

1 d4 ♘f6 2 c4 g6 3 ♘c3 d5 4 ♘f3
♗g7 5 ♕b3 dc 7 ♕xc4 0-0 7 e4
♘a6 8 ♗e2 c5 9 d5 e6 10 0-0 ed 11
ed ♕a5?! 12 a3 ♗f5 13 ♕h4 ♖fe8
14 ♗h6 ♘e4 15 ♗xg7 ♔xg7 16
♘g5! ♘xc3 17 ♕xh7+ ♔f6 18 bc
♔xg5 19 ♕g7!! ♖e4 20 f4+ ♖xf4
21 ♖xf4 ♔xf4 22 ♖f1+ ♔e3 23
♕e5+ ♔d2 24 ♗c4 ♕xa3 25 ♖f2+
1-0

It should be mentioned that
the procedure of transferring the
attack from the centre to the K-
side does not usually depend on
the form of central superiority.

Here is an example with a typical central wedge at e5.

No. 213 Suetin-Ujtelky
Copenhagen, 1965
Pirc Defence

1 e4 g6 2 d4 ♗g7 3 c3 d6 4 f4
♘f6 5 e5! ♘d5 6 ♘f3 0-0 (6...de 7
fe c5!) 7 ♗c4 c6

Black wrongly refrains from
countering in the centre, and as a
result his position becomes
quite unpromising.

8 0-0 a5 9 a4 ♘a6 10 ♘a3 ♘c7
11 ♕e2 h6?

Not only a loss of time, but also a significant weakening of the castled position, which conclusively determines White's subsequent plan of attack.

12 ♗d3! e6 13 ♗d2 ♕e7 14 ♕f2 ♖d8 15 ♘c4 ♘e8 16 g4! *(90)*

90

With his central superiority, White can confidently begin a pawn storm. Black's position is strategically lost.

16...de 17 ♘fxe5 ♘d6 18 ♖ae1 ♕c7 19 ♘xd6 ♖xd6 20 h4! ♘e7 21 h5 gh 22 gh ♕d8 23 ♔h2 f6 24 ♖g1 ♕e8 (after 24...fe 25 fe ♖d7 26 ♖xg7+! ♔xg7 27 ♕f6+ ♔g8 28 ♖g1+ Black is crushed) **25 ♕h4 ♘f5 26 ♗xf5 ef 27 ♖g6 ♔h7 28 ♕g3 ♗f8 29 ♖g1 ♗e6 30 ♖g7+ ♔h8 31 ♖g8+! 1-0**

No. 214 Gipslis-Kostro
Dubna, 1976
Spanish Game

1 e4 e5 2 ♘f3 ♘c6 3 ♗b5 a6 4 ♗a4 ♘f6 5 d4 ed 6 0-0 d6 7 ♘xd4 ♗d7 8 ♗xc6 bc 9 ♘c3 ♗e7 10 ♗f4

0-0 11 e5! ♘e8 12 ♖e1 d5 13 ♘b3 a5 14 ♘a4 f6 15 e6! ♗c8 16 ♘d4 ♗b7 17 ♖e3 c5 18 ♘f5 d4 19 ♖g3 ♔h8

Black's position is completely hopeless. White also wins after 19...♗e4 20 ♘h6+ ♔h8 21 ♘f7+ ♖xf7 22 ef ♘d6 23 ♘xc5

20 ♕h5! ♕d5 21 ♕xh7+! 1-0

Examples with a strong central isolated pawn are also of interest.

No. 215 Botvinnik-Vidmar
Nottingham, 1936
Queen's Gambit

1 c4 e6 2 ♘f3 d5 3 d4 ♘f6 4 ♘c3 ♗e7 5 ♗g5 0-0 6 e3 ♘bd7 7 ♗d3 c5 8 0-0 cd (8...dc 9 ♗xc4 a6 is more flexible) **9 ed dc 10 ♗xc4 ♘b6 11 ♗b3 ♗d7 12 ♕d3 ♘bd5** (12...♘fd5!) **13 ♘e5 ♗c6 14 ♖ad1 ♘b4 15 ♕h3 ♗d5 16 ♘xd5 ♘bxd5** *(91)*

91

17 f4! ♖c8 18 f5! ef 19 ♖xf5 ♕d6

Black's position is already

barely defensible, as the following variations show: 19. . . ☐c7 20 ☐df1 a6 or (20. . .♘b6 21 ♕h4 ♘bd5 22 ♘xf7 ☐xf7 23 ♗xd5 ♘xd5 24 ☐xf7 ♗xg5 25 ♕xg5!! etc) 21 ♘xf7 ☐xf7 22 ♗xd5 ♘xd5 23 ☐xf7 ♗xg5 24 ♕e6!

20 ♘xf7! ☐xf7 21 ♗xf6 ♗xf6 22 ☐xd5 ♕c6 23 ☐d6! ♕e8 24 ☐d7 1-0

No. 216 Spassky-Avtonomov
Leningrad, 1949
Queen's Gambit

1 d4 d5 2 c4 dc 3 ♘f3 ♘f6 4 e3 c5 5 ♗xc4 e6 6 0-0 a6 7 ♕e2 b5 8 ♗b3 ♘c6 9 ♘c3 cd (premature; 9. . .♗b7 is preferable) **10 ☐d1 ♗b7** (10. . .♗e7) **11 ed ♘b4 12 d5! ♘bxd5 13 ♗g5 ♗e7 14 ♗xf6! gf** (14. . .♗xf6 15 ♘xd5) **15 ♘xd5 ♗xd5 16 ♗xd5 ed 17 ♘d4 ♔f8 18 ♘f5 h5 19 ☐xd5! ♕xd5 20 ♕xe7+ ♔g8 21 ♕xf6 1-0**

No. 217 Keene-Miles
Hastings, 1975/76
Queen's Gambit

1 ♘f3 ♘f6 2 c4 c5 3 ♘c3 ♘c6 4 e3 e5 5 d4 d5 6 cd ♘xd5 7 ♗d3 cd 8 ed ♗e7 9 0-0 0-0 10 ☐e1 ♘f6 11 ♗g5 ♘b4?! 12 ♗b1 b6 13 ♘e5 ♗b7 14 ☐e3!! g6 15 ☐g3 ☐c8? 16 ♗h6 ☐e8 17 a3 ♘c6 18 ♘xg6! hg 19 ♗xg6 fg 20 ♕b1! ♘e5 21 de ♘e4 22 ♘xe4 ♔h7 23 ♘f6+ ♗xf6

24 ♕xg6+ ♔h8 25 ♗g7+ ♗xg7 26 ♕xg7 mate.

In the examples given below there occurred a sudden, dynamic opening up of the centre.

No. 218 Suetin-Lyuboshits
Tallinn, 1956
Spanish Game

1 e4 e5 2 ♘f3 ♘c6 3 ♗b5 a6 4 ♗a4 ♘f6 5 0-0 ♗e7 6 ☐e1 b5 7 ♗b3 d6 8 c3 0-0 9 h3 ♘a5 10 ♗c2 c5 11 d4 ♕c7 12 ♘bd2 ♗d7 13 ♘f1 ☐ad8? 14 ♘e3 g6 (92)

15 b4! cb 16 cb ♘c6 17 a3 ☐fe8 18 ♗b2 ♗f8 19 ♘d5 ♘xd5 20 ed ♘e7 21 de ♘xd5 22 e6! 1-0

No. 219 Suetin-Mikenas
Moscow, 1958
Spanish Game

1 e4 e5 2 ♘f3 ♘c6 3 ♗b5 a6 4 ♗a4 ♘f6 5 0-0 ♗e7 6 ☐e1 b5 7 ♗b3 d6 8 c3 0-0 9 h3 ♘a5 10 ♗c2 c5 11 d4 ♕c7 12 b4!? cb 13 cb ♘c6

(13...♘c4) **14 ♗b2 ♘xb4 15 ♗b3 ♘c6 16 ♘c3 ed?** (16...♘a5 17 ♘d5 ♘xd5 18 ♗xd5 ♗b7 was comparatively best) **17 ♘xd4 ♘xd4 18 ♕xd4 ♕a7** (better 18...♗b7) **19 ♘d5 ♗d8** (19...♕xd4? 20 ♘xe7+ or 19...♘xd5 20 ♕xg7 mate!) **20 ♕d3! ♘e8 21 e5! de 22 ♖xe5 ♗e6 23 ♖ae1! ♘f6 24 ♘xf6+ ♗xf6 25 ♖h5 g6 26 ♗xf6 ♗xb3 27 ab ♕b6 28 ♕f3 1-0**

No. 220 Kapengut-Smirnov
Minsk, 1977
Spanish Game

1 e4 e5 2 ♘f3 ♘c6 3 ♗b5 a6 4 ♗a4 ♘f6 5 0-0 ♘xe4 6 d4 ♗e7?! 7 ♖e1 f5(?)

Better is 7...b5 8 ♖xe4 d5 9 ♗xb5 ab 10 ♖xe5 0-0 with a position analogous to the Marshall Attack (Kondratiev-Suetin, Kiev, 1965).

8 d5 ♘b8 9 ♘xe5 0-0 10 d6! ♗xd6

After 10...♘xd6 11 ♗b3+ ♔h8 12 ♕h5 ♕e8 13 ♕xe8 ♖xe8 14 ♘f7+ ♘xf7 15 ♗xf7 ♖f8 16 ♖xe7 ♘c6 17 ♖e8 White wins.

11 ♕d5+ ♔h8 12 ♘f7+ ♖xf7 13 ♕xf7 ♗xh2+ 14 ♔f1! d5 15 ♘c3 c6 16 ♗g5! ♕g8 17 ♕xg8+ ♔xg8 18 g3 ♘d7 19 ♗f4 ♘c5 20 ♗b3 g5 21 ♗e5 ♘xc3 22 ♗xc3 1-0

In the following examples the success of the attack on the king was determined by piece superiority in the centre.

No. 221 Furman-Spassky
USSR Ch., 1957
Sicilian Defence

1 ♘f3 c5 2 c4 g6 3 e4 ♗g7 4 d4 cd 5 ♘xd4 ♘c6 6 ♗e3 ♘h6 7 ♘c3 0-0 8 ♗e2 f5 9 ef ♗xd4!? 10 ♗xd4? (10 ♗xh6!) **10...♘xf5 11 ♗c5 d6 12 ♗a3 ♘fd4! 13 0-0 ♗f5 14 ♖c1** (better 14 ♗d3) **14...♕d7 15 ♘d5 ♖f7! 16 b3 ♖af8 17 ♗b2 e5 18 b4 ♗e6 19 ♗d3?** (better 19 b5) **19...♗g4 20 f3 ♗xf3! 21 gf ♘xf3+! 22 ♔h1 ♕h3 23 ♖f2 ♘e1!! 0-1**

No. 222 Smyslov-Rudakovsky
USSR Ch., 1945
Sicilian Defence

1 e4 c5 2 ♘f3 e6 3 d4 cd 4 ♘xd4 ♘f6 5 ♘c3 d6 6 ♗e2 ♗e7 7 0-0 0-0 8 ♗e3 ♘c6 9 f4 ♕c7 10 ♕e1 ♘xd4 11 ♗xd4 e5? 12 ♗e3 ♗e6? 13 f5 ♗c4?

After this White forces a strategically won position. Comparatively best was 13...♗d7 14 g4 ♗c6 15 ♗f3 d5!? 16 ed e4 17 ♘xe4 ♘xd5 18 ♗d4, although here too White has the advantage.

14 ♗xc4 ♕xc4 15 ♗g5! ♖fe8 16 ♗xf6 ♗xf6 17 ♘d5 ♗d8 18 c3 b5 19 b3 ♕c5+ 20 ♔h1 ♖c8 21 ♖f3 ♔h8 22 f6! gf (22...g6 23 ♕d2! and ♕h6!) **23 ♕h4 ♖g8 24 ♘xf6 ♖g7 25 ♖g3! ♗xf6** (White was threatening 26 ♕xh7+!, as well as 26 ♖×g7 ♔×g7 27 ♕×h7+ ♔×f6 28 ♖f1+ etc) 26 ♕×f6 ♖g8 27 ♖d1 d5 28 ♖×g7! 1-0

No. 223 Veröci-Lemachko
Roosendaal, 1976
Sicilian Defence

1 e4 c5 2 ♘f3 d6 3 d4 cd 4 ♘×d4 ♘f6 5 ♘c3 a6 6 f4 e5 7 ♘f3 ♘bd7 8 a4 b6? (8...♕c7) 9 ♗c4 ♗e7 10 0-0 0-0 11 ♕e2 ♗b7 12 fe de 13 ♗g5 h6 (13...♕c7) 14 ♗×f6! ♘×f6 15 ♖ad1 ♕c7 16 ♔h1 ♖fc8 17 ♗b3 ♗b4? 18 ♘h4! ♗×c3 19 ♖×f6! gf 20 ♘f5 ♗d4 21 ♕f4+ ♔f8 22 ♕g7+ ♔e8 23 ♕g8+ ♔d7 24 ♕×f7+ ♔d8 25 ♕f8+ 1-0

In the last two cases with a backward pawn in the centre; the success of the attack was aided by strong piece pressure on the centre (in No. 222 — the establishment of a knight at d5, and in No. 223 — the presence of a powerful light-square bishop) in combination with effective operations on the f-file. As a result of this combination, Black's castled position became a fruitful target of attack for White.

But this formation does not in itself guarantee the success of White's attack. Instructive in this respect is the following example, where one significant detail — Black's king had not yet castled! — sharply changed the assessment of this plan.

No. 224 Byrne-Fischer
Sousse IZ, 1967
Sicilian Defence

1 e4 c5 2 ♘f3 d6 3 d4 cd 4 ♘×d4 ♘f6 5 ♘c3 a6 6 ♗c4 e6 7 ♗b3 b5 8 f4 ♗b7 9 f5 e5 10 ♘de2 ♘bd7 11 ♗g5 (11 ♘g3!?) 11...♗e7 12 ♘g3? (correct was 12 ♗×f6! ♘×f6 13 ♕d3 with equal chances) 12... ♖c8 13 0-0 h5 14 h4 b4! 15 ♗×f6 ♗×f6 16 ♘d5 ♗×h4 17 ♘×h5 ♕g5 18 f6 g6! 19 ♘g7+ ♔d8 20 ♖f3 ♗g3 21 ♕d3 ♗h2+ 22 ♔f1 ♘c5 23 ♖h3 ♖h4! 24 ♕f3 ♘×b3! 25 ab ♖×h3 26 ♕×h3 ♗×d5 27 ed ♕×f6+ 28 ♔e1 ♕f4 0-1

Switching the attack to the Q-side

Instances of attacks not directed against the king are fairly common, as for example in the Scheveningen Variation of the Sicilian Defence, if Black tries too early for Q-side activity by ...b5.

No. 225 Smyslov-Kottnauer
Groningen, 1946
Sicilian Defence

1 e4 c5 2 ♘f3 d6 3 d4 cd 4 ♘×d4 ♘f6 5 ♘c3 a6 6 ♗e2 e6 7 0-0 b5?
This Q-side pawn offensive is premature, as it is not supported

by the pieces, and it can prove successful only if White plays passively. But White has available a concrete and very effective way of refuting his opponent's plan, involving a determined counter-offensive on the Q-side and in the centre.

8 ♘f3 ♖a7 9 ♕e2! ♖c7 10 ♖d1 ♘bd7 11 a4! ba 12 ♘xa4 ♗b7 *(93)*

93

In a few moves White destroys the opponent's Q-side and gains a decisive advantage.

13 e5! ♘xe5 14 ♗xb7 ♖xb7 15 ♕xa6 ♕b8 16 ♘c6!

Events develop by force.

16...♘xc6 17 ♕xc6+ ♘d7 18 ♘c5!

The concluding combinational blow. If 18...♖c7 there follows 19 ♘xd7 ♖xd7 20 ♖a8.

18...dc 19 ♗f4! ♗d6 (White also wins after 19...♕xf4 20 ♕c8+ ♔e7 21 ♕xb7 ♔f6 22 ♖xd7 ♔g6 23 g3 ♕f5 24 ♖a7 etc) 20 ♗xd6 ♖b6 21 ♕xd7+ 1-0

Here Black's crushing tactical defeat resulted from his over-

confidence in the opening (8...b5?)

In the majority of cases the switching of the attack to the Q-side is assisted by the presence of weak squares in the defending side's position. Here events do not develop so forcibly, but the defensive problems are no easier.

No. 226 Rubinstein-Salwe
Lodz, 1908
Queen's Gambit

1 d4 d5 2 c4 e6 3 ♘c3 c5 4 cd ed 5 ♘f3 ♘f6 6 g3 ♘c6 7 ♗g2 cd(?) 8 ♘xd4 ♕b6 9 ♘xc6! bc 10 0-0 ♗e7 11 ♘a4

After achieving an early piece superiority in the centre, White quickly (and quite correctly) transfers the weight of the offensive to the Q-side. Black's c-pawn is now weak, and the c5 square becomes a strong outpost for White. It is on this that White builds his plan, which he carries out with exceptional accuracy.

11...♕b5 12 ♗e3 0-0 13 ♖c1 ♗g4 14 f3 ♗e6 15 ♗c5 ♖fe8 16 ♖f2 ♘d7 17 ♗xe7 ♖xe7 18 ♕d4 ♖7e8 19 ♗f1 ♖ec8 20 e3 ♕b7 21 ♘c5 ♘xc5 22 ♖xc5 ♖c7 23 ♖fc2 ♕b6 24 b4 a6 25 ♖a5 ♖b8 26 a3 ♖a7 27 ♖xc6! ♕xc6 28 ♕xa7

As a result of the 'overloading' of Black's defences, he has had to part with a pawn. The game is decided.

28. ...♖a8 29 ♕c5 ♕b7 30 ♔f2
h5 31 ♗e2 g6 32 ♕d6 ♕c8 23 ♖c5
♕b7 34 h4 a5 35 ♖c7 ♕b8 36 b5 a4
37 b6 ♖a5 38 b7 1-0

No. 227 Pillsbury-Mason
Hastings, 1895
Queen's Gambit

1 d4 d5 2 c4 e6 3 ♘c3 ♘f6 4 ♗g5
♗e7 5 ♘f3 b6 6 e3 ♗b7 7 ♖c1
dc(?) 8 ♗xc4 ♘bd7 9 0-0 0-0 10
♕e2 ♘d5 11 ♗xe7 ♕xe7 12
♘xd5 ed 13 ♗b5! ♕d6 14 ♖c2 c6
15 ♗d3 ♘f6

Here too the vulnerable point
in Black's position is his c6 pawn.
At the same time, the attempt to
advance it by 15. . .c5 16 dc bc 17
♗f5! leads to the creation of new
weaknesses.

16 ♖fc1 ♖ac8 17 ♗a6! *(94)*

A typical procedure. By exchanging the black bishop, the
chief defender of the c6 pawn,
White soon gains a decisive
advantage.

17. ...♗xa6 18 ♕xa6 ♖c7 19
♘e5! c5 20 ♖xc5! ♖xc5 21 ♖xc5
♘d7 22 ♖c6 ♘b8 23 ♖xd6 ♘xa6
24 ♘c6 g6 25 ♘xa7 ♖a8 26 ♘c6
1-0

No. 228 Suetin-Kamyshov
Tbilisi, 1951
Spanish Game

1 e4 e5 2 ♘f3 ♘c6 3 ♗b5 a6 4
♗a4 ♘f6 5 0-0 ♗e7 6 ♖e1 b5 7
♗b3 0-0 8 c3 d6 9 h3 ♘a5 10 ♗c2
c5 11 d4 ♕c7 12 ♘bd2 ♘c6 13 dc
dc 14 ♘f1 ♗e6 15 ♘e3 ♖ad8 16
♕e2 g6 (16. . .c4 is more active)
17 ♘g5 ♗c8 18 a4 c4 19 ab ab 20
b3! ♘a5 21 bc bc 22 ♗a3

The start of a lengthy offensive on the Q-side, the main target of which ultimately becomes
the c4 pawn.

22. ...♖fe8 23 ♗xe7 ♖xe7 24
♖ed1 ♖ed7 25 ♖xd7 ♖xd7

An interesting situation. In
defending his Q-side, Black must
also concern himself over his K-
side. Thus on 25. . .♗xd7 there
would have followed 26 ♕f3 ♔g7
27 ♘xf7! ♔xf7 28 ♘d5!, when
White wins.

26 ♖a4! ♗a6 27 ♕f1! ♗b5 28
♖b4 ♕c5 29 ♕b1 ♖b7 30 ♗a4
♗a6 31 ♘f3! (the knight aims for
d2, to attack the c4 pawn) 31. . .
♕d6 32 ♗b5! ♗xb5 33 ♖xb5 ♕c6
34 ♖xb7 ♘xb7 35 ♘xe5 ♕xe4 36
♕b5!

The decisive manœuvre. Loss

of material for Black is now inevitable.

36...♘d6 37 ♕b8+ ♘de8 38 ♘5xc4 ♕d3 39 ♕e5 ♕b1+ 40 ♔h2 ♔f8 41 ♘d6 ♕b8 42 ♘xf7 ♕b2 43 ♘d6 ♕xf2 44 ♘d5! ♘xd5 45 ♕xe8+ ♔g7 46 ♕e5+ 1-0

The preparation of pawn breaks

In closed positions with pawn chains, great importance is assumed by the organization of pawn breaks on the main sector of the chess front. Of course, such breaks usually occur deep into the middlegame, but right from the opening a serious foundation must be laid for them. An example of this is provided by a number of games arising in a sharp line of the King's Indian Defence: 1 d4 ♘f6 2 c4 g6 3 ♘c3 ♗g7 4 e4 d6 5 ♘f3 0-0 6 ♗e2 e5 7 0-0 ♘c6 8 d5 ♘e7 (95)

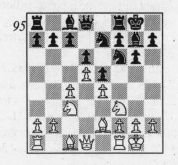

95

In this position White exploits his spatial advantage to begin active play on the Q-side (which in addition he has blocked with gain of tempo!), for which he has several ways of quickly concentrating his forces and preparing to open up the game on this part of the board. But Black too has very real possibilities of beginning a pawn storm on the K-side.

Although the plans of the two sides are largely determined, the intensity of the struggle grows with every move. The subsequent play is very lively and sometimes forcing, and exceptional accuracy is demanded. The difficulty of the problems facing the two sides is due to the necessity for a skilful combining of attack with economical defence. On no account should a player go entirely onto the defensive; the only thing that can save him here is the organization of an attacking breakthrough.

Practice shows that the play in this variation proceeds with alternating success, the player who wins usually being the one who is the first to organize an effective breakthrough. And it should also be mentioned that, although initially the Q-side offensive develops more easily, the consequences of Black's counter-offensive on the K-side can be more dangerous.

We give some examples of this variation, which resemble a race with different finishes (from Diag. 95).

No. 229 Taimanov-Aronin
USSR Ch., 1952

9 ♘e1 ♘d7 10 ♗e3 f5 11 f3 h5? 12 ♘d3 d4 13 ♗f2 g5 14 c5 ♘f6 15 ♖c1 g4 16 ♕b3! ♗h6 17 cd cd 18 ♘xe5! g3 19 ♗e1 de 20 d6+ ♔h8 21 de ♕xe7 22 ♘b5 ♗e6 23 ♗b4 ♕f7 24 ♕c3 gh+ 25 ♔h1 ♖g8 26 ♕xe5 ♕g6 27 ♖f2, and White had a significant advantage.

No. 230 Taimanov-Najdorf
Zurich C, 1953

9 ♘e1 ♘d7 10 ♗e3 f5 11 f3 f4 12 ♗f2 g5 13 ♘d3 ♘f6 14 c5 ♘g6 15 ♖c1 ♖f7!

Black switches his rook to the 7th rank, where it joins the attack on the K-side and assists in the defence of the important c7 square. Simultaneously f8 is vacated for the bishop.

16 ♖c2 ♗f8 17 cd cd 18 ♕d2 g4 19 ♖fc1 g3!, and by this pawn sacrifice Black firmly seized the initiative, which here is very important.

No. 231 Taimanov-Ciocaltea
Moscow, 1956

9 b4 a5?!

Better is 9. . .♘h5 10 g3 f5 with the aim of carrying out his plan as quickly as possible. Here Black merely helps White to open lines on the Q-side.

10 ♗a3! ♘h5 11 g3 f5 12 ♘g5!

A good idea, forcing the exchange of Black's light-square bishop, and thereby weakening his attack on the K-side.

12. . .♘f6 13 c5! h6 14 cd cd 15 ♘e6 ♗xe6 16 de fe 17 ba ♘f5 18 ♘b5 d5 19 ♗xf8 ♗xf8 20 ♖c1 ♖xa5 21 ♕b3 b6 22 ♕b2. White has retained the advantage.

No. 232 Vaganian-Vukić
Odessa, 1975

9 ♘d2 c5?! 10 dc! bc 11 b4 ♘e8? (11. . .d5!?) 12 ♘b3 f5 13 ♗a3 fe 14 ♘xe4 ♗f5 15 ♘g3 ♗e6 16 ♖c1 ♔h8 17 ♘e4 ♖f4?! 18 f3 ♗g8 19 ♕d2 ♗h6 20 ♕c3 ♗g7 21 ♖fd1 d5 22 b5! d4 23 ♕a5! ♕d7 24 ♘bc5 ♕c8 25 ♘d3 ♖f7 26 ♘g5 (Black is clearly losing) 26. . .♗f6 27 ♘xf7+ ♗xf7 28 bc ♕e6 29 c7 ♖c8 30 ♖b1! ♖xc7 31 ♖b8 ♖c6 32 ♘c5 ♕d6 33 ♖d8 ♕c7 34 ♕xc7 ♖xc7 35 ♖b1 1-0

The forms of pawn breaks can be very varied. In modern play they are becoming more and more tactical, and sometimes involve a pawn sacrifice as early as the transition stage from opening to middlegame.

In this respect the development of the following game is instructive.

No. 233 Tal-Hecht
Varna OL, 1962
Queen's Indian Defence

1 d4 ♘f6 2 c4 e6 3 ♘f3 b6 4 ♘c3 ♗b4 5 ♗g5 ♗b7 6 e3 h6 7 ♗h4 ♗xc3+ 8 bc d6 9 ♘d2

The alternative is 9 ♗d3 g5 10 ♗g3 ♘e4 11 ♕c2 f5, where again there is the possibility of a pawn break in the centre, introduced by Keres: 12 d5! ed 13 cd ♗xd5 13 ♘d4 ♕f6 15 f3 etc., with the initiative for White.

9...e5 10 f3 ♕e7 11 e4 ♘bd7 12 ♗d3 ♘f8 13 c5! *(96)*

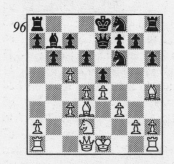

By this move White sharply activates his pieces, e.g. 13...bc 14 ♖b1, and it is dangerous for Black to castle long.

13...dc 14 de ♕xe5 15 ♕a4+ c6 (15...♘8d7 is somewhat better) **16 0-0 ♘g6**

It is dangerous to play 16... ♕xc3 17 ♘c4 ♕xd3 (17...b5 18

♘d6+ ♔d7 19 ♘xb5! favours White) 18 ♖fd1 b5 19 ♖xd3 ba 20 ♘d6+ ♔e7 21 ♘f5+ ♔e8 22 ♘xg7+ ♔e7 23 ♘f5+, when White wins.

17 ♘c4 ♕e6 18 e5! b5 19 ef! ba 20 fg ♖g8 21 ♗f5!

White's splendid positional queen sacrifice on move 19 involved some highly interesting combinational variations. Thus bad is 21...♕xc4 22 ♖fe1+ ♔e6 23 ♖xe6+ fe 24 ♗xg6+ ♔d7 25 ♖d1+ ♔c7 26 ♗g3+ ♔b6 27 ♖b1+ ♔a6 28 ♗d3+ ♔a5 29 ♗c7 mate, or 21...♕xf5 22 ♘d6+ ♔d7 23 ♘xf5 etc., when White wins.

21...♘xh4 22 ♗xe6 ♗a6 23 ♘d6+ ♔e7 24 ♗c4 ♖xg7 25 g3 ♔xd6 26 ♗xa6

The result is a dynamic situation, where Black is a pawn up, but White has strong piece play and the initiative, factors which give him the advantage.

26...♘f5 27 ♖ab1! f6 28 ♖fd1+ ♔e7 29 ♖e1+ ♔d6 30 ♔f2 c4 31 g4 ♘e7 32 ♖b7! ♖ag8 33 ♗xc4 ♘d5 34 ♗xd5 cd 35 ♖b4 ♖c8 36 ♖xa4 ♖xc3 37 ♖a6+ ♔c5 38 ♖xf6 h5 39 h3 hg 40 hg ♖h7 41 g5 ♖h5 42 ♖f5! ♖c2+ 43 ♔g3 ♔c4 44 ♖ee5! d4 45 g6 ♖h1 46 ♖c5+ ♔d3 47 ♖xc2 ♔xc2 48 ♔f4 ♖g1 49 ♖g5 1-0

Pawn storms on opposite flanks

As a result of castling on opposite sides, mutual attacks on the king can arise quite regularly in the opening. In many cases the strategic picture is similar to that in the examples from the preceding section. Both there, and here, a game is often decided by pawn breaks.

The beauty of the struggle in the event of mutual pawn storms is shown by the following game.

No. 234
Nezhmetdinov-Taimanov
Baku, 1951
Sicilian Defence

1 e4 c5 2 ᐃf3 ᐃc6 3 d4 cd 4 ᐃ×d4 ᐃf6 5 ᐃc3 d6 6 ᐃg5 e6 7 ₩d2 ᐃe7 8 0-0-0 0-0 9 ᐃb3 ₩b6 10 ᐃe3 ₩c7 11 f3 a6 12 g4 b5 13 g5 ᐃd7 14 f4 ᐃc5 15 ₩f2 ᐃb8 16 h4 ᐃa4! 17 ᐃd2 ᐃ×c3 18 ᐃ×c3 b4 19 ᐃd2 a5 20 ₩b1 a4! 21 ᐃc1 ᐃd7 22 ᐃd3 ᐃfc8 23 h5 ᐃa5 24 f5 ᐃc4 25 f6 ᐃf8 26 g6 ₩c5! *(97)*

The culmination of the strategic struggle. White's pawn storm is slightly ahead of the opponent's, which should have given him the advantage. This could have been achieved by 27 ₩g2! a3 28 gh+ ᐘh8 29 ᐃ×c4 ₩×c4 (29...₩d4 30 ᐃc3!)

30 ᐃh6!, with an irresistible attack.

97

But White failed to find this continuation, and played differently.

27 gh+? ᐘh8 28 ₩×c5 ᐃ×c5 29 ᐃf4 gf 30 ᐃe2 ᐃe5 31 ᐃe3 ᐃcc8 32 ᐃhg1 ᐘ×h7 33 h6 b3!

The initiative has passed to Black, which in such situations decides the outcome.

34 cb ab 35 a3 ᐃ×d3 36 ᐃ×d3 ᐃb5 37 ᐃd2 ᐃc2, and Black gained a decisive advantage.

We give a few further examples on this theme.

No. 235 Keres-Alexander
Hastings, 1954/55
Petroff's Defence

1 e4 e5 2 ᐃf3 ᐃf6 3 ᐃ×e5 d6 4 ᐃf3 ᐃ×e4 5 d4 d5 6 ᐃd3 ᐃe7 7 0-0 ᐃc6 8 ᐃe1 ᐃg4 9 c3 ᐃf6? (9...f5) 10 ᐃg5 ₩d7 11 ᐃbd2 0-0-0? (11...0-0) 12 ₩a4 h6 13 ᐃh4 g5 14 ᐃg3 ᐃ×f3 15 ᐃ×f3 g4 16 ᐃe5! ᐃ×e5 17 ᐃf5!! ₩×f5 18

罝xe5 ♕d3 (White also wins after
18...♕d7 19 ♕xa7 ♕d6 20 c4!
♘d7 21 c5 ♕xc5 22 dc ♕xc5 23
♕a8+ ♔d7 24 ♕xb7) 19 罝xe7
罝d7 20 罝e3! ♕a6 21 ♕xa6 ba 22
♗e5 1-0

No. 236 Nadezhdin-Boleslavsky
Tashkent, 1965
Sicilian Defence

1 e4 c5 2 ♘f3 ♘c6 3 d4 cd
4 ♘xd4 ♘f6 5 ♘c3 d6 6 ♘g5 e6
7 ♕d2 a6 8 0-0-0 h6 9 ♗f4 ♗d7 10
♗g3 ♗e7 11 ♗e2 ♘xd4 12 ♕xd4
e5 13 ♕d3 ♕c7 14 f4 0-0 15 f5(?)
♗c6 16 ♗f2 罝fc8 17 h4 b5 18 罝d2
♕a5 19 a3 b4 20 ♘d5 ♗xd5 21 ed
罝c3! 0-1

No. 237 Yuferov-Grozdov
Lvov, 1966
Sicilian Defence

1 e4 c5 2 ♘c3 ♘c6 3 ♘ge2 g6
4 d4 cd 5 ♘xd4 ♗g7 6 ♗e3 ♘f6
7 ♗c4 0-0 8 ♗b3 d6 9 f3 ♗d7 10
♕d2 ♕b8 11 h4 罝c8 12 0-0-0 b5?
(better 12...a5 with the threat of
...a4) 13 h5! ♘a5 14 hg ♘xb3+
15 ♘xb3 hg 16 ♗h6 ♗h8 17 ♗f8!
罝xf8 18 罝xh8+! ♔xh8 19 ♕h6+
♔g8 20 ♘d5! 1-0

No. 238 Kupreichik-Mukhin
Kirovabad, 1973
Sicilian Defence

1 e4 c5 2 ♘f3 d6 3 d4 cd 4 ♘xd4

♘f6 5 ♘c3 a6 6 ♗c4 e6 7 ♗b3 ♘c6
8 ♗e3 ♗e7 9 f4 0-0 10 ♕f3 ♘d7?!
11 g4 ♘c5 12 0-0-0 ♗d7 13 g5 b5
14 ♔b1 ♘xb3 15 ab ♘xd4 16
♗xd4 b4! 17 ♘a4 罝b8? (17...
♕c7 followed by...e5 was correct) 18 罝hg1 ♗c6 19 罝d3! ♕c7
20 f5! ef 21 ♕h5! 罝fc8 22 罝h3 ♔f8
23 g6! fg 24 ♕xh7 罝xe4 25 ♕xg6
♗h4 26 ♘c5 dc 27 ♗xg7+ ♔e7 28
罝xh4 ♕d6 29 ♗f8+ 1-0

As can be seen, in such cases
the struggle develops very
quickly and at times dramati-
cally. The player who wins is the
first who manages to organise a
decisive storm. Here sharpness
and energy in attack must be
combined with prophylactic
measures in defending one's
own king.

During the transition from
opening to middlegame, such a
plan sometimes demands considerable flexibility of thought,
as the following example
demonstrates.

No. 239 Botvinnik-Alatortsev
Leningrad, 1934
Queen's Gambit

1 d4 e6 2 c4 d5 3 ♘f3 ♗e7 4 ♘c3
♘f6 5 ♗g5 0-0 6 e3 a6 (better
6...♘bd7 or 6...c6) 7 cd ed
8 ♗d3 c6? (8...♘bd7 9 ♕c2 罝e8
followed by...♘f8 is correct)
9 ♕c2 ♘bd7

White has available a highly

promising plan: a K-side pawn storm in combination with Q-side castling. But with what should he begin? Does he have a strong move, which will immediately set Black difficult problems?

The answer to these questions was provided by White's next move.

10 g4!

Much more energetic than 10 h3 or 10 0-0-0. Now there is the immediate threat of 11 ♗xf6 ♘xf6 12 g5!, winning the h7 pawn, and in the event of 10. . . h6 11 ♗f4! ♘xg4 12 ♖g1 White has a very strong attack; on 12. . . ♘gf6 there follows 13 ♗xh6. The most tenacious defence was probably 10. . .g6, although even then after 11 h3 White has clearly the better chances.

Black however, lost his head, and chose the weakest continuation.

10. . .♘xg4? **11 ♗xh7+ ♔h8 12 ♗f4 ♘df6 13 ♗d3 ♘h5 14 h3! ♘gf6 15 ♗e5 ♘g8 16 0-0-0 ♘h6 17 ♖dg1 ♗e6 18 ♕e2 ♗f5 19 ♗xf5 ♘xf5 20 ♘h4! 1-0**

Incidentally, this type of temporary pawn sacrifice, where a storming pawn move is made without preparation, is typical in many situations. Here is a further example.

No. 240 Petrosian-Estrin
Moscow, 1968
English Opening

1 c4 e5 2 g3 ♘c6 3 ♗g2 d6 4 ♘c3 ♗e6 5 d3 g6 6 b4! ♕d7 (6. . .♘xb4 7 ♖b1 a5 8 a3 ♘c6 9 ♖xb7 favours White) **7 b5 ♘d8 8 ♘f3 ♗g7 9 ♘g5! e4 10 ♗b2 ed 11 ♕xd3 a6 12 h4! ab 13 cb ♘e7 14 ♕d2 0-0 15 h5**

Having gained superiority on the K-side, White switches to a decisive attack on this wing.

15. . .gh 16 ♖xh5 ♗f5 17 ♗e4 ♗g6 18 ♖xh7! ♗xh7 19 ♗xh7+ ♔h8 20 0-0-0 ♘g8 21 ♖h1 ♘h6 22 ♘d5 f6 23 ♘e4 ♖xa2 24 ♖xh6! ♗xh6 25 ♕xh6 ♕g7 26 ♕h4! 1-0

An attack on the king is always the No. 1 threat

As we have seen, during the transition from opening to middlegame the attack on the king has various standard forms, the number of which can probably be multiplied.

It should be remembered that the threat of an attack is always hanging over the king, especially if it is caught in the centre, and in this respect the following examples are instructive.

In the first of these (No. 241) Black appeared to have successfully completed his development in the opening. But instead of castling as soon as possible (which, incidentally, is the insistent recommendation of theory) he prematurely and inappropriately initiated counterplay in the centre. His 'wish' was carried out – the centre was opened. But the consequences of this proved dismal for Black: he provoked an attack on his own king.

In the second game (No. 242) Black again largely overcame his opening difficulties. But when he needed to stabilize the position in the centre – 19. . . e5, he made a tactical oversight (19. . . h6?), overlooking the crushing tactical stroke 20 ☐×e6+, after which his king came under an irresistible attack.

No. 241 Kupreichik-Castalloni
Student Olympiad, Ybbs, 1968
Caro-Kann Defence

1 e4 c6 2 d4 d5 3 ②c3 de 4 ②×e4 ♗f5 5 ②g3 ♗g6 6 h4 h6 7 ②f3 ②d7 8 h5 ♗h7 9 ♗d3 ♗×d3 10 ♕×d3

98

♕c7 11 ♗d2 ♗gf6 12 ♕e2 e6 13 0-0-0 c5?! 14 ♔b1 cd? *(98)*

Prematurely opening up the game. He should have castled.

15 ②×d4 a6 16 ②×e6! fe 17 ♕×e6+ ♔d8 18 ☐he1 ☐c8 19 ♗c3 ♕c6 20 ♗×f6+ gf 21 ☐×d7+! ♕×d7 22 ♕b6+! ♕c7 23 ♕×f6+ ♔d7 24 ♕e6+! 1-0

No. 242 Suetin-Hulak
Ljublin, 1976
Sicilian Defence

1 e4 c5 2 ②f3 e6 3 d4 cd 4 ②×d4 ②c6 5 ②c3 d6 6 g3 ♗e7 7 ♗g2 a6 8 0-0 ♗d7 9 ②×c6 ♗×c6 10 ♕g4 g6 11 ♕e2 ♕c7 12 a4 ②f6 13 ♗h6 ♗f8 14 ♕d2 ☐d8 15 ☐fe1 ♗×h6 16 ♕×h6 ♕b6 17 ♕g5 ②d7 18 ②d5 ♗×d5 19 ed h6? 20 ☐×e6+ ♔f8 (Black is crushed after 20. . . fe 21 ♕×g6+ ♔f8 22 de or 20. . .♔e7 21 ♕g7+) 21 ♕e7+ ♔g7 22 ♗e4 1-0

In games 243, 244 and 245 the main target again becomes the king in the centre, a noteworthy feature of the first two being the combining of an attack on the king with play against a weak complex of dark squares in the opponent's position.

In No. 247 there is a dashing piece attack on the black king, while in No. 248, although the king manages to castle, even there it is caught by the white piece offensive.

No. 243 Alekhine-Bogoljubow
World Championship, 1929
Slav Defence

1 d4 d5 2 c4 c6 3 ᐩf3 ᐩf6 4 ᐩc3
dc 5 a4 e6 6 e4 ♗b4 7 e5! ᐩd5 8
♗d2 ♗xc3? (better 8...b5) 9 bc
b5 10 ᐩg5! f6 11 ef ᐩxf6 12 ♗e2
a6 13 ♗f3! h6 14 ♗h5+! ᐩxh5 15
♕xh5+ ♔d7 (99)

16 ᐩf7 ♕e8 17 ♕g6! ♖g8 18
♗f4 ♗b7 19 ♗g3 ♔e7 20 ♗d6+
♔d7 21 0-0 c5 22 dc ♗d5 23 ab! ab
24 ♖xa8 ♗xa8 25 ♖a1 ᐩc6 26
ᐩe5+! 1-0

No. 244 Suetin-V. Chistyakov
USSR, 1947
French Defence

1 e4 e6 2 d4 d5 3 ᐩc3 ᐩf6 4
♗g5 ♗b4 5 e5 h6 6 ♗d2 ♗xc3 7 bc
ᐩe4 8 ♕g4 g6 9 ♗c1 c5 10 ♗d3
ᐩxc3 11 dc ᐩc6? (11...♕a5!) 12
ᐩf3 ♕a5 13 0-0 ♕xc5 14 a4 a5 15
♕f4! ᐩb4 16 ♕f6 ♖h7 17 ♗xg6!
ᐩe4 (17...fg 18 ♕xg6+ ♖f7 19
♗xh6, and against the threats of

20 ♕g8+ and 20 ᐩg5 there is no
defence) 18 ♗xe4 de 19 ᐩd2!
♕xc2 20 ♕f4! ᐩd5 21 ♕g4! ♔f8
22 ᐩxe4 b6 23 ᐩf6! ᐩxf6 24
♗a3+ ♔e8 25 ef ♕g6 26 ♕f3! 1-0

No. 245 Balashov-Miles
Bugojno, 1978
Queen's Gambit Accepted

1 d4 d5 2 ᐩf3 ᐩf6 3 c4 dc 4 ᐩc3
a6 5 e4 b5 6 e5 ᐩd5 7 a4 ᐩxc3 8 bc
♕d5 9 g3 ♗e6 10 ♗g2 ♕b7 11 0-0
♗d5 12 e6 ♗xe6 13 ᐩg5 ♗d5 14
♗xd5 ♕xd5 15 ab ab 16 ♖xa8
♕xa8 17 ♕g4 ᐩc6 18 ♕f3 f6 19
ᐩe6 ♕b7 20 ♕d5 g5 21 ♗f4 ♗h6
22 ♖e1 ♕b6 23 ᐩxc7+ ♔f8 24
♖e6 gf 25 ♖xc6 ♕b8 26 ᐩe6+
♔e8 27 ♖c7 ♔f7 28 ᐩxf4+ ♔f8 29
♕c5 1-0

No. 246 Matanović-Kieninger
Hamburg, 1954
Petroff's Defence

1 e4 e5 2 ᐩf3 ᐩf6 3 d4 ed 4 e5
ᐩe4 5 ♕xd4 d5 6 ed ᐩxd6 7 ♗d3
ᐩc6 8 ♗f4 ♕e7+ 9 ♗e3 g6 10 ᐩc3
♗e6 11 0-0 ♗g7 12 ♖fe1 0-0
(12...0-0-0?! 13 ♕a4!) 13 ♗c5 b6
(13...♕d7 14 ♖ad1 ♖fd8 is somewhat better) 14 ♗a3 ♗xc3 15 bc
♕d7 16 ♖ad1 ᐩa5 17 ♕h6 f6

White should also win after
17...f5 (after 17...♗c4 18 ᐩe5!
or 17...♗xa2 18 ♗b5! he has an
obvious advantage) 18 ♗xd6 cd
19 ♗b5! ♕xb5 20 ᐩg5 ♖f7 (or

20...♕d7 21 ♖×d6) 21 ♖×e6 ♖g7 22 ♖e×d6 ♕e8 23 ♘e6

18 ♗×g6! hg 19 ♕×g6+ ♔h8 20 ♗×d6 cd 21 ♖×e6 ♕×e6 22 ♖d4 1-0

No. 247 Rashkovsky-Kosikov
Daugavpils Otborochnii, 1978
Slav Defence

1 ♘f3 ♘f6 2 c4 c6 3 d4 d5 4 cd cd 5 ♘c3 ♘c6 6 ♗f4 ♗f5 7 e3 e6 8 ♗b5 ♘d7 9 ♕a4 ♕b6 10 ♘h4 ♗e4 11 ♖c1 ♖c8 12 0-0 a6 13 ♗×c6 ♖×c6 14 ♘×e4 de *(100)*

15 d5! ed 16 ♘f5 g6 17 ♘d4 ♖×c1 18 ♖×c1 ♕×b2 19 ♖c8+ ♔e7 20 ♘b3 g5 21 ♗×g5+ f6 22 ♕b4+ ♔f7 23 ♕×b7 ♗e7 24 ♕×d5+ ♔g7 25 ♕×d7 ♖×c8 26 ♕×e7+ 1-0

No. 248 Kupreichik-Babev
Student Teams, Dresden, 1969
Sicilian Defence

1 e4 c5 2 ♘c3 ♘c6 3 ♘ge2 e6 4 d4 cd 5 ♘×d4 ♕c7 6 ♗e2 a6 7 f4

♘×d4 8 ♕×d4 ♘e7 9 ♕f2 ♘c6 10 ♗e3 ♗e7? (10...b5 is correct) 11 ♗b6 ♕b8 12 e5! d6 13 ed ♗×d6 14 ♘e4! ♗e7 (or 14...♗×f4 15 0-0 ♗×h2+ 16 ♔h1 f5 17 g3 with advantage to White) 15 0-0-0 0-0 16 ♔b1 ♗d8 17 ♗×d8 ♘×d8 18 ♘f6+ gf 19 ♕g3+ ♔h8 20 ♕h4 ♔g7 21 ♖d3 ♖e8 22 ♖h3! h5 23 ♗×h5 ♖g8 24 ♖g3+ ♔f8 25 ♕×f6 1-0

Thus the threat of an attack on the king is always in the air.

Counterattacks and defensive barriers

In the transitional stage, to an even greater extent than in purely opening activity, one should not become carried away by attacking plans. Counter activity by the opponent must always be taken into account, and it can sometimes be very difficult to anticipate. This is shown by the following examples, where the 'victims' were such great masters of attack as Geller and Tal.

No. 249 Geller-Euwe
Zurich C, 1953
Nimzo-Indian Defence

1 d4 ♘f6 2 c4 e6 3 ♘c3 ♗b4 4 e3 c5 5 a3 ♗×c3+ 6 bc b6 7 ♗d3 ♗b7 8 f3 ♘c6 9 ♘e2 0-0 10 0-0 ♘a5 11 e4 ♘e8! 12 ♘g3 cd 13 cd ♖c8 14 f4

♘xc4 15 f5 f6! 16 ♖f4 b5 17 ♖h4 ♕b6! 18 e5! ♘xe5 19 fe ♘xd3 20 ♕xd3 ♕xe6 21 ♕xh7+ ♔f7 22 ♗h6 *(101)*

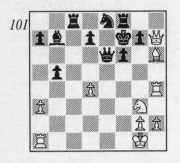

101

22...♖h8!
This emphasizes the ephemeral nature of White's attack. By shutting the white queen out of play, Black decisively seizes the initiative.

23 ♕xh8 ♖c2! 24 ♖d1 (24 d5 was somewhat better) **24... ♖xg2+! 25 ♔f1 ♕b3 26 ♔e1 ♕f3 0-1**

No. 250 Tal-Petrosian
USSR Ch., 1973
Caro-Kann Defence

1 e4 c6 2 d4 d5 3 ♘c3 de 4 ♘xe4 ♘d7 5 ♗c4 ♘gf6 6 ♘g5 e6 7 ♕e2 ♘b6 8 ♗b3 a5!? 9 a4?! h6 10 ♘5f3 c5 11 ♗f4 ♗d6 12 ♗e5 0-0 13 0-0-0? (a dangerous decision; it soon transpires that the white king is the first to come under attack) 13...c4! 14 ♗xc4 ♘xa4 15 ♘h3 ♘b6 16 g4 a4! 17 g5 hg 18

♘xg5 a3 19 b3 ♗b4! 20 ♖hg1?
White's position is very difficult. 20 ♖dg1 may possibly have been comparatively better.

20...a2! 21 ♔b2 ♘xc4+ 22 ♕xc4 ♘d5 23 ♘e4 f6 24 ♗f4 ♗a3+ 25 ♔a1 ♘xf4 26 h4 ♖f7 27 ♖g4 ♕a5 0-1

No less frequently, defences may be erected in the path of an attack (a perfectly correct one!), and often at a fairly early stage. Such 'barriers' may involve material sacrifices of a positional nature.

No. 251 Reshevsky-Petrosian
Zurich C, 1953
Nimzo-Indian Defence

1 d4 ♘f6 2 c4 e6 3 ♘c3 ♗b4 4 e3 0-0 5 ♗d3 d5 6 ♘f3 c5 7 0-0 ♘c6 6 a3 ♗xc3 9 bc b6 10 cd ed 11 ♗b2 c4 12 ♗c2 ♗g4 13 ♕e1 ♘e4 14 ♘d2 ♘xd2 15 ♕xd2 ♗h5 16 f3 ♗g6 17 e4 ♕d7 18 ♖ae1 de 19 fe ♖fe8 20 ♕f4 b5 21 ♗d1 ♖e7 22 ♗g4 ♕e8 23 e5 a5 24 ♖e3 ♖d8 25 ♖fe1 *(102)*

102

The storm clouds appear to be gathering over Black's position, but the following original manœuvre, which involves a sacrifice of the exchange, emphasizes his flexible blockade on the light squares.

25...♖e6! 26 a4 ♘e7 27 ♗xe6 fe 28 ♕f1 ♘d5 29 ♖f3 ♗d3 30 ♖xd3 cd 31 ♕xd3

A counter exchange sacrifice. White was threatened with 'suffocation' on the light squares.

31...b4 32 cb ab 33 a5 ♖a8 34 ♖a1 ♕c6 35 ♗c1 ♕c7 36 a6 ♕b6 37 ♗d2 b3 38 ♕c4 h6 39 h3 b2 40 ♖b1 ♔h8 41 ♗e1 ½-½

In the above examples White's initiative quickly, directly from the opening, became threatening, and each time Black found an interesting way of impeding it. This involved considerable sacrifice of material, the practical effect of which proved pretty convincing. Although in each of these examples White did not make any direct mistake, and, moreover, played with the utmost energy, in the end Black was able at the least to hold the position.

seven

DYNAMIC ATTACKS AND THE TACTICAL STRUGGLE FOR THE INITIATIVE IN MODERN OPENING SYSTEMS

Sharp ways of struggling for the initiative in the centre

In recent decades middle-game ideas, characteristic of positions with mobilization already completed, have been penetrating more and more into the opening stage. The struggle for the initiative in the opening is sharply tactical and at times combinational, and thus tactics are acquiring independent and ever greater importance in the initial stage of the game.

In itself this idea is not new. From early times a sharp tactical struggle for the initiative strongly attracted the 'romantics' in many of the Open Games. Thus the combinational complications arising, for example, in the King's Gambit, Italian Game, Evans Gambit, Two Knights Defence, Danish and Göring Gambits and in many other Open Games were thoroughly, if not exhaustively, studied back in the last century.

In the Semi-Open and Closed Games, which are now the most popular, for a long time players avoided (or were not aware of) the immediate sharpening of the play, and preferred first the systematic (at times pedantic) deployment of the pieces.

And yet, long before the modern treatment of opening play was established, it was found in practice that the scope for combinational creativity at an early stage in the Closed Games was not less, and was perhaps even greater, than in the ancient Open Games. Incidentally, from the modern viewpoint the complications in the ancient openings often resemble a 'storm in a teacup'.

The new approach, presupposing a sharp struggle for the initiative, led to the flourishing of many variations in popular modern openings, where tactical play begins before the mobilization of the forces is complete.

This is reflected in bold and sharp plans, proposed by one

side and uncompromisingly accepted by the other.

For example, the development of the ideas in many variations of the Slav Defence is instructive: after 1 d4 d5 2 c4 c6 3 ♘f3 ♘f6 4 ♘c3 e6 White must either relieve the tension in the centre by 5 cd, or allow Black's sharp counterplay with . . .dc, . . .b5 etc.

Thus in the Botvinnik Variation (5 ♗g5 dc 6 e4 b5) and the Meran Variation (5 e3 ♘bd7 6 ♗d3 dc 7 ♗×c4 b5) Black not only actively contests the centre, but in a number of lines is active over the entire board, the play being highly combinational.

On the other hand, as if in anticipation of this counterplay, in certain variations of the Slav Defence White is the first to begin sharp gambit play. This is the case, for example, in the variation 1 d4 d5 2 c4 c6 3 ♘c3 ♘f6 4 ♘f3 dc 5 e4 b5 6 e5 ♘d5 7 a4 c6 etc.

It is a curious fact that the Boleslavsky Variation in the Sicilian Defence: 1 e4 c5 2 ♘f3 ♘c6 3 d4 cd 4 ♘×d4 ♘f6 5 ♘c3 d6 6 ♗e2 e5, which gives Black very active counterplay, led to a much greater practical use and study of aggressive variations for White: 6 ♗g5 (the Richter/Rauzer Attack) and 6 ♗c4! (the Sozin Attack). These moves were

employed long before the appearance of the Boleslavsky Variation, but it is only in recent times that they have been especially thoroughly studied. It was found that in this way White has better chances in the struggle for the initiative than after 6 ♗e2, despite the fact that the opening play becomes tactical and double-edged.

In such cases the coordination of the forces takes shape during very tense play, often with the further course of the battle already being determined in the opening.

Take, for example, the development of events in the following popular variation of the Sicilian Defence, where in a number of lines an extremely sharp combinational struggle develops right from the opening: 1 e4 c5 2 ♘f3 d6 3 d4 cd 4 ♘×d4 ♘f6 5 ♘c3 a6 6 ♗g5 e6 7 f4! *(103)*

103

In reply to 7. . .♗e7 there can follow 8♕f3!, and 8. . .0-0

9 0-0-0!, when White threatens not only the flank attack 10 g4, but also an energetic blow in the centre.

An exceptionally sharp situation arises in the line 7. . .♗e7 8 ♕f3 h6 9 ♗h4 g5!? 10 fg ♘fd7 11 ♘xe6 fe 12 ♕h5+ ♔f8 13 ♗b5! etc. In general the assessment of this variation is still far from clear, although it has been intensively studied now for many years.

It must be mentioned that sharp play in the opening cannot be isolated from, or opposed to, positional ways of developing. Variations abounding in sharp play are closely associated with others, in which there is a slow battle for the accumulation of small positional advantages.

It can be said that the tactical struggle in modern opening systems is characterized by being positionally well-founded. This is its significant distinction from the ancient variations with sharp play in Open Games, where often only tactical ideas were pursued.

Typical in this respect is the following position, arising in the Nimzo-Indian Defence after 1 d4 ♘f6 2 c4 e6 3 ♘c3 ♗b4 4 ♕c2 d5 5 a3 ♗xc3+ 6 ♕xc3 ♘e4 7 ♕c2 c5 8 dc ♘c6 *(104)*

Here White has available two basic paths.

104

The first, 9 e3 ♕a5+ 10 ♗d2 ♘xd2 11 ♕xd2 dc! 12 ♗xc4 ♕xc5 or 12 ♕xa5 ♘xa5 leads to quiet play with roughly equal chances.

The second, 9 ♘f3 ♕a5+ 10 ♘d2!? ♘d4 11 ♕d3 e5! 12 b4 ♕a4 13 ♖a2 ♗f5 results in a very sharp tactical struggle, in which the chances of the two sides are extremely difficult to assess.

These variations are quite different in character, but they are closely connected, and a player choosing the Nimzo-Indian Defence must be equally prepared both for the one and the other.

Consider also a topical variation of the Sicilian Defence: 1 e4 c5 2 ♘f3 ♘c6 3 d4 cd 4 ♘xd4 ♘f6 5 ♘c3 e5 6 ♘bd5 d6 *(105)*

Here too White has several plans of different character. Thus 7 ♗g5 a6 8 ♗xf6 gf 9 ♘a3 b5 10 ♘d5 f5 leads to a very sharp struggle, e.g. 11 ♗xb5!? ab 12 ♘xb5 etc.

After 7 a4 a6 8 ♘a3 ♗e6 9 ♘c4, on the other hand, a more

positional, 'square-controlling' battle develops.

105

Here too the player must be ready for both types of struggle.

Such a range can essentially be found in any modern opening. Take a classical opening such as the Queen's Gambit Accepted. A white player with a rational, strictly positional style will normally choose the variation 1 d4 d5 2 c4 dc 3 ♘f3 ♘f6 4 e3 e6 5 ♗×c4 c5 6 0-0 a6 7 a4 *(106)*, restricting Black's Q-side counterplay and aiming for the subsequent concentration of his forces in the centre.

The positive features of this

106

are demonstrated by the following example.

No. 252 **Gligorić–Portisch**
Pula, 1971

7... ♘c6 8 ♕e2 cd 9 ♖d1 ♗e7 10 ed 0-0 11 ♘c3 ♘d5 12 ♗d3 ♘cb4 13 ♗b1 b6 14 a5! ♗d7 15 ♘e5 ba 16 ♖a3! f5 17 ♘×d5 ♘×d5 18 ♘×d7 ♕×d7 19 ♖×a5

White has obtained appreciable pressure in the centre, which he consistently increases by purposeful play.

19... ♘c7 20 ♗a2 ♗d6 21 ♗c4 ♔h8 22 ♕f3 ♗b4 23 ♖a1 a5 24 ♗f4 ♘d5 25 ♗e5 ♖fc8 26 ♕e2 ♕b7 27 h3 ♖c6 28 ♖ac1 ♖ac8 29 ♗×d5 ed 30 ♖×c6 ♕×c6 31 ♖d3 ♕d7 32 ♖g3 ♗f8 33 b3! ♖a8 34 ♕c2 ♖c8 35 ♕d2 ♖a8 36 ♕g5 ♔g8 37 ♖f3 g6 38 ♖c3 ♕d8 39 ♕c1 ♗d6 40 ♕f4 ♗×e5 41 ♕×e5 ♖a7 42 ♖c5! ♖e7 43 ♖×d5 ♕c7 44 ♕×c7 ♖×c7 45 ♖×a5 ♖b7 46 ♖a3! ♖b4 47 d5 ♔g7 48 ♔f1 ♔f6 49 ♔e2 ♔e5 50 ♔d3 ♔×d5 51 ♔c3 ♖e4 52 ♖a4 ♖e2 53 ♖d4+ ♔c5 54 b4+ ♔b5 55 ♖d5+ ♔c6 56 ♖d2 ♖e1 57 f3!, and White safely realized his advantage.

By contrast, a player with a sharp style will be more attracted here by variations such as 1 d4 d5 c4 dc 3 ♘f3 ♘f6 4 ♘c3 a6 5 e4!? b5 6 e5 ♘d5 7 a4 ♘×c3 8 bc ♕d5 9 g3! *(107)*, where the opening strategy is sacrificial and 'irrational'.

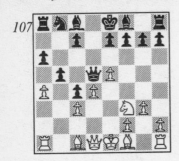

107

In this respect the development of the following game is instructive.

No. 253 Kavalek-Miles
Wijk aan Zee, 1978

From diagram 107: **9. . .♗b7 10 ♗g2 ♕d7 11 ♘h4! c6**

White also has the advantage after 11. . .♗×g2 12 ♘×g2 e6 13 ♕f3 ♖a7 14 ab ♕×b5 15 ♘f4, with the strong threat of d4-d5.

12 f4 e6 13 f5! ef 14 0-0 g6 15 ♗g5 ♗e7 16 ♗f6 ♖g8 17 ♕d2 ♕e6 18 ab ♗×f6 19 ef ♕×f6 20 ♖ae1+ ♔d8

And here, by playing 21 ♕h6 with the threat of 22 ♘×f5, White could have consolidated his advantage.

Or the variation 1 d4 d5 2 c4 dc 3 ♘f3 ♘f6 4 e3 e6 5 ♗×c4 c5 6 0-0 a6 7 ♕e2 b5 8 ♗b3 ♗b7 9 ♘c3 ♘bd7 10 ♖d1 ♕c7 11 e4 cd 12 ♘d5!? etc.

In short, there is ample scope for White to seek an initiative, although, of course, in each case

Black too has resources for counterplay.

It is interesting that, in many cases, an avoidance of sharp play offered by the opponent is objectively unfavourable and signifies a passive approach.

Thus if White tries to avoid complications provoked in the opening stage by Black, he often risks losing the initiative and even handing it to Black. For example, in the line 1 e4 c5 2 ♘f3 ♘c6 3 d4 cd 4 ♘×d4 ♘f6 5 ♘c3 g6, if instead of the sharp 6 ♘×c6 bc 7 e5! White prefers quiet and routine development: 6 ♗e2 ♗g7 7 ♗e3 0-0 8 0-0, then by the energetic 8. . .d5! Black gains an important tempo for this counter-blow in the centre, and easily equalizes.

A similar avoidance by Black can have even more undesirable consequences. For example, in the variation 1 e4 e6 2 d4 d5 3 ♘c3 ♗b4 4 ♗d2!? de 5 ♕g4 it is clearly unfavourable for Black to avoid the complications resulting from the acceptance of the pawn sacrifice 5. . .♕×d4, and to continue 5. . .♗f8, since after 6 ♕×e4 followed by 0-0-0 White has an obvious positional superiority.

These examples show that in modern opening play it is impossible to avoid sharp variations. Therefore, irrespective of his style of play, a player should study with particular care the problems of a sharp tactical struggle in the opening. Such an approach is undoubtedly very important and promising for the further development of theory.

In modern opening variations there are a number of tactical means for enabling the forces quickly to gain manœuvring freedom, which makes for very sharp play.

The attainment of manœuvring freedom and the initiative at the cost of material sacrifices or positional concessions

In the 'main' lines of opening variations with sharp tactical play, where there is a basic and crucial struggle for the initiative, a sharp clash of plans takes place and the events on the board take on a forcing or even a combinational nature.

Often in the opening, if one player is aiming for the initiative, which he considers will be persistent and increasing, for the sake of this he may make positional weakenings or even sacrifice material.

Instructive in this respect are gambit lines of the Benoni Defence (1 d4 ♘f6 2 d4 c5 3 d5 d6 4

♘c3 g6 5 e4 ♗g7 6 ♘f3 0-0 7 h3 b5!? 8 cb a6 9 ba ♕a5), the Benko Gambit (1 d4 ♘f6 2 c4 c5 3 d5 b5!?), and certain lines of the Spanish Game where Black sacrifices a pawn: 1 e4 e5 2 ♘f3 ♘c6 3 ♗b5 a6 4 ♗a4 ♘f6 5 0-0 ♗e7 6 ♖e1 b5 7 ♗b3 0-0 8 c3 d5!? etc. (of the old openings, this tendency is seen in many lines of the King's Gambit Accepted, Evans Gambit and so on).

We will examine a few examples in more detail. The development of events in the following comparatively new variation of the Queen's Gambit is typical: 1 d4 d5 2 c4 e6 3 ♘c3 ♘f6 4 ♗g5.

For a long time in this position Black chose only purely defensive ways of developing — 4...♗e7 or 4...♘bd7.

Then they were joined by a sharp way of battling for the centre, worked out by Keres: 4...c5!?

If White avoids the complications and prefers the quiet continuation of his development by 5 e3, then after 5...cd 6 ed ♗e7 Black transposes into a not unfavourable position from the Caro-Kann Defence (1 e4 c6 2 d4 d5 3 ed cd 4 c4 ♘f6 5 ♘c3 e6 6 ♗g5 ♗e7).

The crucial continuation, which can be regarded as the main line of this variation, is

5 cd! cd!? 6 ♕×d4 ♗e7! 7 e4! ♘c6 *(108)*. The struggle for the

108

initiative in this critical position is sharply tactical, and in the following interesting variations an assessment is possible only after an accurate analysis of the resulting complications: 8 ♕e3 ♘×d5! 9 ed ♗×g5 10 f4 ♘b4, or 8 ♕d2 ♘×e4! 9 ♘×e4 ed 10 ♗×e7 ♕×e7! 11 ♕×d5 0-0!?

Instead of 11...0-0!? Black can regain his piece by 11...f5, but then after 12 0-0-0 fe 13 ♖e1! White gains a strong initiative in the centre, while if in reply to 12 0-0-0 Black plays 12...♕×e4, then after 13 ♗c4 ♕×d5 14 ♗×d5 ♗d7 15 ♘f3 0-0-0 16 ♘g5 it is difficult for him to avoid loss of material in view of the threat of 17 ♘f7!

Therefore Black deliberately chooses a sharp path, aiming at all costs to retain the initiative.

Practice has shown that after 11...0-0!? 12 f3 ♘b4 13 ♕c5! White has the better chances,

and that Black's initiative is most probably only of a temporary nature. However, the complications arising still contain considerable scope for research, and it is possible that the 4...c5 variation is merely experiencing a temporary crisis.

Probably more promising for Black is the similar central thrust in the variation 1 d4 d5 2 c4 e6 3 ♘c3 ♘f6 4 ♘f3 c5 5 cd cd!?

The point is that, as regards the struggle for the important d5 and e4 squares, 4 ♘f3 is a much more neutral move than 4 ♗g5.

For example, in the main line after 6 ♕×d4 ed 7 e4 ♘c6 8 ♗b5 ♘×e4 9 0-0 ♘f6 10 ♖e1+ ♗e7 11 ♕e3 ♔f6 Black retains his extra pawn with a quite defensible position, and it is not easy for White to mount an attack on the king.

It is from a similar viewpoint that the 3...f5 variation in the Spanish Game is studied, where, as in the previous example, Black counters White's 'pressurizing' aims in the centre with a sharp struggle from the very first moves.

Such paths are, of course, by no means lacking in danger. If the opponent should succeed in overcoming his period of difficulties and in neutralizing the initiative, for the sake of which concessions of a permanent nature have been made, such a set-up may prove strategically lost. For example, the decisive influence on the outcome of the game may be the material sacrificed for the initiative in the opening.

Another problem, closely associated with this, is the case where, by contrast, one side aims to achieve in the opening a permanent positional advantage by temporarily conceding the initiative to the opponent (by 'provoking' him into taking action).

An illustration of this is provided by the following line of the Sicilian Defence: 1 e4 c5 2 ♘f3 ♘c6 3 d4 cd 4 ♘xd4 ♘f6 5 ♘c3 g6 6 ♘xc6! bc 7 e5 ♘g8 8 ♗c4 ♗g7 9 ♕f3 f5 10 ♗f4

Black has acquired a very solid pawn mass in the centre, but his mobilization is retarded and for the moment his pieces are significantly restricted.

An interesting continuation is 10...e6 11 0-0-0 ♕c7 12 ♕g3 ♘h6 13 ♔b1 ♘f7 14 ♖he1 ♖b8 15 ♗b3? (15 a3 is correct, not allowing Black's subsequent manœuvre) 15...♖b4! 16 a3 ♖xf4! 17 ♕xf4 ♗xe5, and at a slight cost in material Black very strongly set his central pawns in motion, and soon gained a decisive advantage.

Here Black exploited White's poor play to transform his central pawn majority into a real

force. The correct method of play for White is demonstrated in the following game.

No. 254 Andersson-Bilek
Teesside, 1972
Sicilian Defence

1 e4 c5 2 ♘f3 ♘c6 3 d4 cd 4 ♘xd4 ♘f6 5 ♘c3 g6 6 ♘xc6 bc 7 e5 ♘g8 8 ♗c4 ♗g7 9 ♕f3 f5 10 ♗f4 ♖b8 11 0-0! e6 12 ♖ad1 ♕c7 13 ♖fe1 ♘e7 14 b3 0-0 15 ♕e3, and after reinforcing his critical e5 point, White stands better.

An important part is played in such variations by questions of dynamics. An as yet static advantage is opposed by the initiative and concrete tactical threats of the opponent, who often has a considerable lead in development.

The following example is also typical.

No. 255 Boleslavsky-Flohr
Moscow, 1950
Caro-Kann Defence

1 e4 c6 2 ♘f3 d5 3 ♘c3 ♗g4 4 h3 ♗xf3 5 ♕xf3 e6 6 d4 ♘f6 7 ♗d3 *(109)* 7...de 8 ♘xe4 ♕xd4

Here Black decided to win a pawn, reckoning subsequently on neutralizing White's very strong initiative. In the given case, however, White's initiative increases with every move.

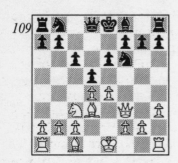

109

9 ♗e3! ♕d8 (accepting the second pawn is extremely risky: 9...♕xb2 10 0-0!, and it is very difficult to defend against the threat of 11 ♖ab1) 10 0-0-0 ♘bd7 11 ♗c4 ♕a5 12 ♗d2 ♕b6 13 ♖he1 ♘xe4 14 ♖xe4! ♘f6 15 ♗xe6!, and White created an irresistible attack.

In this example Black did not succeed in neutralizing White's initiative. On the contrary, it very quickly grew and developed into a very strong attack on the black king.

Thus Black's plan was refuted, an important part being played here by White's tactical possibilities. When aiming in the opening for positional (or material) gains to the detriment of rapid mobilization, what one has to fear primarily is a tactical refutation, in which the most important part is played by the dynamic features of the position.

In this respect the development of the following game is instructive.

No. 256 Matanović–Barcza
Yugoslavia v Hungary, 1957
Sicilian Defence

1 e4 c5 2 ♘f3 d6 3 d4 cd 4 ♘xd4 ♘f6 5 ♘c3 a6 6 ♗g5 e6 7 f4 ♕b6 8 ♕d2 ♕xb2 9 ♖b1 ♕a3 10 e5 de 11 fe ♘fd7 12 ♗c4 ♕c5? (12...♗b4 is correct) 13 ♗xe6!

This tactical blow, which is White's chief threat in the given variation, ensures him a decisive advantage.

13...fe 14 ♘xe6 ♕xe5+ 15 ♕e3! ♕xe3+ 16 ♗xe3 ♗d6 17 ♘d5! ♘f6 18 ♘xg7+, and White created a very strong attack on the opponent's king.

A study of the problems of sharp opening play shows that in such cases the main thing to take into account is whether the initiative will fade or, on the contrary, will increase and develop.

Generalizing this, we can draw the following conclusion: the basic criterion of the viability of this or that sharp plan in modern opening play is how persistent and firm the initiative is, and what resources for counterplay are available to the defending side.

The following sharp variation of the Slav Defence is a typical example: 1 d4 d5 2 c4 c6 3 ♘c3 ♘f6 4 ♘f3 dc 5 e4!? b5 6 e5 ♘d5 7 a4 e6 8 ab ♘xc3 9 bc cb 10 ♘g5 ♗b7 11 ♕h5 *(110)*

110

At the cost of a pawn White gains a highly dangerous initiative.

Practice shows that, if Black tries to neutralize this initiative positionally, aiming mainly to retain his material advantage, it can gradually grow into a strong attack. This is confirmed by the following game.

No. 257 Geller-Unzicker
Stockholm IZ, 1952

From diagram 110: **11...g6 12 ♛g4 ♝e7 13 ♝e2 ♞d7 14 ♝f3 ♛c7 15 ♞e4 ♞b6 16 ♝h6 ♜g8 17 ♝g5 ♝xe4 18 ♝xe4 ♞d5 19 ♝xd5 ed 20 ♝f6!,** and White placed his opponent in a very difficult position.

Much more promising, in our opinion, is the as yet little-studied **11...♛d7!?** (instead of the passive 11...g6), e.g. 12 ♞xh7 ♞c6! 13 ♞f6+ gf 14 ♛xh8 fe!

It is now Black's strong initiative which is threatening to develop into an attack.

This example shows how, in a sharp tactical struggle, the defending side is not at all obliged to neutralize the opponent's threats positionally. Very often the only way of parrying the initiative is by a timely counter-sacrifice of material. Each time he should seek sharp resources for counterplay — the best way of fighting against an initiative.

Dynamics of the modern opening

The struggle in modern opening variations is full of inner dynamics, and abounds in unexpected tactical turns.

We have already talked about the changing of various outward features — the transformation of positional factors. In dynamic variations this is especially marked, the changes sometimes being of an unexpected, explosive nature. But in the process of outward changes (as also in transformations in classical variations), dynamics by no means signifies an arbitrary, accidental change of situation, but, on the contrary, emphasizes the regularity and strict logic of chess.

As a rule, dynamic variations are distinguished by the fact that they aim for not only a complex, but also a highly aggressive struggle. Under the influence of these ideas, many variations, which used to be considered exclusively positional, have been reappraised.

An example of this is provided by the following variation of the Reti Opening, which used to enjoy a solid reputation: 1 ♘f3 ♘f6 2 g3 d5 3 ♗g2 ♗f5 4 c4 c6 *(111)*. Until recent times, in this variation middlegame play would begin rather late. White would first deploy his dark-square bishop on the other long diagonal (b2-b3 and ♗b2), then complete the mobilization of his flanks, and so on.

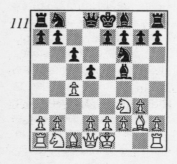

111

This makes the dynamic plan in the following game even more interesting.

No. 258 Smyslov-Bronstein
USSR Teams Ch.,
Moscow 1974

From diagram 111: **5 cd cd 6 ♕b3 ♕c8 7 ♘c3 e6 8 d3! ♘c6 9**

♗f4 ♗e7 10 0-0-0 0-0 11 ♖ac1

White gradually prepares the opening of the centre, which gives a sharp, dynamic nature to this formerly slow variation.

11...♕d7 12 ♘e5 ♘xe5 13 ♗xe5 ♗g6

Now comes a veiled and long-planned blow in the centre, which gives White the advantage.

14 e4! ♖ad8

White also has a powerful initiative in the centre and on the Q-side after 14...de 15 de ♖ad8 16 ♖fd1.

15 ed ed 16 ♗xf6 ♗xf6 17 ♘xd5 ♗e5 18 d4! ♗b8

In the event of 18...♗xd4 19 ♖fd1 ♗e5 20 ♘f6+ White would have gained a material advantage, by winning queen for rook and bishop. This may have been the lesser evil.

19 ♖fe1 ♖fe8 20 ♖xe8+ ♖xe8 21 ♘e3 ♕xd4 22 ♕xb7 h5 23 ♖c8 ♕e5 24 ♘c4 ♕e1+ 25 ♗f1 ♔h7 26 ♖xb8 ♗d3 27 ♘d2 ♖e2 28 ♕f3 1-0

In this respect the following game is also instructive.

No. 259 Smyslov-Darga
Amsterdam IZ, 1964
Reti Opening

1 ♘f3 ♘f6 2 g3 d5 3 ♗g2 ♗g4 4 c4 c6 5 cd cd
Already this is probably the

root of Black's difficulties. Better was 5...♗×f3 6 ♗×f3 cd followed by ...e6 with a solid position.

6 ♘e5 ♗c8 7 0-0 e6 8 ♘c3 ♗e7 (8...♘bd7 or 8...♘c6 was preferable, aiming to neutralize the strong white knight as quickly as possible) 9 d4 0-0 10 ♗f4 ♗d7 11 ♕b3! ♕b6?

11...♗c6 was essential. Like a fleeing ostrich, Black wishes to 'hide' in the endgame, but it proves completely unpromising for him.

12 ♕×b6 ab 13 ♘×d7 ♘b×d7 14 ♖fc1 ♖fc8 15 a3 ♖c6 16 ♗d2!

Here too the decisive events come to a head in the centre. The e3-e4 break is prepared.

16...♖d8 17 e3 ♘e8?

This eases White's task, but Black's position was already very difficult.

18 e4! de 19 ♗×e4 ♖c4 20 ♘b5 ♖×c1+ 21 ♖×c1 ♘c5 22 dc ♖×d2 23 cb ♖×b2 24 a4! ♔f8 25 ♖c8 1-0

We will now turn to an examination of the features which characterize dynamic attacks at the start of the game.

Dynamic attacks in the opening and during the transition to the middlegame

In Steinitz's positional theory, an attack was regarded chiefly as a means of realizing an advantage. It was supposed though to crown other offensive means: pressure, initiative, siege, restriction of the mobility of the enemy forces, and so on. This was perhaps the source of Steinitz's rule: the player with the advantage is obliged to attack!

In recent times, under the influence of dynamic ideas, the concept of attack has grown considerably broader. In the modern understanding, the origin of an attack is assisted (generally speaking) not so much by an objective advantage, as by how the forces are deployed (the advantage is of a localized nature, i.e. it is of significance on a certain part of the board). In all these cases the starting of an attack is a moral duty.

The modern interpretation of attack did not arise by accident. In addition, it cannot be considered that the reason for such an interpretation was the appearance of new, sharp opening variations.

Here we are obliged to encounter a problem on which little research has been done: what is it that advances theory — the development of opening or middlegame ideas? This significant question can be answered categorically: it is middlegame ideas which are the main driving force, while opening ideas are merely functional in this respect.

Of course, the absence of necessary opening patterns was a serious hindrance to the development of dynamic ideas. The creators of new ideas were obliged to experiment, take risks, and sometimes even go to extremes.

But the dynamic interpretation paved a way for itself throughout a very long, preparatory period. This is shown by the many chess masterpieces created in particular by Anderssen, Morphy, Zukertort, Pillsbury and Charousek. And in many of the best games by the leaders of the positional school — Steinitz, Tarrasch, Schlechter and others — dynamic ideas are very apparent.

Chigorin regarded dynamic ideas as a creative method. He approached the principles and rules of the positional school from the viewpoint of their real strength in a particular position. This is shown by his critical comments regarding the dogmatic impressions of the time about the centre, the advantage of the two bishops, the 'weakness' of cramped positions, and so on.

As a determined opponent of dogmatism, Chigorin regarded a game of chess as a living process, and he considered the most important factor in assessment to be a concrete approach to the given position.

Besides carrying out complex strategic opening ideas (e.g. piece pressure on the centre in connection with active counterplay, the blockade of a pawn centre, the preparation of pawn storms on the flanks, and so on), in the opening Chigorin sometimes went in for very sharp gambit continuations, laying a concrete path of dynamism. Thus his favourite openings as White were the Evans Gambit, the King's Gambit, and the Ponziani Opening, the theory of which he enriched and broadened. Even today, when these openings have become largely the property of history, Chigorin's ideas in them have not lost their topicality.

Subsequently the advance of dynamics took place mainly in the implementation of middlegame ideas, as the following games confirm.

No. 260 Breyer-Esser
Budapest, 1917
Slav Defence

1 d4 d5 2 c4 c6 3 e3 ♘f6 4 ♘c3 e6 5 ♗d3 ♗d6 6 f4!? 0-0 7 ♘f3 dc 8 ♗b1?!

A paradoxical decision, the point of which was not appreciated by Black. In fact White intends a sharp dynamic attack on the K-side, while allowing Black a monopoly on the Q-side.

8...b5? (8...c5 is correct) **9 e4 ♗e7 10 ♘g5! h6 11 h4! g6 12 e5 hg**

Black's position is already very difficult. Thus after 12... ♘d5 13 h5 ♘xc3 14 bc hg 15 hg fg 16 ♗xg6 ♔g7 17 ♖h7+! ♔xg6 18 ♕h5+ ♔f5 Black is prettily mated: 19 g4+ ♔e4 20 ♕h1+ ♔d3 21 ♖h3+ ♔c2 ♕g2 mate!

13 hg ♘d5 14 ♔f1! *(112)*

A 'quiet' move, which, however, sets Black very difficult concrete problems: White prepares the following astounding combination, crowning his attack on the king.

14...♘xc3 15 bc ♗b7

It would have been better to try and buy White off with a counter-sacrifice: 15...f5 16 gf

♗xf6 17 ef ♖xf6, although even here his attack is very dangerous.

16 ♕g4 ♔g7 17 ♖h7+! ♔xh7 18 ♕h5+ ♔g7 19 ♕h6+ ♔g8 20 ♗xg6 fg 21 ♕xg6+ ♔h8 22 ♕h6+ ♔g8 23 g6!

This is where the point of White's 14th move is revealed! Were the king still at e1, Black would have a defence: 23... ♗h4+ and 24...♕e7.

23...♖f7 (otherwise mate is inevitable) **24 gf+ ♔xf7 25 ♕h5+ ♔g7 26 f5! ef 27 ♗h6+ 1-0**

And in the following game the initiative gained by White in the opening grows as though 'out of nothing' into a powerful attack over the entire front.

This game, which won a brilliancy prize over 60 years ago, has a completely youthful appearance even today.

No. 261 Reti-Bogoljubow
New York, 1924
Reti Opening

1 ♘f3 d5 2 c4 e6 3 g3 ♘f6 4 ♗g2 ♗d6 5 0-0 0-0 6 b3 ♖e8 7 ♗b2 ♘bd7 8 d4 c6 9 ♘bd2 ♘e4?

Now White commences a lengthy and very fine pressurizing combination.

10 ♘xe4! de 11 ♘e5 f5 12 f3! ef 13 ♗xf3 ♕c7 14 ♘xd7 ♗xd7 15 ed e5 16 c5! ♗f8 17 ♕c2 ed 18 ef! ♖ad8 19 ♗h5! ♖e5 20 ♗xd4

♖xf5 21 ♖xf5 ♗xf5 22 ♕xf5
♖xd4 23 ♖f1 ♖d8 24 ♗f7+ ♔h8
25 ♗e8!! 1-0

The next significant step in the development of the dynamic interpretation of the opening was made by Alekhine, the founder of modern dynamism. One of the main features of the modern opening is the sharp re-appraisal of many closed set-ups, owing to a significant increase in their tactical sharpness.

It was Alekhine who made the positional sacrifice of material in the opening into an effective method of play. In the early 1930s when he began making his first experiments of this type, gambits in the Closed Games were rather rare. Moreover, even the eccentric experiments of his which succeeded were given a hostile reception by the conservative critics of that time.

But in essence, all that Alekhine lacked was a sufficiency of dynamic opening patterns, e.g. gambits of the type 1 d4 d5 2 c4 e6 3 ♘c3 c6 4 e4 de 5 ♘xe4 ♗b4+ 6 ♗d2!

In this position Alekhine usually replied with the prosaic 6 ♘c3, which allows Black a comfortable game after 6...c5 etc. This shows that even the great master could not overcome the routine thinking of his time.

6...♕xd4 7 ♗xb4 ♕xe4+ 8 ♗e2, or 1 d4 d5 2 c4 c6 3 ♘f3 ♘f6 4 ♘c3 dc 5 e4 b5 6 e5 ♘d5 7 a4 ♘xc3 8 bc ♗b7 9 ♘g5!? etc.

At the time Alekhine had to make do with 'one-off' gambit variations, one of which is given below.

No. 262 Pirc-Alekhine
Bled, 1931
Von Hennig-Schara Gambit

1 d4 d5 2 c4 e6 3 ♘c3 c5 4 cd cd
5 ♕a4+ ♗d7 6 ♕xd4 ed 7 ♕xd5
♘c6 8 ♗g5

This activity is inappropriate. 8 e3 ♘f6 9 ♕d1 etc. is better.

8...♘f6 9 ♕d2 h6 10 ♗xf6
♕xf6 11 e3 0-0-0 12 0-0-0? ♗g4
13 ♘d5 ♖xd5! 14 ♕xd5 ♗a3!
15 ♕b3 ♗xd1 16 ♕xa3 ♕xf2
17 ♕d3 ♗g4! 18 ♘f3 ♗xf3
19 ♕f5+ ♔b8 20 ♕xf3 ♕e1+
21 ♔c2 ♖c8 22 ♕g3+ ♘e5+!
23 ♔b3 ♕d1+ 24 ♔a3 ♖c5!
0-1

Or there were dangerous experiments, such as the sensational 6th game from Alekhine's 1937 return match with Euwe. Here Alekhine with White played what was undoubtedly an improvized gambit: 1 d4 d5 2 c4 c6 3 ♘c3 dc 4 e4 e5 5 ♘f3 ed 6 ♗xc4?

The practical effect of this puzzling sacrifice was very great.

Euwe not only failed to find the refutation of White's idea, but even made a decisive error, by playing 6...b5?, on which there followed a further, this time purely tactical blow 7 ♘×b5!, when it transpired that 7...cb failed to 8 ♗d5!, winning the rook.

It is curious that, in their analysis of this game, the critics regarded White's idea as an 'unlawful attempt' on their orderly positional conceptions. Later a refutation was found: 6...dc! 7 ♕b3 cb! 8 ♗×f7+ ♔e7 9 ♗×b2 ♕b6!, after which it was established that Alekhine's experiment was dubious.

Alekhine's eccentric pawn moves in the opening came in for particular criticism. The following game is instructive in this respect.

No. 263 Alekhine-Euwe
World Championship, 1935
French Defence

1 e4 e6 2 d4 d5 3 ♘c3 ♗b4 4 ♘e2 de 5 a3 ♗e7 6 ♘×e4 ♘c6 7 g4!? *(113)*

This move, which at the time was subjected to wholesale criticism, proved highly effective in practice. Its idea is to combine the flank development of the bishop with a possible pawn storm on the K-side.

7...b6 (better 7...♘f6) **8 ♗g2 ♗b7 9 c3 ♘f6 10 ♘2g3 0-0**

113

(better 10...0-0-0) **11 g5 ♘×e4 12 ♘×e4 ♔h8 13 ♕h5! ♕e8 14 ♘f6! ♗×f6**

After 14...gf 15 gf ♘a5 16 fe ♕×e7 17 ♗×b7 ♘×b7 18 ♗g5 f6 19 ♗h6 ♖g8 20 0-0-0 ♘d6 21 ♖de1 White has an obvious advantage.

15 gf gf 16 ♕h4 ♕d8 17 ♗f4! e5 18 ♗g3 f5 19 de and White had an undisputed advantage.

Such searchings by Alekhine essentially began much earlier. This is strikingly shown by the following game, which to this day remains a model of dynamism.

No. 264
Alekhine-Rubinstein
Carlsbad, 1923
Queen's Gambit

1 d4 d5 2 c4 e6 3 ♘f3 ♘f6 4 ♘c3 ♗e7 5 ♗g5 ♘bd7 6 e3 0-0 7 ♖c1 c6 8 ♕c2 a6 9 a4 ♖e8 10 ♗d3 dc 11

♗xc4 ♘d5 12 ♗f4!?

An original and innovative idea for that time. Of course, this decision is debatable, and 12 ♗×e7 was probably stronger.

But against Rubinstein, one of the classics of positional play, Alekhine's method proved highly effective and psychologically justified. In return for his spoiled pawn formation, White gains the initiative.

12...♘×f4 13 ef c5 14 dc ♕c7 15 0-0 ♕×f4 16 ♘e4 ♘×c5

A mistake. 16...♗×c5 17 ♗d3 (or 17 ♘eg5 h6) 17...♗e7 would have been correct, with approximate equality.

17 ♘×c5 ♗×c5 18 ♗d3 b6 19 ♗×h7+ ♔h8?

A further significant error. It would have been better to go to f8. Now White step by step increases his initiative, which eventually develops into a powerful dynamic attack over the entire front.

20 ♗e4 ♖a7

White also wins after 20...♖b8 21 g3 ♕f6 22 b4 ♗d6 23 ♖fd1 ♕e7 24 ♗c6 ♖d8 25 ♖d4 g6 26 ♕d2! ♔g7 27 ♖d1

21 b4! ♗f6 22 ♕c6 ♖d7 23 g3! ♕b8

After 23...♕d6 24 ♖fd1 ♕×d1+ 25 ♖×d1 ♖×d1+ 26 ♔g2 ♗d7 27 ♕×b6 ♗×a4 28 ♕×a6 ♗d7 29 ♘g5 ♔g8 30 ♕e2! White wins.

24 ♘g5! ♖ed8 *(114)* 25 ♗g6!!

A crushing blow! In the event of 25...fg 26 ♕e4! ♗×b4 27 ♕h4+ ♔g8 28 ♕h7+ ♔f8 29 ♕h8+ ♔e7 30 ♕×g7+ ♔e8 31 ♕g8+ ♗f8 32 ♕×g6+ ♔e7 33 ♕e6 Black is mated!

114

Black played **25...♕e5,** but after **26 ♘×f7+ ♖×f7 27 ♗×f7 ♕f5 28 ♖fd1!** White gained a decisive material advantage.

The finish was **28...♖×d1+ 29 ♖×d1 ♕×f7 30 ♕×c8 ♔h7 31 ♕×a6 ♕f3 32 ♕d3+ 1-0**

Thus it is the development of middlegame ideas which has assisted the establishment of the dynamic interpretation. As a result the preconditions have been created for the appearance of new opening forms, which in turn have further influenced the development of dynamic ideas. The flourishing of the dynamic interpretation is notable in all stages of the game today, having been sharply stimulated by a plentiful supply of new ideas.

We will now examine certain modern forms of dynamic attacks.

'Shock' central attacks against the Sicilian

In modern variations of the Sicilian Defence, where at an early stage Black aims as soon as possible for active play on the Q-side, and as a consequence delays the development of his K-side, typical attacks by White have become a standard feature. Here Black has to reckon with sharp and sudden attacks in the centre by White, often involving sacrifices which are most often aimed at the e6 and d5 squares.

Here are a few examples of this type.

No. 265 Keres-Kotov
Budapest C, 1950
Sicilian Defence

1 e4 c5 2 ♘f3 d6 3 d4 cd 4 ♘xd4 ♘f6 5 ♘c3 a6 6 ♗e2 ♕c7 7 ♗g5 ♘bd7 8 0-0 e6 9 ♗h5!? ♕c4? (after 9...g6 10 ♗e2 White has slightly the better game) 10 ♘xe6! ♕xe6 11 ♘d5! ♔d8 (11...♘xd5 12 ed ♕f5 13 ♕e1+ ♘e5 14 f4! also gives White a very strong attack) 12 ♗g4 ♕e5 13 f4 ♕xe4 14 ♗xd7 ♗xd7 15 ♘xf6 gf 16 ♗xf6+ ♔c7 17 ♗xh8 ♗c6 18 ♕d2, and White won.

No. 266 Keres-Sajtar
Amsterdam OL, 1954
Sicilian Defence

1 e4 c5 2 ♘f3 d6 3 d4 cd 4 ♘xd4 ♘f6 5 ♘c3 a6 6 ♗g5 ♘bd7 7 ♗c4 e6 8 0-0 ♕c7? (better 8...♘b6) 9 ♗xe6! fe 10 ♘xe6 ♕c4 11 ♘d5! ♔f7 (after 11...♘xd5 12 ed ♘e5 13 b3 ♕c3 14 ♗d2 ♕b2 15 ♘c7+! White advantageously regains his material, with an unceasing attack) 12 ♗xf6 ♔xe6 (White wins quickly after 12...gf 13 ♕h5+! or 12...♘xf6 13 b3) 13 ♗c3! ♘f6 14 ♗xf6 gf 15 ♘b6 ♕c6 16 ♘xa8 ♗e7 17 a4! b6 18 ♕d5+! ♔d7 19 ♖a3! ♗d8 20 ♘xb6+! 1-0 (20...♕xb6 21 ♕f5+! or 20...♗xb6 21 ♕f7+ ♔d8 22 ♕xf6+! etc).

No. 267 Fischer-Rubinetti
Palma de Mallorca IZ, 1970
Sicilian Defence

1 e4 c5 2 ♘f3 d6 3 d4 cd 4 ♘xd4 ♘f6 5 ♘c3 e6 6 ♗c4 a6 7 ♗b3 b5 8 0-0 ♗b7? (better 8...♗e7) 9 ♖e1 ♘bd7 10 ♗g5 h6 11 ♗h4 (11 ♗xf6 ♕xf6 12 a4! was even stronger) 11...♘c5? *(115)*

11...g5 12 ♗g3 ♘e5 was essential, erecting a barrier on the e-file.

12 ♗d5! ed 13 ed+ ♔d7 14 b4! ♘a4 15 ♘xa4 ba 16 c4 ♔c8 17 ♕xa4 ♕d7 18 ♕b3 g5 19 ♗g3 ♘h5 20 c5! dc 21 bc ♕xd5 22 ♖e8+

♔d7 23 ♕a4+ ♗c6 24 ♘xc6
1-0

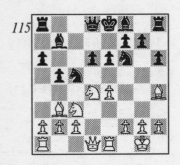

115

Sudden 'explosive' piece attacks

This type of attack, directed mainly at the opponent's king, is highly characteristic of modern variations in the transition from opening to middlegame and in the early middlegame.

As an example, the development of events in the following game is instructive.

No. 268 Holmov-Keres
USSR Ch., 1959
Sicilian Defence

1 e4 c5 2 ♘f3 ♘c6 3 ♗b5 ♘f6
4 e5 ♘g4 5 ♗xc6 dc 6 0-0 g6 7 ♖e1
♗g7 8 h3 ♘h6 9 ♘c3 b6 10 d4 cd
11 ♘xd4 *(116)*

Not sensing the danger, Black played 11...c5?, on which there came an unexpected knight move: 12 ♘c6!

116

It now transpires that 12...♕xd1 is bad because of 13 ♖xd1 ♗b7 (or 13...♗d7) 14 ♘d5!, when 14...♗xc6 fails to 15 ♘c7+ ♔f8 16 ♘xa8.

12...♕d7 13 ♘xe7!!

This knight performs miracles. Out of the great wealth of combinations, there are few where a knight demonstrates such murderous strength.

13...♔xe7 (13...♕xe7 is no better in view of 14 ♘d5, when 14...♕d7 fails to 15 ♗xh6 and 16 ♘xf6+, winning the queen) **14 ♗xh6 ♗xh6 15 ♕f3 ♗g7 16 ♘d5+! ♔d8 17 ♖ad1 ♗b7 18 ♕b3!**

This emphasizes Black's helplessness. The knight at d5 dominates, and material loss for Black is inevitable.

18...♗c6 19 ♘xb6 ab 20 ♕xf7 ♗xe5 21 ♖xd7+ ♗xd7 22 ♖xe5, and Black shortly resigned.

Alekhine left a number of model examples of this type (cf.

No. 264), and the following game is typical. Black appears to play the opening soundly and even more soundly to hide his king away. But (a characteristic feature of dynamic attacks!) White gradually prepares a powerful, dynamic piece attack, under the influence of which Black's solid defences unexpectedly collapse.

No. 269 Alekhine-Lasker
Zurich, 1934
Queen's Gambit

1 d4 d5 2 c4 e6 3 ♘c3 ♘f6 4 ♘f3 ♗e7 5 ♗g5 ♘bd7 6 e3 0-0 7 ♖c1 c6 8 ♗d3 dc 9 ♗xc4 ♘d5 10 ♗xe7 ♕xe7 11 ♘e4 ♘5f6 12 ♘g3 e5 13 0-0 ed 14 ♘f5 ♕d8 15 ♘3xd4 ♘e5 16 ♗b3 ♗xf5 17 ♘xf5 ♕b6? (better 17...g6) 18 ♕d6! ♘ed7 19 ♖fd1 ♖ad8 20 ♕g3! g6 21 ♕g5! *(117)*

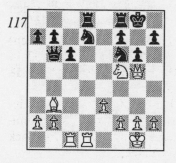

117

21...♔h8 22 ♘d6 ♔g7 23 e4! ♘g8 24 ♖d3 f6

This leads to an immediate loss, but White's attack is also

decisive after 24...h6 25 ♘f5+ ♔h7 26 ♘xh6 f6 27 ♘f5!! fg 28 ♖h3+.

25 ♘f5+ ♔h8 26 ♕xg6!! 1-0

Here are some further examples on this theme.

No. 270 Gaprindashvili-Hartoch
Amsterdam, 1976
Sicilian Defence

1 e4 c5 2 ♘f3 d6 3 d4 cd 4 ♘xd4 ♘f6 5 ♘c3 e6 6 f4 ♘c6 7 ♗e3 ♗e7 8 ♕f3 e5 9 ♘xc6 bc 10 f5!? ♕a5 11 ♗c4 ♖b8 12 ♗b3 0-0 13 0-0-0 ♖xb3 14 cb d5 15 ed cd 16 ♖xd5! ♘xd5 17 ♘xd5 ♗d6 18 ♖d1! ♕xa2 19 ♘f6+ gf 20 ♗h6! ♔h8 21 ♗xf8 ♕a1+ 22 ♔c2 ♕xd1+ 23 ♔xd1 ♗xf8 24 ♕e3 1-0

No. 271 Stein-Portisch
Stockholm IZ, 1962
Sicilian Defence

1 e4 c5 2 ♘f3 e6 3 d4 cd 4 ♘xd4 a6 5 ♗d3 ♘f6 6 0-0 ♕c7 7 ♘d2 ♘c6 8 ♘xc6 bc (better 8...dc 9 f4 e5) 9 f4 ♗c5+ (9...d6 is more circumspect, although here too after 10 ♘f3 e5 11 fe de 12 ♘h4 White has persistent pressure on the K-side) 10 ♔h1 d6 11 ♘f3 e5 12 fe de 13 ♘h4! 0-0 14 ♘f5 ♗e6 15 ♕e2 a5 16 ♗c4 ♔h8 17 ♗g5 ♘d7 18 ♖ad1 ♘b6 *(118)*

This leads to a rapid defeat. The lesser evil was 18...♗xf5 19 ♖xf5 ♘b6.

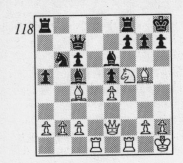

19 ♘xg7! ♗xc4

This allows a pretty finish, but White would also have won after 19...♔xg7 20 ♗f6+! ♔g8 21 ♕h5 ♖fc8 22 ♕h6! or 19...♘xc4 20 ♗f6! ♔g8 21 ♘xe6 fe 22 ♕g4+ ♔f7 23 ♕g7+.

20 ♗f6! ♗e7 21 ♕f3! 1-0 (21...♗xf1 22 ♘h5+ or 21...♗xf6 22 ♕xf6 ♔g8 23 ♘h5!).

No. 272 Schmidt-Kuligowski
Poland, 1978
Nimzo-Indian Defence

1 d4 ♘f6 2 c4 e6 3 ♘c3 ♗b4 4 g3 c5 5 ♘f3 ♘e4 6 ♕d3 d5!? 7 dc ♕a5 8 ♘d2? ♘xc5! 9 ♕e3 0-0 10 cd ed 11 ♘xd5 ♘c6 12 ♗g2 ♗h3!! 13 ♗xh3 (after 13 ♘e7+ ♘xe7 14 ♗xh3 ♘d5 15 ♕d4 ♖ad8 Black has the advantage) **13...♖ae8 14 ♕g5 ♖e5 15 ♘f6+ ♔h8 16 ♕h4 gf 17 ♕xf6+ ♔g8 18 ♗f5 ♘e6! 19 ♗d3 ♖d8 20 ♔d1 ♖xd3! 21 ed ♗xd2 22 ♗xd2 ♕d5 23 ♖e1 ♖xe1+ 24 ♗xe1 ♕xd3+ 25 ♗d2 ♘cd4 0-1**

Switching the weight of the attack from another target to the king

This is a strategic procedure, closely linked to the preceding one, which can perhaps be considered merely as a more complicated instance of a sudden attack. But while in the examples examined above there was a clear predominance of tactical features, here the strategic aspect is more definite. Moreover, such an attack does not arise spontaneously, but develops from an offensive begun on other parts of the board.

As has already been mentioned, such a procedure is often the logical transformation of a positional advantage, such as the exploitation of a central superiority to transfer the weight of the attack onto the opponent's king.

Such a procedure will often take on a very sharp form, and then the play will be highly dynamic.

No. 273 Fischer-Gligorić
Havana OL, 1966
Spanish Game

1 e4 e5 2 ♘f3 ♘c6 3 ♗b5 a6 4 ♗xc6 dc 5 0-0 f6 6 d4 ♗g4 7 c3 ed 8 cd ♕d7 9 h3 ♗e6 10 ♘c3 0-0-0 11 ♗f4!

White has acquired a pawn centre, and his last move clearly demonstrates his active intentions on the Q-side.

Now after 11...g5 12 ♗g3 .h5 13 d5! cd 14 ♖c1! a sharp attack on the opponent's king could already have arisen. In this respect, the variations given by Fischer are instructive:

(a) 14...♗d6 15 ♘a4! ♔b8 16 ♘c5 ♕e7 17 ♘×a6+! ba 18 ♘d4 ♗d7 19 ♕b3+ ♔a7 20 ♖×c7+!! ♗×c7 21 ♗×c7 ♗b5 22 ♘c6+! ♗×c6 23 ♕b6+ and mate next move.

(b) White also wins prettily after 14...de 15 ♘a4! ♔b8 16 ♖×c7!! ♕×d1 17 ♖c8++!! ♔a7 (17...♔×c8 18 ♘b6+) 18 ♗b8+ ♔a8 19 ♘b6 mate.

The game in fact developed as follows:

11...♘e7 (11...♗d6 12 ♗×d6 ♕×d6 is safer) **12 ♖c1 ♗g6 13 ♗g3 ♗d6 14 ♘a4! ♗×g3?**

After this White's outpost at c5 gains markedly in strength. 14...♔b8 15 ♘c5 ♕e7 would have been better.

15 fg ♔b8

15...b6 is bad in view of 16 d5! ♗f7 17 ♕e2! etc.

16 ♘c5 ♕d6 17 ♕a4! ♔a7?

This leads to a rapid showdown. After 17...♗c8 18 ♖c3 ♘f8! Black could still have defended.

18 ♘×a6!

The decisive blow, destroying the black king's defences.

18...♗×h3 19 e5! ♘×e5 20 de fe 12 ♘c5+ ♔b8 22 gh e4 23 ♘×e4 ♕e7 24 ♖c3 b5 25 ♕c2 1-0

Such a transfer of the attack is sometimes assisted by weaknesses in the king's pawn screen, created early in the game. Although up to a certain time these weaknesses do not play any significant part in the play, nevertheless the king's position is always to a certain extent uncomfortable. Of course, one could give a large number of positions where this latter factor has practically no influence on the outcome of the game. But nevertheless, such a strategic feature must always be borne in mind.

Such a situation arose in the following game.

No. 274
Uhlmann-Pietzsch
East Germany, 1976
English Opening

1 c4 e5 2 ♘c3 c5?! 3 g3 ♘c6 4 ♗g2 d6 5 e3 ♗f5 6 a3 ♘f6 7 d3 ♕d7 8 h3! g6 9 ♘ge2 ♗g7 10 ♖b1 0-0 11 b4 h5 12 ♘d5 ♖ab8 13 ♘ec3 ♖fc8 14 ♖b3 ♗e6 15 ♗d2 b6 16 ♕f3! ♘h7 17 b5! ♘a5? 18 ♖b1 ♖f8 19 e4! ♘b7 *(119)*

Better 19...f5 20 ef! ♖×f5 21 ♕e2, although here too White's chances are preferable.

119

20 g4! hg (20...h4 21 g5!) 21 hg ♗xg4 22 ♘e7+!! ♔h8 23 ♕g3 ♖be8 24 ♘f5! gf 25 ♕h4 ♗h6 26 ♗xh6 1-0

Also typical in this respect are some famous 'switching' attacks by Alekhine (e.g. No. 153), and the following two examples.

No. 275 I. Zaitsev-Krogius
Sochi, 1976
Queen's Gambit

1 d4 ♘f6 2 c4 e6 3 ♘f3 d5 4 ♘c3 ♗e7 5 ♗g5 h6 6 ♗h4 0-0 7 ♕c2 b6 8 ♗xf6 ♗xf6 9 e4! c5 10 e5 ♗e7 11 cd ed 12 dc bc 13 0-0-0 d4 14 ♕e4 ♘a6 15 ♕xa8 ♗g5+ 16 ♘xg5 ♕xg5+ 17 ♖d2 dc 18 bc ♖d8 19 ♗d3! c4 (after 19...♖xd3 20 ♕xc8+ ♔h7 21 ♖d1 ♖xc3+ 22 ♔b2 ♕xe5 23 f4! ♕f6 24 ♕d8! White wins) 20 f4! ♕xf4 21 ♕e4 ♕g5 22 h4 ♕g3 23 ♕xc4 ♕xe5 24 ♗c2 ♖e8 25 ♕e4 ♕xe4 26 ♗xe4 ♗g4 27 ♗d5 ♘c5 28 ♖f1 ♖e7 29 ♗xf7+ 1-0

But in the following game, by contrast, White's offensive begins against the black king and concludes successfully on the Q-side.

No. 276 Sax-Vadasz
Budapest, 1977
Caro-Kann Defence

1 e4 c6 2 d3 d5 3 ♘d2 ♘f6 4 ♘gf3 ♗g4 5 h3 ♗h5 6 ♕e2!? ♕c7 7 g4!? ♗g6 8 ♗g2 e6 9 0-0 ♗e7 10 ♘h4 de 11 de ♘bd7 12 ♘f5! ef?! (12...♗f8 followed by 0-0-0 was more circumspect) 13 ef ♗xf5 14 gf ♘b6?! 15 ♖e1 ♘bd5 16 ♘b3 b5 17 a4 b4? (17...0-0 was essential) 18 c4! bc 19 bc 0-0 (on 19...♘xc3 there follows 20 ♗xc6+!) 20 c4 ♗b4 21 cd ♗xe1 22 ♕c4!? ♕e5 23 dc! ♕c3 24 ♕xc3 ♗xc3 25 ♖b1 ♗e5 26 ♘c5 ♗d4 27 ♘a6 ♖ac8 28 c7 ♗b6 29 ♗f4 ♖fe8 30 ♗b7! g5 31 fg hg 32 ♗xc8 ♖xc8 33 ♖b5 ♔f8 34 a5 1-0

A broad tactical offensive

A further feature of early attacks in modern opening variations is their combinational scope, which sometimes encompass the entire chess front.

This is shown in the following games.

No. 277 Smyslov-Botvinnik
World Championship, 1954
French Defence

1 e4 e6 2 d4 d5 3 ᑐc3 ᔔb4 4 e5 c5 5 a3 ᔔa5 6 b4 cd 7 ♕g4 ᑐe7 8 ba! dc 9 ♕×g7 ᖞg8 10 ♕×h7 ᑐd7 11 ᑐf3 ᑐf8?

A passive continuation, which merely assists the development of White's initiative; 11...♕c7! was essential.

12 ♕d3 ♕×a5 13 h4! ᔔd7 14 ᔔg5! ᖞc8 15 ᑐd4! ᑐf5 16 ᖞb1! ᖞc4 17 ᑐ×f5 ef 18 ᖞ×b7 ᖞe4+ 19 ♕×e4! de 20 ᖞb8+ ᔔc8 21 ᔔb5+ ♕×b5 22 ᖞ×b5 ᑐe6 23 ᔔf6 ᖞ×g2 24 h5 ᔔa6 25 h6 1-0

No. 278 Petrosian-Taimanov
USSR Ch., 1955
Slav Defence

1 d4 d5 2 c4 e6 3 ᑐf3 ᑐf6 4 ᑐc3 c6 5 e3 ᑐbd7 6 ᔔd3 ᔔb4 7 0-0 0-0 8 ♕c2 ᔔd6? (better 8...dc 9 ᔔ×c4 ᔔd6 followed by...e5) 9 b3! dc 10 bc e5 11 ᔔb2 ᖞe8 12 ᑐe4! ᑐ×e4 13 ᔔ×e4 h6 14 ᖞad1! ed 15 ᔔh7+! ♔h8 16 ᖞ×d4 ᔔc5 17 ᖞf4 ♕e7 18 ᔔe4 ♕f8 19 ᖞh4 f6 20 ᔔg6 ᖞe7 21 ᖞh5! ᔔd6 22 ᖞd1 ᔔe5 23 ᔔa3 c5 24 ᑐh4! 1-0

No. 279 Vitolins-Yuferov
USSR, 1972
Sicilian Defence

1 e4 c5 2 ᑐf3 d6 3 d4 cd 4 ᑐ×d4

ᑐf6 5 ᑐc3 a6 6 ᔔg5 e6 7 f4 ᑐbd7 8 ♕f3 ♕c7 9 0-0-0 b5 10 e5!? (in recent times 10 ᔔd3 followed by ᖞhe1 has been more often played, intending ᑐd5!) 10... ᔔb7 11 ♕h3 de 12 ᑐ×e6!? fe 13 ♕×e6+ ᔔe7 14 ᔔ×b5 ab 15 ᑐ×b5 ♕c6 16 ᑐd6+ ♔d8 17 fe ♔c7 *(120)*

120

Strangely enough, a position of equilibrium has been reached!

18 ♕×e7 ᖞ×a2! 19 ef ᖞa1+ 20 ♔d2 ♕d5+ 21 ♔c3 ♕a5+ 22 ♔d3 ♕d5+ 23 ♔c3, and the game ended in a draw.

No. 280 I. Zaitsev-Pokojowczyk
Sochi, 1976
French Defence

1 e4 e6 2 d4 d5 3 e5 c5 4 c3 ᑐc6 5 ᑐf3 ♕b6 6 a3 c4 7 ᑐbd2 ᑐa5 8 g3 ᔔd7 9 ᔔh3 f6? 10 ef gf 11 0-0 0-0-0?! 12 ᖞe1 ᔔg7 13 ᖞb1 ♔b8 14 b4! cb 15 ᑐ×b3 ᑐ×b3 (after 15...ᑐa4 16 ᖞ×e6 ᔔ×b3 17 ♕f1 ᔔc4 18 ᔔf4+ ♔a8 19 ♕e1! Black

stands badly) 16 ☐×b3 ♗a4

White's attack is already very strong, e.g. 16...♕c6 17 ♗f4+ ♔a8 18 ♕e2 ☐e8 19 ☐eb1 ♗c8 20 ☐b5! etc.

17 ☐×b6 ♗×d1 18 ☐b×e6 ♗×f3 19 ♗f4+ ♔a8 20 ♗c7! ♘h6 21 ♗×d8 ☐×d8 22 ☐e8 1-0

The dominant role of tactics in attack

The majority of the above samples were notable for their lively and complex tactical skirmishes, and it is this feature which large distinguishes the dynamic nature of an attack.

Here we give several samples of very sharp skirmishes at an early stage of the game, in which behind the game of 'chance' a strategic pattern is nevertheless concealed.

No. 281 Tal-Donner
Wijk aan Zee, 1973
English Opening

1 c4 c5 2 ♘f3 ♘f6 3 ♘c3 ♘c6 4 d4 cd 5 ♘×d4 d5?! 6 ♕a4!?

An alternative was 6 cd ♘×d5 7 ♘×c6 bc 8 ♗d2!, obtaining a slight but persistent advantage.

6...♕b6? (better 6...e6) 7 ♘db5 e6 8 ♗f4 e5 9 cd ef 10 ♕×f4 ♘b4 11 ♘c7+ ♔d8 12 ♘×a8 ♕a5 13 0-0-0!? (13 ☐d1! was

even stronger) 13...♕c5 14 e4! ♘×a2+ 15 ♔c2 ♘×c3 16 bc ♗d6 (16...♘g4 came into consideration) 17 e5 ♘×d5 18 ♕c4! ♗f5+ 19 ♔d2 ♕×f2+ 20 ♗e2 ♕e3+? (the decisive mistake; 20...♗c5 would have led to a draw) 21 ♔e1 ♗×e5 22 ☐×d5+ ♔e7 23 ♘c7 ♗×c3+ 24 ♔d1 ♗e4 25 ♗f3! 1-0

No. 282
Tseshkovsky-Browne
Manila IZ, 1976
Sicilian Defence

1 e4 c5 2 ♘f3 d6 3 d4 cd 4 ♘×d4 ♘f6 5 ♘c3 a6 6 ♗e3 e6 7 ♗e2 ♘bd7 8 g4!? h6 9 f4 b5 10 g5 hg 11 fg ☐h3?! 12 ♗f2! ☐×c3 13 gf! ☐h3

It was essential to play 13... ☐c5!? 14 ♘×e6 ♕a5+ 15 c3 fe 16 b4 ♕a3 17 bc ♕×c3+ 18 ♔f1 ♘×c5 with a double-edged game.

14 ♘×e6!! ♕a5+ 15 c3 fe 16 fg! ♗×g7 17 ♕×d6 ☐h6 18 ☐g1 ♗f8 19 ☐g8 ♕d8 20 0-0-0! *(121)*

121

20...♕e7 21 ♕c6 ♖b8 22 ♗a7!
♔f7 23 ♖g2! ♖b7 24 ♕×c8 ♖×a7
25 ♖f1+ ♘f6 26 e5 ♕d7 (on 26...
♖c7 White has the decisive 27
♖×f6+! ♖×f6 28 ♗h5+ ♖g6 29
♖×g6 ♖×c8 30 ♖g5 mate) 27
♖×f6+ ♖×f6 28 ♗h5+ ♖g6 29
♗×g6+♔e7 30 ♕c5+ 1-0

No. 283 Balinas-Tarjan
Odessa, 1976
Sicilian Defence

1 e4 c5 2 ♘f3 d6 3 d4 cd 4 ♘×d4
♘f6 5 ♘c3 a6 6 ♗g5 e6 7 f4 b5 8 e5
de 9 fe ♕c7 10 ♕e2 ♘fd7 11 0-0-0
♗b7 12 ♕g4 ♕×e5 13 ♗e2 ♘f6 14
♗×f6 gf 15 ♖he1 ♕g5 16 ♕×g5 fg
17 ♗h5! ♔e7 18 ♖f1 f5 19 ♖fe1
♗×g2 20 ♖×e6+ ♔d7 21 ♖e2
♗b7 22 ♘d×b5+ ♔c6 23 ♖e6+
♔c5 24 b4+ ♔×b4 25 ♖d4+ ♔c5
26 ♖e5+ 1-0

No. 284 Sax-Vogt
Budapest, 1976
Scotch Gambit

1 e4 e5 2 ♘f3 ♘c6 3 d4 ed 4 c3
d5 5 ed ♕×d5 6 cd ♗g4 7 ♘c3!?
♗×f3?! 8 ♘×d5 ♗×d1 9 ♘×c7+
♔d7 10 ♘×a8 ♗h5 11 d5! ♗b4+
(better 11...♘d4 12 ♗d3 ♗b4+
13 ♗d2 ♗×d2+ 14 ♔×d2 ♘e7 15
♖ac1 ♖×a8 16 ♖c4 ♘df5 17 g4
♘d6 18 gh with only slightly the
better game for White) 12 ♗d2
♗×d2+ 13 ♔×d2 ♘b4 14 ♗b5+
♔d6 15 ♖ac1 ♘f6 16 ♘c7 ♘×a2

17 ♖c4 a6 18 ♗a4 b5 19 ♖c6+
♔e5 (19...♔d7 20 ♘×a6!) 20
♗b3 ♘b4 21 ♖cc1 ♖d8 22 f3 ♗g6
23 ♖he1+ ♔d4 24 ♖ed1 ♖d7 25
♖c3 ♔e5 26 ♔e2 h5 27 d6! 1-0

No. 285
Lutikov-Ermenkov
Albena, 1976
Sicilian Defence

1 e4 c5 2 ♘f3 ♘c6 3 ♗b5 g6
4 0-0 ♗g7 5 c3 ♘f6 6 d4!? cd 7 cd
♘×e4 8 d5 ♘d6 9 ♘a3 ♘e5?! 10
♘×e5 ♗×e5 11 ♖e1 ♘×b5?!
(better 11...♗f6) 12 ♖×e5! f6 13
♘×b5 fe 14 d6 0-0 15 ♗g5 ♕b6 16
de ♕×b5 17 ef♕+ ♔×f8 18 ♕d6+
♔g8 19 ♗h6 1-0

Psychological factors of dynamic attacks

The modern dynamic style is
notable for its great number of
tactical and combinational
means. At the same time, a characteristic feature of this style is
unexpected changes of plan,
which can have a psychological
effect on the opponent. Such
sudden storms are especially
noteworthy for the further
development of attacking
principles.

The following game confirms
this.

No. 286 Kupreichik-Planinc
Sombor, 1970
Spanish Game

1 e4 e5 2 ♘f3 ♘c6 3 ♗b5 ♗e7
4 0-0 ♘f6 5 ♖e1 d6 6 c3 0-0 7 d4
♗d7 8 h3 ♖e8 9 ♘bd2 ♗f8 10
♗c4!? *(122)*

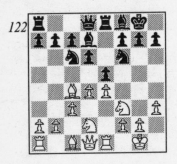

122

In this position Black took an apparently natural decision by playing 10...ed 11 cd d5, but then came 12 ♗b3! (of course not 12 ed? ♖xe1+ 13 ♕xe1 ♘b4 with an excellent game for Black) 12...de 13 ♗xf7+!?

A typically 'irrational' sacrifice, which, however, should have led only to equality after correct play by Black. Note that after 13 ♘g5 ♗e6 14 ♘xe6 fe the game would have been level.

13...♔xf7 14 ♕b3+ ♔g6?

The difficulty in defending such positions lies in the psychological effect of sudden changes of attack. Hence the rapid catastrophe. Black should have played 14... ♗e6! 15 ♘g5+

♔g8 16 ♘xe6 ♘a5 17 ♘xd8
♘xb3 18 ab ♖exd8 with an equal game.

15 ♘h4+ ♔h5 16 ♘xe4!

The decisive blow. In view of the threat of 17 ♕f3+, Black's king comes under an irresistible attack.

16...♖xe4 17 ♖xe4 g5 (after 17...♘xe4 18 ♕f3+ ♔xh4 19 ♕xe4+ ♔h5 Black would have been mated by 20 ♕xh7) 18 ♕f7+ ♔h6 19 ♘f5+! 1-0

The 'brittleness' of dynamic attacks

Dynamic attacks are among the most 'brittle' of strategic means, which demands that they be carried out with particular subtlety. Sometimes, in spite of all the apparently favourable factors, the aim of such an attack proves unrealizable, on account of some unforeseen detail.

Here is an instructive example.

No. 287 Taimanov-Larsen
Vinkovci, 1970
Nimzo-Indian Defence

1 d4 ♘f6 2 c4 e6 3 ♘c3 ♗b4
4 ♕c2 c5 5 dc 0-0 6 ♗f4 ♗xc5
7 ♘f3 ♘c6 8 e3 d5 9 a3 ♕a5 10
♖c1 ♗e7 11 ♗e2 dc 12 ♗xc4

♘d5!? 13 ♗×d5 ed 14 ♕b3

Here Black literally shocked his opponent:

14...g5!? 15 ♗g3 g4

In addition to his organic weakness in the centre, Black creates an even more unpleasant weakness on the K-side. Naturally, in such cases the opponent is 'dazzled' by the wealth of possibilities, and his ambitions increase sharply. Later analysis showed that White should have limited himself to 16 ♘e5, and if 16...d4 17 ed ♘×d4 18 ♕d5 with the initiative. But it was not easy to foresee that the chosen plan of switching to a sharp attack on the king, at first sight very dangerous, would prove unfounded!

16 ♘d4 ♘×d4 17 ed ♗g5 18 0-0 ♗×c1 19 ♖×c1 ♗e6 20 h3 (20 ♕×b7 is parried by 20...♕b6) **20...gh 21 ♗e5**

White was counting on this attack when he sacrificed the exchange.

21...f6 22 ♘e4 fe 23 ♕g3+ ♗g4!!

A splendid defensive resource, which eloquently testifies to the practical strength of Black's plan. Now the game swings sharply in his favour.

24 ♕×g4+ ♔h8 25 ♘g5 ♕d2 26 ♖c7 ♕×f2+ 27 ♔h2 ♕×g2+ 28 ♕×g2 hg 29 de ♖ac8 30 ♖×b7 ♖c2 31 ♘f7+ ♔g7 32 e6 ♔f6 33 e7 g1♕+ 34 ♔×g1 ♖g8+ 0-1

Dynamic counterattacks

Nowhere does the early counterattack play such a part as in sharp dynamic opening variations. An eloquent example of this is the Taimanov-Larsen game just given.

In the general case a counterattack here is a reaction to a violent attacking measure, which at the same time is very brittle.

To illustrate the sudden tactical counterblow, we will consider the following interesting example.

No. 288 Poulsson-Farago
Gausdal, 1976
Queen's Gambit

1 d4 e6 2 ♘f3 ♘f6 3 c4 d5 4 ♘c3 c5 5 cd ♘×d5 6 e3 ♘c6 7 ♗c4 cd 8 ed ♗e7 9 0-0 0-0 10 ♖e1 ♘×c3 11 bc b6 12 ♗d3 ♗b7 13 ♕c2 g6 14 ♕d2?! ♗f6 15 h4?! ♖c8! 16 h5 *(123)*

A strictly strategic battle appears to be in progress. Here Black would usually play for square control on the Q-side, for example with 16...♘a5 etc. In turn, White would aim to build up a piece attack on the black king. But here we see a completely new interpretation of this position, as now, like a bolt from the blue, there came:

16...♘xd4!! 17 ♘xd4 (after 17 cd ♗xf3 18 gf ♗xd4 19 ♗a3 ♗c3!! 20 ♕e3 ♗xa1 21 ♖xa1 ♖c3! Black wins) 17...♖xc3!! 18 ♕xc3 ♗xd4 19 ♕c2 ♗xa1 20 ♗a3 ♕g5! 21 ♗e4 ♖c8 22 ♕e2 ♗xe4 23 ♕xe4 ♗g7, and Black had a winning position.

No. 289 Uhlmann-Veresov
East Germany-Byelorussia
1969
Queen's Gambit

1 d4 d5 2 c4 e6 3 ♘c3 ♘f6 4 ♗g5 ♗e7 5 ♘f3 0-0 6 ♖c1 h6 7 ♗h4 b6 8 cd ♘xd5 9 ♗xe7 ♕xe7 10 ♘xd5 ed 11 g3!?

Before this game the given system of development was considered one of the most effective for White, e.g. 11...♗e6 12 ♗g2 c5 13 ♘e5 ♕b7 14 ♘d3 ♘d7 15 0-0 ♖ac8 15 dc bc 17 ♖c2, and it is not easy for Black to deploy his forces (Uhlmann-Rodriguez, Havana, 1969).

But here Veresov finds a deep and highly combinational plan.

11...♖e8! 12 ♗g2 ♗a6! 13 ♘e5 ♘d7! 14 ♖xc7 ♖ac8!!

A brilliant move. It transpires that after 15 ♖xd7 ♕b4+ 16 ♔f1 (16 ♕d2? ♖c1 mate) 16...♕xd4!! Black wins.

15 ♖xc8 ♖xc8 16 0-0 ♘xe5 17 de ♕xe5 18 ♖e1 d4 19 ♕d2 ♖e8 20 f4 ♕c5 21 b4 ♕d6 22 ♗f3 ♗c4 23 a3 b5 24 ♖d1 ♖d8 25 ♔g2 a5 26 ♕b2 a4 27 ♖d2 g5!

After the dynamic introduction, the play has become purely classical, and Black has gained the initiative.

28 fg hg 29 ♕c2 ♕e5 30 ♕e4 ♕xe4 31 ♗xe4 ♔g7 32 e3?

The decisive mistake. It was essential to play 32 ♔f3.

32...♖e8! 33 ♔f3 (33 ♖xd4 ♖xe4! 34 ♖xe4 ♗d5 35 ♔f3 f5! leads to a win for Black) 33...de 34 ♖d1 e2 35 ♖e1 ♔f6 36 ♗c6 ♖e6 37 ♗d7 ♖d6 38 ♗g4 ♖d3+ 39 ♔e4 ♖xa3 40 ♗xe2 ♗xe2 41 ♖xe2 ♖b3 0-1

The following two examples are also typical in this respect.

No. 290 Justolisi-Primavera
Italy, 1976
King's Indian Defence

1 ♘f3 ♘f6 2 g3 g6 3 ♗g2 ♗g7 4 0-0 0-0 5 d4 c5 6 d5 d6 7 c4 b5 8 cb a6 9 ba ♗xa6 10 ♘c3 ♘bd7 11 ♗f4 ♕a5 12 ♕c2 ♖fb8 13 h3?

This carelessness has serious

consequences. 13 罝ab1 was necessary.

13...罝xb2! 14 營xb2 ②e4! 15 營c2 ②xc3 16 ♗d2 ②xe2+ 17 ♔h2 營a3! 18 營e4 ②e5! 19 ②xe5 ♗xe5 20 罝ae1 ②xg3! 21 fg 營xg3+ 22 ♔g1 營h2+ 23 ♔f2 ♗xf1 24 ♔xf1 罝xa2 25 ♗e3 營g3 26 罝b1 罝xg2 27 罝b8+ ♔g7 28 營xg2 營xe3 0-1

No. 291 Popov-Suetin
Daugavpils, 1974
Sicilian Defence

1 e4 c5 2 ②f3 e6 3 d4 cd 4 ②xd4 ②c6 5 ②c3 a6 6 g3 d6 7 ♗g2 ♗d7 8 0-0 ②f6 9 ②ce2 ♗e7 10 c4 0-0 11 b3 罝c8 12 ♗b2 b5 13 cb ②xd4 14 營xd4?

White made this move without thinking, almost automatically. He clearly overlooked the counterblow which Black now interposes.

14...罝c2! 15 ②c1 ♗xb5 16 ②d3 e5 17 營e3 d5 (17...營a5 was even stronger) 18 ed e4 19 ♗xf6 ♗xf6 20 ②xe4 ♗xa1 21 罝xa1 f5 22 ♗g2 營f6, and Black retained much the better chances.

Dynamic seizing of the initiative

The dynamic seizing of the initiative also occurs very frequently in a number of modern variations. Normally one side (more often Black, of course), which has up till then been defending, boldly goes in for a positional sacrifice of material. The following examples are instructive in this respect.

No. 292 Mnatsakanian-Veresov
Lvov, 1968
Sicilian Defence

1 e4 c5 2 ②f3 ②c6 3 d4 cd 4 ②xd4 g6 5 ②c3 ♗g7 6 ♗e3 ②f6 7 ♗c4 d6 8 f3 0-0 9 營d2 ♗d7 10 ♗b3 營a5 11 0-0-0 罝fc8 12 g4 ②e5 13 h4 罝c4!? (124)

14 ♗xc4 ②xc4 15 營d3 b5 16 ②b3 營a6 17 ♗d4? (better 17 a3) 17...e5! 18 ♗f2 b4 19 ②d5 ②xd5 20 營xd5 ♗c6 21 營d3 ♗b5 22 ②d2? (22 營d5 was essential) 22...②xb2 23 營d5 ②d3+! 24 ♔b1 ♗a3! 0-1

A sudden counterattack may occur not only against the king, but also against other targets. The following game is an example of a sudden attack in the centre.

No. 293 Botvinnik-Smyslov
World Championship, 1954
King's Indian Defence

1 d4 ♘f6 2 c4 g6 3 g3 ♗g7 4 ♗g2 0-0 5 ♘c3 d6 6 ♘f3 ♘bd7 7 0-0 e5 8 e4 c6 9 ♗e3 ♘g4 10 ♗g5 ♕b6 11 h3

In reply to this natural move, Black began a sudden, sharp and risky attack on White's centre:

11...ed! 12 ♘a4 ♕a6 13 hg b5 14 ♘xd4 ba 15 ♘xc6 ♕xc6 16 e5 ♕xc4 17 ♗xa8 ♘xe5 18 ♖c1 ♕b4 19 a3 ♕xb2 20 ♕xa4 ♗b7!

20...♗xg4 is weaker − 21 ♕xa7!

21 ♖b1?

Sudden attacks of this type have a psychological effect on the defender.

Correct was 21 ♗xb7 ♕xb7 22 ♖c3 ♘f3+ 23 ♖xf3 ♕xf3 24 ♗e7 ♖c8 25 ♗xd6, with a probable draw. This is a typical example of a modern attack as a playing method (rather than as the realization of an advantage), where objectively, perhaps, it is difficult to count on an advantage.

21...♘f3+ 22 ♔h1 ♗xa8 23 ♖xb2 ♘xg5+! 24 ♔h2 ♘f3+ 25 ♔h3 ♗xb2 26 ♕xa7 ♗e4 27 a4 ♔g7 28 ♖d1 ♗e5 29 ♕e7 ♖c8! 30 a5 ♖c2 31 ♔g2 ♘d4+ 32 ♔f1 ♗f3

33 ♖b1 ♘c6 0-1

No. 294 Capablanca-Alekhine
World Championship, 1927
Queen's Gambit

1 d4 d5 2 c4 e6 3 ♘c3 ♘d7 4 ♘c3 ♘gf6 5 ♗g5 c6 6 e3 ♕a5 7 ♘d2 ♗b4 8 ♕c2 0-0 9 ♗h4 c5 10 ♘b3 ♕a4 11 ♗xf6 ♘xf6 12 dc ♘e4 13 cd ♗xc3+ 14 bc ♘xc5 15 ♖d1 ed 16 ♖xd5 ♘xb3 17 ab ♕c6 18 ♖d4 ♖e8

Black has sacrificed a pawn, and seems thereby to have restricted the development of White's K-side. But Capablanca finds an effective and elegant plan, involving a counter pawn sacrifice for the sake of an attack on the black king. This attack is very dangerous, although the white forces participating in it are quite modest.

19 ♗d3! ♕xg2 20 ♗xh7+ ♔f8 21 ♗e4 ♕h3 22 ♕d2! ♗e6 23 c4 a5 24 ♖g1! ♕xh2 25 ♖h1 ♕c7 26 ♕b2!

White continually comes up with highly concrete threats, in this case 27 ♕a3+ ♔g8 28 ♗h7+ ♔h8 29 ♖dh4 etc.

26...♕c5 27 ♗d5!

And now there is the threat of 28 ♗xe6 fe 29 ♖f4+ ♔g8 30 ♕c2.

27...♖a6 (27...♖ad8 is more tenacious, although even here White has every chance of winning after 28 ♗xe6!) **28 ♖e4!**

♖d6 29 ♖h7! ♔e7 30 ♕xg7 ♔d8 31 ♗xe6 fe 32 ♕xb7, and White won.

No. 295 Estrin-Veresov
USSR, 1962
Sicilian Defence

1 e4 c5 2 ♘f3 d6 3 d4 cd 4 ♘xd4 ♘f6 5 ♘c3 g6 6 ♗e3 ♗g7 7 ♗e2 0-0 8 f4 ♘c6 9 ♘b3 ♗e6 10 g4!? ♖c8!? (the immediate central counterblow 10...d5 has been analyzed more) 11 g5 ♘d7 12 ♕d2 ♘b6 13 0-0-0 ♘b4! 14 ♔b1 ♘c4 15 ♗xc4 ♖xc4 16 ♗d4! ♗g4 17 ♖de1 ♗xd4 18 ♘xd4 ♕b6 19 ♘b3 ♖fc8 20 a3(?) ♘xc2 21 ♕xc2 ♗e6! 22 ♔a1 ♖xc3! 23 bc ♗xb3 24 ♕b2 ♖c4! 25 ♖b1 ♕a5! 26 ♕xb3 ♖xc3 27 ♖hc1 ♖xb3 28 ♖xb3 ♔g7 29 ♖1c3 b5 30 h4 ♕b6 31 ♖e3 ♕d4+ 32 ♖bc3 a5 33 ♔b1 ♕d1+ 34 ♔b2 ♕g4 35 f5 ♕xh4 36 e5 de 37 fg hg 38 ♖f3 ♕d4 39 ♖d3 b4! 0-1

No. 296 Goodman-Nunn
England, 1978
English Opening

1 c4 e5 2 ♘c3 ♘f6 3 ♘f3 ♘c6 4 e3 ♗b4 5 ♕c2 0-0 6 ♘d5 ♖e8 7 ♕f5 d6 8 ♘xf6+ gf 9 ♕h5! d5 10 a3 ♗f8 11 d4 ♗e6 12 ♗d3 e4 13 ♗c2 ♘e7 14 ♘d2 f5!? 15 cd ♕xd5 16 f3 ♕c6?
An outwardly active, but incorrect plan. Better was 14...f4!

15 ♘xe4 ♕xh5 16 ♘f6+ ♔h8 17 ♘xh5 fe. Now White not only firmly seizes the initiative, but also develops a very strong attack.

17 ♘xe4! ♕xc2 18 ♘f6+ ♔g7 19 e4! ♕xc1+ 20 ♖xc1 ♔xf6 21 ♕xh7 ♘g6 22 e5+ ♔g5?! 23 h4+ ♔f4 24 ♔f2 1-0

Belief in defensive resources

Often, in certain sharp variations of the Sicilian Defence, for example, Black deliberately exposes himself to a sharp attack by White. Many such problems arise in the Polugayevsky Variation: 1 e4 c5 2 ♘f3 d6 3 d4 cd 4 ♘xd4 ♘f6 5 ♘c3 a6 6 ♗g5 e6 7 f4 b5!?

Black draws the enemy fire, believing not only in the wealth of defensive resources in this position, but also in its latent active possibilities. In a number of cases Black as though invites his opponent to go in for a sacrifice of material, but if White's attack misfires, the material factor will triumph.

An instructive example is provided by the following game.

No. 297 Sakharov-Polugayevsky
USSR Ch, 1960
Sicilian Defence

(1 e4 c5 2 ᗏf3 d6 3 d4 cd
4 ᗏ×d4 ᗏf6 5 ᗏc3 a6 6 ᗒg5 e6
7 f4 b5) 8 ᗒd3 ᗏbd7 9 ᗕe2 ᗕb6
10 ᗏ×e6!? fe 11 e5 de 12 fe ᗕc5!
(125)

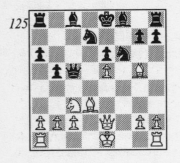

It transpires that White's seemingly threatening initiative peters out move by move.

13 ᗒf4 ᗏd5 14 ᗏ×d5 ed 15
0-0-0 ᗕc6!

An excellent move, which simultaneously achieves three aims — control over e6 and, even more importantly, over g6, and vacating of the c5 square.

16 ᗒf5 ᗒe7 17 ᗕg4 g6 18 e6
ᗏc5 19 ᗒ×g6+ hg 20 ᗕ×g6+ ᗕd8
21 ᗕhe1 ᗒ×e6 22 b4 ᗕd7 23 bc
ᗕag8 24 ᗕd3 ᗕ×g2 25 ᗕf3 ᗕg6
0-1

No. 298 Bellon-G. Garcia
Orense, 1976
Sicilian Defence

1 e4 c5 2 ᗏf3 ᗏc6 3 d4 cd
4 ᗏ×d4 ᗏf6 5 ᗏc3 e5 6 ᗏbd5 d6
7 ᗒg5 a6 8 ᗏa3 b5 9 ᗒ×f6 gf 10
ᗏd5 f5 11 ef ᗒ×f5 12 ᗕf3?! ᗏd4!
13 ᗏc7+ ᗕ×c7 14 ᗕ×a8+ ᗒc8 15
ᗒd3? (15 c3) 15...d5! 16 0-0
ᗒ×a3 17 ba 0-0 18 f4 ᗒb7 19
ᗒ×h7+ ᗕg7 20 ᗕ×f8+ ᗕ×f8 21 fe
ᗏe2+ 0-1

No. 299 Levchenkov-Gorelov
Riga, 1977
Sicilian Defence

1 e4 c5 2 ᗏf3 ᗏc6 3 d4 cd
4 ᗏ×d4 ᗏf6 5 ᗏc3 e5 6 ᗏbd5 d6
7 ᗒg5 a6 8 ᗒ×f6 gf 9 ᗏa3 b5 10
ᗏd5 f5 11 ᗒ×b5!? ab 12 ᗏ×b5

A problematic piece sacrifice. On the basis of Pereypskin-Sveshnikov (1973), in which Black gained the advantage after 12...ᗕa7 13 ᗏ×a7 ᗏ×a7 14 ᗕf3 ᗏc6 15 0-0-0 ᗒh6+ 16 ᗕb1 fe 17 ᗕ×e4 0-0, the *Encyclopaedia of Chess Openings* regarded this sacrifice as dubious. But it was successfully employed in Vitolins-Katishonok, Latvian Ch., 1977 (White played 14 ef), which appeared to shake the theoretical assessment. But now comes a fresh duel — and the scales tip the opposite way.

12...ᗕa4! 13 ᗏbc7+ ᗕd7 14 ef

♘e7 15 0-0 ♖d4 16 ♕e2 ♘xd5 17 c3 ♘xc7 18 cd ♗a6 19 ♕g4 ♗xf1 20 f6+ ♔e8 21 ♖xf1 ♕d7 22 ♕e4 d5! 23 ♕xe5+ ♔d8, and Black won.

Under the microscope of analysis

As a result of analysis, the theory of certain modern sharp opening variations develops not only quickly, but also with radical changes in fortune, as first attack triumphs, and then counterattack.

Typical in this respect is the development of a sharp and topical variation of the Benko Gambit: 1 d4 ♘f6 2 c4 c5 3 d5 b5 4 cb a6 5 ♘c3 ab 6 e4!? b4 7 ♘b5!? *(126)*

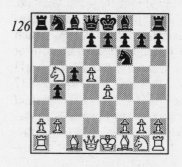

126

The idea of this continuation belongs to GM Igor Zaitsev. In certain lines White voluntarily gives up his e4 pawn with the aim of opening the e-file.

Then in a number of cases the 'incomprehensible' white knight at b5 becomes a formidable force.

7...d6 8 ♘f3 (8 ♗f4, which appears very strong, is parried by 8...g5!) **8...♘bd7**

The basic idea of the pawn sacrifice lies in the following tactical operation (which is how many of the early games proceeded): **8...♘xe4 9 ♗c4 g6** (after 9...♘d7 10 ♕e2 ♘df6 11 ♗f4 White has the very strong threats of 12 ♘g5 and 12 ♘d2) **10 ♕e2 ♘f6** (things are also difficult for Black after 10...f5 11 ♘g5!) **11 ♗f4 ♖a6 12 ♘xd6+!**

As the dramatist Anton Chekhov expressed it, if in the first act of a play there is a gun hanging on the wall, it is bound to be fired sooner or later!

12...♖xd6 13 ♗b5+, and White gains a great advantage.

But nowadays after 8...♘bd7 White's initiative does not prove so effective. Moreover, the white knight often proves to be cut off from its main forces.

No. 300 I. Zaitsev-Benko
Szolnok, 1975

From diagram 126: **7...d6 8 ♘f3 ♘bd7 9 ♗f4 ♘h5 10 ♗g5 ♘hf6 11 ♕e2 ♖a5! 12 e5 ♗a6 13 ef ♗xb5 14 fe ♗xe7 15 ♗xe7 ♕xe7 16 ♕xe7+ ♔xe7 17 ♗xb5 ♖xb5 18 0-0 ♘b6 19 ♖fe1+ ♔d7. The** endgame favours Black.

Here the counterattack proved stronger, but this by no means signifies that the given assessment is conclusive. Many sharp, dynamic variations are constantly being reassessed under the microscope of sharper and ever deeper analysis. Thus instead of 11 ♕e2 White can consider the immediate central pawn thrust: 11 e5!? de 12 ♕e2 ♖a5 (12...e4 13 ♘d2! ♗a6 14 ♘xe4 favours - White) 13 ♘xe5 ♘xe5 (not 13...♗a6 14 ♘c4! ♗xb5 15 ♘d6 mate) 14 ♕xe5 ♕b6 15 ♘c7+ ♔d8 16 ♗f4! (but not 16 d6? ♕xd6! 17 ♖d1 ♔xc7! 18 ♖xd6 ed with advantage to Black) 16...♖a7 17 ♘b5 ♖d7 18 ♗c4 etc., with the better chances for White (recommended by Zaitsev).

Here too it is early to draw the line. Despite the tempting variations, the plan with 6 e4!? remains at the least double-edged. In this sense the development of the following game is instructive.

No. 301 Gligorić-Dezě
Novi Sad, 1976

From Diagram 126: **7...d6 8 ♘f3 g6 9 e5 de 10 ♘xe5 ♗g7 11 ♗c4 0-0 12 0-0 ♘fd7!? 13 f4?** (13 ♘xd7 ♘xd7 14 d6 leads to an equal game) **13...♘b6! 14 b3**

♗b7 15 ♗e3 ♘8d7 16 ♘c6?! ♗xc6 17 dc ♗xa1 18 ♕xa1 ♘xc4 19 c7 ♕c8 20 bc ♕b7!, and Black had the advantage.

The following example is also typical.

No. 302 Stean-Sigurjonsson
England-Iceland, Telex, 1977
Sicilian Defence

1 e4 c5 2 ♘f3 d6 3 d4 cd 4 ♘xd4 ♘f6 5 ♘c3 a6 6 ♗g5 e6 7 f4 b5 8 e5 de 9 fe ♕c7 10 ♕e2 ♘fd7 11 0-0-0 ♗b7 12 ♕g4 ♕xe5 13 ♗e2 ♗c5!

A prepared innovation. Balashov-Quinteros (Manila, 1976), where 13 ♗e2 first occurred, continued 13...h5?! 14 ♕h4 f6 15 ♗f4 g5 16 ♕xh5+ ♖xh5 17 ♗xh5+ ♔e7 18 ♗xe5, and White won on move 42.

14 ♗f3 (14 ♖he1 is probably better) **14...♗xd4 15 ♗xb7 ♗xc3 16 bc ♖a7 17 ♖he1 h5** (if 17...♕xc3 18 ♖xe6+ ♔f8 19 ♗e7+ ♔g8 20 ♗f6 ♕a3+ 21 ♗b2 ♕f8 22 ♖e8) **18 ♕h4 ♕xc3 19 ♖e3 ♕a1+ 20 ♔d2 ♕xa2 -** defending e6) **21 ♕b4 f6 22 ♕d6 ♖xb7 23 ♖xe6+ ♔d8 24 ♗f4 ♔c8 25 ♖de1 ♕a5+ 26 ♔c1! ♖d8 27 ♖e8 ♕a1+! 0-1**

If 28 ♔d2, then 28...♕xe1+! (29 ♔xe1 ♖xe8+ or 29 ♖xe1 ♘c5).

Of course, here too research continues. It was not by accident that the winner of this game advised the loser; make a careful study of 13...♗c5!

A necessary measure of caution in active intentions

Sharp dynamic plans, both in attack and counterattack, involve a considerable risk, the degree of which is most probably determined intuitively. It is largely intuition which should suggest the necessary sense of measure in the choice and implementation of a particular dynamic plan.

Below we give some examples of this sense of measure being lost.

No. 303 Dely-Horvath
Hungary, 1977
Sicilian Defence

1 e4 c5 2 ♘f3 ♘c6 3 d4 cd 4 ♘xd4 ♘f6 5 ♘c3 e5 6 ♘bd5 d6 7 ♗g5 a6 8 ♘a3 b5 9 ♗xf6 gf 10 ♘d5 f5 11 ♗d3 ♗e6 12 0-0 ♗g7 13 c4?! bc 14 ♘xc4 0-0 15 ♘cb6 fe 16 ♗xe4 ♖b8 17 ♗xh7+ ♔xh7 18 ♕c2+ e4! 19 ♕xc6 ♗d4

This is evidently what White was aiming for, when he embarked on his sharp and risky plan on move 13. He has won a pawn, but has overlooked Black's powerful counterattack, which in fact decides the game.

20 ♘a4 ♖c8 21 ♕b7 ♕h4 22 ♕b4 ♖g8!

And here is the refutation! On 23 ♕xd4 there follows 23... ♖xg2+! 24 ♔xg2 ♕g4+ 25 ♔h1 ♕f3+ 26 ♔g1 ♖g8+.

The game concluded: 23 ♘e3 ♗xe3 24 fe ♖xg2+ 25 ♔xg2 ♖c2+ 0-1

No. 304 Heinsohn-Espig
East Germany, 1977
Alekhine's Defence

1 e4 ♘f6 2 e5 ♘d5 3 d4 d6 4 c4 ♘b6 5 ed cd 6 h3 g6 7 ♘f3 ♗g7 8 ♗e2 0-0 9 0-0 ♘c6 10 ♘c3 ♗f5 11 ♗e3 d5 12 c5 ♘c4 13 ♗xc4 dc 14 ♕a4 ♗d3 15 ♖fd1 f5?

In search of active counterplay, Black loses his sense of danger and soon runs into a decisive counter. Correct was 15...♕a5 16 ♕xa5 ♘xa5 17 ♘e1 ♗f5 18 ♖ac1 ♘c6, maintaining equality (Dvoretsky-Bagirov 1973).

16 d5 f4 *(127)*

17 ♖×d3! cd 18 dc fe 19 cb ef+ 20 ♔f1 ♖b8 21 ♕c4+ ♔h8 22 c6 ♕b6 23 c7 ♕×b7 24 cb♕ ♕×b8 25 ♘d1 d2 26 ♕b3 ♕c7 27 ♘×f2 ♕c1+ 28 ♕d1 ♗×b2 29 ♖b1 ♖d8 30 g3 ♖d6 31 ♔g2 h6 32 ♘e4 1-0

Here are two further instructive examples of risky, although active plans by Black being refuted. In the first of these he was wrongly tempted at an early stage by unrealizable dreams of an attack in the centre, and overooked the loss of a rook. In the second, instead of setting up a determined defence, he began superficial active play in the centre, which led to a crushing defeat.

No. 305 Karpov-Miles
Tilburg, 1977
English Opening

1 c4 c5 2 ♘f3 ♘f6 3 ♘c3 ♘c6 4 d4 cd 5 ♘×d4 e6 6 g3 ♕b6 7 ♘b3 ♘e5 8 e4 ♗b4 9 ♕e2 a5?! 10 ♗e3 ♕c6 11 f3 0-0 12 ♘d4 ♕a6 13 ♘b5 d5 14 ♘c7 ♕d6 15 ♘×a8 de 16 fe ♘×e4 17 ♖d1 ♕c6 18 ♗g2 ♘×c4 19 ♗d4 ♗×c3+ 20 bc f5 21 0-0 ♘cd6 22 ♘b6 e5 23 ♘×c8 ♖×c8 24 ♗×e5 ♕c5+ 25 ♗d4 1-0

No. 306 Petrosian-Kupreichik
USSR Ch., 1976
Slav Defence

1 d4 d5 2 c4 c6 3 cd cd 4 ♘c3 ♘f6 5 ♘f3 ♘c6 6 ♗f4 e6 7 e3 ♗d6

8 ♗g3 ♘e4 (8. . . 0-0) 9 ♘×e4 de 10 ♘d2 ♗×g3 11 hg e5? 12 de ♕a5 13 ♕b3! ♕×e5 14 ♗e2 ♕e7 15 ♖c1 0-0 16 ♘×e4! ♕×e4 17 ♗d3 ♕b4+ 18 ♕×b4 ♘×b4 19 ♗×h7+ ♔h8 20 ♗b1+ ♔g8 21 ♖c4! a5 (21. . . ♘c6 also fails to save Black: 22 ♗h7+ ♔h8 23 ♗d3+! ♔g8 24 ♖ch4! etc) 22 ♗h7+ ♔h8 23 ♗f5+! 1-0

Attack as a playing method

Above we have examined a whole series of dynamic attacks, many of which gave a positive result to one side, but this by no means signifies that there is no room for compromise (cf. No. 279). In the majority of cases defeat was by no means predestined by the preceding logic of the opening struggle. Moreover, at the start of the sharp skirmish the chances of the two sides were roughly equal. It was a question of one side having a dynamic initiative.

But this initiative, as if at the waving of a magic wand, very often was quickly transformed into an irresistible attack. This, of course, was assisted by mistakes by the opponent, who was overwhelmed by the onslaught.

This suggests that dynamic attacks are effective in the practical sense. In this type of situation the probability of mistakes by both sides is very great (although, as already mentioned, the attacker has a certain psychological advantage).

What is required here is great combinational ingenuity and a particular tactical accuracy in defence.

In such variations a primary role is played by deep and concrete calculation, as shown by the following line of the Slav Gambit: 1 d4 d5 2 c4 c6 3 ♘c3 e6 4 e4 de 5 ♘xe4 ♗b4+ 6 ♗d2 ♕xd4 7 ♗xb4 ♕xe4+ 8 ♗e2 ♘a6 9 ♗c3 *(128)*

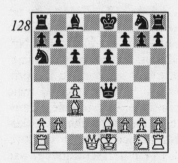

128

In this critical position exceptional accuracy is demanded of Black. Imperceptible but instructive mistakes were made by Black in the games Rovner-Kotov (Leningrad, 1949) and Bronstein-Kotov (Budapest, 1950), in which he was lost right from the opening.

The first went 9...♘e7 10 ♗xg7 ♕xg2? (10...♖g8 is the correct defence) 11 ♗f6!! ♘c5 (11...♕xh1 12 ♕d6! 0-0 13 ♕g3+, winning the queen) 12 ♕d6 0-0 13 ♗f3 ♕g6 14 ♗xe7 ♘d3+ 15 ♔e2 ♘xb2 16 ♖c1, and White won.

In the second there followed: 10...♖g8 11 ♗c3! ♕xg2? (the combinational 11...♘d5! is correct) 12 ♕d2 ♕xh1? (here too 12...♘d5! is better) 13 0-0-0 ♘d5 14 ♘f3 ♕xd1+ 15 ♗xd1 ♘xc3 16 ♕xc3 ♔e7 17 ♘e5!, and again White won.

From the examples given it is apparent that, in opening variations with concrete tactical play, in many cases the outcome can be decided very quickly.

In these variations, where usually there is no formal boundary between opening and middlegame, it is rather difficult to establish any lasting features of the positions arising from the opening struggle. The assessment of such set-ups can be revealed only by their concrete study.

Thus the variation in the games just considered can lead to the following unusual position with approximate equality (cf. Diag. 128): 9...♘e7 10 ♗xg7 ♖g8 11 ♗c3 ♘d5! 12 cd ♕xg2 13 de (in the event of 13 ♗f3 ♕xg1+ 14 ♖xg1 ♖xg1+ 15 ♔e2 ♖xd1 16 ♖xd1 ed the advantage passes to Black) 13...♗xe6 14 ♗f6

♕×h1 15 ♕d6! ♖×g1+ 16 ♔d2 ♕d5+! 17 ♕×d5 ♗×d5 18 ♖×g1 ♔d7 etc.

Thus in a number of cases a sharp tactical attack is not a final aim, but a playing method, necessary for the gaining of this or that positional advantage. Sometimes with an attack of this type a game does not conclude, but merely moves into a new stage of the struggle for an advantage. It may lead to a superior ending, the seizure of important squares, the spoiling of an enemy pawn chain, the winning of a pawn in return for which the opponent may temporarily gain the initiative, and so on.

Reflected here is a deep and truly realistic penetration into the specific character of the chess battle. After all, it happens comparatively rarely, only after serious opening mistakes by one of the sides, that there is a sharp disturbance of the equilibrium. At the same time, with modern technique, success can be achieved even after an outwardly insignificant disturbance of the equality line. There are many possible plans for achieving this. Along with the accumulation of small advantages, a dynamic path is also possible, making use of all typical attacking procedures. Thus the overal aim of an attack, in its modern under-

standing, lies not in the obligatory destruction of the enemy position, but in the attainment of the initiative, certain positional gains, or perhaps simply a comfortable position or one conforming to a player's style of play. But in carrying out such a plan he sets concrete problems, over which his opponent can stumble at literally every step.

Instructive in this respect is a line of the Richter/Rauzer Attack in the Sicilian Defence: 1 e4 c5 2 ♘f3 ♘c6 3 d4 cd 4 ♘×d4 ♘f6 5 ♘c3 d6 6 ♗g5 e6 7 ♕d2 ♗e7 8 0-0-0 0-0 9 f4 ♘×d4 10 ♕×d4 h6 11 ♗h4 ♕a5 12 e5!? de 13 ♕×e5 ♕×e5 14 fe ♘d5 15 ♗×e7 ♘×e7 16 ♗d3.

On his 12th move in this line White begins a sharp plan, which involves various tactical nuances. Thus, for example, on his 13th move Black cannot avoid the exchange of queens (13. . . ♕b6 14 ♘a4!), and the game goes by force into an ending, which, however, is not easy to assess. In return for the definite weakness of his e5 pawn, White has a spatial advantage, which ensures him a certain initiative. Black must still overcome numerous difficulties in solving the problem of completing the mobilization of his forces.

Thus the direct development 16. . . ♗d7? creates additional

difficulties for Black, even though the game is further simplified. After 17 ♗h7+! ♔xh7 18 ♖xd7 ♘c6 19 ♖xb7 ♘xe7 20 ♖e1 the endgame clearly favours White.

Theory recommends 16. . . ♘c6 17 ♖he1 ♖d8! 18 b4 ♗d7 19 b5 ♘a5 20 ♘e4 ♖ac8 21 ♘d6 ♖c5

followed by . . .♔f8-e7, trying to become established on the d-file and gradually to create counterplay against White's e5 pawn. Black has good chances of equalizing.

It can be considered that subsequently a positional struggle develops.

eight

OPENING PRINCIPLES IN THEIR SECOND APPROXIMATION

Dynamic play and a new approach to opening principles

The method of sharp struggle for the initiative does not contradict the implementation of important general tasks in the initial stage of the game.

With this type of play, opening and middlegame (and sometimes even endgame) are closely linked. In variations of this sort the transition from opening to middlegame appears to take place imperceptibly, before the completion of mobilization. This is assisted by the implementation of an active strategic plan at an early stage of the game, to which even mobilization tasks are subordinate.

Since each side has the aim of taking play along the sharpest, most crucial path, in such variations the desire to disrupt the coordination of the opponent's forces is very clearly seen. At the same time, the harmonious and purposeful coordination of one's own forces is especially important.

But the solving of general problems also demands the observance of basic elementary opening principles, and in this respect deviations are often noticed in dynamic variations. Thus often the principle of rapid development is not strictly observed, or else the queen (and sometimes one of the rooks) is brought into play early, and so on.

In such opening set-ups the use of opening principles often depends on the early implementation of active operations, which are usually characteristic of a full-blooded middlegame. It is here that a concrete approach to opening principles is important.

It is natural that the struggle in dynamic variations differs from that in opening set-ups where forcing events develop only after the completion of mobilization. Such opening set-ups are especially dynamic, and the handling of them, sometimes from a very early stage, demands deep and accurate concrete calculation. When analyzing them, 'constant' factors such as disturbance of material balance, 'persistent' weaknesses in the position, and so on, should be primarily assessed from the dynamic point of view.

In sharp opening variations one should place the least trust in general assessments. It is for this reason that in 'refuted' lines one can often find a concrete path to obtain a good game, while many set-ups with 'equal chances' prove to favour one of the sides.

Thus the struggle in variations with sharp tactical play takes on unusual forms. These include: the deviations from the principles of development just mentioned; the rapid switching of the weight of the struggle from the centre to one of the flanks; leaving the king in the centre for a long time, retaining the right to castle on either side, depending on circumstances, or saving an important tempo, up to a certain point, for the development of active operations.

In many cases a sharp tactical struggle for the initiative is possible only at the cost of material sacrifice. For this reason the balance is often disturbed early in the game, and unusual balances of forces arise, such as queen against rook, minor piece and pawn.

This allows us to single out new strategic problems in the opening, which to some extent contradict basic opening principles, in particular: 1) manœuvres by the forces at an early opening stage; 2) the rapid disturbance of material equality, and an opening struggle with unbalanced material; 3) a dynamic struggle in the opening over the entire board.

It should be noted that these problems are often closely linked. Thus if the play becomes sharp at an early stage, the struggle may develop over the entire board. This may be accompanied by pawn sacrifices, and by the early development of the heavy pieces. And in general in such situations, what occurs is not so much development, as opening manœuvring. In this respect the following topical variation of the French Defence is typical: **1 e4 e6 2 d4 d5 3 ♘c3 ♗b4 4 e5 c5 5 a3 ♗xc3+ 6 bc ♘e7 7 ♕g4 cd!? 8 ♕xg7 ♖g8 9 ♕xh7 ♕c7! 10 ♘e2 ♘bc6 11 f4 ♗d7 12 ♕d3 dc** *(129)*

Here Black's pawn screen on the K-side has been destroyed, while White's pawn formation on the Q-side has been significantly disrupted. In such positions the number of pawns does not matter — what is important is to carry out your own plan.

129

White's subsequent plan will be a pawn offensive on the K-side, combined with play on the dark squares. Black in turn intends a counter-offensive in the centre and on the Q-side, invariably combined with threats to the white king, which usually remains in the centre for a long time.

Both plans are seen in the following examples.

No. 307 Bronstein-Uhlmann
Tallinn, 1976

From diagram 129: **13 h4?! 0-0-0 14 h5 ♘f5 15 h6 ♖g6 16 ♖h3 d4 17 h7 ♖h8 18 ♖b1 ♗e8 19 ♕f3 ♕d8 20 g4 ♘h4 21 ♕h1 ♖xg4 22 ♘g3 ♖xh7 23 ♘e4 ♘xe5! 24 fe ♘c6 25 ♗d3 ♔c7 26 ♔f2 ♖h5 27 ♖f3 ♕g8 28 ♗f4 ♘xf3 29 ♕xh5**

♖xf4 30 ♕h6 ♘g5+ 0-1

No. 308 Mecking-Uhlmann
Manila IZ, 1976

From diagram 129: **13 ♖b1 0-0-0 14 ♕xc3! ♘f5 15 ♖g1 f6 16 g4 ♘h6 17 ef ♖xg4 18 ♗e3 ♖xg1 19 ♗xg1 ♘f5 20 ♖d1 ♖f8 21 ♖d3 b6 22 ♖h3 d4 23 ♘xd4 ♘fxd4 24 ♗xd4 ♕xf4 25 ♗e3 ♕xf6 26 ♕xf6 ♖xf6 27 ♗g2 e5 28 ♖h6 ♖xh6 29 ♗xh6 ♘d4 30 ♔d2 ♗f5 c3 ♘b5 32 ♗f8**

As a result of an exceptionally dynamic struggle, White has gained a favourable ending, which he confidently converts into a win.

32...♔d7 33 ♗f1 ♘c7 34 h4 ♗g4 35 ♗g7 ♔e6 36 ♗c4+ ♔f5 37 ♔e3 e4 38 ♗g8 ♗f3 39 ♗h7+ ♔g4 40 ♗xe4 ♗xe4 41 ♔xe4 ♔xh4 42 c4 ♘e6 43 ♗e5 ♘c5+ 44 ♔d5 ♔g4 45 ♗b8 a6 46 ♗e5 ♔f5 47 ♗c3 ♘a4 48 ♗d4 ♔f4 49 ♔c6 ♔e4 50 ♗xb6 ♔d3 51 c5 ♔c4 52 ♗a7 a5 53 ♗b6 ♔b3 54 ♔b7 ♘c3 55 ♗xa5 ♘d5 56 ♗b4 ♘e7 57 c6 1-0

We have seen a whole complex of modern ideas, full of bold risks. But in each case one of these factors is the starting point (in the given examples — the destruction of the flanks), bringing about the 'disruption' of opening principles. It is from this viewpoint that the following problems should also be considered.

Minor piece manœuvres in the opening. Opening exchanges

Certain interesting features of opening play, where an erroneous tendency was punished by energetic manœuvres with one and the same piece, have already been examined.

Here we will be analyzing cases where a disruption in the position has not yet occurred. Piece manœuvres have the aim not of refuting the opponent's plans (which may be quite correct), but of achieving positional advantages by the method of opening struggle.

In this connection, before the completion of overall mobilization, an already developed and actively placed piece is sometimes transferred to another position, sometimes even to its initial square, in order to redevelop it according to a different scheme.

In such an obvious 'breaking' of the principle of rapid development, the concrete features of the resulting opening set-up are taken into account. In the main such manœuvres are only possible in positions with a blocked or stable pawn centre.

The basic aim of such manœuvres is to improve the coordination of the forces. This is the case with Black's knight manœuvre on move 9 in a topical variation of the Spanish Game, suggested back in his time by Breyer: 1 e4 e5 2 ♘f3 ♘c6 3 ♗b5 a6 4 ♗a4 ♘f6 5 0-0 ♗e7 6 ♖e1 b5 7 ♗b3 d6 8 c3 0-0 9 h3 ♘b8!? *(130)*

130

The Breyer Variation has been regularly employed in practice since the early 1950s, which confirms its soundness, and its evolution is also instructive. Initially White attempted to exploit his temporary lead in development by 10 a4, and particularly by 10 d4 ♘bd7 11 c4!? For a certain time this line seemed to be the most promising, but later games and analysis in the second approximation showed that after 11...c6 12 c5!? ♕c7 13 cd ♗×d6 14 ♗g5 ed 15 ♘×d4 ♘e5! 16 ♗×f6 gf Black had highly attractive counterplay.

It is no accident that in recent times White has almost given up trying to refute Black's knight manœuvre, and has turned to a purely positional method of development: 10 d4 ♘bd7 11 ♘bd2 ♗b7 12 ♗c2 etc., satisfying himself with a slight initiative.

A similar situation can occur in the French Defence: 1 e4 e6 2 d4 d5 3 ♘d2 ♘c6 4 ♘gf3 ♘f6 5 e5 ♘d7 6 ♘b3 ♗e7 7 ♗b5 ♘cb8!?

With the central pawns blocked, Black temporarily withdraws his knight (which has played an active part in the initial struggle for the centre) to its initial square, making way for the important pawn advance ...c5! At the same time, in some lines the active white bishop at b5 proves unexpectedly to be out of play.

In the variation 1 e4 e6 2 d4 d5 3 ♘c3 ♗b4 4 e5 b6 5 ♕g4 it is Black's bishop which returns to its initial square: 5...♗f8!? Then in many cases he does not aim for the traditional undermining of White's centre by...c5 etc., but plays completely non-standardly: ...♗b7, ...♘c6, ...♕d7, and ...0-0-0 (an alternative plan involves the exchange of light-square bishops by...♗a6 etc).

The formation arising is typical of the King's Indian Defence, but with flanks reversed. In that case it is well known that White's plan involves a pawn offensive on the Q-side (here – on the K-side). And in this respect the position of the white queen at g4 is not altogether happy, and may sometimes even assist Black's counterplay on the K-side.

Such manœuvres are also typical of certain modern opening variations for White: he can permit himself a few more liberties than Black (for example, he can carry out manœuvres with a fairly open formation in the centre).

This is well illustrated by a variation of the Spanish Game: 1 e4 e5 2 ♘f3 ♘c6 3 ♗b5 a6 4 ♗a4 d6 5 c3 ♗d7 6 d4 ♘ge7 7 ♗b3 h6 *(131)*

131

Here, along with the purely developing moves 8 0-0 or 8 ♗e3, the manœuvre 8 ♘h4!? is possible, and practice shows that it is precisely this plan which sets Black the most difficult, and immediately highly concrete problems.

Long before completing his opening development, White directs an already developed piece towards an outpost — f5. At the same time, unpleasant tactical threats arise: 9 ♕f3 or 9 ♕h5, which enable White to gain time for carrying out the operation mentioned.

For a long time Black used to counter this plan rather passively: with 8...♘a5 or 8...♘c8, which gave White a persistent initiative, as demonstrated by the variations 8...♘a5 9 ♗c2 g5 10 ♘f5 ♘xf5 11 ef ♘c6 12 ♗e3! ♕f6 13 d5 ♘e7 14 g4 ♘xd5 15 ♕xd5 ♗c6 16 ♗a4 ♗xa4 17 ♕xb7 ♕d8 18 ♕e4!, with clearly the better chances for White (analysis by Boleslavsky and Suetin), or 8... ♘c8 9 ♘f5 g6 10 ♘g3 ♗g7 11 0-0 ed 12 f4 dc 13 ♘xc3 with a strong initiative for White (Geller-Keres, 18th USSR Ch., 1950).

Perhaps more promising for Black is the tactical plan consisting in a sudden counterblow in the centre: 8...ed 9 cd ♘xd4!? 10 ♕xd4 ♘c6! It transpires that the currently undefended position of the knight at h4 plays an important role.

The possibility of such operations is something of which one should beware, when carrying out this type of early improvement in the placing of the pieces (in the given case ♘f3-h4, aiming at f5).

Thus in Tal-Bannik (23rd

USSR Ch., 1956), where this variation was first employed, after 11 ♗xf7+ ♔xf7 12 ♕d5+ ♗e6 13 ♕h5+ ♔g8 14 0-0? ♘e5! White found himself in a difficult position.

This plan for Black also came through later tests fairly successfully. In the battle for the initiative, White should evidently go in for a pawn sacrifice, e.g., 11 ♕d5 ♕xh4 12 ♕xf7+ ♔d8 13 ♘c3 ♘e5 14 ♕d5 ♕g4 15 ♗e3 ♕xg2 16 0-0-0 etc.

In many cases the problem of improving the coordination of the forces is decided in the opening by exchanging important enemy pieces for less valuable pieces of one's own, which compensates (sometimes with interest) for a slight delay in mobilization.

The following examples show Black 'ridding himself' of a 'bad' bishop. Such a problem can arise after the closing of the centre (by d4-d5) in the King's Indian Defence. Here the dark-square bishop at g7 has little mobility, and it is often useful for Black to exchange it, particularly for its opposite number guarding the dark squares in White's position.

This is what happens in the variation 1 d4 ♘f6 2 c4 g6 3 ♘c3 ♗g7 4 e4 d6 5 ♘f3 0-0 6 ♗e2 e5 7 0-0 ♘bd7 8 d5 ♘c5 9 ♘d2 a5 10 ♕c2 ♗h6! 11 ♘b3 ♗xc1 12

♖a×c1 ♘fd7.

It is not in vain that Black has wasted a few tempi. He has provoked the important exchange of the dark-square bishops, which gives him fair prospects for the future.

The following game is also instructive.

No. 309 Zukharov-Gurgenidze
Tbilisi, 1956
King's Indian Defence

1 d4 ♘f6 2 c4 g6 3 ♘c3 ♗g7 4 e4 d6 5 f3 e5 6 d5 ♘fd7!? 7 ♗e3 ♗h6!
(132)

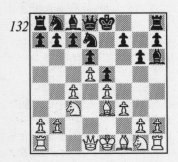

8 ♕d2

8 ♗×h6 ♕h4+ 9 g3 ♕×h6 favours Black. Perhaps White should have preferred 8 ♗f2, retaining his good bishop, although Black would have achieved a definite success, his bishop being better placed at h6 than at its usual square g7.

8...♗×e3 9 ♕×e3 a5 10 ♗d3 ♘a6 11 0-0-0 ♕e7 12 ♘ge2 ♘dc5

13 ♗b1 ♗d7 14 ♘b5 ♗×b5 15 cb ♘b8 16 h4 ♘bd7 17 h5 0-0-0 18 b3 ♘b6 19 ♖d2 ♕d7 20 ♘c3 f5 21 ef gf 22 ♕g5 ♖df8 23 g4 e4!

After setting up a solid blockade on the dark squares, Black does not intend to be content with what he has achieved, but wishes to exploit his advantages in dynamic play. He begins energetic action in the centre, with the aim of seizing the initiative.

24 gf ♖×f5 25 ♕g4 ♖×f3 26 ♕×d7+ ♘b×d7 27 ♘×e4 ♘×e4 28 ♗×e4 ♖f4

In the resulting ending Black has a small, but persistent advantage. His knight is obviously stronger than the white bishop, the opponent's pawns are more exposed, and the black rook is slightly more active. The concluding stage of the game is highly instructive.

29 ♗g2 ♔d8! (29 ♗h3 was threatened) 30 ♔c2 ♖g8 31 ♖h3 h6 32 a3 ♖g5 33 ♖f3 ♖×f3 34 ♗×f3 ♘e5 35 ♗d1 b6 36 ♖f2 ♔e7 37 ♖d2 ♖g3 38 ♖d4 ♖g2+ 39 ♔c3 ♖f2 40 ♗c2 ♖f3+ 41 ♔b2 ♔f6 42 ♖d1 ♖g3 43 ♖c1 ♖g2 44 ♔c3 ♔g5 45 ♗g6 ♔f4! 46 ♖f1+ ♘f3 47 b4 ab 48 ab ♔e3 49 ♖a1 ♖g1! 50 ♖a8 ♖c1+ 51 ♔b2 ♖c4 52 ♔b3 ♘d2+ 53 ♔a3 ♘d4 54 ♖e8 ♖c3+ 55 ♔b2 ♘c4+ 56 ♔b1 ♖e3 57 ♖h8 ♔c3 58 ♖×h6 ♖e1+ 59 ♔a2 ♖e2+ 60 ♔a1 ♘d2 0-1

This game shows clearly how the exchange of even one important enemy piece can promote a general improvement in the coordination of one's own forces. At the decisive stage of the game the harmony of the black pieces was fully revealed.

Early development of the heavy pieces

As has often been mentioned, in the opening it is difficult to play actively with the heavy pieces, since normally they quickly come under attack by the opponent's pawns and minor pieces. Usually the heavy pieces develop their power later, at the height of the middlegame, without being particularly active in the opening.

Therefore here we will be talking mainly about exceptions, or, more precisely, about a different interpretation of the rules as applied to dynamic variations. Very characteristic of certain modern opening variations is the active role of the heavy pieces, if their manoeuvres disrupt the opponent's plans and assist the favourable coordination of one's own forces.

Instructive in this sense is a line of the English Opening, worked out by A. Cherepkov:

1 c4 c5 2 ♘c3 ♘f6 3 g3 d5 4 cd ♘×d5 5 ♗g2 ♘c7 6 ♘f3 ♘c6 7 ♕a4!? *(133)*

White brings his queen into play in order to hamper the opponent's basic plan, which is to set up a piece-pawn centre by . . . e5 and . . .f6 etc., and he thus seizes the initiative.

The following sequel is also typical: 7. . .♗d7 8 ♕e4! e6? (better 8. . .g6 9 ♘e5 ♗g7, reconciling himself to a slightly inferior game after 10 ♘×d7 ♕×d7) 9 0-0 ♗e7 10 d4! cd 11 ♘×d4 0-0 12 ♖d1 ♕c8 13 ♗e3, with strong pressure for White in the centre.

The following example illustrates a modern opening variation, where at a very early stage the white queen penetrates into the opponent's position, and although for a long time it does not have any direct effect, it strongly influences the course of play.

No. 310
Nezhmetdinov-Sakharov
Moscow, 1957
Sicilian Defence

1 e4 c5 2 ♘f3 ♘c6 3 d4 cd
4 ♘×d4 e5 5 ♘b5 a6 6 ♘d6+
♗×d6 7 ♕×d6 ♕f6

A highly dynamic variation, which should not be underestimated. Thus after 8 ♕×f6 ♘×f6 9 f3 (9 ♘c3 d5! 10 ed ♘b4) 9. . .d5 Black could have seized the initiative. White's problem is to prevent the opening of the centre and then to exploit the weakness of the dark squares in Black's position. One of the ways of achieving this is by the following unusual manoeuvre.

8 ♕c7! ♘ge7 9 ♘c3 ♘b4 10 ♗d3 d5 11 0-0 d4 12 ♘e2 ♘×d3 13 cd g5?!

Black wishes radically to prevent the opening of the centre which was possible after 14 f4. But, as the further course of the game shows, the weakening of his castled position proves a more serious drawback. 13. . . ♘c6 was better.

14 ♗d2 ♘c6 15 ♖ac1 0-0 16 ♘g3 h6 17 b4 ♖e8 18 a4 ♘d8 19 ♖c5! ♕g7 20 ♖d5 ♗g4 21 ♖c1 ♔h7 22 ♘f5! ♗×f5 23 ef ♕f6 24 g4

Black is in a positional zugzwang: his position is hopeless.

24. . .♖e7 25 ♖d7 ♖×d7 26 ♕×d7 ♔g7 27 ♖c5! b6 28 ♖c7 b5

29 a5! ♔g8 30 ♕d5 ♖b8 31 ♗e1 ♕g7 32 ♕c5 ♕f8 33 ♕a7 1-0

And now an example which confirms the strength of the other form of chess 'heavy artillery'.

No. 311 Petrosian-Bertok
Stockholm IZ, 1962
Queen's Gambit Accepted

1 d4 d5 2 c4 dc 3 ♘f3 ♘f6 4 e3 e6 5 ♗×c4 c5 6 0-0 a6 7 ♘c3 b5 8 ♗b3 ♗b7 9 ♕e2 ♘bd7 10 ♖d1 ♗d6 11 e4 cd *(134)*

134

12 ♖×d4!
The capture with the rook is much stronger than the usual 12 ♘×d4, when, for example, Petrosian-Smyslov (Candidates Tournament, 1959) continued 12. . . ♕b8 13 ♘f3 b4! with good counterplay for Black.

12. . .♗c5 (if 12. . .♕c7 13 ♖×d6! ♕×d6 14 e5 ♗×f3 15 ♕×f3 ♕×e5 16 ♗f4! and White wins) 13 ♖d3! (the rook is irrepressible — it is not only active in

the centre, and also has its sights set on the K-side) **13...♘g4 14 ♗g5 ♕b6 15 ♘d5! ♕a5?** (this loses; comparatively best was 15...♗×d5! 16 ed e5 17 ♗h4 0-0 with chances of equalizing, Veresov-Suetin, Novgorod, 1961) **16 ♖f1 ♖c8 17 ♘f4 ♘ge5 18 ♘×e5 ♘×e5 19 ♖h3 ♘c4 20 ♖d1 ♕b6 21 ♘h5 ♖g8 22 ♖hd3! ♘d6 23 e5 ♘e4 24 ♗e3 ♗×e3 25 ♖×e3 ♕c6 26 ♕g4 ♔e7 27 ♖de1 f5 28 ef gf 29 ♕h3! f5 30 f3 ♘g5 31 ♕×f5 ♖cf8 32 ♖×e6+ ♘×e6 33 ♖×e6+ ♔d8 34 ♕d3+ 1-0**

Delayed castling. Leaving the king in the centre

In certain modern opening variations one of the players (or sometimes even both!) leaves his king in the centre for a rather long time, so as not only to retain the possibility of castling on either side, but also to do so at the necessary moment, and before this to engage in concrete operations.

Leaving the king in the centre is often associated both with a more complicated interpretation of its safety, and with a new approach to the struggle for the initiative in the opening stage of a game.

Here is an example of the centre 'armour' which the black king often acquires in the Richter/Rauzer Variation of the Sicilian Defence: 1 e4 c5 2 ♘f3 ♘c6 3 d4 cd 4 ♘×d4 ♘f6 5 ♘c3 d6 6 ♗g5 e6 7 ♕d2 a6 8 0-0-0 ♗d7 9 f4 ♗e7 10 ♘f3 b5 11 ♗×f6 gf 12 ♗d3 ♕b6 13 ♔b1 b4 14 ♘e2 a5 etc.

In this and similar set-ups, Black sometimes leaves his king in the centre for a long time and begins a persistent battle for the initiative, mounting an energetic offensive on the Q-side, where the white king has taken shelter.

Such a situation is one of the most complicated in modern opening strategy, but practice shows that Black has fair chances of obtaining a good game, and possibly even more. For the moment only approximate assessments are possible here.

It also happens that one of the players will often refrain from castling, in order to save an important tempo in the opening and be the first to go onto the offensive, forcing the opponent to give up his active plan (cf. No. 239, Botvinnik-Alatortsev). The following example is also instructive.

No. 312 Vasyukov-Parma
USSR v Yugoslavia
Rijeka, 1963
Sicilian Defence

1 e4 c5 2 ♘f3 d6 3 d4 cd 4 ♘×d4
♘f6 5 ♘c3 g6 6 ♗e3 ♗g7 7 f3 ♘c6
8 ♕d2 0-0 9 ♗c4 ♗d7 10 h4

Although the central position is not blocked, for the moment White leaves his king in the centre, so as to begin his K-side offensive as quickly as possible and seize the initiative.

10...♖c8 11 ♗b3 ♘e5 12 h5!
(all in the same attacking style)
12...♘×h5 13 0-0-0 (this is the moment to castle) 13...♘c4 14
♗×c4 ♖×c4 15 g4 ♘f6 16 ♖dg1
(16 ♗h6! is stronger) 16...e6
(here Black misses the moment for counterplay by 16...b5!) 17
♔b1 ♕a5 18 ♘b3 ♕c7 19 ♗f4! e5
20 g5! ♘h5 21 ♘d5 ♕d8 22 ♗e3
♗e6 23 ♘f6+!

The decisive opening of lines for the attack.

23...♘×f6 24 gf ♕×f6

Equally bad is 24...♗×f6 25
♕h2 h5 26 ♕×h5 ♖e8 27 ♖×g6+!
fg 28 ♕h7+ ♔f8 29 ♗h6+ and mate next move.

25 ♗g5! ♕×f3 26 ♕h2 ♕h5 27
♕f2 ♗h3 28 ♕e3 h6 29 ♘d2 1-0

The central position of the king in the above examples was either a convenient or an insignificant feature of the position, and it did not constitute a break-

ing of opening principles.

There are many nuances of this type in modern opening variations, and this applies equally to other forms of the breaking of old rules. For example, of no small importance is the choice of moment for castling, and depending on circumstances it may be on one side or the other.

No. 313 Sokolsky-Zhukovitsky
Kiev, 1945
Sokolsky Opening

1 b4 e5 2 ♗b2 f6 3 b5 d5 4 e3
♗d6 5 c4 c6 6 ♘f3 ♘e7 7 d4 e4
8 ♘fd2 0-0 9 ♘c3 f5 10 g3 ♘d7 11
a4 ♘f6 12 ♗a3 ♗c7 (better 12...
♗×a3 13 ♖×a3 dc 14 ♗×c4+
♘ed5 with a good game for Black, but he clearly failed to anticipate White's subsequent strategic plan) 13 a5! a6 14 b6 ♗b8 15
♘b3 ♖f7 16 ♘c5 g5 17 ♕b3 ♗d6
18 0-0-0!

The point of White's plan. Although he has just been mounting a pawn offensive on the Q-side, it is here that the white king will feel safest.

18...h6 19 cd cd 20 h4 g4? 21
♖d2 ♖b8 22 ♖c2 ♗×c5 23 ♗×c5
♘c6 24 ♕a3 ♗d7 25 ♔b2 ♖c8 26
♗e2 ♗e6 27 ♘a2 ♘e8 28 ♖hc1
♘b8 29 ♗b4 ♖×c2+ 30 ♖×c2
♕d7 31 ♘c1! ♘c6 32 ♘b3 ♘×b4
33 ♕×b4 ♕d6 34 ♕a3 ♕×a3+ 35
♔×a3 ♘d6 36 ♘c5 ♖e7 37 ♔b4!

Now the white king embarks on a decisive raid. It is interesting that it is precisely on the Q-side that the fate of the game is decided.

37...&f7 38 &xa6! ba 39 &xa6 &e8 40 &c6 &d7 41 &c5 1-0

However, the active side should be aware that in such 'exceptional' cases he is always on the verge of a real breaking of principles.

Thus at times even the most solid central barriers cannot ensure a safe shelter for the king, since, apart from purely positional attacking methods, there are also sharp, tactical ones. It is a dynamic type of struggle that strikingly reveals not only the advantages, but also the drawbacks of new procedures.

The sacrifice of a pawn in the opening

In a dynamic struggle there is often a close connection between material and positional factors, and the material balance may be disturbed for a long time as a result of a positional sacrifice.

For the sake of achieving certain positional gains and seizing the initiative, it is most often a pawn which is sacrificed, and the concrete aims and the forms of this sacrifice may be very varied. Typical, for example, are pawn sacrifices with the aim of developing the pieces rapidly, eliminating strong enemy pieces or maintaining one's own active pieces, opening important lines and diagonals, gaining space, and so on. Usually these factors are closely linked and often they successively replace one another.

The innovator of this procedure, which until comparatively recently was regarded as an exception but has now become a method, was Alexander Alekhine.

Here are some of his first opening experiments of this type.

No. 314 Alekhine-Reshevsky
Kemeri, 1937
Alekhine's Defence

1 e4 &g6 2 e5 &d5 3 &f3 d6 4 d4 &g4 5 c4 &b6 6 &e2 de 7 &xe5!? (a problematic pawn sacrifice) 7...&xe2 8 &xe2 &xd4 9 0-0 &8d7 10 &xd7 &xd7?

10...&xd7 was correct, when Alekhine was intending to play 11 a4! &c6 12 &a3 e6 13 a5 &d7 14 &b5 with the initiative for the pawn.

11 &c3 c6 12 &e3 &e5 13 &ad1 e6 14 &f3! 0-0-0 15 &xa7

As a result of his novel play White has regained the pawn, while retaining the initiative.

15... ♕a5 16 ♗d4 ♕f5 *(135)*

135

17 ♕g3!?
Here Alekhine rejects a favourable positional decision: by 17 ♕xf5 he could have obtained a clear if slight end-game advantage. Instead he continues playing in the same dynamic style.

17...e5 18 ♗e3 ♗b4 19 ♘a4 ♗a5 20 f4! ♗c7 21 b3 f6 22 fe ♕e6 23 h3 ♖hg8 24 ♗d4 ♘xe5 25 ♕c3! ♘d7 26 c5! ♖ge8 27 b4! ♘b8 28 ♘b6+ ♗xb6 29 cb ♕xa2 30 ♕g3!

White conducts a broad offensive, forcing his opponent to think for himself at every move.

30...♖d7 31 ♗c5 ♕f7 32 ♖a1 ♕g6 33 ♕h2! ♖e5 34 ♖a8 ♖d2 35 ♖xb8+! ♔xb8 36 ♕xe5+! 1-0

No. 315 Alekhine-Fine
Hastings, 1936-37
Spanish Game

1 e4 e5 2 ♘f3 ♘c6 3 ♗b5 a6 4 ♗a4 ♘f6 5 0-0 ♗e7 6 ♖e1 b5 7 ♗b3 d6 8 c3 ♘a5 9 ♗c2 c5 10 d4 ♕c7 11 ♘bd2 0-0 12 ♘f1 ♗g4 13 ♘e3! ♗xf3 14 ♕xf3 cd 15 ♘f5!? *(136)*

136

Again a problematic pawn sac-rifice for the initiative.

15...dc 6 ♕xc3 ♖fc8 17 ♕g3 ♗f8 18 ♗d3 ♘c6 19 ♗g5 ♘e8 20 ♖ac1 ♕b7 21 a3 g6 22 ♘h6+ ♗xh6 23 ♗xh6 ♘d4 24 ♖cd1 b4 25 f4! ef 26 ♕xf4 ba 27 ba ♖c3! 28 ♕f2 ♘e6?

Black fails to withstand the tension of constant calculation. 28... ♘c6 was correct, retaining roughly equal chances.

29 a4 ♖ac8 30 ♖f1 ♖3c7 31 ♖b1 ♕c6 32 a5! ♘c5? (the deci-sive error; 32...♖a8 was more tenacious) 33 ♗c4 ♕d7 34 ♕a2! ♘xe4 35 ♖xf7 ♕xf7 36 ♗xf7+ ♖xf7 37 ♕e6! 1-0

No. 316 Alekhine-Flohr
Nottingham, 1936
French Defence

1 e4 e6 2 d4 d5 3 ♘c3 ♗b4
4 ♗d2 de 5 ♘xe4?! ♕xd4 6 ♗d3
♗xd2+ 7 ♕xd2 ♕d8?

Inconsistent: Black should
have played 7...♕xb2. Now
White's initiative becomes
dangerous.

8 0-0-0 ♕e7 9 ♘f3 ♘f6 10
♖he1 ♘xe4 11 ♖xe4 ♘d7 12
♖g4! f5 13 ♗f4 ♘f6 14 ♖e1 ♗d7
15 ♗xf5 0-0-0 16 ♖a5 ♔b8 17
♘e5 ♗e8 18 g3!

Showing a deep penetration
into the position. White goes in
for the exchange of queens, foreseeing excellent opportunities
for developing his initiative.

18...♘d5 19 ♖e4 ♘b6 20 ♕e3
♖d5 21 ♖a3 ♕c5 22 ♕xc5 ♖xc5
23 f4 ♖d5 24 ♘f3! ♗d7 25 ♘g5
♖e8 26 c4 ♖f5 27 ♖d4 ♖5f8 28 c5
♘d5 29 ♗xh7 ♗c6 30 ♗g6 ♖e7 31
♘f3 ♘f6 32 ♘e5 ♗d5 33 ♖e3 ♖h8
34 h4 c6 35 ♗c2 ♖d8 36 ♗b3 ♖c7
37 ♘f3 ♖e8 38 ♘e5 ♖ec8 39 ♗c4
♔a8 40 b4 ♖b8 41 g4! b6 (41...
♗xc4 fails to 42 ♘xc4 ♘xg4 43
♘b6+!) 42 g5 bc 43 bc ♘d7 44
♘xd7 ♖xd7 45 h5 ♖f7 46 ♖xe6!
♗xe6 47 ♗xe6 ♖fb7 48 ♗b3 ♖e8
49 h6 gh 50 g6 ♖g7 51 f5 ♖f8 52
♗c2 h5 53 ♖d6 ♖e7 54 f6 ♖e1+
55 ♔d2 ♖f1 56 f7 h4 57 ♖d7
1-0

In the given case it would be
absurd to try to determine even
the most characteristic instances
of the pawn sacrifice. Without
exaggeration it can be said that
this is a topic of encyclopaedic
dimensions. We can merely conclude that the general aim
uniting such sacrifices consists
in the obtaining of more active
coordination of the forces, ensuring a certain initiative and
facilitating the carrying out of a
concrete plan.

From this angle many classical variations with long-standing
assessments have also been re-
vised, in particular the following
line of the Spanish Game: 1 e4
e5 2 ♘f3 ♘c6 3 ♗b5 a6 4 ♗a4 d6
5 c3 f5!?, which was introduced
by Capablanca. For a long time
in this variation theory mainly
considered the strictly positional
defensive method with 5...♗d7
and the plans ensuing from it.

But then in the late 1940s interest in 5...f5!? grew, and it
transpired that, by handling it in
modern gambit style, Black
could count on rich counterplay.

Instructive in this respect are
the variations 6 ef ♗xf5 7 d4 e4
8 ♘g5 d5 9 f3 e3!? 10 f4 ♗d6 11
♗xe3 ♕f6, or 9...h6!? 10 fe hg
11 ef ♗d6! 12 ♕g4 ♘f6 13 ♕xg5
♔f8!, in both cases with an excellent game for Black.

In recent times gambit ideas
have 'spread' to the Q-side,

where earlier the opening struggle was of a strictly positional nature.

No. 317 Geller-Mikenas
USSR Ch., 1955
Reti Opening

1 ♘f3 d5 2 c4 d4 3 g3 c5 4 ♗g2 ♘c6 5 0-0 e5 6 d3 ♗e7 7 b4!? cb 8 a3 ba 9 ♕a4 ♗d7 10 ♗xa3 ♘f6 11 ♕b5! 0-0 (better 11...♗xa3 and 12...♕e7) 12 ♘xe5 ♘xe5 13 ♕xe5 ♗xa3 14 ♖xa3! ♗c6 15 ♗xc6 bc 16 ♖e1 ♕b6 17 ♘d2 ♕b4? 18 ♕a5! ♕d6 19 ♖b3 ♖fe8 20 ♖b7 ♖e5 21 ♕c7 ♕e6 22 ♘f3 ♖h5 23 ♘xd4 ♕e8 24 ♖eb1 1-0

22 years later Yefim Geller again employed his plan to great effect, only this time with Black.

No. 318 Rashkovsky-Geller
Sochi, 1977
King's Indian Defence

1 d4 ♘f6 2 c4 g6 3 ♘c3 ♗g7 4 e4 d6 5 h3 0-0 6 ♗g5 c5 7 d5 b5! 8 cb a6 9 ba ♕a5 10 ♗d2 ♕b4! *(137)* 11 ♕c2 ♗xa6 12 ♗xa6 ♘xa6 13 a3 ♕c4! 14 ♖b1 ♘b4! 15 ab cb 16 ♘ge2 bc 17 ♘xc3 ♖fc8 18 f3 ♘h5 19 g4 ♘g3 20 ♖g1 ♘e2! 21 ♖g2 ♘d4 22 ♕d1 ♕d3 23 ♔f2 ♘xf3 24 ♕xf3 ♕xd2+ 25 ♔g1 ♗d4+ 26 ♔h1 ♕e3! 27 ♕xe3 ♗xe3 28 ♖c2 ♖ab8 29 ♔g2 ♖b3 30 ♖a1 ♗d4 31 ♖ac1 ♖cb8 32 ♘d1 ♔g7 33 ♖c7 ♗f6 34 ♖1c2 ♖d3 35 ♘f2 ♖e3 36

♖a7 ♖bb3 37 ♖ac7 h6 38 ♖a7 ♗h4 39 ♖ac7 ♗xf2 40 ♖xf2 ♖xe4, and Black won.

137

As the above examples indicate, in each specific case one must not only very carefully, but also deeply weigh up the consequences of the pawn sacrifice. This also applies equally to its acceptance.

It can also be difficult to draw the line between the correct acceptance of a pawn sacrifice and 'pawn-grabbing'.

Here are some such 'tricky' examples.

No. 319 Ivanović-Borkovsky
Pristina, 1976
Pirc Defence

1 e4 d6 2 d4 ♘f6 3 ♘c3 g6 4 ♗g5 ♗g7 5 e5 ♘fd7 6 ed cd 7 ♕d2 0-0 8 0-0-0 ♘c6 9 h4 ♗xd4?

White's initiative would also have been dangerous after 9... ♘xd4 10 h5 ♘e6 11 ♗h6. Here the acceptance of the sacrifice is inappropriate.

10 h5 ♕a5 11 hg hg 12 ♗×e7! ♗g7 (if 12...♗×c3 White wins by 13 ♕h6!) 13 ♗×f8 ♘×f8 14 ♗c4 ♗e6 15 ♗×e6 ♘×e6 16 ♘ge2 ♘cd4 17 ♘×d4 ♘×d4 18 ♖h4! ♘f5 19 ♖a4 ♕c5 20 g4 ♗h6 21 f4 b5 22 ♖e4 ♘g3 23 ♖d4 b4 24 ♘e2!, and White soon won.

No. 320 Bronstein–Geller
Göteborg IZ, 1955
Sicilian Defence

1 e4 c5 2 ♘f3 ♘c6 3 ♗b5 g6 4 c3 ♗g7 5 d4 ♕b6 6 a4 cd 7 0-0!? a6 8 ♗×c6 ♕×c6?! 9 cd ♕×e4?! 10 ♘c3 ♕f5 11 ♖e1 d5 12 a5 ♗d7 13 ♕b3 ♘f6? 14 ♖e5! ♕d3 15 ♖×e7+ ♔×e7 16 ♘×d5+ ♘×d5 17 ♕×d3 1-0

No. 321 Spassky–Fischer
World Championship, 1972
Sicilian Defence

1 e4 c5 2 ♘f3 d6 3 d4 cd 4 ♘×d4 ♘f6 5 ♘c3 a6 6 ♗g5 e6 7 f4 ♕b6 8 ♕d2 ♕×b2 9 ♘b3 ♕a3 10 ♗×f6 gf 11 ♗e2 h5 12 0-0 ♘c6 13 ♔h1 ♗d7 14 ♘b1!? ♕b4? 15 ♕e3 d5? (15...♘e7 16 ♘1d2!) 16 ed ♘e7 17 c4! ♘f5 18 ♕d3! h4? 19 ♗g4! ♘d6 20 ♘1d2 f5? 21 a3! ♕b6 22 c5! ♕b5 23 ♕c3! fg 24 a4! h3 25 ab hg+ 26 ♔×g2 ♖h3 27 ♕f6! ♘f5 28 c6! ♗c8 29 de fe 30 ♖fe1 ♗e7 31 ♖×e6 1-0

While the first of these examples is a typical case of 'pawn-grabbing', the second and third are by no means clear-cut. Despite Black's failures in these games, in each case White's pawn sacrifice was problematic.

With regard to game No. 321, the following variations are significant: 14...♕b2! (instead of 14...♕b4?) 15 ♘c3 (after 15 a3? ♖c8 16 ♖f3 e5 17 ♘c3 ♘b4 only Black has chances) 15...♕a3 16 ♘b1 etc., or 1 e4 c5 2 ♘f3 d6 3 d4 cd 4 ♘×d4 ♘f6 5 ♘c3 a6 6 ♗g5 e6 7 f4 ♕b6 8 ♕d2 ♕×b2 9 ♖b1 ♕a3 10 e5 de 11 fe ♘fd7 12 ♗c4 ♗b4 13 ♖b3 ♕a5 14 0-0 0-0 15 ♗f6!? ♘×f6 16 ef ♖d8 17 ♖×b4 ♕×b4 18 ♕g5 g6 19 ♘e4 ♕f8 20 ♘f3 ♘c6 with a very complicated game.

White's gambit here is problematic, and at any rate the counterattack ...♕b6 and ...♕×b2 cannot be regarded as 'pawn-grabbing'.

At the same time there are many tempting but insufficiently positional pawn sacrifices in the opening. Sometimes the boundary between a correct and an incorrect sacrifice is very fine. This is shown by the example just given, and also by a comparison of two analogous variations of the Spanish Game:

a) 1 e4 e5 2 ♘f3 ♘c6 3 ♗b5 a6 4 ♗a4 ♘f6 5 0-0 ♗e7 6 ♖e1 b5 7

&b3 0-0 8 d4 d6 9 c3 &g4 10 h3 &xf3 11 ♕xf3 ed 12 ♕d1 dc 13 ♘xc3.

b) 1 e4 e5 2 ♘f3 ♘c6 3 &b5 a6 4 &a4 ♘f6 5 0-0 b5 6 &b3 d6 7 c3 &e7 8 d4 &g4 9 h3 &xf3 10 ♕xf3 ed *(138)*.

In the first case White's gambit, although it contains considerable dangers, is objectively hardly convincing. The dangers for Black are illustrated by the following game.

No. 322 Bronstein-Keres
Budapest C, 1950

(1 e4 e5 2 ♘f3 ♘c6 3 &b5 a6 4 &a4 ♘f6 5 0-0 &e7 6 ♖e1 b5 7 &b3 0-0 8 d4 d6 9 c3 &g4 10 h3 &xf3 11 ♕xf3 ed 12 ♕d1 dc 13 ♘xc3) 13...♘a5 14 &c2 ♖e8 15 f4 b4 16 ♘d5 ♘xd5 17 ♕xd5 c6 18 ♕d3 g6 19 ♔h1 &f8 20 ♖f1 &g7 21 &d2 c5 22 &a4 ♖f8 23 ♖ab1 ♕b6 (23...c4 is correct) 24 f5! &d4 25 ♕g3 ♘c4 26 &h6 &g7? Now Black is lost. He would

have had more chances after 26...♘xb2.

27 &xg7 ♔xg7 28 f6+ ♔h8 29 ♕g5 b3 30 ab ♕b4 31 bc ♕xa4 32 ♖f4 ♕c2 33 ♕h6! 1-0

Black's play can easily be improved. Thus instead of 14... ♖e8 he has 14...c5, setting in motion his phalanx of pawns, and so on.

Black can not only successfully defend, but he can also retain his extra pawn, which casts doubts on White's gambit idea.

In the second case White has an extra tempo (he has not played ♖e1, which here is unnecessary), and this allows to develop a powerful initiative which more than compensates for the pawn sacrificed. For example (from diagram 138): **11 ♕g3!**

More active than 11 ♕d1, although even here after 11...dc ♘xc3 White has much better prospects than in the analogous variation given above.

No. 323
Nezhmetdinov-Zhuravlyev
USSR, 1959

11...0-0 (11...g6 12 &d5!) 12 &h6 ♘e8 13 &d5 ♕d7 (or 13...&h4 14 ♕f4! gh 15 &xc6 dc 16 ♘xc3 and then 17 ♕xh6 with advantage to White) 14 ♕g4! ♕xg4 15 hg gh 16 &xc6 dc 17 ♘xc3 ♖b8 18 ♘d5 &d8

Although White is still a pawn down, his position is very strong and it more than compensates for the slight material deficit.

19 f3 ♔g7? 20 b4! ♔g6 21 g3 ♔g7 22 ♖ac1 ♘f6 23 ♘e3 ♘g8 24 ♔g2 ♘e7 25 ♖c2 h5 26 gh f5 27 ef ♘xf5 28 ♘xf5 ♖xf5 29 g4 ♖f4 30 ♗e4 c5? 31 bc dc 32 ♖xc5 h6 33 ♖d1 ♗g5 34 ♖c6 a5 35 ♖a6 b4 36 ♖xa5 b3 37 ab ♖xb3 38 ♖d7+ 1-0

A complex and highly unusual opening problem is provided by the struggle with unbalanced material (e.g. queen against rook, minor piece and pawn, or a piece against several pawns, and so on).

Here one player often has a slight material advantage, but as a result the other has more actively coordinated forces, and hence also the initiative.

With unbalanced material the struggle is not only very sharp, but also of a complex positional nature. Most often this critical balance of material remains on the board for a very long time (during the course of play the same pawn equivalent is usually exchanged on both sides).

Positions of this type have long been known to theory, but until recently they were regarded as exceptions and occurred mainly in 'secondary' lines of certain opening variations. This is the case, for example, with the following line of the Dragon Variation: 1 e4 c5 2 ♘f3 ♘c6 3 d4 cd 4 ♘xd4 ♘f6 5 ♘c3 d6 6 ♗e2 g6 7 ♗e3 ♗g7 8 0-0 0-0 9 f4 ♕b6 10 ♕d3!? (the main line here is known to be 10 e5!? etc) 10. . . ♘g4! 11 ♘d5 ♗xd4! 12 ♘xb6 ♗xe3+ 13 ♔h1 ♗xb6 14 ♗xg4 ♗xg4 15 f5 d5! etc.

In recent times the number of opening lines with unbalanced material has grown considerably. They are not of a secondary nature, but arise during a clash of the most crucial aspirations of the opponents in a number of opening variations.

The result of the struggle in such variations is problematic. In opening positions of this type with unbalanced material and full of combinational possibilities, well known relationships from the middlegame can often facilitate a general assessment. Thus, for example, three minor pieces (if they are able to seize the initiative) are slightly stronger than a queen, and a queen is stronger than a rook and minor piece. These rules have been confirmed in a number of researches of new opening variations. Instructive in this respect is the line of the Dragon Variation given above, which is rightly judged to favour Black. However, in the given situation the concrete and dynamic possibilities of a position are very important.

Queen against rook and minor piece

Such a situation occurs fairly often in modern openings, in particular in the Keres Variation of the Open Defence to the Spanish Game: 1 e4 e5 2 ♘f3 ♘c6 3 ♗b5 a6 4 ♗a4 ♘f6 5 0-0 ♘xe4 6 d4 b5 7 ♗b3 d5 8 de ♗e6 9 ♕e2 ♗e7 10 ♖d1 ♘c5 11 ♗xd5!? ♗xd5 12 ♘c3 ♗c4 13 ♖xd8+ ♖xd8 *(139)*

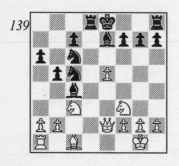

A position with unbalanced material has been reached, where Black has sacrificed his queen for rook and bishop. But it is Black who has the initiative, and soon it is White who must think in terms of equalizing. Events develop by force: 14 ♕e3 b4! 15 b3! ♗e6 16 ♘e4 ♖d1+ 17 ♘e1 ♘d4 18 ♗b2 ♘xc2 19 ♕e2 ♖xa1 20 ♗xa1 ♘xa1 21 ♘xc5 ♗xc5 22 ♘d3

The dynamic struggle continues with its former intensity. Despite the fact that it is propelled by combinational motifs, it remains on the equilibrium line.

The development of events in the following game is typical.

No. 324 Suetin-Geller
25th USSR Ch., 1958

22...♗b6 23 ♘xb4 0-0 24 ♘c6 f6 25 h4 fe 26 ♕xe5 ♖f6 27 g4!? ♗xf2+ 28 ♔h1 ♗xh4 29 ♘e7+ ♔f8 30 ♘f5, with an equal position.

An important factor here is which player has the initiative, and how firm it is. Although a queen is somewhat stronger than rook, minor piece and also a pawn, reverse situations can often arise. The possession of the initative can often more than compensate for the sacrificing of the queen, as is confirmed by the examples below.

No. 325 Sokolsky-Vasiliev
Leningrad, 1947
Queen's Gambit

1 d4 d5 2 c4 e6 3 ♘c3 ♘f6 4 ♘f3 ♗e7 5 ♗g5 h6 6 ♗h4 0-0 7 e3 b6 8 ♕c2 c5 9 0-0-0?! (9 ♖d1) 9...cd 10 ♘xd4 ♗b7 11 ♗xf6 ♗xf6 12 cd ed 13 ♔b1 ♘c6 14 ♘xc6 ♗xc6 15 ♘xd5? ♗xd5 16 ♗c4 ♗xc4! 17

♖×d8 ♖a×d8 18 ♕×c4 ♖d2 19 b4
♖fd8 20 ♖e1 b5! 21 ♕×b5 ♖c8!
0-1

No. 326 Bobotsov-Tal
Student Teams, Varna, 1958
King's Indian Defence

1 d4 ♘f6 2 c4 g6 3 ♘c3 ♗g7 4 e4
d6 5 f3 0-0 6 ♘ge2 c5 7 ♗e3 ♘bd7
8 ♕d2 a6 9 0-0-0 ♕a5 10 ♔b1 b5
11 ♘d5?! *(140)*

This move would have been
stronger after 11 dc dc.

140

11...♘×d5!? 12 ♕×a5 (after
12 cd ♕×d2 13 ♖×d2 c4! Black
has the better ending) 12...
♘×e3 13 ♖c1 ♘×c4 14 ♖×c4 bc
15 ♘c1 ♖b8! 16 ♗×c4 ♘b6 17
♗b3 ♗×d4 18 ♕d2 ♗g7 19 ♘e2 c4
20 ♗c2 c3!

Black's attack reaches its
finale. His mounting initiative is
stronger than White's extra
material.

21 ♕d3 cb 22 ♘d4 ♗d7 23 ♖d1
♖fc8 24 ♗b3 ♘a4 25 ♗×a4 ♗×a4
26 ♘b3 ♖c3! 27 ♕×a6 ♗×b3 28 ab

♖bc8 29 ♕a3 ♖c1+ 30 ♖×c1
♖×c1+ 0-1

No. 327 Hollis-Baumbach
Corr., 1976
Queen's Gambit

1 d4 d5 2 c4 c6 3 ♘f3 ♘f6 4 ♘c3
e6 5 ♗g5 dc 6 e4 b5 7 e5 h6 8 ♗h4
g5 9 ♘×g5 hg 10 ♗×g5 ♘bd7 11 ef
♗b7 12 g3 ♕b6 13 ♗g2 0-0-0 14
0-0 ♘e5 15 de! ♖×d1 16 ♖a×d1
♗c5 17 ♘e4 ♗d4?! 18 ♘d6+ ♔c7
19 ♗f4 ♖f8 20 ♗h6 ♖h8 21 ♗g7
♖d8 22 ♘×f7 ♗×f2+ 23 ♔h1
♖×d1 24 ♖×d1 ♕e3 25 ♘d6 ♕e2
26 ♖a1! ♕h5 27 g4! ♕h7 28 f7
♗g3 29 h3 c5 30 ♘×b7 ♕×g7 31
♖f1 ♕f8 32 ♘×c5 1-0

Queen against three minor pieces

This balance of forces occurs
rather rarely in the opening
stage. Such an exchange of the
queen is normally unfavourable,
since in the opening and middlegame the three minor pieces are
usually stronger.

This situation can arise, for example, in a line of the Sozin
Attack in the Sicilian Defence: 1
e4 c5 2 ♘f3 ♘c6 3 d4 cd 4 ♘×d4
♘f6 5 ♘c3 d6 6 ♗c4 e6 7 0-0 a6 8
♗e3 ♕c7 9 ♗b3 ♘a5 10 f4 b5 11
f5 ♘×b3 12 cb ♗e7 13 ♖c1 ♕d7
14 ♕f3 0-0 15 e5! ♗b7 (Black

also stands badly after 15...
de 16 fe fe 17 ♘xe6!) 16 ef! ♗xf3
17 fe ♕xe7 18 ♖xf3 *(141)*

141

The position obviously favours White, e.g. 18...e5 19 f6! gf 20 ♘f5 etc.

For roughly the same reasons the following line of the Sozin Attack is also dubious for Black: 1 e4 c5 2 ♘f3 ♘c6 3 d4 cd 4 ♘xd4 ♘f6 5 ♘c3 d6 6 ♗c4 e6 7 0-0 a6 8 ♗e3 ♗e7 9 ♗b3 ♘a5 10 f4 0-0 11 ♕f3 b5 12 e5! ♗b7 13 ef ♗xf3 14 fe ♕xe7 15 ♖xf3.

In this case White's initiative is not so clear, but with the possibility of an attack on the K-side by f4-f5 he has the better chances.

It is no accident that this variation, where Black quickly develops his Q-side, soon went out of practice.

For the same reason this variation of the Grünfeld Defence is unfavourable for Black: 1 d4 ♘f6 2 c4 g6 3 ♘c3 d5 4 ♘f3 ♗g7 5 ♕b3 dc 6 ♕xc4 0-0 7 e4 b6 8 e5 ♗a6?

9 ef! ♗xc4 10 fg ♔xg7 11 ♗xc4 etc.

Unusual situations, where a queen is opposed by just two minor pieces, occur rarely in the opening. These are possible only if there is compensation in the form of a strong initiative and some equivalent in pawns. Here is a truly paradoxical example where, despite the great difference in material, the queen is helpless and the attack by the minor pieces proves decisive.

No. 328
Nezhmetdinov-Chernikov
RSFSR Ch., 1962
Sicilian Defence

1 e4 c5 2 ♘f3 ♘c6 3 d4 cd
4 ♘xd4 g6 5 ♘c3 ♗g7 6 ♗e3 ♘f6
7 ♗c4 0-0 8 ♗b3 ♘g4?! 9 ♕xg4
♘xd4 10 ♕h4!?

Theory mainly considered 10 ♕d1, regarding ♕h4 as leading to a draw.

10...♕a5 11 0-0 ♗f6 *(142)*
Here is the theoretically

142

drawn position: it appears that White must repeat moves by 12 ♕h6 ♗g7 13 ♕h4 ♗f6 etc. But, as has already been mentioned, in such situations the theoretical assessments are very relative. White's next move essentially signifies the creation of a new and highly attractive opening variation.

12 ♕×f6! ♘e2+!

Comparatively best. After 12...♘×b3 13 ab ♕×a1 14 ♕×e7! ♕a5 15 ♗h6 ♕d8 16 ♘d5! Black would have lost immediately.

13 ♘×e2 ef 14 ♘c3 ♖e8

Later it was decided that Black should have played 14... d5! The play here is of an 'irrational' nature. Apart from 15 ♘×d5 White would have also had the interesting continuation 15 ♗d4!?

Now White's attack develops inexorably.

15 ♘d5 ♖e6 16 ♗d4 ♕g7 17 ♖ad1 d6 18 ♖d3 ♗d7 19 ♖f3 ♗b5 20 ♗c3 ♕d8 21 ♘×f6! ♗e2 22 ♘×h7+! ♔g8

After 22...♔×h7 23 ♖×f7+ ♔h6 24 ♗×e6 ♗×f1 25 ♗d2+ g5 26 ♗f5 ♕h8 27 h4! White's attack is irresistible.

23 ♖h3 ♖e5 24 f4! ♗×f1 25 ♔×f1 ♖c8 26 ♗d4! b5 27 ♘g5 ♖c7 28 ♗×f7+ ♖×f7 29 ♖h8+ ♔×h8 30 ♘×f7+ ♔h7 31 ♘×d8 ♖×e4 32 ♘c6 ♖×f4+ 33 ♔e2 1-0

Exchange sacrifices in the opening

In the opening stage the queen can comparatively rarely be sacrificed (or exchanged) for an equivalent amount of other material. On the other hand, the possibility of a positional sacrifice of rook for minor piece occurs much more often, and is the most common type of sacrifice after that of a pawn. The aims and forms of it are varied. The point of such sacrifices and the general strategic structure are largely analogous to those in the preceding sections. Important here are the initiative, and the active and harmonious coordination of the forces.

Early in the game there is sometimes a possibility of 'pursuing' the win of the exchange, but in the majority of cases the following advice is true: don't go in for it to the detriment of your development.

Typical in this respect is the following example, where White tried to handle a solid variation of the English Opening in 'ultra-dynamic' style, but essentially he seriously broke the principle of development in pursuit of material.

No. 329 Karasev-Nezhmetdinov
Daugavpils, 1973
English Opening

1 ♘f3 ♞f6 2 c4 c5 3 d4 cd 4 ♘xd4 e6 5 ♘c3 ♗b4 6 ♘db5 0-0 7 ♗f4?!

More logical was 7 a3 ♗xc3+ 8 ♘xc3 d5 9 e3 with a roughly equal game.

7...d5! 8 a3 (after 8 ♘c7 ♞e4 9 ♘xa8 ♛f6! Black's attack in the centre is decisive) **8...♗xc3+ 9 ♘xc3 d4 10 ♘b5?! a6!? 11 ♘c7 ♖a7 12 ♘b5**

White cannot get out of his acquisitive mood, and he soon pays for this. 12 ♘d5 was the lesser evil.

12...ab 13 ♗xb8 bc! 14 ♗xa7 ♛a5+ 15 ♛d2 ♛xa7

The outcome of the opening is dismal for White. In return for the exchange Black has a strong pawn centre, but the main point is that the white king is hopelessly stuck in the centre of the board. The conclusion of the game is highly instructive.

16 e3 d3 17 g3 ♞e4 18 ♛b4 d2+ 19 ♔e2 ♛a6! 20 ♔f3 ♛c6 21 ♔e2 ♛d5 22 ♖d1 e5 23 h3 b6 24 ♖g1 c3 25 bc ♘xc3+ 0-1

In this case the exchange sacrifice occurred in the course of events and was not in itself an active operation, but much more often, of course, this is not the case. Thus in many variations of the Sicilian Defence Black makes a typical exchange sacrifice on c3, e.g: 1 e4 c5 2 ♘f3 d6 3 d4 cd 4 ♘xd4 ♞f6 5 ♘c3 a6 6 g3 b5 7 ♗g2 ♗b7 8 a3 e6 9 0-0 ♘bd7 10 f4 ♖c8 11 f5 e5 12 ♘b3? ♖xc3! 13 bc ♘xe4, and at the cost of a slight material deficit Black breaks up White's pawn position on the Q-side and in the centre, firmly seizing the initiative. White must beware of such sacrifices and take timely measures to forestall them.

A problematic exchange sacrifice in one of the most important variations of the Grünfeld Defence is still topical: 1 d4 ♞f6 2 c4 g6 3 ♘c3 d5 4 cd ♘xd5 5 e4 ♘xc3 6 bc c5 7 ♗c4 ♗g7 8 ♘e2 cd 9 cd 0-0 10 ♗e3 ♘c6 11 0-0 ♗g4 12 f3 ♘a5 13 ♗d3 ♗e6.

In order to forestall Black's active intentions on the Q-side — 14...♗c4 or 14...♘c4 — White must go in for the most critical line, which involves sacrificing the exchange: 14 d5! ♗xa1 15 ♛xa1 *(143)*

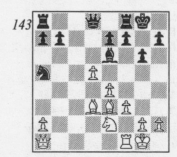

143

In return for the exchange White has obtained a strong pawn centre and real chances of an attack on the opponent's castled position. In the resulting sharp struggle for the initiative, an important part is played by combinational motifs.

For over 40 years the attention of researchers has been fixed on this enigma, and there is still no clear answer to it. The analysis merely goes deeper and becomes more and more intricate.

A possible continuation is 15...f6 16 &h6 &e8! 17 &f4 &f7 18 e5 &×d5! 19 &b1 &c4, with a sharp game where Black has good defensive possibilities.

Rook for two minor pieces

In the opening and middle-game two minor pieces are usually stronger than a rook, even if the latter has two pawns. Therefore such an exchange of minor pieces is unfavourable, although the opportunity for it often occurs.

Thus in a line of Philidor's Defence which has been known for a long time, the following variation is considered unfavourable for White: 1 e4 e5 2 &f3 d6 3 &c3 &d7 4 d4 &gf6 5 &c4 &e7 6 &g5? 0-0 7 &×f7+ &×f7 8 &e6 &e8 9 &×c7 &d8 10 &×a8 ed! etc.

It is quite obvious that in the opening one should not normally make use of such an opportunity. But if at the same time the coordination of the minor pieces is disrupted and permanent weaknesses are inflicted, such an exchange may be favourable. Thus in the Spanish Game after 1 e4 e5 2 &f3 &c6 3 &b5 f5 4 &c3 fe 5 &×e4 d5 6 &×e5 de 7 &×c6 bc!? 8 &×c6+ &d7 9 &h5+ &e7 10 &e5+ &e6 11 &×a8 &×a8 *(144)*, in view of Black's lack of development White's chances are preferable.

144

The sacrifice of a minor piece in the opening

There are many types of minor piece sacrifice in the opening. In the majority of cases the piece is sacrificed for one or two pawns, with the possibility in mind of mounting a strong attack on the opponent's king.

We give some further

examples of this type from the games of Rashid Nezhmetdinov, a striking representative of modern dynamism.

No. 330
Nezhmetdinov-Mikenas
Match, 1948
Alekhine's Defence

1 e4 ♘f6 2 e5 ♘d5 3 c4 ♘b6 4 c5 ♘d5 5 ♗c4 e6 6 ♘c3 d6 7 ♘xd5 ed 8 ♗xd5 c6 9 ♗xf7+ ♔xf7 10 cd ♕e8 11 ♕e2

Events developed in similar fashion in Vasyukov-Spassky (26th USSR Ch., 1959), which continued 11 ♕f3+ ♔g8 12 ♕e3 ♗e6 13 ♘e2 ♘d7 14 0-0, and soon an unusual position of dynamic equilibrium was reached.

11...c5 12 ♘f3 ♗xd6! 13 ♘g5+!

After 13 ed ♕xe2+ 14 ♔xe2 ♖e8+ 15 ♔d1 ♗g4 Black could have gained a dangerous counterattack. White prefers to continue in gambit style.

13...♔g6 14 ♕d3+ ♔xg5 15 ♕xd6 ♕d8?

As already mentioned, in dynamic situations it is easy to go wrong tactically, and it is tactical mistakes which can have the most serious practical consequences. Correct was 15...♘c6 16 d4+ ♔h5 17 ♕xc5 ♕e7 with a double-edged game, whereas now White's attack proves

quickly decisive.

16 d4+ ♔f5 17 g4+ ♔e4 18 ♕xc5 ♖f8 19 0-0 ♔f3 20 h3 b6 21 ♕c3+ ♔e4 22 ♕c4! 1-0

The sacrifice in the following game was even more 'irrational'.

No. 331 Mikenas-Nezhmetdinov
Match, 1948
King's Indian Defence

1 d4 ♘f6 2 c4 d6 3 ♘f3 g6 4 ♘c3 ♗g7 5 e4 0-0 6 ♗e2 c6 7 h3 ♘bd7 8 ♗e3 e5 9 d5 cd 10 cd ♘c5 11 ♘d2 a5?! 12 a3 ♘e8 13 b4 ab 14 ab ♖xa1 15 ♕xa1 *(145)*

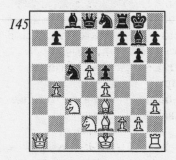

15...♘xe4!?

Frankly speaking, an unusual sacrifice, although highly characteristic of the modern dynamic approach.

16 ♘dxe4 f5 17 ♘d2

On 17 ♗g5 there would have followed 17...♕b6! Had White foreseen just how dangerous Black's attack was, he would have done best to return the piece by 17 0-0!, remaining with a minimal positional advantage.

17...e4! 18 ♘b3 f4 19 ♗d4 f3 20 gf ef 21 ♗d3 ♕g5! 22 ♗e3 ♕h4 23 ♔d2 ♕xb4 24 ♖b1 ♕h4 25 ♕a7 ♗e5 26 ♘d4 ♗f4!

With every move events turn in favour of Black, whose dynamic attack becomes more and more dangerous.

27 ♔c2 ♗xe3 28 fe ♕f2+ 29 ♔b3 ♕xe3 30 ♗f1 f2 31 ♘db5 ♕g3 32 ♕a2

And here, by capturing the h3 pawn, Black would have gained winning chances. After exciting complications the game in fact ended in a draw, but the moral victory went to Black for his bold idea begun on move 15.

Here are some further examples, where the sacrifice is associated with a counterattack.

No. 332 Hebell-Dorniden
West Germany, 1976
Pirc Defence

1 e4 g6 2 d4 ♗g7 3 ♘c3 d6 4 f4 ♘c6 5 ♗e3 ♘f6 6 h3 0-0 7 g4 e5 8 de de 9 f5 ♘d4 10 ♕d2 gf 11 gf ♘xe4 *(146)* 12 ♘xe4 ♗xf5 13 ♘g3 ♘xc2+ 14 ♔e2 ♗g6! 15 ♖c1 ♘xe3 16 ♕xe3 f5! (White's position is indefensible) 17 ♕b3+ ♔h8 18 ♗g2 ♕g5 19 ♖c3 f4 20 h4 ♕g4 21 ♗f3 ♕xg3 22 ♗xb7

♗h5+ 23 ♔f1 f3 24 ♘xf3 e4 25 ♗xe4 ♖ae8 0-1

146

No. 333 Smejkal-Olafsson
Reykjavik, 1978
King's Indian Defence

1 c4 ♘f6 2 ♘c3 g6 3 ♘f3 ♗g7 4 e4 d6 5 d4 0-0 6 ♗e2 e5 7 0-0 c6 8 ♕c2 ♘bd7 9 ♖d1 ♕e7 10 ♖b1 ed 11 ♘xd4 ♘c5 12 f3 ♘h5!? 13 ♗f1 f5! 14 b4 fe! 15 bc dc 16 ♘de2 ef 17 gf ♖xf3 18 ♕e4 ♕f8 19 ♗g5? (19 ♗b2 is correct) 19...♖xc3! 20 ♗e7 ♘f6! 21 ♗xf8 ♘xe4 22 ♖d8 ♖f3! 23 ♗xc5+ ♔f7 24 ♗g2 ♘xc5 25 ♗xf3 ♗f6 26 ♖d2 ♗f5 27 ♖bd1 ♗g5 28 ♖b2 ♗f6 with advantage to Black.

And here is a 50 year-old example which still remains highly instructive.

No. 334 Euwe-Alekhine
World Championship, 1937
Slav Defence

1 d4 d5 2 c4 c6 3 ♘f3 ♘f6 4 ♘c3

dc 5 a4 ♗f5 6 e3 e6 7 ♗×c4
♘bd7 8 0-0 ♗d6? 9 ♕e2 ♘e4 10
♘×e4? (better 10 ♘d2!) 10...
♗×e4 11 ♘d2 ♗g6 12 e4 ♗c7! 13
♗b3 0-0 14 f4? ♘f6 15 ♗c2
♕×d4+ 16 ♔h1 ♕b4 17 g4 ♖ad8!
18 f5 ef 19 ef ♖fe8 20 ♕g2 ♕×g4
21 fg hg 22 ♗d1 ♕×g2+ 23 ♔×g2
♖d4 24 ♘f3 ♖g4+ 25 ♔h3 ♖d8 26
♗g5 ♖b4 27 ♗d2 ♖e4 28 ♗b3?
♖e2! 29 ♗c3 ♖d3 30 ♔h4 ♖×f3!
31 ♖×f3 ♖×h2+ 32 ♖h3 g5+ 33
♔×g5 ♖×h3 34 ♗d1 ♘e4+ 0-1

Tactical destruction of the flanks in the opening

The tactical destruction of the
flanks in the opening mainly results from dynamic attacks,
which often conclude with the
devastation of the pawns (especially in the French and Slav
Defences).

At an early stage of the game,
one of the players often begins
an energetic piece attack on one
of the flanks, based, of course,
on there being real preconditions for its success. The most
energetic strategic plan in reply
is a counterattack in the centre
and on the opposite flank.

Instructive in this respect is
the 'irrational' play which arises
in one of the topical variations of
the French Defence: 1 e4 e6 2 d4
d5 3 ♘c3 ♗b4 4 e5 c5 5 a3 ♗×c3+

6 bc ♕c7 7 ♕g4 f5 8 ♕g3 ♘e7
9 ♕×g7 ♖g8 10 ♕×h7 cd 11
♔d1!?

It is not easy to find criteria by
which to assess this position.
The development of the following game is typical.

No. 335 Gligorić-Petrosian
Zurich, 1959

11...♘bc6 (11...♗d7 is probably better) 12 ♘f3 ♘×e5 13 ♗g5!
♘eg6, and here, by continuing 14
♗f6! (instead of 14 ♗×e7 ♘×e7
15 cd ♗d7) followed by h2-h4,
White would have obtained
strong pressure.

Often the pawn screen on a
flank is destroyed in the opening
as a result of active flank pawn
operations. This is the picture in
many lines of the Slav Defence,
in particular the Botvinnik Variation, the Meran Variation, and
others.

147

In the main line of the Botvinnik Variation after 1 d4 d5 2 c4 c6

3 ♘c3 ♘f6 4 ♘f3 e6 5 ♗g5 dc 6 e4 b5 7 e5 h6 8 ♗h4 g5 9 ♘×g5 hg 10 ♗×g5 ♘bd7 11 ef *(147)* Black permits the destruction of his K-side pawns, but by an energetic pawn offensive on the Q-side he succeeds in creating a strong pawn phalanx.

The subsequent play is very complicated and full of combinational motifs. For example, the following game took an interesting course.

No. 336 Smyslov–Botvinnik
World Championship, 1954

11...♗b7 12 g3 ♕b6 13 ♗g2 0-0-0 14 0-0 ♘e5!? 15 ♕e2 ♕×d4 16 ♗e3 ♕d3 17 ♖fd1 ♕×e2 18 ♖×d8+ ♔×d8 19 ♘×e2 ♘d3, and in the resulting ending Black maintained the balance.

Black carries out a similar idea of a Q-side pawn offensive in the Meran Variation, from which we will consider one interesting line: 1 d4 d5 2 c4 c6 3 ♘f3 ♘f6 4 ♘c3 e6 5 e3 ♘bd7 6 ♗d3 d×c4 7 ♗×c4 b5 8 ♗e2 ♗b7 9 e4 b4 10 e5 bc 11 ef cb 12 fg ba♕ 13 gh♕ *(148)*

Almost by force, a highly unusual position has been reached with four queens on the board, in which the play has been little studied.

A similar, highly unusual idea was carried out in the middle-

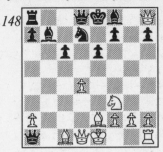

148

game by Alekhine with White in the following game: 1 e4 e6 2 d4 d5 3 ♘c3 ♘f6 4 ♗g5 ♗b4 5 e5 h6 6 ef hg 7 fg ♖g8 8 h4 gh 9 ♕g4! ♗e7 10 g3 c5 11 gh cd 12 h5! dc 13 h6 cb 14 ♖b1 ♕a5+ 15 ♔e2 ♕×a2 16 h7 ♕×b1 17 hg♕+ ♔d7 18 ♕×f7 ♕×c2+ 19 ♔f3 ♘c6! 20 ♕g×e6+ ♔c7 21 ♕f4+ ♔b6 22 ♕6e3+ ♗c5 23 g8♕ b1♕

Here Alekhine found an elegant way to win: 24 ♖h6!! (threatening 25 ♕d8 mate) 24... ♕×f1 25 ♕b4+ ♔b5 26 ♕d8+ ♔a6 27 ♕ea3+, and wins.

Seizure of the centre from the flanks

In modern opening set-ups the flanks are not always functionally dependent with regard to the centre.

Sometimes a complicated flank operation does not have the aim of making purely local gains, but of weakening the opponent's pressure on the centre, in order later to gain superiority there.

Thus in the line of the Spanish Game after 1 e4 e5 2 ♘f3 ♘c6 3 ♗b5 a6 4 ♗a4 ♘f6 5 0-0 ♗e7 6 ♖e1 b5 7 ♗b3 d6 8 c3 0-0 9 h3 ♘a5 10 ♗c2 c5 11 d4 ♕c7 12 ♘bd2 g6? 13 ♘f1 ♖e8 14 ♘e3 ♕g7, the solution lies not in the local offensive on the K-side with 15 g4, for which Black is well prepared, but in the unexpected flank blow 15 b4!, which after 15...cb 16 cb ♘c6 17 ♗b2 enables White to begin an effective attack on the opponent's central defences. This plan has become typical of such set-ups.

It especially gains in strength if White has a lead in development or if his pieces are more actively placed.

For example: 1 e4 e5 2 ♘f3 ♘c6 3 ♗b5 a6 4 ♗a4 ♘f6 5 0-0 b5 6 ♗b3 d6 7 c3 ♘a5 8 ♗c2 c5 9 d4 ♕c7 10 ♘bd2 g6 (149)

149

Here the most energetic plan for White is undoubtedly the flank attack on the enemy positions in the centre by 11 b4! cb 12 cb ♘c6 13 ♗b2 ♗g7 14 ♖c1 ♗b7 15 ♗b3.

White forces a favourable opening of the centre and the Q-side, thus gaining the opportunity to exploit his lead in development. For example, White's attack developed quickly in the following game.

No. 337 Bronstein-Evans
USSR-USA, Moscow, 1955

15...♕e7(?) 16 ♖×c6! ♗×c6 17 de ♘h5 18 g4 ♘f4 19 ed ♕d7 20 ♘e5!, and White soon won.

The following game is also instructive.

No. 338 Kapengut-Mukhin
USSR, 1972
Sicilian Defence

1 e4 c5 2 ♘f3 d6 3 ♗b5+ ♘c6 4 0-0 ♗d7 5 ♖e1 ♘f6 6 c3 a6 7 ♗f1 e5(?) 8 h3 ♗e7 9 d4 0-0 10 ♘bd2 b5 11 d5 ♘a7

A typical structure from the Closed Variation of the Spanish Game has arisen. In the subsequent play, exploiting his spatial advantage, White conducts a combined offensive on both flanks, preparing the main blow against the opponent's king.

12 b4 c4 13 a4 ♘e8 14 ♘h2 g6 15 ♘df3 ♘g7 16 ♗h6 ♕c7 17 ab ab

18 ♕d2 ♖ab8 19 ♘g4 f6 20 ♘h4

The white cavalry is at action stations!

20. . .♗e8 21 g3 ♘c8 22 f4 ♗d8 23 ♘f3 ♘b6 24 ♗g2 ♖a8 25 ♖×a8 ♘×a8 26 ♔h2 ♘b6 27 ♖f1 ♕a7 28 h4! ♗d7 29 ♗h3! ♗c8 30 ♖f2 ♘a4 31 fe fe? 32 ♗e3! 1-0

In the above examples the consequences of the flank blow on the Q-side were felt on the Black's K-side. More often (and this is characteristic of the English Opening) a successful flank operation leads to the achievement of a favourable structure in the centre.

Take, for example, the following variation of the English Opening: 1 c4 c5 2 ♘c3 ♘f6 3 g3 d5 4 cd ♘×d5 5 ♗g2 ♘c7 6 ♘f3 ♘c6 7 a3! e5 8 b4! etc.

After undermining one of Black's supports in the centre, at c5, White later has the real possibility of exploiting his 'extra' pawn in the centre by playing d2d4, which assures him of a persistent initiative.

Undermining pawn moves of this type are Black's strategic theme in a number of lines of the Paulsen Variation of the Sicilian Defence. For example: 1 e4 c5 2 ♘f3 e6 3 d4 cd 4 ♘×d4 ♘c6 5 ♘b5 d6 6 c4 ♘f6 7 ♘1c3 a6 8 ♘a3 ♗e7 9 ♗e2 0-0 10 0-0 ♗d7 11 ♗e3 ♕a5 12 ♕e1 ♖ab8 (interesting here is Boleslavsky's idea of

12. . . ♖fb8!?, and if 13 f3 b5! 14 cb ab 15 ♘a×b5 ♘b4 with adequate counterplay for Black) 13 f3 ♖fd8 14 ♖c1 ♗e8 15 ♕f2 b5! 16 cb ab 17 ♘a×b5 d5!, and Black has splendid prospects.

Also of interest are these variations of the English Opening: 1 c4 c5 2 ♘c3 ♘f6 3 g3 d5 4 cd ♘×d5 5 ♗g2 ♘c7 6 d3 e5 7 ♘f3 ♘c6 8 0-0 ♗e7 9 ♘d2 ♗d7 10 ♘c4 f6 11 f4! when White has a strong initiative, or 1 c4 c5 2 ♘c3 ♘f6 3 g3 d5 4 cd ♘×d5 5 ♗g2 ♘c7 6 d3 e5 7 f4!?, or first 7 ♘h3!? and then 8 f4.

Flank attacks such as g2-g4 (or . . .g7-g5) are more rarely encountered. Instructive in this respect are some examples from Alekhine's games.

No. 339 Alekhine-Euwe
AVRO, 1938
Slav Defence

1 d4 d5 2 c4 c6 3 ♘f3 ♘f6 4 cd cd 5 ♘c3 ♘c6 6 ♗f4 ♗f5 7 e3 a6 8 ♘e5 ♖c8 *(150)*

150

Here White unexpectedly played **9 g4!**, beginning an original offensive plan. **9...♗d7 10 ♗g2 e6 11 0-0 h6** (White's main idea is revealed in the variation 11...h5 12 g5! ♘g8 13 e4!, when, with a spatial superiority, he advantageously opens the centre) **12 ♗g3 h5 13 ♘xd7** (now on 13 g5? there would have followed 13...h4) **13...♘xd7 14 gh! ♘f6 15 ♗f3,** and White attained an obvious superiority in the centre and on the K-side.

Castling on opposite sides

In positions with castling on opposite sides the interrelation of the centre and the flanks is of particular importance. The set-ups which are most interesting and problematic are those where mutual attacks on the flanks are combined with play in the centre, and the pawn structure remains undetermined, without a clear superiority for either side.

Athough the subsequent play will certainly involve attempts to mount an attack on the flank, a player must also constantly reckon with the weight of play being transferred to the centre. If the structure in the centre is undetermined, a player must watch with particular care for possible operations there.

Instructive in this respect is the Yugoslav Attack in the Sicilian Dragon, one of the most 'intriguing' variations over a long period of time: **1 e4 c5 2 ♘f3 d6 3 d4 cd 4 ♘xd4 ♘f6 5 ♘c3 g6 6 ♗e3 ♗g7 7 f3 0-0 8 ♕d2 ♘c6.** For a long time the preferred move here was **9 0-0-0,** to which Black usually replied 9...♘xd4. But then fashion changed decisively in favour of the sharp **9...d5!?.** *(151),* by which a pawn is sacrificed in the interests of the rapid opening of lines on the Q-side, where the white king has taken shelter.

151

Now a very sharp tactical struggle develops, and the white king may find itself in great danger.

Thus in the event of the sacrifice being accepted: 10 ed ♘xd5 11 ♘xd6 bc 12 ♘xd5 cd 13 ♕xd5 ♕c7!, Black develops a very strong attack. White must be on the alert, in order to maintain the balance: 14 ♕c5 ♕b7 15 ♕a3!

♗f5 16 ♗a6 ♕c7 17 ♕c5 ♕b6! etc. (recommended by Averbakh).

The main, problematic struggle develops in the line **10 ed ♘xd5 11 ♘xc6 bc 12 ♗d4! e5!** (but not 12...♗xd4 13 ♕xd4 ♕b6 14 ♘a4! with advantage to White) **13 ♗c5 ♗e6!**

In the interests of developing his attack, Black offers an exchange sacrifice, the acceptance of which probably gives him an irresistible attack.

There was an interesting battle, for instance, in the following game.

No. 340 Trifunović-Averbakh
USSR v Yugoslavia
Belgrade, 1956

After great complications: **14 ♗c4** (14 ♘e4 is possibly stronger) **14...♘xc3 15 ♕xc3 ♕g5+ 16 ♗e3 ♕xg2 17 ♗xe6 fe 18 ♕xc6 ♖ac8 19 ♕e4 ♖xf3 20 ♖hf1 ♖f2 21 ♕xg2 ♖cxc2+ 22 ♔b1 ♖xb2+** the game ended in a draw by perpetual check.

The general comments at the start of this section are also confirmed by other constantly topical variations of the Sicilian Defence.

Thus in the main line of the Richter/Rauzer Variation after **1 e4 c5 2 ♘f3 ♘c6 3 d4 cd 4 ♘xd4 ♘f6 5 ♘c3 d6 6 ♗g5 e6 7 ♕d2 ♗e7 8 0-0-0 0-0** *(152)* the position

in the centre is worthy of note.

152

White has a spatial advantage, and hence greater freedom for manœuvring, but the black d6 and e6 pawns securely defend important squares. One of these pawns may have the opportunity to advance, gaining space and driving away White's centralized pieces. Other important features of Black's position, assisting his active play on the Q-side, are the half-open c-file and the d8-a5 diagonal.

It can be concluded that Black's forces also have sufficient possibilities for active play, and all this lends a particular sharpness to the developing struggle. There is a fierce battle for the initiative. Since White has a somewhat greater choice of possible attacking plans, considerable ingenuity is demanded of Black in finding active resources for counterplay. At all costs he must avoid going over to passive defence.

Interesting play develops, for example, after 9 ♘b3 ♕b6 10 f3 a6 11 g4 ♖d8, when Spassky-Boleslavsky (25th USSR Ch., 1958) continued 12 ♗e3 ♕c7 13 g5 ♘d7 14 h4 b5 15 g6! fg 16 h5 gh 17 ♖×h5 ♘f6 18 ♖g5 ♘e5 19 ♕g2 ♗f8 20 f4 ♘c4 21 ♗×c4 bc 22 ♘d4 ♖b8 23 ♖g1 ♖b7 with a double-edged game.

In the given variation the attack on the castled position is often accompanied, in the opening stage itself, by the sacrifice of pawns or even pieces with the aim of developing operations as rapidly as possible. Usually such sacrifices are made for the rapid opening of lines and diagonals with the aim of attacking on the flank.

Thus in the variation 9 f4 (cf. Diag. 152) 9...♘×d4 10 ♕×d4 ♕a5 11 ♕d2 h6 White has the very active continuation 12 h4!, sacrificing a piece to open lines on the K-side.

As shown by Averbakh-Fridstein (Moscow 1951), the acceptance of the sacrifice by 12...hg gives White a decisive attack: 13 hg ♘×e4 14 ♘×e4 ♕×d2+ 15 ♖×d2 followed by g2-g4 and ♖dh2!

Instead of 12...hg?, correct is 12...b5!, aiming for counterplay on the Q-side. In Zagorovsky-Ilivitsky (Tbilisi 1951) after 13 ♗×b5 ♖b8 14 a4! ♗a6 15 ♔b1

♗×b5 16 ab hg 17 hg ♘×e4 18 ♘×e4 ♕×b5 19 c4 ♕×c4 20 ♕c2 ♖×b2+! interesting complications led to a draw.

Such a piece sacrifice is also typical of many other lines of this variation.

If the central structure is undetermined, possible active operations here should be watched for with particular care. Sometimes the main weight of the struggle is transferred to the centre, with the further play no longer involving an attack on the castled position.

The double-edged nature of pawn expansions

Pawn expansions in the opening, especially in front of one's own castled position, normally create problems, but in modern variations such an advance can be highly effective, and sometimes even an essential plan, ensuring that an opening advantage is retained.

The development of events in the following game was instructive.

No. 341 Karpov-Portisch
Ljubliana Portorož, 1975
Slav Defence

1 ♘f3 d5 2 d4 ♘f6 3 c4 c6 4 ♘c3

dc 5 a4 ♗f5 6 e3 e6 7 ♗×c4 ♗b4
8 0-0 0-0 9 ♘h4 ♗g4 10 f3 ♗h5 11
g4! *(153)*

As Karpov pointed out, only in this way can White fight for an opening advantage. He forces the exchange of his knight for the important enemy bishop, and gains a slight but stable opening advantage — the two bishops, which can prove useful in an open game.

In the given instance the weakening of White's K-side pawns is not important.

11...♗g6 12 ♘×g6 hg 13 ♕b3 ♕e7 14 g5 ♘d5 15 e4 ♘b6 16 ♘a2!

An instructive manoeuvre. White succeeds in forestalling the important advance ...c5!, which would free Black's game. It is unfavourable for Black to play 16...♘×c4, since after 17 ♘×b4 White obtains a marked spatial advantage.

16...♗a5 17 ♗e2 e5 18 ♕c2! ♘6d7 19 de ♕×e5 20 ♔h1 ♖e8 21 ♗c4 ♘b6 22 ♗d3 ♘a6 23 ♗×a6 ba

24 ♖d1!

White very subtly maintains his initiative and at the same time watches carefully for tactical threats by the opponent. If now 24...♖ad8 25 ♗e3, and 25...♘d5 fails to 26 ♗d4! etc.

24...c5 25 ♗e3 ♖ac8 26 ♘c3 ♘c4 27 ♗c1 ♖b8?

Black fails to withstand the tension and loses quickly. It was essential to play 27...♗×c3 28 ♕×c3 ♕×c3 29 bc, although in the endgame too White's chances are preferable.

28 ♘d5! ♘×b2 29 ♗f4 ♕e6 30 ♖db1 ♕h3 31 ♗×b8 ♖×b8 32 ♖×b2 1-0

Even here the 'thorns' were very close to the 'roses'. In the next game a similar weakening of White's castled position proved to be a serious defect.

No. 342 Bagirov-Kupreichik
Leningrad, 1965
Slav Defence

1 d4 d5 2 c4 c6 3 ♘f3 ♘f6 4 ♘c3 dc 5 a4 ♗f5 6 ♘h4?! ♗g4?!? 7 h3(?) (7 f3) 7...♗h5 8 g4 ♗g6 9 ♘×g6 hg 10 g5? (better 10 ♗g2) 10... ♘d5 11 e4 ♘b4 12 ♗e3 e5! 13 de ♘d7 14 f4 ♗c5 15 ♗d2 ♘×e5 16 fe ♕d4 17 ♕e2 (17 ♖h2 ♖×h3! 18 ♗×h3 ♕g1+ 19 ♗f1 ♘d3+ would have given Black a crushing attack) 17...♘c2+ 18 ♔d1 ♘×a1 19 ♕×c4 0-0-0 20 ♖h2 ♕×e5 21

♖e2 ♖d4 22 ♕a2 ♕f4 0-1

In general such situations are highly contradictory. At any rate, provoking the advance of enemy pawns without specific grounds, especially at a cost of time, is sometimes no less dangerous than their reckless advance.

Interesting in this respect is Mikenas-Vasyukov (Moscow 1963), where Black set himself the aim of provoking the early advance of White's pawn phalanx in the centre and on the K-side: 1 d4 d6 2 g3 ♗g4 3 ♗g2 c6 4 h3 ♗h5 5 g4 ♗g6 6 f4! e6 7 e4 f5

This last move was practically forced in view of the threat of f4-f5. The resulting position is difficult for Black: the advanced pawn mass has become a great force. Hence the résumé: the opponent should not be allowed to advance his pawns with gain of tempi.

8 ♕e2 fe 9 ♗xe4 ♕h4+ 10 ♔f1 ♗xe4 11 ♕xe4 ♕e7 12 ♘f3, and White had an undisputed advantage.

Tactical ways of transforming the centre

Early in the game one sometimes has to go in for the breaking up of stable central structures, in order to carry out specific aims. The following examples are instructive in this respect.

No. 343 Boleslavsky-Stoltz
Saltsjöbaden IZ, 1948
Spanish Game

1 e4 e5 2 ♘f3 ♘c6 3 ♗b5 a6 4 ♗a4 ♘f6 5 0-0 ♘xe4 6 d4 b5 7 ♗b3 d5 8 de ♗e6 9 ♕e2 g5? 10 c4! *(154)*

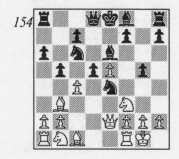

154

An 'explosive' move. White gives up his centre for the sake of more serious gains. Only in this way can he punish Black's flank diversion.

10...bc 11 ♗a4 ♗d7 12 e6! fe 13 ♗xc6 ♗xc6 14 ♘e5 ♕d6 15 ♕h5+ ♔e7 16 ♗xg5+ ♘xg5 17 ♕xg5+ ♔e8 18 ♕h5+ ♔e7 19 ♕f7+ ♔d8 20 ♕f6+, with a crushing attack.

No. 344 Suetin-Donner
Havana, 1968
French Defence

1 e4 e6 2 d4 d5 3 ♘c3 ♗b4 4 e5

c5 5 a3 ♗×c3+ 6 bc ♕c7 7 ♘f3 b6 8 a4 ♗a6 9 ♗×a6 ♘×a6 10 ♕d3 ♘b8 11 0-0 ♘d7 12 a5 ♖c8? (better 12...ba) 13 ab ab 14 dc!

White voluntarily gives up his central base at d4, but he eliminates Black's threatened counterplay on the c-file and creates scope for his pieces.

14...bc 15 ♖e1 ♘e7 16 h4! h5 17 c4! *(155)*

17...dc 18 ♕×c4 ♘f5 19 ♕f4 ♘f8? (19... 0-0 was essential, although here too after 20 ♕g5 g6 21 f4 hg 22 ♕×g4 ♘g7 23 ♗h6 White retains the initiative) **20 ♖d1!**

A 'quiet' but unpleasant move, threatening 21 ♕a4+!

20...♕c6? 21 ♕c4 ♘d7 22 ♖a6 ♘b6 23 ♕b3 ♖b8 24 ♗g5! 1-0

No. 345
Nezhmetdinov-Chistyakov
Kharkov, 1956
French Defence

1 e4 e6 2 d4 d5 3 ♘c3 ♘f6

4 ♗g5 ♗b4 5 e5 h6 6 ♗d2 ♘fd7?! 7 ♕g4 ♗f8 8 ♘f3!

8 f4 looks more solid, consolidating the pawn centre. But White already had in mind the original plan which is revealed on move 11.

8...c5 (8...a6 is more circumspect) **9 ♘b5! g6?**

A serious weakening of the K-side. 9...cd was better, when White intended 10 c3! dc 11 ♗×c3 with compensation for the pawn.

10 ♗d3 ♖g8

On 10...h5 there could have followed 11 ♕×e6+!! fe 12 ♗×g6+ ♔e7 13 ♗g5+ ♘f6 14 ef+ ♔d7 15 ♘e5 mate!

11 c4!

This is the point of White's opening strategy — he literally blows up the centre, rejecting the usual structure typical of the French Defence. But he has taken account of his great lead in development, and so he opens up the position.

11...cd

Black also has a difficult position after 11...dc 12 ♗×c4 a6 13 ♘d6+ ♗×d6 14 ed ♕b6 15 0-0 ♕×d6 16 dc ♘×d5 17 ♗×h6.

12 cd ♘c5 13 ♕×d4 ed

After this Black is quickly crushed. 13...♘c6 was essential, although even here White has the advantage after 14 ♕e3!

14 ♘d6+! ♗×d6 15 ed ♕×d6 16

0-0 ♘xd3 17 ♕xd3 ♘c6 18
♖fe1+ ♗e6 19 ♘d4! g5 20 ♖ac1
♔d7 21 ♘f5! ♕f8 22 ♕b5! ♖c8 23
♕xb7+ ♖c7 24 ♕b5 a6 25 ♕d3
♕b8 26 ♘xh6 ♖g6 27 ♘xf7! ♗xf7
28 ♕f5+ ♔d8 29 ♖xc6 ♖cxc6 30
♗a5+ ♔c7 31 ♕xf7 1-0

Optimal plan or best variation?

It has already been men-
tioned that the achievement of
an obvious advantage in the
opening (and the more so a decisive one) is possible only in the
event of serious mistakes by one
of the players. At the same time,
from an analysis of opening principles, the conclusion suggests
itself that as a result of the
opening, given correct play by
both sides, the position should
be roughly equal. After all, at the
start of the game the struggle is
just beginning, and at the transition to the middlegame there are
usually several objectively equivalent plans.

In the majority of cases this
presupposes the choice of an optimal plan, depending sometimes on the tastes and style of
the player. Experienced players,
taking a realistic viewpoint, content themselves with a slight initiative or counterplay, or else
equal chances, endeavouring to
develop the favourable aspects

of their position.

This relates to the classical
understanding of the process of
completing the opening stage. In
a number of cases the appearance of dynamic new opening
variations demands the introduction of new 'corrections' into
the old rules. It is this that will
now be discussed.

One of the most important
demands of modern analysis is
the necessity for inquisitive research into the possibility of
finding the most effective plan
(or even the best variation!).
From this viewpoint certain
long-standing variations with
routine assessments have been
reconsidered.

Searches of this type prove
the most effective if, by disclosing some serious disruption in
the coordination of the opponent's forces, one can find a
way to obtain a significant
advantage.

With this aim let us consider a
line of the Caro-Kann Defence:
1 e4 c6 2 ♘c3 d5 3 ♘f3. It is well
known that, apart from 3...de,
the generally accepted defence is
3...♗g4, which, incidentally,
gives Black the best counterplay.
But the tempting 3...♘f6? 4 e5
♘e4, despite its apparent
activity, can lead to serious difficulties, if White avoids developing routinely (e.g. 5 ♗d3?, after

which Black's idea would be completely justified: 5... ♘xc3 6 bc ♗g4 etc), and instead searches for an effective plan. With this aim the best continuation is 5 ♘e2!, when 5...♗f5? is bad because of 6 d4 e6 7 ♘fg1! (the point of White's concrete idea on move 5 is revealed: the black knight at e4 is cut off from its main forces) 7... h5 8 h4 ♗e7 9 g3 c5 10 f3, and the knight is trapped!

Also of interest is the development of events in the following game.

No. 346
Nezhmetdinov-Kamyshev
Gorky, 1950

5 ♘e2! ♛b6 6 d4 c5 7 dc ♛xc5 (better 7...♘xc5) 8 ♘ed4 ♘c6 9 ♗b5! ♗d7 10 0-0 ♘xe5 11 ♘xe5 ♗xb5 12 ♘xb5 ♛xb5 13 ♖e1! ♘f6 14 ♗g5 e6 15 c4! ♛a5 16 ♗xf6 gf 17 ♘xf7!! ♔xf7 18 ♛h5+ ♔e7 19 cd e5 20 f4 ♛xd5 21 fe f5 22 e6 ♔f6 23 h4! ♗c5+ 24 ♔h1 ♛xe6 25 ♛h6+ 1-0

Thus in many cases the search for an effective path at the start of the game is just as necessary as the following of mobilization principles in the majority of other situations.

We now give several examples where there is a decisive disruption of the equilibrium at the transition stage from opening to middlegame.

In the first game White found a highly effective plan at the transition stage, which enabled him to disclose a latent lack of coordination in the opponent's forces and to crown his tactical actions with a swift attack on the black king.

No. 347 Botvinnik-Levenfish
USSR Ch., 1940
English Opening

1 c4 e5 2 ♘c3 ♘f6 3 ♘f3 ♘c6 4 d4 ed 5 ♘xd4 ♗b4 6 ♗g5 h6 7 ♗h4 ♗xc3+ 8 bc ♘e5 9 e3 (9 f4 is more energetic) 9...♘g6 10 ♗g3 ♘e4 11 ♛c2 ♘xg3 12 hg d6 13 f4! ♛e7 (13...♘f8 14 ♗e2 ♘e6 15 ♛e4 is slightly better, although here too White retains the initiative) 14 ♔f2 ♘f8 15 c5 dc 16 ♗b5+! ♘d7 *(156)*

156

Already Black's position is barely defensible, e.g. 16...c6 17 ♘xc6! or 16...♔d8 17 ♖ad1 cd

18 ♖xd4+ ♗d7 19 ♘xd7
♘xd7 20 ♖hd1 ♔c8 21 ♖xd7
♕xd7 22 ♖xd7 ♔xd7 23 ♕f5+,
or 16...♗d7 17 ♘f5 ♕f6 18 ♕e4+
♔d8 (18...♘e6 19 ♗xd7+ ♔xd7
20 ♖hd1+) 19 ♖hd1 c6 20 ♖d6!,
each time with a crushing attack
for White.

17 ♘f5 ♕f6 18 ♖ad1 g6

Black also fails to save the
game after 18...c6 19 ♖d6 ♕d8
20 ♕e4+ ♔f8 21 ♕e5! f6 22
♕xc5+! etc.

**19 ♘xh6 ♖f8 20 g4 a6 21 g5
♕e6 22 ♗e2 ♘b6 23 ♘g4 ♔e7 24
♘f6 ♕c6 25 ♖h7 ♗f5 26 e4 ♗e6
27 f5 1-0**

In the following two games
White each time found a tactical
way of refuting Black's active but
unfounded attempts to seize the
initiative in the opening stage.

No. 348 Suetin-Veresov
Byelorussian Ch., 1955
Caro-Kann Defence

**1 e4 c6 2 ♘c3 d5 3 ♘f3 ♗g4
4 h3 ♗h5 5 ed cd 6 ♗b5+ ♘c6 7 g4
♗g6 8 ♘e5 ♕c7?! 9 d4 e6 10 ♕e2
♘f6 11 h4 ♗b4 12 h5 ♗e4 13 f3
0-0 14 ♗xc6 bc 15 g5 c5 *(157)* 16
♗e3!**

This refutes Black's eccentric
opening strategy. Events continue to develop by force, but
White emerges a piece up.

**16...♗xf3 17 ♘xf3 ♘e4 18
0-0 ♘xc3 19 bc ♗xc3 20 ♖ad1**

157

♖ab8 21 ♖f2 ♖b2 22 h6! ♖fb8
23 ♘e5 cd 24 ♗xd4 ♗xd4 25
♖xd4 ♖b1+ 26 ♔g2 ♕c3 27
♖xf7! 1-0

No. 349 Averbakh-Estrin
Moscow, 1964
Queen's Gambit

**1 d4 d5 2 c4 e6 3 ♘c3 ♘f6 4 ♘f3
♗b4 5 ♗g5 dc 6 e4 c5 7 ♗xc4 cd
8 ♘xd4 ♕c7? (8...♕a5) 9 ♕b3!
♗xc3+ 10 ♕xc3 ♘xe4 11 ♘b5!
♕c5 12 ♕xg7! ♖f8 (12...♕xf2+
13 ♔d1 ♖f8 14 ♘c7+!) 13 ♗h6!
♕xf2+ 14 ♔d1 ♘d7 15 ♖e1 ♘ef6
16 ♗xe6! ♕xb2 17 ♖c1 1-0**

In the above games we see a
tactical method of punishment,
which was covered in the section
on typical opening mistakes. Is
this not the same thing? As we
have already seen several times,
in chess it is sometimes very difficult to draw a clear line
between closely-related but different concepts. To a great extent this also applies to the prob-

lems in question of the modern understanding of opening principles (as was mentioned, for instance, when we considered the problem of the pawn sacrifices and 'pawn-grabbing'). In the same way, there is a definite, although sometimes almost imperceptible, boundary between the tactical punishment of elementary opening errors and actions of this type in dynamic situations. In the latter case this is primarily a search, which will not always prove successful, even with the most brilliant combinational vision. After all, there is a considerable difference between a purely tactical operation and a dynamic plan, often highly risky but containing a bold idea.

'Opening fashion' and the origin of the new variations

This is a complex and highly interesting topic, deserving of an independent study. Here we will restrict ourselves to a few characteristic examples.

We will begin with new opening variations.

Even over a short period of time, intensive analysis and practical testing can lead to the origin of completely new opening variations.

Not long ago there was little interest in this variation of the Sicilian Defence: 1 e4 c5 2 ♘f3 ♘c6 3 d4 cd 4 ♘×d4 ♘f6 5 ♘c3 e5 6 ♘db5 d6 7 ♗g5 a6 8 ♗×f6 gf 9 ♘a3.

In opening guides this variation was judged to be unsatisfactory for Black in view of his organic weakness at d5 and his broken K-side. But modern opening analysis relates to obvious external factors with a fair degree of scepticism, and tries mainly to find a lively dynamic approach.

And as a result of such analysis it turned out that after 9. . .b5 10 ♘d5 f5 Black has rich possibilities for sharp counterplay.

Other variations of the Sicilian Defence with long-standing reputations have also undergone many changes in a very short time. They are 'eternally' alive thanks mainly to the oscillation of assessment scales first to one side, and then the other. For example, the Polugayevsky Variation has many times been 'buried': 1 e4 c5 2 ♘f3 d6 3 d4 cd 4 ♘×d4 ♘f6 5 ♘c3 a6 6 ♗g5 e6 7 f4 b5!? White's refutations have been associated with the variations 8 e5 de 9 fe ♕c7 10 ef ♕e5+ 11 ♘e4 and 10 ♕e2 etc., but in general the 7. . .b5!? variation continues to be very much alive.

Or take the Velimirović

Attack in the Sozin Variation, which has had a tempestuous development: 1 e4 c5 2 ♘f3 ♘c6 3 d4 cd 4 ♘×d4 ♘f6 5 ♘c3 d6 6 ♗c4 e6 7 ♗e3 ♗e7 8 ♕e2 a6 9 0-0-0 ♕c7 10 ♗b3 ♘a5 11 g4 b5 12 g5 ♘×b3+ 13 ab ♘d7, with a whole series of intricate continuations.

It can also happen that highly prominent lines, and even entire variations, fade into the past. Thus it can be said, without exaggeration, that during several generations of chess players one of the most important concrete problems in the opening was a sharp line of the Meran Variation: 1 d4 d5 2 c4 c6 3 ♘f3 ♘f6 4 ♘c3 e6 5 e3 ♘bd7 6 ♗d3 dc 7 ♗×c4 b5 8 ♗d3 a6 9 e4 c5 10 e5!? etc.

But then in the late 1940s another pawn blow in the centre came to light: 10 d5!? It soon transpired that here there was no less scope for analysis, and in fact Black still faces very difficult problems.

At the present time the 10 e5!? variation has swelled the ranks of its 'great' predecessors, such as the King's Gambit and the Evans Gambit. However, this archive has not only avoided being covered by the sands of time, but is still very much alive. At any time some variation may be extracted from it and restored to life in the light of new trends.

The given instance is most probably one of chess 'fashion'. It can happen that for a long time theory will be indifferent to many of its creations, even its favourite ones. But it may once again return to them. The only variations condemned to the archives are those which are lacking in strategic content, or which can be exhausted by concrete analysis.

nine

MODERN STRATEGIC PROBLEMS OF THE OPENING STRUGGLE FOR THE CENTRE

New methods of opening struggle for the initiative

In the modern opening the factor of the initiative plays a highly important role. Only if it is held is there a real possibility of putting into effect an intended strategic plan.

Hence the new approach to the role of chess 'time' in the opening, which rejects the mechanical counting of tempi. It is the connection between tempi and concrete ideas which must mainly be taken into account, since only in this way can a particular plan be effectively implemented.

Of course, in the opening the struggle for the initiative most often revolves around control of the central squares.

The method of struggling for the initiative in the modern opening is constantly being improved. This applies both to active means (White's play) and defensive (Black's play), and it is

this that stimulates the development of opening theory.

White's basic opening strategy is still to aim for a protracted and consistent increasing of the pressure on the central squares. This is clearly expressed in the popular openings of our time, such as the Spanish Game and the Semi-Open and Closed Games.

At the same time, White's main problem in the struggle for the centre, while avoiding rapid simplification and the premature liquidation of the central tension, is to hinder Black's free development and gradually deprive him of active play.

Such strategy for White was proposed back in Steinitz's time, but since then it has undergone numerous changes and has been greatly enriched. At the present time it is the path to a complex, dynamic struggle, and not the prelude to the accumulation of small advantages (as was considered earlier).

In the modern opening White conducts a very active

struggle for the initiative, for which he often boldly goes in for complications.

Changes in White's strategy in the direction of aggression and dynamism have largely been induced by Black's much greater activity, and his aiming for counterplay at the very start of the game (it can be said that this is Black's basic modern strategy).

In this mode of play Black does not limit himself in the opening to the passive defence of his central squares, but tries consistently to disrupt White's plan, opposing these with his own active plans in the centre.

With Black aiming for active counterplay in the opening, White must act concretely, and not rely on the advantage of the first move. In the event of routine play, White may not only quickly lose the initiative, but may also get into great difficulties.

The strategy of counterplay is the most effective in modern opening systems for Black. Thus the most popular variations are those where Black clearly aims for active counterplay: in reply to 1 e4 — the 3. . .a6 defence to the Spanish Game, and in particular the splendid Chigorin (Closed) Variation, as well as the Sicilian and French Defences; in reply to 1 d4 — the Nimzo-Indian Defence, Grünfeld Defence, and the various other Indian Defences etc.

From the viewpoint of searching for counterplay, at the present time many 'approved' variations for Black are being reconsidered, as a result of which they are being considerably enriched.

In opening variations with counterplay for Black in reply to White's aim for a lengthy initiative, the mechanical implementation of opening principles is the least acceptable. From the very start of the game each side aims to disrupt the coordination of the opponent's forces in the struggle for the centre, taking account of the concrete prospects for the middlegame, and a very intense struggle for the initiative ensues. In our opinion, in this lies the promise of the modern methods of opening struggle.

In the course of such a struggle, complex positions arise with rich and varied strategic plans. Approximate equality here does not foreshadow simplification and a quick draw (which is characteristic, for example, of many variations of the 'ancient' Open Games). It merely emphasizes that the two sides have aspirations of equal value in the coming struggle.

Thus counterplay is the best way of fighting for the initiative throughout the entire game. Take even the final aim: neutralizing the initiative by purely defensive methods in principle means obtaining a static equality; counterplay signifies a struggle for the initiative, for an advantage.

It is no accident that the method of counterplay has become the most effective in the struggle for the centre. Passive defence is now resorted to only in cases of extreme necessity, since passive play with the aim of neutralizing the initiative restricts Black's possibilities in the opening.

In his opening plans Black must naturally observe a certain caution, nevertheless making his main aim the obtaining of equal chances in the middlegame. But the best way of equalizing (or more accurately, of obtaining a good game) is by active counterplay.

Positions of dynamic balance

Characteristic of the modern opening is the rejection of the mechanical approach to the occupation of the centre.

In many opening set-ups there is an apparent breaking of the principle of occupying the centre, which is expressed, for instance, in conceding the opponent a numerical superiority or in creating a persistent pawn weakness in the centre. Such a breaking of the principle is acceptable, however, if effective piece pressure on the centre can be created.

In such cases complex positions arise with roughly equal chances. If in the subsequent play the approximate equality is retained as the outward positional factors change, such opening positions can be characterised as ones of dynamic balance.

In the subsequent play (of course, provided it takes a logical course) the active side may achieve some gains only by making equivalent concessions, and all the time a state of equality is as though in motion. One side will have certain positional advantages, while the other will have counterplay sufficient to balance them.

It must be mentioned that in such a struggle it is very difficult to maintain the balance, since the resulting concrete tactical and strategic problems are highly complex and demand of the players great mastery.

Typical in this respect is the development of events in the

following variation of the King's Indian Defence: 1 d4 ♘f6 2 c4 g6 3 ♘c3 ♗g7 4 g3 0-0 5 ♗g2 d6 6 ♘f3 ♘bd7 7 0-0 e5 8 e4 ♖e8 9 h3 ed 10 ♘×d4 ♘c5 11 ♖e1 a5 12 ♕c2 a4 13 ♗e3 c6 14 ♖ad1 ♘fd7 15 f4 *(158)*

White has an obvious numerical and spatial superiority in the centre; in Black's position there is an obvious pawn weakness at d6. But White's pieces are tied to the defence of the central squares, and his initiative is not felt. Practice shows that Black has fine counterchances in the coming interesting struggle, and this position can be characterized as one of dynamic balance.

From the diagram position the game Stahlberg-Boleslavsky (Zurich C, 1953) continued:

16 ♗f2 ♘b6 17 ♗f1 ♗d7 18 a3

This move is basically necessary, although it involves a weakening of White's Q-side pawns. Otherwise how else can he consolidate his grouping on the Q-side? It should not be forgotten that without a2-a3 White would be constantly restricted by the possible threat of . . .a3!

18. . .♖ad8 19 ♔h2 ♗c8 20 ♘a2 ♘bd7 21 ♗g2 ♘f6 22 ♘c3 ♖d7 23 ♘f3 ♖de7

The weakness of the d6 pawn is illusory. In order to win it, White must remove his knight from its very important post at d4, where it controls b5, c6, e6 and f5, while simultaneously neutralizing the bishop at g7. After lengthy preparations aimed at repelling Black's various counterattacks (. . .a3, . . . ♗e6, . . .f5, . . .d5) White has at last decided to attack the d6 pawn. But Black has succeeded in regrouping his forces and he gives up the pawn for a worthy price.

24 ♘g1 ♘fd7 25 ♗d4 ♘b6 26 ♗×g7 ♔×g7 27 ♖×d6 ♘×c4 28 ♖dd1 ♗e6

A position of dynamic balance has once more arisen, although its outward contours have changed. There are now more positional weaknesses in White's position (the b3 and d3 squares, and the passive bishop at g2). But White has possibilities of active play against Black's slightly weakened castled position, which equalizes the chances.

After a lively struggle this game ended in a draw.

Of course, one cannot use the name 'dynamic balance' dogmatically, by mechanically transferring it to other, similar positions, arising in different lines of one and the same variation. The main criterion in the assessment of a position must only be concrete analysis.

Typical pawn structures in the centre

A typical position is the name given to a set-up which arises fairly regularly in the opening, and can be obtained from several different opening variations.

Extensive practical experience and theoretical research have disclosed a number of typical structures in the centre, which largely determine the external contours of the position. A knowledge of the general character of the struggle in this or that central pawn structure allows easier orientation in a concrete position of this type. Such structures, which often arise right at the start of a game, have a lengthy influence on the resulting middlegame.

We have in mind, of course, solid, rather stable structures, arising as a result of the opening struggle. Each of these structures can influence the course of events. After all, the struggle for the centre normally takes place throughout the entire game.

A knowledge of the most general strategic features of such positions can not only significantly facilitate the play in these situations and an understanding of the close connection between opening and middlegame, but can also assist the intelligent assimilation and systemization of a complex of opening variations.

Typical, for example, is the following structure with a central outpost for White, arising in a variation of the French Defence after 1 e4 e6 2 d4 d5 3 ♘c3 ♘f6 4 ♗g5 ♗e7 5 e5 ♘fd7 6 ♗xe7 ♕xe7 7 f4 a6 8 ♘f3 c5 9 dc ♕xc5 10 ♕d4 *(159)*

159

This structure is also typical of many other lines of the French Defence, and also of some lines in the Caro-Kann and Sicilian Defences.

This structure can be obtained in various ways. Thus in the Sicilian Defence it can arise from an undetermined pawn structure in the centre, e.g. 1 e4 c5 2 ♘f3 d6 3 d4 cd 4 ♘xd4 ♘f6 5 ♘c3 g6 6 ♗e3 ♗g7 7 f3 0-0 8 ♕d2 d5 9 e5! ♘e8 10 f4 etc.

In such positions the structure in the centre is of great significance. White, with his important central outpost at d4, creates pressure on the dark squares, and intends to restrict the opponent's light-square bishop. White need not fear simplification, nor the exchange of his light-square bishop for an enemy knight.

An important resource for active play is White's spatial advantage on the K-side. It is here that White intends later to make the decisive breakthrough. From this it follows that in such positions Black must act very energetically in the centre, and must aim primarily to undermine White's centre by...f6!

Pawn structures and the inner content of the opening struggle

In many openings at the transition to the middlegame, the problem arises as to which is better —

to block the centre, or to fix the pawn structure and thereby open a central file (for example, in the main line of the Spanish Game). Or there is the still undecided problem in the Sämisch Variation of the King's Indian Defence, the essence of which is what is Black's most expedient course in the main line: 1 d4 ♘f6 2 c4 g6 3 ♘c3 ♗g7 4 e4 d6 5 f3 0-0 6 ♗e3 e5 7 d5. Should he block the centre with 7...c5, which allows White the plan of an attack on the K-side with 8 g4!?, or should he leave his Q-side untouched and try in turn for counterplay on the K-side: 7... ♘h5 8 ♕d2 f5 9 0-0-0 ♘d7? Or, finally, should he open a file on the Q-side: 7...c6 8 ♕d2 cd 9 cd a6, aiming if possible for active play on both sides of the board?

The choice between these decisions is a matter of taste, but the subsequent, now stable structure largely obliges the two sides to take definite action and demands a knowledge of typical procedures.

Of interest, for example, was the course taken by the opening in the following game.

No. 350 Bronstein–Szabo
Saltsjöbaden IZ, 1948
French Defence

1 e4 e6 2 d4 d5 3 ♘d2 ♘c6

4 ♘gf3 ♘f6 5 e5 ♘d7

A blocked pawn position in the centre has arisen, with a certain spatial advantage for White. However, the play in the centre quickly enlivens, and the structure soon changes completely.

6 ♘b3 f6 (had Black played 6...f5, a closed centre would have arisen, but this would have favoured White with his spatial advantage) 7 ♗b5 a6?

Black intends to obtain a central pawn group and later to set up a pawn centre, but this plan is ruined by White's energetic play. 7...♘cb8 was better.

8 ♗×c6 bc 9 0-0 c5 10 c4! (160)

160

In this energetic way, exploiting his lead in development, White advantageously opens the centre and causes a timely disruption of Black's plans. Weaker was 10 ef? ♕×f6 11 ♖e1 c4 12 ♘c5 ♗×c5 13 dc 0-0 14 c6 ♘b8 15 ♘e5 a5! with an excellent game for Black.

10...dc 11 ♘a5 ♘b6 12 ef ♕×f6 13 dc!, and White began a strong piece attack on the black king.

In this example the structure in the centre changed successively over the course of 5-6 moves: first from a tense structure it changed into a closed one (5 e5), then Black obtained a numerical superiority (8 ♗×c6 bc 9 0-0 c5), and finally the centre was opened (10 c4), which was the most logical consequence of the dynamic struggle for the centre. This confirms that the main thing is not the structure, but the inner content of the struggle!

The following examples from the Sicilian Defence are also typical: 1 e4 c5 2 ♘f3 d6 3 d4 cd 4 ♘×d4 ♘f6 5 ♘c3 a6 6 ♗e2 e5 7 ♘b3 ♗e7 8 0-0 0-0 9 a4 b6 10 ♗e3 ♗b7 11 f3 ♘bd7 12 ♕d2 ♕c7 13 ♘d5 ♗×d5 14 ed, or 1 e4 c5 2 ♘f3 d6 3 d4 cd 4 ♘×d4 ♘f6 5 ♘c3 a6 6 g3 e5 7 ♘de2 ♗e7 8 ♗g2 0-0 9 0-0 ♗d7 10 h3 ♗c6 11 ♘d5 ♗×d5 12 ed.

On each occasion here the basis of the opening struggle was for control of the d5 square, and it was for this reason that such a metamorphosis occurred. And in general it can be concluded that the struggle for the critical d5 square often leads to such a creation of an immobile pawn chain in the centre.

Also characteristic of the modern opening are new forms of structures in the centre. Thus until recently it was considered dangerous to concede to the opponent a piece-pawn superiority in the centre, arising, for example, in the following line: 1 e4 c5 2 ♘f3 ♘c6 3 d4 cd 4 ♘×d4 a6!? 5 c4.

It was this 'blockading' move that was feared earlier, when such set-ups were considered unfavourable for Black. Moreover, back in the 1920s and even the 1930s they were simply not taken seriously, but now a major reappraisal has taken place.

The typical result of such a struggle is a position of dynamic balance, where Black's play is fully viable and noted for good possibilities of active counterplay.

Typical structures in the centre include: 1) open centre; 2) closed or fixed centre; 3) numerical superiority in the centre for one of the sides; 4) positions with various pawn weaknesses (pawns and squares). A detailed and systematic review of these typical structures in the centre was made by the author in his book *Modern Chess Opening Theory* (Pergamon, 1965).

In conclusion, we must once again emphasize the somewhat arbitrary nature of typical pawn structures, and the fact that their significance is limited in the analysis of concrete situations where such structures arise. General conceptions (and that includes typical positions) are merely a starting point for a chess player's thinking. The decisive word always rests with concrete analysis.

And now let us turn to 'untypical' topical problems of pawn structures in the opening. In practice they are much more common than those with a clearly defined outward picture.

In such situations it is especially important to be guided by general playing methods. We will consider the problem of pawn tension in the centre.

Tense structures in the centre

In modern positional play a primary role is assigned to the problems of tense or undetermined structures in the centre. Very often in close set-ups, pawn tension is created or else a flexible structure arises, lacking in clear form.

Between these undetermined structures there is a significant difference. Pawn tension in the centre cannot normally be prolonged, and in the transition to the middlegame, or even in the opening, a definite form results after an exchange or the closing of the position.

Up to a certain point the release of the tension is unfavourable to the active side, who holds the initiative or has more space. Often the logic of the struggle demands that Black go in for certain concessions, being the first to release the tension and concede a central outpost (cf. Diag. 159).

On each occasion the elimination of the tension in the centre is a highly important strategic decision for both sides. With Black this normally is associated with freeing his game. Typical in this respect is this line of the Vienna Game: 1 e4 e5 2 ♘c3 ♘c6 3 ♗c4 ♘f6 4 d3 ♗b4 5 ♘ge2 d5 6 ed ♘×d5, and Black has successfully solved both his development problems, and the opening battle for the centre. Of course, it is by no means always that the defending side manages to eliminate the tension in the centre. For example, in the line of the Dragon Variation after 1 e5 c5 2 ♘f3 d6 3 d4 cd 4 ♘×d4 ♘f6 5 ♘c3 g6 6 ♘e3 ♗g7 7 f3 ♘c6 8 ♕d2 the freeing attempt 8...d5? is clearly premature, as the very strong 9 ♗b5! follows, when Black is already in difficulties.

In general the classical rule still remains in force, according to which it is advisable for the defending side to maintain his pawn base in the centre, provided this does not entail any obvious disadvantage. Thus after 1 e4 e5 2 ♘f3 ♘c6 3 ♗c4 ♗e7 4 d4 for the moment Black should play for the maintenance of the critical e5 square with 4...d6, not fearing 5 de de 6 ♕×d8+ ♗×d8, with a sound game.

On the other hand, if White maintains the tension, he cannot avoid reckoning with Black's counterplay, and to avoid it he must often, at the necessary moment, take the optimal decision, closing or fixing the centre.

We give a fairly complicated example of modern strategy from the Keres Variation in the Closed Defence to the Spanish Game: 1 e4 e5 2 ♘f3 ♘c6 3 ♗b5 a6 4 ♗a4 ♘f6 5 0-0 ♗e7 6 ♖e1 b5 7 ♗b3 d6 8 c3 0-0 9 h3 ♘a5 10 ♗c2 c5 11 d4 ♘d7!?

This 'mysterious' manœuvre is made with the aim of preparing an abrupt enlivening of the pawn position in the centre.

Instructive in this respect is the following game.

No. 351 Tal-Keres
Curacao C, 1962

12 ♘bd2 cd 13 cd ♘c6 14 a3(?) ed! 15 ♘b3 ♘de5 16 ♘fxd4 ♗f6 17 ♗d2 ♘xd4 18 ♘xd4 ♘d3! 19 ♘c6 ♘xf2! 20 ♕f3 ♘xh3+ 21 ♔h2 ♗e5+! 22 ♘xe5 de 23 ♖ed1 ♘f4!, after which Black gained a decisive material advantage.

The cause of White's difficulties was the strategic over-looking of Black's strong and lively counterplay, involving the freeing of his position in the centre. Where then did White go wrong? Perhaps he should have radically prevented Black's plan by the timely fixing or closing of the centre? However, practice shows that both after 12 dc dc 13 ♘bd2 f6! 14 ♘f1 ♘b6 15 ♕e2 ♖a7! 16 ♘e3 ♗e6 17 ♘f5 ♖e8 etc., and after 12 ♘bd2 cd 13 cd ♘c6 14 d5 ♘b4 15 ♗b1 a5 16 a3 ♘a6 17 b4 ♘b6! 18 ♕b3 ♗d7 19 ♗d3 ♘c7 Black does not have any difficulties.

The line which causes Black the most problems nevertheless involves maintaining the tension: 12 ♘bd2 cd 13 cd ♘c6 14 ♘b3!

Here we encounter yet another positional factor — the over-protection of critical points. At the same time White clears the way for his bishop at c1, and thus avoids putting off the devel-opment of his own Q-side.

Incidentally, after the possible 14. . .a5 15 ♗d3 ♗a6 the closing of the centre now looks much more appropriate: 16 d5, creating persistent pressure on the Q-side.

A timely release of the pawn tension is seen in an overwhelming number of modern openings and even classical variations of Closed Games.

This is confirmed by a well known line of the Orthodox Defence: 1 d4 d5 2 c4 e6 3 ♘c3 ♘f6 4 ♗g5 ♗e7 5 e3 ♘bd7 6 ♘f3 0-0 7 ♖c1 c6.

Here there is an eternal problem: is it more advisable for White to clarify the position in the centre, e.g. by 8 ♗d3 dc 9 ♗xd4 ♘d5 10 ♗xe7 ♕xe7 11 0-0 ♘xc3 12 ♖xc3 e5 etc., or should he defer forcing events, aiming to gain an important tempo after the possible 8 ♕c2 a6 9 a3 h6 10 ♗h4 ♖e8, where each side awaits a convenient moment to release the tension: 11 ♖d1 dc 12 ♗xc4 b5, or 11 cd ed, after which completely different structures, and hence plans, arise.

Undetermined structures in the centre

One of the noteworthy tendencies in modern strategy is the

creation for a lengthy period of flexible pawn structures, lacking in definite form, but at the same time distinguished by their great inner tension.

Such set-ups take shape right from the opening, and can occur particularly often in the English Opening, Reti Opening, Pirc Defence and so on.

A characteristic feature of such set-ups is their great flexibility in choice and implementation of strategic plan. Here there is a clear tendency towards avoiding clashes in the centre, preference being given to preparatory flank pressure by the pieces. For a long time the central pawns remain on their original squares, or else occupy modest positions.

It was the ideas of Reti, put forward in the 1920s, which confirmed the great potential strength of such positions.

Here is a classic example of such a set-up.

No. 352 Reti-Rubinstein
Carlsbad, 1923
Reti Opening

1 ♘f3 d5 2 g3 ♘f6 3 ♗g2 g6 4 c4 d4 5 d3 ♗g7 6 b4 0-0 7 ♘bd2! c5 8 ♘b3 cb 9 ♗b2 ♘c6 10 ♘bxd4 ♘xd4 11 ♗xd4 b6 12 a3 ♗b7 13 ♗b2 ba 14 ♖xa3 ♕c7

Nowadays such positions have become typical, and are rightly considered to favour White in view of his powerful pawn phalanx in the centre.

15 ♕a1!

Following Reti's example, this queen manœuvre has become characteristic of such positions. The pressure on the a1-h8 diagonal forces Black to seek simplification.

15...♘e8 16 ♗xg7 ♘xg7 17 0-0 ♘e6 18 ♖b1 ♗c6 19 d4! ♗e4 20 ♖d1 a5 21 d5! ♘c5 22 ♘d4

And now White's knight obtains strong outposts at d4 and c8, which leads to a clear superiority in the centre.

22...♗xg2 23 ♔xg2 ♖ad8 24 ♘c6 ♖d6 25 ♖e3 ♖e8 26 ♕e5 f6 27 ♕b2 e5 28 ♕b5! ♔f7 29 ♖b1 ♘d7 30 f3 ♖c8 31 ♖d3!

Preventing 31...♘b8 because of 32 c5!

31...e4 (on 31...♘c5 White has the very strong 32 ♕xb6!) 32 fe ♘e5 33 ♕xb6! ♘xc6 34 c5!, and White gained an overwhelming advantage.

In modern variations with an undetermined structure in the centre, the combining of play in the centre with operations on the flanks is acquiring ever greater importance.

The strategic procedure of rapidly transferring action from one sector of the board to another is becoming more and more common. Such a problem is also typical of many determined structures in the centre, but in the given case it is particularly sharp and dynamic.

For example, in many lines of the Sicilian Dragon an undetermined pawn structure in the centre arises. The course of the following game is typical.

No. 353 Rauzer-Botvinnik
Moscow, 1933
Sicilian Defence

1 e4 c5 2 ♘f3 ♘c6 3 d4 cd 4 ♘xd4 ♘f6 5 ♘c3 d6 6 ♗e2 g6 7 ♗e3 ♗g7 8 ♘b3 ♗e6 9 f4 0-0 10 0-0 ♘a5 11 ♘xa5 ♛xa5 12 ♗f3 ♗c4 13 ♖e1 ♖fd8 14 ♕d2 ♕c7 15 ♖ac1 *(161)*

161

Up till now the two sides have been engaged in preparatory manœuvres, and the pawn position in the centre has remained undetermined. But now Black, who has deployed his pieces much more actively, commences energetic play in the centre. This

plan, which after the present game became typical of such positions, proves especially effective in the event of passive play by White in the opening.

15...e5! 16 b3? (underestimating the coming advance in the centre; 16 fe de 17 ♕f2 was better, fixing the central pawns) **16...d5!!**

The centre is unexpectedly opened, and to the advantage of Black, whose forces combine very harmoniously.

17 ed e4! 18 bc ef 19 c5 ♛a5 20 ♖ed1 ♘g4! 21 ♗d4 f2+ 22 ♔f1 ♛a6+ 23 ♕e2 ♗xd4! 24 ♖xd4 ♕f6! 25 ♖cd1 ♕h4! (Black switches to a decisive attack against White's poorly defended K-side) **26 ♕d3 ♖e8 27 ♖e4 f5! 28 ♖e6 ♘xh2+ 29 ♔e2 ♕xf4 0-1**

If the central pawn structure is undetermined, one must watch with particular care for a counterattack in the centre when attacking on the K-side.

Here is an example of this situation.

No. 354 Alekhine-Botvinnik
Nottingham, 1936
Sicilian Defence

1 e4 c5 2 ♘f3 ♘c6 3 d4 cd 4 ♘xd4 ♘f6 5 ♘c3 d6 6 ♗e2 g6 7 ♗e3 ♗g7 8 ♘b3 0-0 9 f4 ♗e6 10 g4 d5! *(162)*

Against White's sharp attack

on the K-side, Black replies with an energetic blow in the centre, which is the most advisable in the given situation. Now events develop by force, exceptional accuracy being demanded of both players.

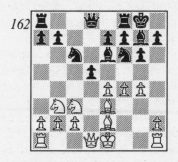

162

11 f5! (11 e5? is very strongly met by 11...d4!) **11...♗c8 12 ed ♘b4 13 d6 ♕xd6 14 ♗c5! ♕f4! 15 ♖f1 ♕xh2! 16 ♗xb4 ♘xg4 17 ♗xg4 ♕g3+,** with a draw by perpetual check.

In the given structure of the Sicilian Defence (the Dragon Variation) other possible structures can also arise, such as a backward pawn in the centre, a piece outpost in the centre, and so on.

With an undetermined structure, a problem of practical importance is that of choosing a convenient moment to achieve a favourable structure in the centre. For example, it is strategically highly promising for White to establish a knight at d5 in front of a backward pawn at d6. But modern practice shows that this is of real value only if there is solid control over the key point, otherwise the opponent may advantageously be able to drive the knight from its insecure post.

An elementary question: why after 1 d4 ♘f6 2 c4 c5 3 d5 e6 4 ♘c3 ed does White not exploit (in master games, of course) the seemingly advantageous opportunity to establish a piece at d5: 4 ♘xd5 ♘xd5 5 ♕xd5, but instead prefers the immediate determining of the central structure by 4 cd d6 5 e4 etc?

The point is that, in the given instance, the queen at d5 feels very much like an uninvited guest, and after 5...♘c6 6 ♘f3 d6 followed by 7...♗e6 Black completes his development with gain of time, and has chances of seizing the initiative.

To sum up: in positions with an undetermined pawn structure, the general problem for each side with regard to the centre consists in obtaining the more favourable pawn formation.

Flexible opening structures

In many opening variations a clash in the centre does not take place. Usually an initial role is place. Usually an initial role is played by flank pressure on the centre. An example of this is provided by the Closed Variation of the Sicilian Defence: 1 e4 c5 2 ♘c3 ♘c6 3 g3 g6 4 ♗g2 ♗g7 5 d3 d6 etc.

In recent times there has been a considerable increase in the number of such set-ups, in which for a long time the pawn structure in the centre is undetermined.

It would be wrong to imagine that the classical opening set-ups have been 'submerged' under the flood of sharp tactical variations. Purely positional opening laws have also been developing in parallel.

Possibly even as a reaction to the sharp tactical variations, a trend in the openings has developed, characterized by great flexibility in the subsequent choice and implementation of strategic plan. Here there is a clear aim of avoiding clashes in the centre, preference being given to preparatory flank action.

Until mobilization is completed, the pawns in the centre occupy modest positions. The struggle is as though transferred to the middlegame. Such opening set-ups are often slightly cramped, but they are fully viable, mainly for the reason that at a convenient moment the central pawns can advance with great force. In general the play is notable for its great flexibility.

Many such variations have been developed in recent years in the English Opening, for example: 1 c4 ♘f6 2 ♘c3 g6 3 g3 ♗g7 4 ♗g2 d6 5 d3 c5 6 a3, preparing a later offensive on the Q-side, or 1 c4 ♘f6 2 ♘c3 d5 3 cd ♘×d5 4 g3 g6 5 ♗g2 ♘b6 6 d3 etc.

This also applies to the Paulsen Variation of the Sicilian Defence: 1 e4 c5 2 ♘f3 e6 3 d4 cd 4 ♘×d4 a6. Here Black avoids an immediate clash in the centre, preferring to prepare gradually for active play, and intending if possible to develop his king's bishop actively along the f8-a3 diagonal.

The modern handling of this variation expresses very clearly the features characterizing such set-ups. In particular one should note Black's great flexibility, which enables him to adapt to White's plans. For example, after 5 c4 ♘f6 6 ♘c3 ♕c7 7 ♘c2 b6 8 ♗d3 d6 9 0-0 ♘bd7 10 ♘e3 ♗b7 11 f3 ♗e7 12 ♗d2 0-0 13 ♖c1 ♖ac8 Black sets up a very flexible defence and subsequently simply does not allow White's initiative to develop.

Although in this variation (and ones similar to it) the events in the opening develop rather slowly and are rarely forcing, nevertheless each move in the opening is very committing and full of concrete meaning. The difficulty of playing White is that, since in many lines the opponent's activity is delayed, he must largely be guided by a clear-cut, concrete plan, in spite of the wide choice of possibilities.

Thus if White plays for the rapid development of his minor pieces, as in the analogous Scheveningen Variation (where instead of 4...a6 Black plays 4... d6), after 5 ♘c3 ♕c7 6 ♗e2 ♘f6 7 0-0 b5 Black already acquires fairly significant counterplay.

The main danger for White is that, in the event of routine play, he can quickly find himself in an unfavourable strategic situation in the middlegame.

In the given variation, for example, an important feature is that Black's d-pawn remains for a long time in its initial position. As a result his dark-square bishop has a wide choice of active development at b4, c5 or even d6. The saving of a tempo in the opening is also significant. At the same time Black's central pawn can be energetically advanced, with the aim of actively joining the battle for the centre.

It is no accident that this variation for Black has become firmly established in the opening repertoires of several leading players.

We must also mention another important feature of flexible positions: the reorganization of the pawn formation at the transition from opening to middlegame, with the aim of improving the coordination of pieces and pawns.

Many lines of the Nimzo-Indian Defence are instructive in this respect, in particular: 1 d4 ♘f6 2 c4 e6 3 ♘c3 ♗b4 4 e3 c5 5 ♗d3 0-0 6 a3 ♗×c3+ 7 bc ♘c6 8 ♘e2 b6 9 e4 d6 followed by ...e5 with a blockade on the dark squares.

Black successfully reorganizes his pawn chain and obtains a convenient structure in the centre.

'Cramped' positions

Fairly often in practice, especially with Black, one has to reckon with having a 'cramped' position. Sometimes it is possible to escape fairly quickly from such a position by a timely freeing pawn advance in the centre. But in a number of variations, for example with solid pawn chains where the active side has a strong pawn wedge in the centre, the cramped position of the defending side is a feature throughout the entire strategic development of the middlegame.

Tarrasch in his time put forward the 'formula': "a cramped position contains the germ of defeat". However, modern strategy does not give a simple answer to this question. Everything depends on the character of the defender's position, since in the transition from opening to middlegame there are a number of cramped positions which contain considerable manœuvring potential. One merely needs to have patience.

Typical in this respect is a position arising in the English Opening: 1 c4 c5 2 ♘f3 ♘f6 3 ♘c3 d5 4 cd ♘×d5 5 e4 ♘b4 6 ♗c4 ♘d3+ 7 ♔e2 ♘×c1+ 8 ♖×c1 e6 9 d4 cd 10 ♕×d4 (better 10 ♗b5+) 10...♕×d4 11 ♘×d4 a6 12 ♖hd1. Although White has a development lead of 6 tempi and a marked superiority in space, practice shows that his advantage is insignificant. The point is that Black has no weak points and this allows him to engage in flexible manœuvring.

* * *

Opening theory has made enormous strides, but this does not mean that opening problems are being exhausted. On the contrary, the preconditions are being created for their ever more deep, and at the same time, fascinating development.

Index of Games

Numbers in **bold** refer to complete games. The numbers given are game numbers. The first-named player is White. Game numbers followed by the letter 'a' indicate that the game will be found in the notes to the main game.